PEAK EVOLUTION

Beyond Peak Performance
and Peak Experience

Lauren Holmes

Second Edition Paperback: Revised in 2010
All rights reserved.
ISBN 978-1-7770524-2-3

SECOND EDITION
Paperback

Requests for permission or further information should be addressed to the Permissions Department info@laurenholmes.com
Published by Naturality.Net, LLC

*Dedicated to all those clients
and individuals who loaned
me their lives for the cause.*

CONTENTS

PART ONE: A New Paradigm

PART TWO: Making the Paradigm Shift

THE KNOWLEDGE TECHNOLOGY

PART ONE

A New Paradigm

1

THE NATURALITY PARADIGM

"All power is of one kind, a sharing of the nature of the world. The mind that is parallel with the laws of nature will be in the current of events, and strong with their strength."
Emerson, "Power,"   The Conduct of Life

The intent of our work together will be to liberate human potential. Your potential. We will be using a breakthrough human development process. It is designed to take each one of us to the highest creative expression of our core being and then beyond it. This new growth science is based on the greatness I encountered within each individual allowed to express his or her natural identity in the most meaningful way. One does not need to be disciplined, controlled, ruled, or educated for this greatness to exist. One needs only to release it. When people are allowed to operate consistent with their natural design, magic happens. Extraordinary achievements. Extraordinary creations. Extraordinary human beings.

Civilization has persistently progressed towards the liberation of the individual. In the twentieth century, this has been evident in the successes of Mahatma Ghandi, Nelson Mandela, Martin Luther King Jr., and the Dalai Lama. The women's movement and, in fact, the whole human rights movement, demonstrate the same trend. Trade sanctions against countries in which individuals are mistreated illustrate the gathering intolerance for those resisting the inevitable trend.

As society evolves, the rights of individuals and what is considered individual freedom will continue to expand. We made great strides in the last millennium to remove oppression and infringements to human freedom. However, in this millennium, we will proactively promote levels of human freedom hitherto not identified. We will see the human potential movement become the platform for the human rights movement in society and business.

All individuals will expect to live lives aligned with their natural identities. The opportunity to do work most expressive of that identity and one's natural talents will be assumed. As a result, societies will emerge to support and promote individual freedom of this magnitude. And, if each of us around the world is free to be the person we are naturally, we will have world freedom. Individual freedom results in world freedom. World freedom propagates world peace. World peace means we will all have the safety to cultivate our personal creativity even more. Individuals will be in a position to have their strongest impact and make their greatest contribution to the world.

Many enlightened peacemakers have begun to focus on the growth of the individual as the means to spawn world freedom and world peace. The technologies presented in this book support their efforts. They promote the grassroots development of individuals aligned with their Naturality and operating at their highest potential by using their greatest talents. The *Peak Evolution* technologies will contribute to the foundations for a new, more evolved civilization.

The rise of entrepreneurialism is evidence of this worldwide evolution. Increasingly, individuals invent companies which allow them to do their *art*, the work that is most expressive of their natural identity and talents. We think of the major corporations detrimentally for their downsizing programs.

Whose life has not been affected directly or indirectly by the suffering of those individuals cast aside? However, this downsizing is the result of the inability of corporations to compete with individuals in entrepreneurial businesses. As this trend advances, large companies will become networks of entrepreneurs and small companies will link up for the same reason – to become networks of entrepreneurs. Welcome to the Age of the Individual.

Society will evolve to encourage each one of us to use our greatest talents to make our greatest contribution. For some, it will suit to congregate together in large companies in order to achieve more significant goals. Business will provide the forums for our personal evolution. Companies will offer contexts for creativity that will allow us to stretch and grow and thus to know ourselves and our potential. Business will benefit from the resulting creativity. Organization goals and personal goals will symbiotically be met by the opportunities for meaningful creativity.

The intent of Peak Evolution is the freeing of both human beings and human potential. Human potential goes far beyond recognized levels of peak performance. The Peak Evolution technologies will raise the bar on the potential for peak performance for individuals and the race. The result will be new, unexpected levels of freedom, functionality, human ingenuity, and personal achievement. What we currently consider "peak experience" doesn't begin to describe what's possible for us.

A Paradigm Shift

How will we accomplish your extraordinary metamorphosis to full power as an evolved human being? We're going to do it with a *paradigm shift*. A paradigm is the lens through which we see our world. They determine our attitudes and behavior. Paradigm shifts happen as a result of changes to the basic, underlying assumptions by which we've been living. They move us from one way of seeing the world to another. Because we see things differently, we think differently, feel differently, behave differently, and believe differently. Paradigm shifts can be instantaneous or progressive, but the result is always dramatic change.

Ptolemy, the great Egyptian astronomer, placed the earth at the center of the universe. When Copernicus made the sun the center, everything in astronomy and beyond needed to be reconnected in a different way. The shift to the new paradigm proposed in *Peak Evolution* will trigger reconnections in every part of your life. It will replace how most of us have been brought up to think the world functions. The trick to learning a new paradigm is to set aside your current worldview. It is unlikely that the new knowledge can be integrated into your existing model. Consider it an "either-or" situation. If you can do this, I believe you'll be intrigued and enriched by the process of experimentation proposed.

With *Peak Evolution*, you can visit the new paradigm, explore its power, and use its tools. The people technologies will help you to make the transition so you can "test drive" the new paradigm. Unfortunately, you can't bring things back to your old paradigm. They'll have no power there. For most people, the old and the new paradigms are mutually exclusive. Therefore, ultimately, you're going to have to choose between the two paradigms. Since a choice is inevitable, let me use this first chapter to lay some foundations for your journey, your experimentation, your evaluation, and your final selection of the ideal paradigm for you.

The new paradigm is based on how I believe we are designed to harmonize with natural dynamics. As an anthropologist, I view evolution as a continual process of systems adapting and re-optimizing to their environment and to each other. Those living systems that can readjust or adapt to changes are the most successful.

Science fiction writers love to weave stories around mutating viruses that adapt to or become immune to each vaccine developed. Think of how our bodies adapt to the intrusion of viruses by developing antibodies to quell the onslaught of a virus invasion. The creative adaptiveness of human beings has made us a successful species. With some adjustments to our cultural constructs, this adaptability can be significantly enhanced in each of us.

There are numerous forces and mechanisms within nature designed to take each system to its optimal or peak performance vis-à-vis its environment. In 1990, I theorized that if we could tap into those natural optimizing processes, we could quickly achieve and sustain peak performance. With extensive real-life experimentation, what emerged was a way to achieve a level of capability not commonly thought to be humanly possible.

This optimizing flow of nature is what I call the *naturality flow*. The technologies you will read about are designed to reintegrate you with that flow. As a result, you'll not only be moving with the flow of nature, you'll have nature's processes, mechanisms and intelligence working for you to extend and augment your capabilities. Your functionality and creative adaptiveness will increase enormously.

This "naturality flow" paradigm or *naturality paradigm* redefines how human beings have evolved to operate in conjunction with optimizing forces in nature. These are the same forces which can, for example, balance a multitude of species in an ecosystem. Operating in partnership with the naturality flow is the basic dynamic of the newly defined paradigm for human operation presented in *Peak Evolution*.

This naturality paradigm is based on living with complete naturalness. The technologies transition us back to the way we are designed to operate with natural dynamics. They help us to undo the damage done by our cultures in removing us from the naturality flow in the first place. The naturality paradigm is simply the way humans have evolved to operate before culture interfered.

The three major technologies of the peak evolution science are the Knowledge Technology, the Reality Creation Technology, and the Growth Technology. Each has a subset technology - the pathfinding technology, the reality design technology, and the quantum leap technology, respectively. Each is based on an uncommon belief.

For the knowledge technology, this uncommon belief is that we have access to all knowledge - ultimately spontaneously - merely by focusing consciousness. For the reality creation technology, the uncommon belief is that beliefs create reality and therefore the reality we experience is 100% self-created. For the growth technology, the belief is that natural forces perpetually pressure us along an evolutionary continuum to the full expression of our naturality.

The reality creation technology chapters are broken into two distinct parts: *De-Creating Undesirable Realities* and *Creating Desired Realities*. These instruct on how to stop creating realities we don't want, and how to proactively create realities we do want. I discovered the naturality paradigm while interviewing hundreds of leaders as the head of an executive search firm dedicated exclusively to the recruitment of change leaders.

I found the most successful leaders had a different relationship with the dynamics of their context than was the norm. They continuously took action consistent with the naturality flow. The more accomplished the leader, the greater I found his or her actions complied with ten telltale signals associated with nature's optimizing flow.

These ten identifiers of the naturality flow are introduced and explored in *Peak Evolution*. You'll learn how to use them to determine directly from nature your personal pathway for peak evolution. You'll learn how to operate at peak potential while continuously evolving beyond that potential. This is an opportunity to have the functionality of future generations now. This is a paradigm shift that can make peak experience a way of life.

We appear to be born fully integrated into the naturality flow. I find that children, leaders and creatives comply with the flow and therefore express the innate creative adaptiveness that is in all of us. As a result, they are more aligned with their authenticity, their naturality. The increased functionality presented in this book emerges when naturality and the compliance with the naturality flow increase. Children and leaders, then, are two ends of an evolutionary continuum we are all designed to be on. It moves us perpetually towards the full expression of our naturality.

Leaders are more aligned with their naturality than most of us and hence are the furthest along this evolutionary continuum. This is what you would expect of leaders. By projecting this continuum out into the future from the most advanced leaders I studied, the direction of human evolution became apparent.

Once I had determined what the natural extension was, I was in a position to develop technologies to not only get us back onto the continuum defined by the naturality flow but to advance people beyond the evolved state for even the best of leaders. This is what you will learn in this book. I believe those making the shift to the naturality paradigm will become the leaders of human evolution. Once a critical mass has made the paradigm shift, it will become a global cultural shift.

The Evolved State

The evolved state you can expect to achieve with the paradigm shift cannot be effectively described until you have greater knowledge of both the paradigm and naturality flow. We need a common language and understanding. For now, let me describe the approach we will use to accelerate individuals to peak performance as a holistic one based on systems theory. The technologies presented will enable you to move with the naturality flow to your most evolved state. You will evolve by becoming a natural extension to the underlying creative dynamic of the universe.

The process used is one of aligning our "internal drives" with "nature's drives" as defined by the naturality flow attempting to optimize our system. Culture has interfered with that natural process. Thus, the technologies help us to release from cultural constructs, so we can shift back to what is natural for us. Once back into the naturality flow, the technologies will no longer be required. Once you initiate the process, cascading quantum leaps will carry you the rest of the way.

This is because natural forces have never stopped pressuring us to move back into nature's flow. Consequently, there are mechanisms inside and outside of us to support the realignment process. Nature prefers quantum leaps for advancements and optimization. Therefore, reintegration into the naturality flow generates a multitude of coincidences and quantum leaps to accelerate our progress.

Many people label our upcoming evolution as spiritual. Accordingly, they follow a spiritual discipline or philosophy in order to evolve. This will not be the approach here. You and your reality are viewed as a seamless system. There is no separation of the system into parts such as mind, body, spirit, or God, for example. If the most evolved states are oneness and unity consciousness, fragmenting yourself and your existence is counter-evolutionary. Further, these are personal beliefs and choices which need to be respected.

Out of respect for the diversity of religious, philosophic, and spiritual schools of thought, the methodologies presented will be purposely kept as generic as possible. They will be purely prescriptive in nature as to actions to be taken in compliance with natural forces. Everything I know of the most evolved states achievable through spirituality and religion appear to be innate in each of us and simply need to be released.

For example, the desire for humanitarian endeavors promoted by many religions is spontaneously released as consciousness evolves in the naturality paradigm. Another example, the oceanic experience of oneness with the universe, is also innate. The author of *The User's Guide to the Brain* (Pantheon Books, 2001), John Ratey, M.D., says medical professionals are now able to electrically stimulate certain parts of the brain to achieve this same oceanic experience. The naturality flow formula for accelerated growth will trigger unity consciousness in such a way that it is a sustained modus operandi for your life.

One thing I can reveal this early about our most evolved state is that it is not a passive state of serene inactivity. Rather, we are an extension of the underlying creative dynamic of the universe. Evolved states, then, arise from the activity fusion or *flow* consciousness that emerges from pure creativity in doing the things that best reflect our naturality. The evolved state then is an active creative state of full expression of your naturality in compliance with the naturality flow. Naturality is known only by its expression. What do we know of the naturality and full potential of a flower from a seed, or a butterfly from a cocoon?

> *"There is nothing in a caterpillar that tells you it's going to be a butterfly."*
> Buckminster Fuller

This highlights one of the surprising discoveries that emerged as I returned people to the naturality flow and then accelerated their evolution. We are creative beings who are an extension of the creative and creating flow of the universe. As such, ours is a dimension of physical materialization. The underlying human dynamic appears to be a continuous cycle of growing ourselves to grow our creations and then to be grown by those creations.

Our performance in this dimension is based on our legacy of creations - whether that is the nurturing of a child to adulthood or the redesign of society. What is changed by your existence here is the theme, opportunity and focus of this dimension.

In this dimension, the underlying dynamic is self-creation for the purpose of better reality creation. Our creations reinforce our new growth and increase it more so that our next creations increase again. I call this basic dynamic of human existence the self-creation/creation dynamic or the self-growth/creation- growth dynamic. If we all share a generic purpose, this is it. We pursue the greatest expressions of our naturality. We grow to create better realities and that creation process grows us more. We *know* ourselves by our creations. We *grow* ourselves by our creations. We are creative beings.

Another fascinating finding in my experimentation was that the closer you come to alignment with your naturality and integration into the naturality flow, the more spontaneous knowledge you will experience. If you are doing things that express your naturality, you may find whole systems of information emerging complete into your awareness. Information coincidences or quantum leaps will abound. Spontaneous knowledge is part of the increase in quantum leaps that occur when we partner with the naturality flow.

In addition, it would appear that if we have expertise for how to grow, and then we partner with nature, the expert on growth, growth becomes safe. And if growth is safe, we want to do it all the time. We have so many drives to transcendence, new learning, and new levels of achievement, that we become benevolently addicted to growth. We quickly become growth addicts as a way of life. When we release ourselves to these "internal drives" in partnership with "nature's drives" represented by the naturality flow, evolution proceeds at exponential rates by cascading quantum leaps.

Exploring the Naturality Paradigm

Now, let's get you ready for, what will be for many of you, an exploration of new territory. The naturality paradigm and the "people" technologies designed to transport you there, will attempt to restore you to the way you were evolved to operate in harmony with nature's optimizing mechanisms. However, let me propose one important rule first: where you're not sure about any part of the model presented in *Peak Evolution, let nature be your guide.*

If something feels unnatural, or, in any way, tedious or draining, then return to what feels natural and energizing for you. The naturality paradigm is designed to increase your integration into natural dynamics, not to create a whole new set of rules which serve to further disrupt your natural functioning.

The strategy behind *Peak Evolution* is to teach you to read ten identifiers of the naturality flow. You can then capitalize on the ongoing optimizing process rather than to try to duplicate nature's capabilities. The goal is to enable you to harness natural forces to surpass peak performance and peak experience. You'll be able to duplicate nature when you've seen how nature operates and have gained knowledge experientially.

As you partner with nature, you will internalize a big picture perspective of the perpetual cycle of optimization. Therefore, each individual optimization challenge that arises will not be a new problem to deal with. Instead, it will be business as usual in a world of continuous re-optimization. Rather than having to develop "tool kits"or competencies to handle a multitude of problems, you can have one set of optimization tools to handle variations on a theme. This single toolkit for harmonizing with natural forces is what is provided in *Peak Evolution.*

Think back for a moment to when you first learned to drive. Initially, it was a bit overwhelming because you had so many stimuli demanding your attention. With experience, your responses to the various stimuli became unconscious and instinctive. You no longer had to *think* about driving. Since it was no longer required for driving, your conscious mind could actually be applied to numerous other tasks - conversations, music, planning a presentation, or looking at the scenery. You'll grow into operating within the naturality paradigm in the same way.

Initially, you'll be concentrating on a multitude of new stimuli that you might have ignored in the past - signals from nature about optimization, growth, your beliefs, quantum leaps, new information, learning, and safety. You'll be internalizing new ways to react to these various stimuli. Gradually, however, your response will become conditioned and unconscious. Your new repertoire of reflex reactions will be instinctive and automatic. You'll have internalized the reflexes of someone adapted to moving with the dynamic processes of nature.

Internalizing the paradigm shift is more satisfying than learning to drive because of the emotional rewards inherent in complying with natural human drives. Doing the activities associated with these drives yield some of the highest emotional rewards we can experience. Hence, these activities can engender some of the strongest cravings. These emotional states serve to condition you to want to take action on those drives again and again - to move further into the naturality paradigm. So, the more you release yourself to complying with your natural drives, the stronger they'll get until you'll find yourself perpetually in the naturality paradigm. You'll have become an extension of the naturality flow.

I want to keep this book focused on your personal evolution to your full potential. Therefore, I'm going to leave out a lot of the scientific proofs on which this model was founded. Since many of these proofs are in dispute as part of ongoing scientific debates, this may be a prudent tactic in any event. Those to whom the model comes naturally will instantly "feel" its truth. Many will already "know" that parts of the model are true and just need the other parts to connect all of the dots into a cohesive, logical whole. The paradigm is basically self-provable. Therefore, I've tried to set up instructions to permit you to prove each component to yourself.

There are two additional things the *Peak Evolution* methodology requires. The first is a willingness to change - not just to *do* things differently but to *be* different and to *believe* differently. Growth involves a change of beliefs. In addition, you'll need to be willing to experiment. One of the limitations of attempting to evolve individuals through a book is that I can't provide you with the benefits of just-in-time learning. Therefore, I urge you to revisit the parts of the book relevant to what you're experiencing at any point in time in your life. Further, when you experience one facet of the paradigm, it will change your understanding of the other facets. Therefore, it's likely you'll want to reread sections of *Peak Evolution* as you evolve because they will take on new meaning.

Many of the elements in the naturality model result in quantum leaps and exponential changes that can't be described in a logical and linear fashion. Also, we'll be letting nature and reality be our guide as to what needs to grow next or to be done next for you. Consequently, there can be no predefined route for everyone to follow universally. The goal is to teach you how to read and use nature's messages, signals, and intelligence to permit the most evolved expression of your naturality at any point in time. We want nature to be your guide.

Again, there is no prescribed linear process for learning the information presented in *Peak Evolution*. Rather, your knowledge of all parts of it, more or less, will be learned and experienced and internalized at one level of sophistication and then all will move up a notch to operate at a new level of sophistication, and so on. Experiences with one part of the paradigm will shift how you operate with another part. You have to do the steps at one level, experience the resulting transformation, and then, from that transformed state, do other sets of instructions. You can read the instructions for all levels but they'll have limited meaning until you are transformed by having "experienced" the results of the instructions for a previous level.

Let me emphasize this point again in another way. Experiential learning or experiential knowledge will be more important to your conversion to operating in the new paradigm than simply "knowing new information." This means that knowing the information required to cause change may not be enough to trigger the necessary belief changes required for your permanent transformation.

Usually, the prescribed activities need to be "experienced" for quantum leaps to occur. You are unlikely to evolve simply by some intellectual change. You must experience the world differently, experience new ways of being, before you will truly quantum leap to peak performance and peak evolution.

If you try to make this a book only about *doing* different things as opposed to *being* different inside, I don't believe you'll experience the dramatic transformations presented. For emphasis again, let me isolate another aspect of the need for experiential learning: you can't lock in change without a change in beliefs. If you've had a lifetime of believing reality or human beings operate one way, you are unlikely to be able to permanently change your beliefs about this by reading about a potentially new way of operating. It won't be "real" or "true" until you prove it

to yourself, no matter how persuasively I might present it.

Because there is no required route for learning this material, you may choose to proceed with whatever sections of *Peak Evolution* appeal to you most. There is no need to force yourself to work on parts of the model that generate negative emotions in you. In fact, that would countermand the modus operandi proposed. If you encounter blocks or discomfort as you advance, try working with another sector of the paradigm.

Because the naturality paradigm consists of a completely integrated and cohesive worldview, every part of it is logically interconnected just as in nature. Every part of the paradigm can therefore be deduced from other parts of it. Knowing one part will automatically lead to your knowledge about and ability to use other parts. Ultimately, all of the parts will come together and you will understand how we are designed to operate with the naturality flow.

There will be a point when you will simply "leap" to a comprehension of the paradigm as a whole. Once you have a critical mass of beliefs and knowledge from any part of the naturality paradigm, you will experience a quantum leap to understanding how the entire paradigm operates and, indeed, how nature operates. You will simply *know* how it all works, whether I've written about all of it or not. *Peak Evolution* presents a holistic approach to your optimization as a human being. It is the means to discover what it truly means to be human. It's a powerful new way for living, creating and being.

So let's begin. In the next chapter, we'll find out more about this naturality flow that is the underlying dynamic of the universe. In the third chapter, we'll learn about the ten signals from nature that will help you to identify the naturality flow in your life so you can hop aboard. We're then ready for Part Two of the book which details how to evolve to your highest form by shifting into the naturality paradigm. Good luck!

> *"What does reason demand of a man? A very easy thing –*
> *to live in accord with his own nature."*[1]   Seneca

2

DYNAMIC STABILITY

"According to everything taught by the exact sciences about the immense realm of nature, a certain order prevails – one independent of the human mind . . . . this order can be formulated in terms of purposeful activity. There is evidence of an intelligent order of the universe to which both man and nature are subservient."[2]
Max Planck, Nobel Prize winner, founder of modern physics

Ancient cultures saw people as an integral part of nature. As civilization progressed, however, our worldview became increasingly one in which we assumed we were separate from nature. Nature was viewed as an adversary to be subdued, controlled, and conquered. It's possible to increase one's functionality and power by reversing this trend. *Peak Evolution* proposes a reintegration into nature in a more evolved way befitting the current, more advanced state of human consciousness. The "people" technologies presented in *Peak Evolution* provide a means for such a reintegration for the purpose of releasing our full potential.

Our cultures have generated a number of interferences to each of us operating naturally. Society's institutions, mores, norms, beliefs, values, and modi operandi have often pressured us to be someone we're not or to do things that are unnatural to us. Consequently, a function of the peak evolution science is to remove the impediments to our returning to our natural state. They facilitate the "unlearning" and "relearning" required to re-integrate us into nature so that we may operate the way we were designed to, in harmony with larger universal processes and themes. They are the means to transition from our old paradigm to the naturality paradigm.

Communicating a New Paradigm

The naturality paradigm is the worldview or understanding of the world used by successful leaders and creatives. Though they may not be able to describe it, they take actions consistent with understanding the world as you would in this paradigm. It is still a challenge for me to take someone to this totally new paradigm, even when I work one-on-one with them.

Needless to say, I find the prospect of attempting it through a book somewhat daunting. The Greek mathematician and physicist, Archimedes, once claimed, *"Give me a lever long enough and . . . single-handed I can move the world!"* I liked his thinking. What I needed was a lever that would make it easy for me to shift people to a world of naturality. Since I didn't know of such a tool, I have invented one to use experimentally in *Peak Evolution*.

Naturality is the emotion of "naturalness." "Living naturally" emerges from doing the thing most natural to you moment after moment after moment. Therefore, in developing this new tool, it would be imperative for me to refrain from prescribing a lot of rules about how to operate in the new paradigm, or how to use the peak evolution science. Rules are what caused us to come out of sync with the naturality flow in the first place. Ideally this tool should provide gentle guidelines to allow you to "feel" your way back to what is natural for *you*.

It would also be counterproductive to burden you with a lot of scientific theory to explain how nature operates. That would be a digression from our purpose. What I needed to develop was a vehicle that would permit you to be able to deduce how nature will operate and to intuitively know how to use the technologies to partner with nature. What I was seeking was a means to simplify my communication to you while promoting your assimilation and use of processes that were highly complex.

To develop such a communication tool, I examined all of the ways I'd seen nature respond in the lives of people using the peak evolution science. I then "retrofitted" my findings into a hypothesis as to how the universe must be operating for the results we'd observed to have occurred. I reasoned that if I could tell you how to expect the universe to operate, you would know how to use the technologies to harmonize with that operation for your own advancement. You would automatically be functioning in the naturality paradigm.

If I was successful, then, even if I had not addressed a specific challenge you were facing, you'd be able to deduce what was likely going on and how to handle it. The resulting communication tool is a model I call the *Optimization Theory*.

There's a great deal of disagreement and speculation about how the universe operates. While I've tried to be consistent with some of the most popular scientific theories, the Optimization Theory allows us to bypass all the controversy. It's a working hypothesis designed to increase the power and predictability of your use of the peak evolution science to simplify your transition to the naturality paradigm. These technologies are designed reintegrate you back into nature's continual re-optimization process – the naturality flow – so you can conscript powerful systems, processes and mechanisms already in existence in nature for your advancement.

The Optimization Theory

The purpose of the Optimization Theory as a communication tool is to instill in you an intuition about what nature is going to do next so you can proactively capitalize on the ongoing processes. By identifying some natural cycles, directions, and themes for you, it's my hope you'll be in a better position to grow and optimize yourself in harmony with the naturality flow – nature's *dynamic stability*. Here, then, is my theory of the ongoing optimization of the universe.

According to Webster's dictionary, to "optimize" means "to make as perfect, effective, or functional as possible." *Optimization* is an activity that aims to find the best – the "optimal" solution to a problem. Every system seeks optimization vis-à-vis its environment. Every system wants the most favorable conditions for purposeful continuance. Optimization is the best compromise between opposing forces among the system's internal components, and between its internal system and the external environmental system. Systems tend to evolve towards an increase in equilibrium. Optimization is a stable state of balance. However, it's seldom a static state.

A system's stability arises because forces which tend to break the system down are compensated for by processes internal to the system which keep it operating. In other words, a system's stability is achieved actively through mobility. System stability then is "dynamic." Hence, this chapter about the universal optimization process has been named *Dynamic Stability*. *Re-optimization* is the perpetual process of re-balancing opposing forces.

Think of the universe as composed of a multitude of systems all interacting and affecting each other – the solar system, ecosystems, our circulatory and immunological systems, to name a few. Some are hierarchical in that they are systems within systems. These systems can be dependent or interdependent as a result. Other systems interact in a shared environment. They co-exist, co-evolve, and compete for resources. The degree of competition depends on the scarcity of resources and the degree to which systems are similar in their need for specific resources. Uniqueness, therefore, has benefits in terms of competitiveness.

So, too, does "fitness" as it pertains to the concept of the "survival of the fittest" associated with Darwinian evolutionary theory. "Fitness" indicates a system's ability to keep as many options open as possible to adapt to future environmental changes. When operating in a shared context, an improvement in the "fitness" of one system will lead to it having an advantage over competing systems.

Therefore, continuing development is a "must" just to maintain a system's *"fitness"* relative to the rest of the systems it's co-evolving and competing with. This concept is called *The Red Queen Principle* and it was proposed by the evolutionary biologist L. van Valen (1973). The Red Queen Principle is based on the observation to Alice by the Red Queen in Lewis Carroll's *"Through the Looking Glass"* that, "in this place it takes all the running you can do, to keep in the same place."[3] Therefore, re-optimization is a never-ending process for every system and for us. We are systems too.

Another dimension of this interactivity is reflected by the fact that every improvement to a system will also change that system's own

context.   Therefore,
a system can never "arrive" at an optimally adapted state vis-à-vis its environment since the very evolution of the system will itself change its environment so that a new adaptation is needed. Because optimization is a balance of forces between a system and its environment, co-evolution is the norm. There is seldom just one system evolving in isolation. There is usually a multitude of systems evolving simultaneously – partially autonomously, and partially in interaction. There is a "network" structure for evolutionary processes. This will be true for us as well.

The universe has evolved powerful mechanisms to remain in balance. Consequently, all the successful systems which comprise the universal system must be linked somehow to this optimization process. If optimization is a universal theme echoed in every successful system, then we should be able to see in our own systems the same reflection of that theme. This is, in fact, the case. The operation of the human body perfectly reflects the universal optimization process just described. Many miraculous systems and processes have evolved to keep our bodies optimized and fit for optimal performance – the respiratory system, the circulatory system, the nervous system, and the immunological system, to name a few. The part does indeed reflect the whole.

If these optimizing processes are mirrored from the entire universe to each of our bodies, then it would seem logical to hypothesize that they must exist at every level in-between. Again, the consistency of the logic prevails. There are a multitude of examples confirming this to be the case. For example, we have all observed nature's ability to perfectly optimize multiple species and systems within a biological ecosystem to create equilibrium. When human beings have impacted even one species of predator or prey, we have often wreaked havoc on the ecosystem's equilibrium.

The existence of universal optimizing processes means there are powerful forces already trying to move us to peak performance and the highest expression of our authenticity or naturality. If we knew how to harmonize with them and conscript them to our cause, they could take us to peak performance. This is the strategy proposed in *Peak Evolution*. As it turns out, just like every other system in the universe, we come equipped with links into this underlying dynamic of the universe. The ten *Optimizers* introduced in the next chapter are our links to the naturality flow.

Creativity is the means nature uses to resolve challenges to optimization. Nature is, by definition, creative. The interconnectedness of all systems, each continuously pursuing re-optimization, results in a universal theme of endless creativity. As systems ourselves, many of us do not feel creative. We could not achieve peak performance if left to our own creative means. However, if we could become expert at linking to nature's ongoing creative process, we could become creative enough to promote and capitalize on the continuous re-optimization process. This is a more rational approach to peak performance and evolution than trying to duplicate nature's superior expertise.

Nature re-balances and re-optimizes within a level of complexity we are only beginning to be capable of. Compare nature's ability to run universal re-optimization of trillions of systems to Man's ability to run a very tiny subset of this – a market, for example, where companies re-optimize to the changing contexts resulting from the creativity of competitors. Obviously, we don't yet command sufficient predictability in our market control to indicate a proficiency in optimization expertise.

How many of us can accurately predict the activity of the stock market? As another example, ask yourself how Man has done with a multitude of ecosystems in which nature previously sustained optimization. I think you'll agree that, at this stage of our evolution, it would be more strategic to partner with nature's optimizing processes than to attempt to duplicate them. This is the philosophy behind the peak evolution formula.

I've had the good fortune of spending years watching nature's optimization processes in action in the lives of hundreds of people. I've also had the pleasure of educating a multitude of individuals on how to see for themselves the patterns and models by which nature tends to resolve similar optimization challenges. With experience, you'll be able to predict, from various telltale signs, what natural processes are likely to do next to bring your individual "system" back into equilibrium. There is a logic to nature.

The patterns are so orderly you can project them into the future to know, with great accuracy, which directions will and will not be supported by the naturality flow. Many times my clients think I must be psychic because of my accuracy in predicting the future. Intuition helps, but basically the interpretation of the orderly events in reality can be rationally and logically ascertained. Why not write down recent important events in your life and see if you can't see where nature has been trying to direct you?

I play a game with my clients to prove the existence of the naturality flow that is optimizing individuals. Each session I arrive with presentation material on the subject I believe they need to learn next. I determine what's next based on my having studied the pattern of growth and optimization events in their lives. The patterns of events in reality for both of these are very orderly when you know what to look for. At the beginning of each session, I always ask about recent events in their lives. If I'm tuned in correctly, I should have arrived ready to talk on the subject relevant to the events they have just told me about for which I had no previous knowledge. This is almost always the case.

Through 20/20 hindsight, I can tell them what past events served as signals to enable me to project what would happen next. By reviewing these, they start to be able to perceive the future from past patterns too. We are basically testing whether it's possible to consistently predict nature's optimizing process. The answer is *yes*! This is a skillset you'll find prevalent among excellent leaders and is one of the indicators that leaders operate in harmony with the naturality flow – in other words, in the naturality paradigm.

The underlying fabric of the universe is one of creativity. Interacting systems continuously de-optimize each other. Nature uses creativity to resolve optimization challenges for individual systems and for the universe as a whole.

We need to understand these creative processes in order to work with nature to achieve the creative changes required for our personal system. We'll want to capitalize on them to expedite our personal re-optimization process. Let's take a closer look at the natural flow of creative processes which continually assist re-optimization. You'll want to be able to recognize the processes operating in your own life, then, to harmonize with them, and, finally, to proactively capitalize on them to advance yourself. This is your route to the naturality paradigm.

Emergence - Progress by Wholes

Science is uncovering an increasing number of demonstrations that progression in nature is not linear. Instead, nature appears to progress by *wholes* – systems with irreducible properties. There is a rapid transition between stable states rather than a continuous evolution at slow and steady rates. Instead of a gradual progression, evolution appears to have occurred, and to be occurring, by a number of abrupt leaps to new levels of order.

Advancement entails a series of iterations of completely integrated, whole systems in which significant change has occurred. If we are wanting to decipher nature's directions for the evolution of our system, it is critical to understand that nature seldom advances us in a straight line.

We thought there were missing links in the fossil records of living history. Instead, those transitional beings may never have existed. When you think about it, how could a human eye, for example, gradually come into existence? It would be easier to imagine that the fully functioning human eye spontaneously emerged when the genes of separately evolving component systems were brought together. Their recombination could then have erupted synergistically into a novel *whole* which was greater than the sum of the parts.

At every level of science, the spontaneous emergence of new levels of order is a common theme. Consequently, there are numerous scientific theories which have recognized that nature advances by quantum leaps. Let me give you a few examples to motivate you to experiment with the quantum leap operating style proposed in *Peak Evolution*.

The science of nonlinear dynamics was originally christened "chaos theory" because unpredictable solutions emerged from nonlinear equations. In mathematical terms, a system is said to exhibit the property of chaos if a slight change in the initial conditions generates large-scale differences in the result. Very disordered systems can spontaneously crystallize into a higher degree of order.

Catastrophe theory studies what happens when a system goes from one state to a radically different state without passing through any intermediate states. This sudden, discontinuous jump is called a "catastrophe." This accelerated form of evolution is what we will be attempting to trigger in you. However, "catastrophe" is not a very endearing label for our significant growth events, so I call them quantum leaps.

A phenomenon known as the *Bernard Instability* occurs when a liquid is heated from below. At a certain point during heating, the randomly ordered molecules in the liquid suddenly "self-organize," arranging themselves into hexagonal cells. Again, order emerges out of chaos – an order that is not always predictable from the start point.

Dramatic self-organizations are evident throughout chemistry and biology. Nobel Prize winning chemist, Ilya Prigogine used the Bernard Instability to demonstrate that combining some chemicals causes them to suddenly transform into a more ordered arrangement. He calls these "spontaneously appearing ordered systems," "self-organizing systems," and "dissipative structures."

But how can a new system just suddenly erupt into existence? Prigogine and others have speculated that, rather than materializing out of nowhere, "they are an indication of a deeper level of order in the universe."[4] In *The Holographic Universe* (1991), Michael Talbot suggests that "If this is true, it could have profound implications and . . . lead to a deeper understanding of how new levels of complexity pop into existence in the human consciousness and even how that most intriguing complexity of all, life itself, appeared on the earth several billion years ago."[5]

The *hundredth monkey effect* is representative of the spontaneous spread of information to an entire species. The concept derives from observations of the communication of new knowledge through a species of Japanese monkeys despite their dwelling on separate islands. Once a critical mass of individuals – theoretically, the hundredth monkey – had the new knowledge, beliefs, or modus operandi, the entire species spontaneously had it. Even subsequent generations appeared to be born with it.

Quantum physics also confirms that things don't change slowly over time, but rather they make quantum leaps. German Physicist, Max Planck, spawned the first crucial idea of quantum theory in 1900 when he described the processes of energy absorption and emission in terms of "quantum chunks" or "quanta." Until then, radiated energy, like light and heat, was thought to be wavelike. Einstein postulated that energy itself is "quantized." This means that energy is not emitted continuously but appears in the form of "energy packets."

When an electron orbiting the nucleus of an atom absorbs a packet or quantum of energy of the correct size, it spontaneously leaps to an orbit of a higher frequency with no transition states. Accordingly, everything in the quantum mechanical universe happens in quantum leaps. Nature jumps from one quantum amount to another, never traversing the area in-between. What goes on between those quantum states – in the moment of the quantum leap – is still uncertain.

There is now speculation that, at some point, these multi-disciplined theories may be unified into a new science of emergence. Emergence is a classical concept in systems theory which is the prevailing dynamic at work in the naturality paradigm. As the name suggests, it's a special category of change in which something new emerges. A new whole emerges by combining existing parts such that *the whole is greater than the sum of those parts – the total effects are greater than the individual effects – the combined effect exceeds the sum of the individual effects.*

These, of course, are also descriptions of *synergy*. I call emergence an evolution by *wholes*. To *progress by wholes* means that we move from one stable state to the next. One system iteration is replaced by a new iteration which comes into being by recombining all or part or none of the original system components with other existing information units. The more we can reduce the chaos of the transitions in between the stable states, the faster and more effectively we'll grow, evolve, adapt, and optimize. This is the work of the peak evolution science. And this is the art of quantum leap living that you will learn about at the end of this book.

Most people operate in paradigms in which solutions are achieved through a linear process based on linear time and space. Culturally, we're taught to build solutions to a specified design, a clearly defined goal, or a well-thought-out plan. We tend not to begin unless we clearly know the best solution and precisely how we're going to get there. This limits us to our purely rational intelligence.

Using the peak evolution science to follow the signals to the naturality flow gives us access, not only to nature's intelligence and proven mastery of the emergent process, but to other aspects of our own natural intelligence and creativity. As you gain expertise with the technologies, you'll discover that nature has a plethora of creative ways to solve problems where our limited minds can see only one linear solution.

Synergy, on the other hand, results from an emergent process – a creativity, if you will – that emerges seemingly unexpectedly from bringing component systems together. This is how nature "builds" things, how evolution progresses, and how growth occurs – not to a plan, but by combining the ideal pieces at each juncture in time and space to solve the immediate problems of adaptation and optimization. An emergent process unifies available information units at each stage to deal with the immediate optimization issue in such a way as to improve the "fitness" of the whole for the future.

Nature does this so well that when you view a series of products of a system's emergence, it may appear that nature is evolving the system to a plan . . . that nature already knows the highest order possible for the system. With the interactive creativity of all the creating systems of the universe, it would be impossible to work to such a specific design. You can only combine the best information options that exist at any point of time to resolve the immediate optimization challenge through emergence. This is the way of our best entrepreneurs and creatives. This will be your way if you capitalize on nature's ten signals of the naturality flow presented in this book.

It is amazing to see emergence in action in your life or to review it in 20/20 hindsight. You will misread some of nature's messages if you don't know this is the way nature is operating. Nature's solutions to optimization challenges are nonlinear and based on emergence by wholes. Nature will take you to the information units to be recombined if you know what to look for. This is the power of the knowledge technology you will begin to learn about in Chapters 4 to 6. The necessary new information units are usually acquired through a series of information coincidences which the technology is designed to make available to you.

As your experience leads you to increasingly trust this process, you'll collect every information coincidence and flow event even if you can't understand the connection, until they spontaneously combine through emergence into an "Aha!" event. As you align with your naturality, coincidences will increase in frequency, intensity and meaning, thereby speeding your re-optimization through emergence. Coincidences and quantum leaps can save you hundreds of steps in achieving your goals. And quantum leaps take you from one stable state to the next, thus bypassing the chaos of the transitioning gaps between the stable states. This makes growth and advancement so much more enjoyable.

Merging with the naturality flow will automatically make you an expert in creating new *wholes* because nature is an emergence expert. Becoming an emergence expert means you are a master of creativity, growth, learning, evolving, entrepreneuring and, of course, leading. By using the knowledge technology to comply with nature's signals, you'll find yourself bringing together the right components at the right time to permit them to spontaneously bond to create new *wholes* that are greater than the sum of their parts. You'll be able to operate on a practical level with greater expertise at both triggering and surviving emergence.

Tools of Emergence

Emergence is the essence of the creative process of the universe. It is the recombining of existing pieces or "information units" in new, and perhaps, unexpected ways. Quantum leaps, coincidences, synchronicities, spontaneous knowledge, intuitive inspirations, "Aha!" experiences, and paradigm shifts are tools of emergence, whether initiated by nature or by you. These are all names for the same emergent process of creativity used to resolve optimization problems. The exact same process underlies each. We are going to make full use of all of these emergence tools to accelerate your progress to peak performance, peak experience, and peak evolution.

You may not have thought of intuitive inspirations or spontaneous knowledge as quantum leaps. Think in terms of the right information coming together for you to "leap" to sudden comprehension of entire solutions — or, *knowledge of wholes*. We'll use the knowledge technology to bring together the component information units that will catalyze the spontaneous emergence of new knowledge. As your capabilities advance, you will find systems of new information emerging complete in your head in territories you know nothing about yet you will *know* are accurate.

Coincidences too are the result of emergence as the right elements *collide* in time and space to create meaningful events. They can catapult you to your goal, even if you haven't been able to clearly define that goal. As you learn how to use coincidences and to create them, they'll become one of the most powerful emergence tools in your arsenal. The number and significance of the coincidences in your life increase dramatically along the naturality flow. Therefore, clusters of coincidences also offer the means for you to identify the direction of the naturality flow in your life. Follow the pattern of coincidences to accelerate your evolution.

With quantum leaps, spontaneous knowledge, and coincidences you are beginning to see how you could have some significant enhancements to your functionality and advancement in the naturality paradigm. In order to accelerate your re-creation as an evolved being, we'll be attempting to cultivate a proficiency in the art of the quantum leap and a modus operandi supporting your rapid transitions between stable states. We'll be attempting to *advance you by wholes* – "*wholistically,*" if you will.

What I'm proposing, for you, then, is the rapid release of more expanded and intensified versions of the authentic "you" by emergent leaps rather than through a gradual development process. Requiring your growth to be linear may, in fact, put unnecessary steps and stages into the pathway to the goal with no guarantee of your evolution. It will also take you right out of the naturality flow where natural mechanisms and forces can support your progress.

With our current level of successful adaptation, human beings, like all successful systems, come equipped with mechanisms to link us to the universal optimization process. Ten major signals flagging the naturality flow will be discussed in the next chapter, *The Ten Optimizers*. The very existence of these *Optimizers* makes a compelling argument for human beings being designed to operate in nature in the ways described by the naturality paradigm, the Optimization Theory and emergence theory. It may well be that reformulating our perception of our place in nature will trigger a new phase of human evolution.

> *"True wisdom consists in not departing from nature and in molding our conduct according to her laws and model."*[6] Seneca

3

THE TEN OPTIMIZERS

"In unity consciousness, in no-boundary awareness, the sense of self expands to totally include everything once thought to be not-self. One's sense of identity shifts to the entire universe, to all worlds, high or low, manifest or unmanifest, sacred or profane. And obviously this cannot occur as long as the primary boundary, which separates the self from the universe, is mistaken as real."[7]   Ken Wilber

The universe has evolved powerful mechanisms to maintain its optimal balance. Consequently, all the successful systems which comprise the universal system must be linked to this optimization process. We are no different. Like every other system, we too come equipped with links into this underlying dynamic of the universe. The existence of universal optimizing processes means there are powerful forces already trying to move us to peak performance and the highest expression of our naturality. If we knew how to harmonize with them and conscript them to our cause, they could take us to full power in our most evolved state. This is the intent of *Peak Evolution*.

In this chapter, I want to give you a brief introduction to the key links to optimization we'll be using in *Peak Evolution*. They provide not only direction for our personal ongoing re-optimization, but fuel for it as well. As you would expect, human beings have evolved built-in reward systems for using these ten *Optimizers*. We're both enticed by natural drives to optimize and emotionally rewarded for doing so. When you see the optimizing links collected together as they are in this chapter, it becomes difficult to refute their intent. The Optimization Theory establishes a new level of dynamic order in our lives which makes peak performance, peak experience, and peak evolution accessible.

This overview of the ten *Optimizers* provides a framework for the naturality paradigm into which to plug the more detailed discussions and techniques of subsequent chapters. Integration into the naturality flow is the underlying dynamic of the naturality paradigm. The shift into the new paradigm is based on reordering your life around the naturality flow. The ten *Optimizers* flag the direction of this universal optimizing dynamic.

One of the more evolved states of living offered in the *Growth Acceleration* chapter is a technique called the *growth horizon window*. An oversimplified explanation of this approach is that vision is narrowed to living totally and precisely in the immediate present simply taking action on these ten *Optimizers* as they occur. In other words, we are in deep *flow* with our lives perfectly aligned with both our naturality and the naturality flow. This is a state of unity consciousness fused with the activity of actioning the ten *Optimizers* as a way of life.

Growth-horizon-window living offers exponential and accelerating evolution and peak performance. All of the advanced functionality presented in this book is available in this powerful state. This includes the automatic creation of adaptive realities; spontaneous knowledge in which whole systems of information emerge complete in your consciousness; a multitude of quantum leaps and coincidences accelerating your progress; immense creativity in the service of your most meaningful humanitarian contributions; complete abundance; transcendence as a way of life; and oceanic oneness with the universe. This powerful formula for living may offer a new perspective on how you internalize the information of this chapter. Could you change your life to simply reacting to the instructions of the naturality flow?

OUR TEN LINKS TO UNIVERSAL OPTIMIZATION

1. The Natural Growth Path
2. Our Growth Drive
3. The Naturality Drives: Your *Art*

4. Our Drive for Meaning
5. Our Creativity Drives
6. Reality is an Optimizing System
7. *Flow*
8. Resonance
9. The Emotional Drives
10. The Knowledge Drive

1. The Natural Growth Path

Science is routinely discovering new hierarchies of order out of chaos. The natural growth path is an underlying order that exists in the lives of all human beings. This order is based on the two directions that the naturality flow *Optimizers* pressure us to grow – first, to expand the expression of our naturality and second, to clear the interferences to the expression of our naturality.

First, the naturality flow, as identified by all ten *Optimizers*, continuously channels us to the highest expression of our naturality. This makes sense when you realize that naturality is the optimization of our system. The orderliness is most evident by examining the pattern of events in reality "corralling" each of us into alignment with our naturality. Blocks will occur whenever we attempt to do things which are inauthentic or "off-path." There are flow events, coincidences, spontaneous knowledge, and lots of positive emotional states when we are doing activities that express our natural identity. Reality is also one of the *Optimizers*.

I might have missed identifying this natural growth path had I not been working with some exceptional leaders. Powerful leaders are further along this evolutionary growth continuum towards the full expression of naturality. They live in alignment with their naturality. Hence, I could more clearly see the orderliness and consistency of the ten *Optimizers* acting on their lives to increase their naturality. When I brought "would-be leaders" into alignment around their naturality, they too became leaders.

Obviously, the only possible foundation for peak performance and peak evolution is naturality and its creative expression. Once you know this is what nature is trying to accomplish, you can help it, accelerate it, and, more importantly, stop interfering with it. When you master the art of quantum leaps, you can use them to catapult yourself along your natural growth path at great speeds. The enhanced capabilities described in *Peak Evolution* that may have seemed unattainable can, in fact, be only a quantum leap away.

Since the natural growth path entails the expansion of the expression of your naturality, it is not a linear progression or gradual unfoldment. It is better represented by an expansion by concentric circles of your authentic core or naturality. Growth then can be defined as the amplification of the expression of our naturality. Rather than transitioning in a straight line from one identity to another, we intensify the expression of the naturality that makes us who we are. The Optimizers become more positive and supportive whenever we are doing activities that expand our naturality.

Second, let me introduce an even more incredible level of dynamic order associated with the natural growth path. Over the years, we've all collected a number of interferences to the expression of our true or authentic selves – interferences caused by acculturation, life events, and trauma. As a result, we've accumulated all sorts of toxic emotions, and conflicting, limiting or fear beliefs. All of these conspire to keep us from being whom we are designed to be.

Now, here's the amazing thing. Amid what appears to be our random existence, *nature moves in a very orderly fashion to clear each of these interferences from our being, one after the next after the next.* Nature is meticulously systematic about clearing, in priority order, interferences to an individual's full expression of his or her naturality.

Test it in your own life. This order is entirely self-provable. Write down all recent problem events. Assume that beliefs create reality and therefore that there is a one-to-one relationship between your beliefs and these events. What beliefs would you have had to have to create each of the negative events? I think you'll find that one belief in particular seems to be the current culprit for most of your recent troublesome events.

It will likely be a belief associated with your not being valued, free, safe, or included, or not having power, capability, respect, or abundance. Change this belief and watch that pattern or category of problem events disappear from your life. When you've cleared your current interference to expressing your naturality, the next one will begin creating a cluster of events in your reality until you again make the necessary belief change.

Let's say the most significant impediment to you expressing your naturality right now was that you didn't believe you were valued or valuable. Events would begin to occur in your reality reflective of this. These events would start off small but would gradually increase in number and intensity until you made the change to believing you are valued and valuable – the necessary state for naturality. Once that belief change happens, the "not-valued/not-valuable" events would decrease in intensity and frequency until they disappeared.

The people "created" by your not-valued belief will transform before your eyes or disappear from your life. There would no longer be a belief inside of you to create them in your reality. As this happens, the next interfering belief to be cleared would begin generating a cluster of events of increasing intensity. Imagine! Order in what appears to be a life of chaos! It is unfortunate that some of us might have had a lifetime of being plagued by events created by a specific interference, never identifying it, and never knowing those events could be so easily eliminated from our lives.

Think of the power of knowing what nature is trying to do! For example, now that you know that this belief clearing mechanism is operating, you can quickly respond to a cluster of message events gathering in your reality, make the necessary belief change, and proceed to the next interfering belief to be cleared. Very shortly, you're going to be catching these clusters in their early stages when the problem events are still very small. Very quickly, you'll find your life starting to work better with fewer problems. Very quickly, your naturality will be increasing in strength and clarity without these interferences holding it back.

This natural clearing mechanism is discussed in greater detail in Chapter 8, *Reclaim Your Reality*. It is a means for significantly reducing the number of emotionally negative events in your life while accelerating growth. There appears to be no "arrival" at the full intensity of your naturality. In a dynamic universe of interacting systems creatively re-optimizing and co-evolving in response to each other, I suspect that no such arrival is possible. Humans are designed to grow continuously and they actually become dysfunctional when deprived of opportunities for growth and creation.

"As human beings we are made to surpass ourselves and are truly ourselves only when transcending ourselves."
Huston Smith

2. Our Growth Drive

One of the reasons that we, as a species, have been so successful at adapting to our environments is that we come equipped with a natural drive for growth and advancement. We love to learn. New knowledge and new experiences fascinate us. We enjoy incredible emotional rewards when we achieve new levels of performance. The growth drive is another *Optimizer* linking us to the naturality flow and the universal optimization process.

While the growth-path *Optimizer* is most easily identified by external pressures in reality, the growth-drive *Optimizer* is an internal pressure. The growth-path *Optimizer* flags the direction of growth. The growth-drive *Optimizer* signals the need for adaptive, optimizing growth. Nature's drives and our internal drives are both trying to re-optimize our system and bring it into peak performance and peak evolution.

Unfortunately, we rarely allow ourselves to be governed by this desire for growth. As a result, we de-optimize our system and throw everything out of balance. We are designed for growth. Ignoring our need for growth transgresses against our natures. Suppress your growth drive, and peak performance and peak evolution will never be possible. You will die never knowing whom or what you could have become or what you could have contributed to the world.

Unfortunately, we both crave and fear growth and change. Culture interferes with our pursuit of this Optimizer. Society makes growth too risky. I often come across executives whose fear of change, the unknown, and the possibility of rejection or failure or criticism has totally suppressed their growth drive. They have therefore shut themselves off from the re-optimization process of the naturality flow. This results in negative consequences and repercussions on many fronts.

If we perceived growth as safe, there is no doubt that we'd do it all the time. We would let this natural growth drive order our lives the way it's supposed to. The growth technology is designed to improve your skill at growth thereby reducing the risks associated with it. Its intent is to enable safe growth. Growth expertise and safe growth invariably result in growth addiction – the more growth we experience, the more we want.

As our growth expertise improves with the growth technology, the same effort will yield greater measures of growth. Our rate of growth will "feel" the same, but the actual quantifiable growth achieved will continue to increase. Over time, our rate of effective growth will accelerate exponentially. Because of this acceleration process, the advanced capabilities presented in *Peak Evolution* are actually much more accessible than you might initially think.

In addition, inherent quantum leaps, coincidences and exponential changes can project you to levels of evolution that can't be visualized as linear projections from where you might be starting as you read this. As a result of turning your life over to the naturality flow, you can find yourself operating at unexpected levels of evolution and achievement. This is the power of the quantum leap technology.

3. The Naturality Drives

Naturality is optimization. The naturality flow is always towards optimization and naturality. Therefore, all *Optimizers* pressure us to naturality. This includes a series of innate naturality drives – drives to self-knowledge, self-expression, self-creation and self-valuing; drives to creativity, creations, achievement, contribution, service, and meaning; drives to being valued for who you are and what you contribute or achieve; drives to being free to be you, to belonging – with your uniqueness intact. As mentioned for the growth drive, all drives are trying to re-optimize our system. They emerged for an adaptive survival reason.

Therefore, proactively pursuing naturality will mean we'll be moving with nature rather than fighting it. Your growth will accelerate as you partner with nature to achieve the highest expression of your natural core. As your life aligns with your naturality, you'll be doing only those things you are passionate about and that are reflective of who you truly are. Accordingly, your performance can't help but improve. Naturality is the only reliable foundation for sustainable peak performance and peak evolution.

In the language of systems theory, our authentic identity is the "attractor" at the center of our personal *system* which bonds all of our parts together. Naturality is the "emotion of naturalness." While the emotion of naturalness is a constant, the attractor or authentic core of our system is dynamic depending on the balance of the system at any point in time. Naturality is fluid and changeable. This will become easier to comprehend as you proceed through the book.

However, it is necessary to realize that you are unlikely to be able to put a permanent identity label on your naturality. Trying to say you are a "this" or a "that" is a misunderstanding of the naturality concept. Naturality is just a natural "feeling" when you are behaving in a certain way that causes your whole "system" to harmonize and feel right. Naturality feels as if you are vibrating at your natural or intended frequency. You *know* when something feels natural or not – whether it is the "authentic you" or not. You *know* whether what you're doing is an expression of your natural identity.

Let this "feeling of naturalness" be enough of a definition of your naturality for now. Naturality is dynamic and evolving. The ambiguity of naturality will diminish as you learn how to use it to optimize yourself and to accelerate growth. Naturality is known by experiencing it rather than by defining it intellectually.

Your *Art*

Your "*art*" is the natural creative expression of your naturality. Your *art* is what I describe as that thing or category of things you love to do and you're naturally good at. Other people might think of your *art* as work if they had to do it, but for you, doing your *art* is its own reward. You would put in long hours of work for no pay in order to do it. It is something you would describe as "the effortless effort." You continually seek opportunities to do it. You have undoubtedly enjoyed doing your *art* since you were a small child. If you can't determine what it is, think back to your childhood and look for the common themes among the things you enjoyed doing.

Even though I call it your "*art*," it is rarely "artistic" as per the common usage of this term. For some people, their *art* might be their gift for parenthood or building relationships or growing people. The expressions of your *art* – your creations – are a form of self-expression. You know who you are by your creations. Your creations, in turn, reinforce your naturality. You tend to create yourself through your creations. Your creations, therefore, serve to facilitate "self-expression," "self-knowledge," and "self-creation."

4. Our Drive For Meaning

Naturality is known by what is meaningful to you and your passion.

Therefore, pursuing something that is meaningful to you is another way to enter the naturality flow. Meaning is the way to reorder and re-prioritize your life around your naturality. It doesn't matter which of the *Optimizers* you use, if your life is aligned to your naturality and you are complying with the *Optimizer* messages, you will be on an accelerated and accelerating path to peak performance and peak evolution.

Accordingly, I often give clients not yet in alignment with their naturality, noble causes with which they resonate in order to trigger that alignment. The cause motivates creations reflective of their natural identity which serve to strengthen that identity. And, here was an intriguing finding: no matter how scattered the collection of meaningful projects might be that you begin with, they will ultimately link up into a common theme. If they are meaningful, it means they are reflective of your naturality. Therefore, as the projects develop, they will ultimately converge in some way around your naturality. The pattern of meaningful projects you are drawn to is another way to come to know your naturality.

Consciousness evolves with alignment with naturality and nature's flow. As a result, humanitarian tendencies emerge with no cultivation. It would seem to be innate that the highest motivation for our growth and our creations is associated with meaningful contributions to the world. As you get a taste of doing meaningful creativity expressing your naturality, it will become impossible to resist. It will become impossible to do work that isn't meaningful and thus an expression of your naturality.

5. Our Creativity Drives

Because of the Optimization Theory, our creative impulse may be the single most important factor in the successful adaptation and evolution of the human race – past, present, and future. Creativity is the means to resolve optimization challenges and succeed in any environment, individually and as a species. Since we are surviving and flourishing, the human species appears to be innately endowed for creativity. We are not only designed for creativity, but we thrive on it.

I have so much evidence that creativity normalizes and optimizes that it has become one of my most powerful tools for causing major transformation. Even executives in crisis can be restored to optimization and naturality in record time by having them operate creatively – especially if I can get them doing their *art*. So many executives have been blocked from expressing their creativity that once they've had a taste of creatively expressing themselves, they're quickly addicted to it. This is how I'm able to kick-start their growth process to naturality and its accompanying powers.

In a profound sense, all of our creative acts express who we are at any moment in time. Our creations reinforce our identities by their very existence. Creativity is a dance of interdependence between the creator and the creation. Each time you create something more advanced than before, you can use your creation to lock in that level of advancement of your system.

There is some scientific evidence for my discovery of the power of creativity. In a 1963 paper by V.J. Papenek entitled "Solving Problems Creatively," the results of a study are reported which indicates that 90% of children aged 5 test as highly creative. As our children spend a couple of years in the formal education system, this drops to 10% by age 7 and to 2% over the age of 7. I find this rather frightening. When creativity is blocked, dysfunction, disease and aging result. If I have been able to put a dysfunctional executive back into balance by having him focus on being creative, then blocking creativity in our children as they enter the formal education system may account for many of the ills that we all seem to carry into adulthood. Their systems would immediately come out of balance.

And, what about corporations who stifle any form of creativity in their employees by making it too risky to experiment; by sabotaging attempts to introduce change; by managing with an authoritarian hand; or by wanting employees to operate like machines that just run faster and more efficiently doing the same outmoded activities? I view our innate craving for creativity as a driving force in the current evolution of society away from oppressive institutions and monolithic corporations to smaller, more entrepreneurial organizations where creativity is nurtured and valued. Perhaps the great inventor, Buckminster Fuller, aptly assessed our human situation, "Everyone is born a genius. Society degeniuses them."[8]

I've found creation and creativity so effective in optimizing, normalizing and transforming individuals that I now believe that the *will to creativity* is the major motivational force in human beings. Sigmund Freud's psychoanalysis was based on the *will to pleasure*. Alfred Adler's psychology and Friedrich Nietzsche's philosophy promoted the *will to power*,[9] and the foundation of psychologist Viktor Frankl's logotherapy is the *will to meaning*. No matter which of these I tried to identify for a client, it always came back to *the power or freedom to create*.

What was innately meaningful to a client turned out to be the creation of a new reality or just a creation in general. This is why I believe that the *will to creation*, or the drives to creativity and creation, are actually what motivates us. We crave to change the world with our meaningful creations. We seek to be part of something greater than ourselves. We seek to know ourselves by our creative expression. Creativity and creation are an underlying theme of *Peak Evolution* since the naturality paradigm mirrors the same underlying theme in the universe.

6. Reality is an Optimizing System

Reality itself is one of nature's most powerful optimizing systems. There is actually an unexpected degree of "dynamic order" in what we have generally perceived to be a random or even chaotic reality. Thus far in *Peak Evolution*, we have been gradually identifying a number of signals and messages in reality reflective of that order that guide us to optimization.

First, we learned that events in reality perfectly shepherd us along our natural growth path to naturality and optimization. There will be "block events" when you try to go in the wrong direction. On the other hand, there will be "flow events" or facilitating events when you're "on path." These latter events include coincidences that accelerate your progress and events that stimulate the experience of emotional highs.

You can check the accuracy of the pattern of blocks and flows right now. Revisit some project you were trying to accomplish that ended up badly. Examine the events leading up to it. Were there lots of events blocking your progress? Take a look at other projects. Can you think of one which ended well? With 20/20 hindsight, can you see the pattern of signals from events in your reality which tried to warn you when you were going in the wrong direction and encourage you when you were going in the right direction? Were there signals early on in the pattern of blocks and flows of what you ultimately found to be the solution or the answer or the direction that made the project successful?

Once you've proved reality's reliability to yourself, you'll stop yourself when you keep hitting blocks in the future and proactively honor the directions indicated by flow events. As a result, you'll find your projects moving along much more quickly and pleasantly. Not only will you be enjoying increased creation, creativity, naturality and growth, but you'll also be gratifying your emotional needs more often.

In addition to *direction messages* such as these, there are also *growth-related messages* in reality. The discussion of the natural growth path has already suggested that clusters of events appear in reality to perfectly reflect the next interference to be cleared on your route to naturality. Reality also signals when quantum leaps are necessary in the growth and optimization processes.

We can't always read our internal messages to grow. Therefore, what we appear to have evolved is a mechanism for "objectifying" our growth or optimization process into actual events in our physical reality to assist us in facilitating, rather than inadvertently resisting, the indicated changes. What is going on "inside" of us, is being reflected "outside" of us into reality, apparently to assist us in optimizing our system.

This messaging phenomenon, however, is part of an even greater phenomenon concerning the role of reality as an *Optimizer*. Reality is just a reflection of our beliefs. Our reality is "created" by our beliefs. This means the reality we experience is 100% self-created. Since we create it, we have total power to change it. If you don't like what's in your reality, you can simply recreate yourself in order to recreate your reality. Change your beliefs inside and something different will be reflected outside. This is a very powerful foundation for the naturality paradigm. It will likely require you to reconnect everything you know about the world in a new way.

In studying the partnership between leaders and their realities, I came across a great deal of scientific information that indicated that beliefs create reality. For example, quantum physics and Einstein's Theory of Relativity suggest that the observer creates the observed. There are also a number of scientific studies proving that a patient can be "cured" by taking a placebo, an inert substance which the patient "believes" is a cure.

Subjects who have been given hypnotic suggestions as to what to believe about their reality, experience that suggested reality. In addition, there are numerous studies that have shown that hypnotic suggestion can cause subjects to control allergic reactions, blood flow patterns, nearsightedness, heart rate, pain, and body temperature. In other words, their beliefs determined their physical body.

The same is true of those with multiple personality disorder (MPD). As they flick from one personality to another, there are measurable changes in their bodies. One personality might be allergic or inebriated while the next is not. One may speak a particular language or know scientific information and the next will not. I am anxious to see research on the changes in the realities created by the changed belief blueprints of each personality.

While we think of MPD as an illness resulting from trauma, it could well represent an example of how all human beings could evolve to more sophisticated reality creation. The technique of reincarnation that I have developed for creation and growth is a powerful affirmation that this may, indeed, be the case. More about reincarnation in the reality creation technology and the growth technology chapters.

When I started experimenting in 1990, I simply assumed that if beliefs created reality in some situations then it must be the case in all situations. I then began rigorously applying this new understanding of reality to my life and the lives of others. What resulted was the Reality Creation Technology. To save you the time of rediscovering what I did from scratch, I'll provide you with some tests in Chapter 7 to assist you in proving it to yourself.

In the interim, you can start to make the paradigm shift by simply assuming a one-to-one relationship between an event in your reality and a belief you might have. The orderliness of the reflection in what appears to be a random reality will astound you. If there are some pairings of beliefs and events that you can't figure out, don't let that deter you. These are likely events being created by *systems* of interrelated beliefs and/or conflicting beliefs. We'll be taking a look at how to deal with these in Chapter 9 when we discuss the "powerlessness belief system."

In my scientific readings, I had encountered a recurring theme throughout the universe of "the part reflecting the whole." For example, every cell in our bodies contains the genetic blueprint for the entire individual. I therefore assumed that our beliefs and "systems of beliefs" map our realities in the same way that genes in our chromosomes map the human body. I call the "map" defining the reality we experience our *belief blueprint.*

Once you can see the relationship between your beliefs and reality, you'll want to master the art of creating that reality in the way human beings have been designed to. In other words, you'll want to reclaim your birthright! This is the function of the reality creation technology.

As soon as I tell executives about our ability to create the realities we will experience, the vast majority invariably make creating money their immediate goal. Incredible as it might seem to you now, once individuals optimize around their naturality so they are expressing their identity and doing what they love and what is meaningful to them, there is no amount of money you can pay them to leave this "naturality groove."

Quite often, however, because they are doing what they love and are designed for, they command their greatest incomes. It is my experience that people have been pursuing money in order to be free to do what they love to do. Yet, paradoxically, money comes by doing what they would do if they had all the money in the first place. In the naturality paradigm, money comes easiest as a result of expressing your naturality.

Let's continue our exploration of the messaging phenomenon that makes reality an *Optimizer*. In addition to messages for *optimization, direction, growth, and creation*, reality also provides *information*. Information causes de-optimization and is also the fuel for the creativity required to re-optimize. Reality can actually be used like a giant computer to provide information for optimization as and when you need it.

Peak Evolution will help you to comprehend whole new categories of nature's messages about growth, optimization, creativity and reality creation, pathfinding, emotional goals, accessing information and diagnosing problems. You'll soon realize that both systems – ours and that of our reality – optimize to each other through a two-way information exchange.

While, as children, we might be a product of our reality, the revised process of maturation and reaching your full potential in the naturality paradigm is one of reality becoming our product. What I would like to propose, as you enter the naturality paradigm, is that you treat both yourself, with your internal belief blueprint, and reality, the "objectification" of that belief blueprint, as one single system.

Your identity extends beyond your "skin," so to speak, to include everything inside of you and everything you experience outside of you. This is your total personal system. Your being-reality system. This is the *system* which is addressed throughout *Peak Evolution*. Any individual evolves tremendously at the moment they "own" their reality in this way. For most people, this is a quantum leap.

Creating reality versus being created by one's reality is one of the pivotal quantum leaps I look for an executive to internalize en route to becoming a leader. It requires a shift from being externally referenced to being internally referenced. Internally referenced means one is operating in harmony with internal drives and your naturality. Externally referenced means that your identity, goals, and emotions are determined externally by what others say, or by circumstances in your current reality. Your ability to create any reality improves dramatically when you become internally referenced because of the power and precision of your instructions to reality.

7. Flow

One of the leading scientists working on the study of *flow* is psychologist Mihaly Csikszentmihalyi, author of the book *Flow* (1990). He calls *flow* the "the optimal experience." In *Emotional Intelligence* (1995), psychologist Daniel Goleman calls *flow* the "neurobiology of excellence." Some athletes call it "the zone."

I call it activity fusion since you and the activity you are doing become one. Awareness merges with action. In *flow*, all that exists for you is the activity and your masterly control of what you're doing. *Flow* is an altered state of consciousness. It is an egoless state in which we achieve unity consciousness and oneness. It is a state of positive emotions.

Children seem to operate in *flow* constantly, indicating that this is an innate capability of human beings. This would make sense since, in the naturality paradigm, *flow* is the means for our systems to re-optimize. And *flow is optimization*.

In the naturality paradigm, *flow* is pure naturality and growth. *Flow* is the number one *Optimizer* to signal when you have reached optimization within the naturality flow. All of the processes, capabilities, and mechanisms inherent in the naturality flow are therefore supporting us. Coincidences abound, thus expediting our progress. Consequently, in *flow*, it can feel as if we can do no wrong.

If you want to grow and evolve more quickly and to optimize, *flow* is one of the most powerful forces for transformation. *Flow* is an addictive state with growth built-in. We have to be stretched in order to enter this highly gratifying state. Individuals can be dramatically enhanced by increasing their time in *flow*, whether it's on the golf course or in the boardroom. Most of the best athletes rely on *flow* for exceptional performance. Imagine the quality of your life if you made that level of performance a way of life.

The naturality paradigm offers profound new ways for achieving and sustaining *flow* . . . . with evolutionary consequences. *Flow* is our modus operandi in the naturality paradigm. Follow any *Optimizer* to the naturality flow and you will be led into *flow* state. Being in *flow* means you are operating at your peak.

Sustaining yourself in *flow* while doing your *art* – the expression of your naturality – allows you to shift to the depths of *flow* that will initiate peak evolution. Because *flow* is optimization within the naturality flow, this entire book is designed to help you achieve a life of 100% *flow*. When *flow* is fully mastered and exists in every part of your life, you are living in the naturality paradigm.

8. Resonance

We all have a powerful, built-in guidance system. If we honor our resonance each moment, we will be automatically led to operating in alignment with our naturality and the naturality flow. Achieving naturality can be that simple. It's a navigational device that will quickly accelerate us along our natural growth path to full power.

Resonance is the best *Optimizer* to take us into the deepest *flow* states. Resonance allows us to operate as if we have access to all knowledge – past, present, and future. It tells us the fastest route to any goal. It links us to coincidences that can accelerate our progress exponentially. Resonance can keep us safe in any situation. If you're not using it, you can't be operating at your full potential.

Technically, resonance is "the reinforced vibration of a body exposed to the vibration of another body." If you can recall your high-school physics, you'll undoubtedly remember the experiment demonstrating "resonance." When a tuning fork is struck it begins to vibrate. The vibration emits a tone.

As the vibration/tone "travels" through the air to another identical tuning fork, the second tuning fork starts vibrating until it, too, emits the same tone. A vibrating tuning fork will "resonate with" or "set up a vibration in" another tuning fork *only* if the second tuning fork is inherently the same frequency. It appears that human beings have a physical ability to "resonate" in the same way.

Think of your resonance as an indication of your natural vibration or frequency. You want to only do activities with the same frequency. As you choose each activity to do next, pretend you are one of the tuning forks. Look down your to-do list, your project plan or your options and choose your next task based on resonance – that is, when you *feel* the surge of the second tuning fork starting to resonate as you contemplate selecting a particular task.

Resonance can be experienced as a "frequency change" in your energetic structure – an almost "pre-emotional" state. Alternatively, it can be a full "emotional shift" to enthusiasm and excitement. At minimum, your resonance is an internal "knowing" that something is "you." Your ability to "read" your resonance increases with use, so don't be discouraged if you make a few mistakes in the beginning. However, as a precaution, you might want to practise on less important things for awhile before risking major decisions.

The goal is to only do activities we resonate with one hundred percent of the time. This may require extensive "unlearning" and a release from all sorts of rules and habits and fears we've accumulated. To "hear" the instructions of our resonance, we must operate totally in the present. Surrender to your resonance whenever you can to build up your expertise with this powerful built-in guidance system.

All of my words and concepts and technologies in Peak Evolution are designed to get you to exactly the same natural state that your resonance would take you to directly if you would follow it moment after moment. This is one of the confirmations I have that the naturality paradigm may indeed be an accurate representation of the way we have evolved to operate. This is also suggestive of how fundamentally powerful your resonance is. It is the "mother" of all of the *Optimizers*.

9. The Emotional Drives

Our emotional drives are also *Optimizers* leading us to the naturality flow for optimization. As with all drives, they emerge to incite us to take actions which will re-optimize our system. According to neuroscientist, Candace B. Pert as documented in book, *Molecules of Emotion* (1997),[11] all emotions are traceable biochemical events and, at the time of her book, likely electromagnetic events.

Therefore, in applying the Optimization Theory, I speculated that, as our system tries to re-optimize itself biochemically and electromagnetically, it generates the drives for us to seek specific emotional states in order to come back into balance. Our system is trying to biochemically and electromagnetically optimize by "asking" us to pursue an emotion or a symbol of that emotion.

In addition, human beings unfortunately adapt to stimuli, whether they invoke pleasure or pain. This means that a stimulus ceases to be sensed after a period of time. We need stronger intensities of stimulation to sustain our experience of the same emotional state. Therefore, sustaining a positive emotional state is a dynamic process. Emotions are the fundamental source of all motivation. The only reason we choose to do anything is to achieve a change in our emotional state.

Since emotional change is our only goal, all goals are emotional goals. Therefore, anything we pursue in reality is only a symbol of our current preferred emotional state. We can use these symbols, then, to identify our emotional needs for optimization. We can then achieve the emotional goals by the fastest route rather than insisting they come through the original symbol. In this way, we can proactively support the optimization process for our system. We can also better understand what the naturality flow is trying to accomplish at any point in time so that we do not fight the process.

10. The Knowledge Drive

The drive for information or knowledge is the fundamental survival mechanism for all systems. The company with the best market intelligence is usually the most successful. A system's knowledge of the environment is critical to its longevity. The information sourcing mechanisms of a system determine its evolutionary fitness – its ability to adapt to change and unknown future realities. Hence, evolutionary mechanisms have tended to select in favor of making the human system feel good whenever something new is discovered.

The drives and information sourcing mechanisms we have evolved are one of the greatest reasons for the adaptive success of our species. Unfortunately, we no longer use them to the fullest. Our cultural deference to information products derived from rational logical thinking has reduced our reliance on other information sources. Most people won't even begin a project without a project plan. If you know how to use the *Optimizers*, you can use them in conjunction with the pathfinding technology – without a plan – to move into unknown territory or to create what you are seeking.

As with all drives, the knowledge drive urges us to take action in order to re-optimize our systems. Information is both the fuel and the product of the emergence process nature uses to resolve optimization challenges. Accordingly, the drive to information is the engine that makes everything work in the naturality paradigm.

Because we don't understand this, we often resist our knowledge drive and don't pursue the information our system needs. We don't realize that, through the *Optimizers*, we are connected to nature's greater intelligence and knowledge. We cannot perceive of why an urged action is logically connected to our goals or needs and thus dismiss it.

The knowledge technology and the pathfinding technology are designed to restore you to full access to all knowledge through the naturality flow. This is essential for peak performance and peak evolution. As long as you are taking action with your knowledge drive and the *Optimizer* messages, you will have the information needed to fuel your growth and your creations.

The Optimizing Drives

The *Optimizers* link us to the universe's underlying optimizing dynamic. They are predominantly a set of innate drives that are consistent with the directions in which nature wants to optimize us. The ten *Optimizers* consist of the following eight drives: growth, naturality, meaning, creativity and creation, *flow*, resonance, positive emotions, and knowledge.

The two remaining *Optimizers* are reality and the natural growth path. Both of these relate to optimizing through directions from patterns of events in reality. They represent reflections or objectifications in reality of what's going on inside of us as a means to consciously assist the process of optimization.

Sigmund Freud is the most famous of the discoverers of human drives. Previously, philosophers believed that humans were completely rational. Freud, however, theorized that many of people's actions are caused by completely irrational impulses, which he called drives. Freud said, "There is no more urgent need in psychology than for a securely founded theory of the instincts on which it might then be possible to build further."[10]

Perhaps the description of the *Optimizers* in *Peak Evolution* will raise drives and instincts to a new understanding. All drives are simply trying to optimize our systems consistent with universal optimization. Once we learn how to recognize and use them to comply with the direction of the naturality flow, we will have found a new level of rational order.

Once we have understood nature's order, we will discover that, thanks to that order, we are once more rational beings. Ignoring the signals of the naturality flow will be irrational behavior.

> *"The world is not to be put in order; the world is order incarnate. It is for us to harmonize with this order."*   Henry Miller

Part Two

Making the Paradigm Shift

THE KNOWLEDGE TECHNOLOGY

"The factory of the information age is the human mind."
Donna Partow

Each of the three major technologies presented in *Peak Evolution* is based on an uncommon belief. For the Knowledge Technology, this uncommon belief is that we have access to all knowledge – ultimately spontaneously – merely by focusing consciousness. This is an imperative skill in a world of accelerating change. It is also an evolving skill of the human race.

From organisms to organizations, the ability to access information about changing environments determines success or failure. Aren't the most successful corporations those with the best market intelligence? The knowledge technology promotes a new level of human functionality with respect to sourcing and utilizing information. It accelerates the ongoing evolution of human adaptiveness.

The knowledge technology permits us to pioneer any new territory quickly and safely as if we had access to all knowledge – past, present and future. If we can learn to conquer the challenge of the unknown, we will have mastered the underlying dynamic inherent in entrepreneurship, leadership, innovation, creativity, idea generation, informationless decision-making, learning, pathfinding, pioneering, growth, and strategic planning. Do you recognize any of the capabilities sought by corporations facing today's volatile world?

In the Age of Reason, the logic and deductive reasoning of rational, linear thought prevailed. In the Knowledge Age, we are no longer limited to man's intelligence or even that of technology. We are quickly gaining the means to also conscript nature's knowledge and intelligence to our goals. The bar is being raised on human peak performance. Discover capabilities you never knew you had.

Techniques presented in *Peak Evolution* help you to comply with the inevitable pressures in nature to be who you are . . . . to be the authentic you. As you submit to this naturality imperative, you will find new and existing knowledge spontaneously emerging in your consciousness and your reality. You are about to discover how to use naturality to not only foster superior performance but more advanced human functionality.

> *Challenging evidence is being offered from a number of different directions that information, not mass or energy, is the ultimate fabric of the cosmos. . . . . The laws of physics that govern the seemingly objective world also break down, cause and effect as we know them no longer apply, and even the boundaries of time evaporate.12*   Michael Talbot

4

RESONANCE

Access to Nature's Intelligence

*The more carefully we listen to the voice inside of us, the more
clearly we will hear what is sounding outside.*
Dag Hammarskjöld

If you are not using your resonance, you cannot operate at your full
potential. Period! If you perfectly mastered and executed all of the peak
evolution science, you would achieve exactly the same evolved state as
would result from following your resonance moment by moment.

If you did nothing but follow the dictates of your resonance, you
would end up with a life in alignment with your naturality in the naturality
flow, doing what you love, and what is most meaningful to you. In other
words, you would progress along your natural growth path.

This is one of the confirmations I have that the naturality
paradigm is an accurate representation of the way we have evolved to
operate. This is also suggestive of how fundamentally powerful this
Optimizer is. We are all born with resonance. When you know what to look
for, you can observe how very well our children harmonize with their
resonance. Unfortunately, for most of us, our resonance has been
"culturally disabled." To reconnect to our resonance, many of us will need
to do extensive "unlearning" to release us from the interfering rules, habits,

and fears we've accumulated.

This is why I developed the six technologies and the other nine *Optimizers*. There are many routes to the naturality paradigm and peak evolution. However, let's not give up on our resonance just yet. It's like a muscle: the more you use it, the stronger, more effective, and more reliable it becomes. Let's explore resonance in greater depth so you can begin to rebuild your connection to this powerful information source today.

Experimentation and experiential learning are the best methods I can suggest for reclaiming your resonance connection to the naturality flow. Therefore, the thrust of this chapter will be to stimulate experimentation with your resonance as you go about your daily living. Out of that experimentation, you will develop new beliefs about how nature operates and your own enhanced functionality. A number of the quantum leaps listed in the *Quantum Leap Living* chapter will occur automatically as a result of conforming to your resonance. Our ultimate goal is for you to do only activities you resonate with one hundred percent of the time.

WHAT IS RESONANCE?

Think of resonance as a powerful built-in guidance system that is frequency-based. It is a kind of "navigational device" taking us in the right direction for optimization, growth and naturality. Resonance is our connection to nature's intelligence, pulse and knowledge. It is a source of information which transcends the bounds of time and space. It is the voice that directs us from the deepest point of naturality within us. Omniscient resonance can tell us the fastest route to any goal. It can link us to coincidences that can accelerate our progress exponentially. It can keep us safe in any situation.

Technically, resonance is "the reinforced vibration of a body exposed to the vibration of another body." If you can recall your high-school physics, you'll undoubtedly remember the experiment demonstrating "resonance." When a tuning fork is struck, it begins to vibrate. The vibration emits a tone. As the vibration/tone "travels" through the air to another identical tuning fork, the second tuning fork starts vibrating until it, too, emits the same tone. A vibrating tuning fork will "resonate with" or "set up a vibration in" another tuning fork only if the second tuning fork is inherently the same frequency.

It appears that human beings have a physical ability to "resonate" in the same way. Science may ultimately find that our resonance is a built-in frequency-sensing device. It may operate like the "echo-location sensing" of dolphins and bats, the navigational mechanism of migratory birds and homing pigeons, or the way a lost dog can walk miles to the exact location of its master. There is growing evidence beyond the scope of this book that we are not only evolving towards the ability to operate at higher frequencies, but that we are learning to operate with the most basic frequency reality of the universe. For now, I would like to just introduce the first step in this direction, resonance.

Resonance can be experienced as a "frequency change" in your energetic structure – a "pre-emotional" state. Alternatively, it can be a full "emotional shift" to enthusiasm and excitement. At minimum, your resonance is an internal "knowing" that something is "you." Like all *Optimizers*, resonance identifies the naturality flow for us and the ideal actions for re-optimizing our system. By using your resonance, you'll observe first hand, that there is indeed a "dynamic order" to the universe and, by reflection, to your life.

Resonance is part of the new frequency-sensing capabilities that human beings are evolving. Resonance enables us to select adaptive, optimizing action based on frequency. It is a pre-intuition, pre-belief, pre-cognitive, and often pre-emotional state. Resonance and intuition are on the same continuum for providing us information, but resonance is more purely an expression of nature's intelligence. It provides instructions without words, knowledge, beliefs or explanation. By comparison, intuition usually has all of these. Intuition is much more developed. Intuition is knowledge gained without rational thought. Intuition is part of the spontaneous knowledge portion of the knowledge technology that will be discussed in the next chapter.

With resonance, there is no knowledge to act on, just a feeling or a vibration when your consciousness has focused on something that is the same frequency. Yet, once you have experimented with this frequency-matching ability and seen what it can do, you will know it has access to all information – past, present and future. Therefore, as you reconnect with your resonance, you can operate as if you have access to all knowledge including nature's intelligence. Resonance adds nature's capabilities to your own to take you beyond your full potential.

HEARING YOUR RESONANCE

Think of your resonance as an indication of your natural vibration or frequency at any point in time. You want to do only those activities which have this same frequency. As you are choosing activities, pretend you are one of the tuning forks. Assume that the most adaptive activity for you to be doing next will feel like the second tuning fork has just begun to resonate.

If you scan down a list of possible actions, you will find the one that most represents the frequency of the second tuning fork. Review your to-do list, your project plan or your options and choose your next task based on resonance. Which activity, when you contemplate doing it, *feels* like it generates the surge of energy of a second tuning fork starting to resonate? This is the most adaptive activity for you at the moment. It is the same frequency that you are right now.

Communications from your resonance can be as *loud* as "great enthusiasm" or as *quiet* as an "inner knowing" that an action reflects the "authentic you." It can be experienced as a surge of energy when an adaptive action is contemplated or a complete energy drain when you're considering an action which goes contrary to the flow of optimization for your personal system. The strength of the sympathetic surge of energy will demonstrate the degree the activity will promote the optimization of your system.

Review times you did things in the past that "didn't feel right." Did they work out? If the larger percentage did not, then you already have proof that your resonance was accurately warning you not to proceed. Now, what about the reverse? Think of times when you did something because it "felt right" – even though all logic, all rules, and all the people in your life disagreed with you. Did these work out?

Again, you can gage the accuracy of your resonance from your own experience. Thirdly, review times in which you were drawn to a particular activity but didn't follow through. Did you later find out that this was precisely the activity you should have done? With practice, resonance can become a reliable tool for decision-making and determining your direction to optimization. Experience helps you to feel your resonance better.

If you feel that someone or something is pressuring you from the upper back and neck region to take a particular action, resist it. This is old cultural programming and fear, not your resonance. If it feels like something out in front of you is magnetizing you into proceeding in a direction which energizes you, that is likely your resonance. Follow that urge in order to speed yourself towards your goals. External pressures or fears can corrupt the communications from your resonance. Try to release yourself from these to better "hear/feel" the messages from your resonance.

Resonance has an "on" switch and an "off" switch. It is important to honor the exchange of a resonance "on" switch for an "off" switch. When an activity that once had resonance energy now drains you, it's time to stop. Signals of pain, tension, stress and fatigue are indications that you are violating some elemental force of nature.

Your resonance is indicating that this is no longer the activity you should be doing given the optimization needs of your system. It may simply be time to rest. It may be there is something else you should be doing right now. You may also be off track; or a delay is necessary until some other event occurs before you can continue; or you have achieved what you needed to with this particular activity. With experience, you'll come to understand the distinctions in what your resonance is communicating.

The Resonance-Rating Exercise

The Resonance-Rating Exercise is a means to combine resonance, intuition and rational thought to understand current situations better or to take safe, adaptive, effective action into the future or the unknown. When you have a list of activities you need to do, you can use resonance-sensing to rate each of the activities. Or, make a list of every activity possibility you can think of for a major project or to enter a new territory. With any list of activities in hand, take your consciousness or awareness down to the center of your chest. This is to try to minimize the work of interfering fears and beliefs in your head where, for many of us, we tend to focus our consciousness. Taking it to your chest will change your pattern.

Now, from the center of your chest, quickly scan down the list rating the degree of energy surge you feel for each of the activities out of ten, with ten being high. Ensure you do not engage your mind. Disengage judgment and analysis. Moving quickly down the list to capture your initial reaction increases your accuracy. We are trying to "hear" what nature has to say rather than be limited by *our* knowledge and intelligence. We are looking here for simply a visceral reaction to the activities based on the strength of their resonance.

Review the activities you rated a ten or the ones with the highest numbers. Write down a number of possible sub-activities you could do under each of these. Again, take your awareness to your chest and repeat the resonance rating. Now look at the activities with high ratings again in your normal consciousness. These are your hypotheses to be actioned based on your resonance.

Do a bit of analysis to see if you can figure out what nature is trying to tell you about how to accomplish your goals. Give yourself a moment for intuitive knowledge to spontaneously appear while you are so focused on the activities. Eliminate the activities from your list which have low resonance-ratings.

Now, find a safe way to action each of the high-rated activities to test out the accuracy of your resonance-rating while proactively trying to accomplish the goals of your list. Only by taking action on these hypotheses will you gain the experiential learning about what your resonance knows and doesn't know. Only by taking action will you be able to discover new levels of peak performance for yourself based on your resonance. This resonance-rating process can be used for any project that requires you to go into unknown territory safely and quickly. This is why it is a key component of the pathfinding technology.

It will only be necessary to write things out like this until you have clear communication with your resonance and you have proven to yourself how it works. As you build your resonance muscle, you will eventually be able to "hear" your resonance on the fly within the process of living. You will have become accustomed to operating in the present. You will have built up a trust in your resonance that allows you to take actions when you have no idea where you are going. When you have reached this level of proficiency, you can still return to the Resonance-Rating Exercise when you have an emotionally charged situation in which it is difficult for you to reconnect with your resonance.

The Resonance-Rating Exercise can also be used to sense out into the future; to see what your resonance thinks is going to happen. List off all potential possibilities that you can imagine occurring and resonance-rate them out of ten. When you review the high-rated items, you may find spontaneous knowledge occurring giving you further insight into the future. Because we live in a very volatile world, things may change in the future and some of the events will not come to pass as indicated by the exercise. However, see if your resonance-rating of future events is not giving you what you need to know right now for your current peak performance.

Operate in the Present

To "hear" the instructions of your resonance, you must operate totally in the present. This may be no easy feat – especially for those of us accustomed to worrying about the future, or who insist on wearing past failures at all times. You need to just *stop everything*. Move entirely into the present. Feel, this moment, precisely what it is that you would like to do next if you were 100% free; 100% safe; guaranteed to succeed; if the world was perfect; if you couldn't hurt anyone, no matter what you did, nor be hurt; if the world was entirely abundant; if there were no restrictions whatsoever. It's not easy for a novice, but it's important to jettison all of your baggage for the moments you are trying to "hear/feel" your resonance.

Operating as if you have Total Knowledge

Once you start to operate with your resonance, you will get the feeling you're linked to all knowledge and events – past, present and future. Your resonance appears to be omniscient. You will find yourself preparing for future events you don't yet know about. You'll find yourself in the right place to collide with the exact information coincidence you were seeking. You can take decisions based on your resonance with no information yet feel absolutely safe. Later you will have confirmation that your resonance was accurate. You'll find out information that, had you known it before the decision, you would have made the same decision as with your resonance. As a result, you will begin to operate as if you are more intelligent than you are. You will have added nature's intelligence and knowledge to your own.

Allow Resonance to be Nonlinear

In order to get the maximum benefit from your resonance as an information source and an evolutionary guidance system, you will want to refrain from requiring it to give you step after step in a linear progression. It is advisable to relinquish beliefs in linear time, linear space, or linear process for the duration of *Peak Evolution*. Remember, nature is nonlinear and your resonance is connecting you into the flow of nature. Let nature show you how to bypass a multitude of intermediate steps to more effectively arrive at a goal state.

Releasing a belief in continuity means you cease to view life as a linear series of separated events. Rather you can begin to evolve the consciousness that ultimate will view everything as one homogenous event that occurs simultaneously. An analogy can be made with a reel of movie film. Rather than experiencing each frame one after the other in order to understand the whole picture, you will come to view/know all frames, simultaneously, from the *present*. Linear time and space are cultural constructs. In the naturality paradigm, we have to think in terms of how nature does things.

As you comply with your resonance more often, you will gradually through experience, the infinite number of nonlinear ways you have observed nature using to get you to your goals. By following your resonance, you will actually experience the powerful results of nature's nonlinear action. Nature will teach you to be nonlinear so that you too can operate by emergence and quantum leaps. Experiment with your resonance until you can trust it above your rational linear thinking. At this point you will move to a new level of active intelligence. You will have absorbed nature's intelligence. Release the habit of needing a linear pathway.

Resonance may make a walk attractive in the middle of a crisis because there may have been no place for creative, unlimited or nonlinear thinking in your previous stressed mode. You may have been driving yourself to pursue a single channel that was the wrong channel. Or, you may have been pushing against block after block in the wrong direction without realizing it. You needed some distance in order to notice you had been breaking the rules of the Pathfinding Methodology in honoring the blocks and flows. Or you needed the walk to actually "collide" with an information coincidence that would solve everything. Keep checking how your resonance operated with 20/20 hindsight to improve its use going forward.

STRENGTHEN YOUR RESONANCE MUSCLE. *EXPERIMENT !!*

I'd like to give you lots of ideas about how to experiment with your resonance in order to release it to full power. The more you use it, the more powerful it becomes. For many of us, living by the dictates of our resonance is a dramatic change. Give yourself some space to make mistakes. As a precaution, you might want to practise on less important things for awhile before risking major decisions. You are learning a new language and a new modus operandi. The key is to keep experimenting with your resonance.

You could record decisions or actions that your resonance has recommended. Then do what you would have done without the resonance and compare the results on an ongoing basis. Which was more accurate – your rational mind or your resonance? Once you have enhanced your communication with it, you'll find your resonance outperforming your mind. Ultimately, however, it will be the combined power of your resonance, intuition, and rational thinking that will have you operating at dramatically augmented levels of intelligence.

Why not derive numerous tests through your daily living to stretch and strengthen your resonance "muscle" until you can trust it for increasingly larger decisions. Make a game of playing with it all day. Assume it has access to all knowledge and ask for its directions as you go about your day. Follow an urge to call someone even though you don't know why. Follow an impulse to pick up a book or magazine and open it at a particular page *knowing* the page will have important information for you. Assume you have this capability and you will soon discover you do.

If you want to purchase a particular piece of apparel or find a particular book, for example, assume you can do a geographical scan in your mind to sense where the item is located, regardless of whether you know of a store existing in that location. Follow your urges after that, for example, to open the Yellow Pages to see if there is an appropriate store in the identified location or to call someone or, as your skills and trust develop, to simply drive to the identified area following your urges to make right and left turns as they arise.

When you are rushing through your day, stop to check if you are driving yourself to do things you don't enjoy or that make your energy "nosedive" when you think of having to do them. Let's say there is a task that you absolutely despise doing but which must be done. When you've released yourself to living by your resonance, here's what might happen. Your resonance will direct you to a time to do the task where you can move into *flow* state and do the whole task "in the effortless effort." In fact you will be enjoying all of the usual benefits of being in *flow* state – noticing neither time nor space nor effort, experiencing emotional highs, feeling refreshed and reintegrated, etc. If a negative task must be done, resonance will signal the time to do it that is advantageous for your system.

Alternatively, you may find you are experiencing real resistance with your resonance to do a particular job. Where you used to struggle and push yourself to get through it, now you honor your resonance and wait to see what happens. Events could occur to entirely remove the necessity for doing the work – which somehow your resonance *knew* but intellectually you had no information to suggest the task would not need to be done. Perhaps procrastination is not the discipline failure we might have assumed. Rather, it might be a more adaptive approach of waiting for more resonance information or honoring your resonance "off" switch.

Another reason why your resonance may be fighting you on a job that must be done is because you're attempting to do it before some other events unknown to you have to occur to make it easier for you to do the undesirable deed. Therefore, your resistant resonance is trying to get you to delay. You have the right task but the wrong timing. Eventually, your understanding of your resonance will become so acute that you are able to differentiate between its communications to "not do a task" as opposed to "delay doing a task." To perceive distinctions of this nature will require a real commitment to operating in the present.

One of the hardest instructions from your resonance – especially for Type A personalities – is to "take no action" – especially after a pretty active set of instructive messages from your resonance. Go with the flow on this and trust your resonance. Many of us tend to want to work on a task until completion. Nature, and hence your resonance, likes to multitask and interleave various projects in order to maximize all resources available.

It could be there are activities occurring elsewhere that will make the tasks in a project you were about to do next unnecessary or even dead wrong. Watch for this. Pay attention as information becomes available in the future if there is an explanation for why your resonance halted a pathway that it had been enthusiastic about to that point. You will discover reasons to trust your resonance even more.

Resonance can also be used to "edit" which meetings you will attend. Resonance novices often begin by cancelling meetings at the last minute when they no longer have resonance to attend. This sends out negative messages to colleagues you might not have intended to communicate. Therefore, I suggest attempting to bypass this stage of your resonance development and insist that your resonance determine whether you need to attend the meeting at the time of booking. If you have an assistant who books meetings, review your schedule periodically to weed out those meetings you don't resonate with, with a respectful lead time.

Over time, you will come to see that your resonance seems to be operating in compliance with future events which you have no knowledge of. You will come to trust this. By the same token, if you had positive resonance at the time of booking a meeting, trust that. There is information in that positive resonance event to be considered if you feel like cancelling a meeting later.

Are your emotions or intellect interfering with your reading the resonance that is continuing to tell you to attend the meeting? Often the reason you set up the meeting is not the real purpose of the meeting as far as your resonance is concerned. Therefore, just because the original rational reason for attending the meeting disappears, if your resonance still flags it, go. Find out what your resonance knows that you don't.

Parking spots are another good place to test out and strengthen your resonance. When you're pulling into a crowded shopping mall on a Saturday afternoon, aerial view the parking lot in your head. Where is the unknown vacant parking spot that you resonate with? Drive directly there. If this method doesn't work for you, use your resonance at each intersection to tell you whether to go left, right or straight. For some people, this is also a visual exercise. They picture the three directions possible at the intersection and determine which one generates the little energy surge of their resonance or seems visually more vivid in their mind.

Reading with Resonance

A key part of the knowledge technology has to do with a new relationship with books and the written word based on resonance. As you are better able to understand the communication of your resonance, you should be drawn to the book with the answer to one of your outstanding information requests and you should be able to open the book at the right page. Then you should be able to let your eyes fall on the right paragraph without knowing the content on the open page. Your ability to do this will increase as you are living in alignment with your naturality. Your passion for the subject will also affect this ability. Therefore, give yourself some time to practise this, but keep striving.

As part of your development on this front, it is important to begin to read with resonance. Since we are attempting to have you do only those things you resonate with, it is important to release your need to read complete books cover to cover. When your energy declines, stop reading! Pay attention to your resonance "off" switch. Open the book at another page if your resonance suggests you are not yet finished with this book. You can use resonance to go to only those sections of the book you need to read. It can also tell you when you've gotten everything you need out of a book.

Many people have great difficulty not reading a book in the sequential order in which it is written. This is an example of the kinds of rules and habits we have to release to begin to experience the benefits of resonance. The faster you can let them go, the faster you will transition to the new instantaneous connection to information promoted by the knowledge technology. You will want to learn to read only those passages that you resonate with – where your energy goes up with the prospect of reading them. As your energy drops, you need to stop.

Test this out. After your resonance drop, continue to read just to verify that your resonance was accurate in telling you that you had gleaned all of the benefit out of the material. Eventually you will be unable to read material you don't resonate with. You will know it will be a waste of time. Also, it can be pretty exhilarating when, through following your resonance, you begin to consistently read the right thing at the right time. The old method of reading the good and the bad in linear order will seem primitive and unsatisfying by comparison.

There are other applications of this new resonance-based modus operandi with written material. If you are a person with a substantial "in-basket," for example, you could use your resonance to determine what you need to read and what you don't. As soon as you pick up an item, try to increase the speed with which your resonance determines that it need not be read. To do this, you need to switch from this being an intellectual activity to a resonance activity.

In the beginning, anything you discard could be kept in a storage place elsewhere and reviewed some weeks later to make certain that, at the time it was discarded, it was not important for it to be read. In other words, that your resonance was accurate. Going through your "in-basket" is a great place to experiment with your resonance. Keep items, read items, throw items out, or forward them, all based on your resonance, unconstrained by habits, rules, fears and old programming.

Trust Comes with Use

It's a little unnerving to take actions without knowing why or where the action will take you. This is something you can only trust with experience. You have to build a relationship with your resonance. The more you experiment with your resonance, the more you will learn to trust it. The more you trust it, the greater the risks you can take based on your resonance. For example, you can make increasingly more significant decisions with less information as your communication with your resonance develops. To get to this point, however, you will want to start out small and take as little risk as possible. Trying to source information is a nice safe way to get started.

Be very scientific about testing your resonance. Operate as if you have access to all knowledge and the strengthening of your resonance will accelerate. Beliefs create reality. Deciding that resonance information is not valid before testing it is very unscientific and will create a reality reflective of your belief. Be as objective as you can. Record your result and use it to fine tune your capabilities.

If you find yourself in an undesirable reality, retrace the steps in your mind that got you there. At each point, did you follow your resonance over your fears, for example, or your rules, or your habits or what seemed logical? If the answer is "yes," you may be in a more adaptive reality than you might have initially realized. Wait to see. If the answer is no, you have more proof that your resonance was accurate and should be followed. This audit will help you gain trust in your resonance and improve your ability to understand its messages.

Each check into your resonance creates a message event which can be added to actual events in reality that can be tracked for patterns. If you have been operating consistent with your resonance and suddenly you reach a point where you are questioning your direction or position, you can look back over the pattern of positive resonance events and *know* you are in a safe place *on path*.

If you never transgressed against your resonance to arrive at your current situation, you must be in the right place. Nature is much more orderly and consistent than we assume. There is information in the pattern of your resonance events. If you can't figure out what to do next or the situation is too emotionally charged for you to trust your resonance, the other nine *Optimizers* can be used to determine the direction of the naturality flow. They can back up your resonance. They are all signals of the same optimization dynamic for your system.

Resonance Blocks Wrong Actions

Resonance can provide a new level of safety by having you do activities needed for you to be safe in the future or not do activities that will make your life less safe. As you cease to edit the actions your resonance is enticing you to do, you will find yourself doing things without having a logical reason.

Let the scientist in you go ahead and do these activities so you can check in the future if these activities were actually adaptive. Once you begin to prove they were, you will have moved to a new level of safety in your life. You will be hooked into the process of preparing in the present for unknown future events.

With 20/20 hindsight, you may find your resonance prevents you from doing something "unsafe" which only becomes apparent to you as future events unfold. Phillip had been waiting for a promotion for two years. He didn't feel very valued by the executive team at his current employer. Unexpectedly, he got a job offer from outside that was precisely the job he wanted at his current company – with a 20% pay increase. His wife was ecstatic about their good fortune.

Phillip really liked everyone he talked to at the new company. Logically, everything was telling him to take the job. However, his resonance said "no." He had this nagging feeling inside of him that something was wrong but he couldn't put his finger on it. Because he had a longstanding relationship with his resonance and knew how accurate it was, Phillip turned down the job.

One month later, his employer was taken over and the senior management team was ousted. A key player in the new parent company was one of Phillip's mentors from the past who thought the world of him. He recommended Phillip for the job of president of the newly formed organization with a 40% increase over his previous compensation package. Needless to say Phillip's trust in his resonance increased. Two years later, the parent company bought the company Phillip almost joined and merged the two under Phillip. He now runs them both.

Resonance Promotes Preparation for Future Events

The ability of resonance to prepare you for action required for unknown future events has to be experienced to be believed. Your resonance might suggest that the best activity for you to be doing this moment is preparing a presentation even though you know of no upcoming speaking requirements and you have a number of other time-pressured things to do. Two days later, you may find that all of the time pressured items you thought you needed to do were unnecessary.

Out of the blue, your boss is asking you to present with no preparation time, the exact presentation you prepared. Alternatively, you might be working at high speed on a major problem situation that urgently requires resolution. In the middle of your struggle with the various alternatives, your resonance signals you to go for a walk or to talk to a particular friend. With some trepidation you let go of your previous modus operandi and honor your resonance. When you either make the phone call to your friend or take the walk, all of a sudden you learn or figure out the solution to the problem.

Roger is an excellent entrepreneur and so was frequently reliant on his resonance even before I became his career manager. From his development of software on his home computer, he had spawned a technology company with revenues of $100 million in 6 years. However, the increasing number of lenders and venture capitalists on his board were squeezing the entrepreneurial spirit out of the company. The company had been in the red for a few quarters before Roger and I began to work together.

Some Board members were intent on replacing Roger as President at their next board meeting, one month away. They had given Roger several deliverables they said would be the deciding factor. As intelligent as Roger was, his rational mind could not come up with the means to achieve the demanded deliverables. In the midst of the immense pressure, I worked to release Roger's ability to access spontaneous knowledge to solve the problems.

One of our first tasks was to remove the interferences to his connection with his resonance. Thus freed, his resonance could augment him to new levels of performance. I encouraged him to trust his resonance and take action on its dictates moment by moment. All *Optimizers* lead to naturality, and resonance is no exception.

Resonance would take him to his naturality, intuitiveness, creativity, and the passion that had made his company successful in the first place. These, of course, are also the ingredients in the formula for increasing receptivity to spontaneous knowledge as you will learn in the next chapter. In addition, I encouraged the use of the pathfinding technology you will read about shortly as well as the reality creation techniques in the reality creation technology chapters.

One day, when he was up to his neck in alligators, Roger followed the direction of his resonance to go out to his country home for a break. While contemplating the beauty and stillness of the lake, a speech emerged from within him. It was about the future of the nation resting on the entrepreneurial spirit of individuals like he and his colleagues working at his company.

The next day, he received a call from one of the local financial associations asking if he would be a last-minute replacement to speak that week. Since the speech was ready, Roger was in a position to accept the opportunity.

Roger presented what he had prepared at the lake with immense pride and fervor. The day after his presentation, he received a call from a group of investors and venture capitalists who had been impressed by Roger and moved by what he had to say. The net result was they bought out his current investors and injected the capital he needed to not only turn around his company but take it to new levels of explosive growth and success.

Removing Interferences to Resonance

Often there are all sorts of reasons why we can't get in touch with our resonance, especially as novices. Fears, stress, dysfunctional habits, rules, and interfering beliefs can all distort or annihilate your connection to your resonance. I find that I am able to read a client's resonance better than he or she may be able to because I don't have the same restrictions and interferences as they do. Perhaps, you have a friend who could do the same for you to expedite the building of your relationship with your resonance.

The peak evolution science is always channeling you along your natural growth path in harmony with nature's optimizing systems. If you will recall from *The Ten Optimizers* chapter, one of the two directions of the natural growth path is the systematic clearing of interferences to naturality. As a result, you will gradually be clearing the fears, conflicting and limiting beliefs, and toxic emotions that might have interfered with your ability to listen to your resonance in the past.

The methods of clearing these interferences are discussed in the *Reclaim Your Reality* chapter. This ongoing process will gradually help you to "hear" your resonance more clearly. In the interim, here are some additional elements to pay heed to in order to ensure accurate communication from your resonance.

Eliminating your judged-judging reflex will also assist with hearing your resonance. Our fear of being wrong is so deeply ingrained that our minds tend to become preoccupied with not making mistakes rather than finding something that will work. And resonance is about finding what will work. The *Judged-Judging Reflex* chapter is designed to help with this. In addition, can you suspend your knowledge and expertise as to the "right way to proceed?" One needs to operate precisely in the present for resonance accuracy.

Resonance sometimes functions as an early warning system. Unfortunately, we don't always want to hear the news, preferring safe untruths to an uncomfortable truth. Not only your fears but your desires may interfere with your ability to read your resonance. Neutrality and detachment are your best friends when it comes to living by your resonance. Your ability to distinguish the messages of your resonance will increase with practice as you move from using it on unimportant, non-emotional issues to higher risk, emotionally charged decisions.

Often, we miss the messages that are trying to prepare us for a different outcome than we expect. Practising neutrality eliminates the emotional and intellectual attachments to a particular outcome which block the messages from our resonance.

As part of the reality creation technology, you will come to pursue the achievement of your desired emotional goal but not demand that it come through a specific channel. Rather you'll be getting used to the infinitely creative means that nature takes us to our desired goals. Therefore, as you progress on this front, you will also be freeing yourself to hear your resonance more objectively.

"It is our business to go as we are impelled."   D.H. Lawrence

Resonance can be thought of as your link to the larger integrated information systems of the universe. You can limit your capabilities to your own intelligence with your limited view of your world. Alternatively, you can use your resonance to tap into the naturality flow and be able to operate as if you have unlimited knowledge and access to all systems, blueprints and levels of expression in the universe. Your choice.

The ways of our cultures have prevented many of us from retaining our resonance connection to nature's intelligence and the naturality flow. The peak evolution science is designed to release us from cultural constraints so we can transition back to the way we were designed to operate.

By understanding the capabilities of resonance, hopefully, we will learn how to restructure our world so we do not interfere with the resonance connection our children are born with. We will want to assist future generations to retain their full capabilities without the restraints and limitations that we might have experienced.

*At the heart of each of us, Whatever our imperfections, There
exists a silent pulse of perfect rhythm, A complex of wave
forms and resonances, Which is absolutely individual and*

unique, And yet which connects us to everything in the
universe.   George Leonard

5

SPONTANEOUS KNOWLEDGE

"The only conclusion the unbiased observer can come to must be that there are people who obtain knowledge existing in other people's minds, or in the outer world, by means that are yet unknown to science."2   H.J. Eysenck, department head, Psychology, Maudsley Hospital, London

As human consciousness evolves, so too does our ability to access information. The Knowledge Technology is the means to develop the information access skills now that won't be prevalent in the human population for decades. Quantum physics declares all information is nonlocal or distributed. It is unfortunate, then, that we have limited our access to only that information which we believe to be in our "local" memories. As you begin to operate as if you have access to all knowledge, you will discover that you do.

We have all experienced spontaneous knowledge. New information, to which we know we have never been exposed, spontaneously emerges in our heads. Sometimes it's just an information tidbit. Other times it's the complete comprehension of a whole complex system of information – an "Aha!"experience.

And somehow we just know the information is accurate, even if it turns out the information is brand new to the rest of the world as well as to us. My episodes of spontaneous knowledge increased in frequency and magnitude as I began to develop the technologies in this book through my executive career management work. I wondered why that happened and if this was a transferrable skill. The spontaneous knowledge formula emerged from my subsequent investigations.

THE SPONTANEOUS KNOWLEDGE FORMULA

I am perpetually fascinated by exceptions in human capabilities. It has always been my contention as an anthropologist that if there are individuals who have supernormal capabilities, or, alternatively, if there are supernormal capabilities we all have occasionally, then I assume we could all have these capabilities all of the time . . . . *if we could duplicate the circumstances*. I therefore assumed that if *any* individuals have access to spontaneous knowledge under *any* circumstances, then we might *all* have this capability. I began scanning my experience to develop the model for enabling this periodic occurrence to become more widespread. I wanted a formula for making spontaneous knowledge a way of life rather than something that occurs inexplicably on rare occasions.

As an executive growth accelerator, my work usually entails taking individuals to peak performance through naturality in the ways described in this book. As a result, I had an opportunity to see the difference in the functionality of my clients before and after they shifted to naturality. The occurrences of spontaneous knowledge in their lives increased exponentially. What I had discovered was an incredible link between naturality and the occurrence of spontaneous knowledge. I therefore had the *spontaneous knowledge formula*:

First, individuals need to have the beliefs they can access information instantly. Then, they need to be able to flow with nature's ten *Optimizers* to naturality. If beliefs create reality, then we will have to have the beliefs that will create a reality of spontaneous knowledge. Further, as we learned in Chapter 3, all *Optimizers* conspire to take us to increasing expressions of our naturality. This is the integrative orderliness of nature attempting to optimize our system, and indeed, all systems. Therefore, pursuing the peak evolution science would automatically increase the occurrence of spontaneous knowledge.

Naturality

I had often observed that while people were doing what they love, they tended to experience spontaneous knowledge with greater frequency than at other times. Of course, when we are passionate about something we have, by definition, identified an activity which expresses our naturality. Have you ever found yourself speaking on a subject for which you had great passion, only to discover you are presenting information you *know* you have never heard before . . . . yet you *know* it's true?

Have you noticed that when you are doing things you are passionate about, you tend to slip into *flow* state more often? *Flow* is pure naturality. This was another state where I observed complete systems of information emerging in individuals. I was definitely seeing a pattern of spontaneous knowledge surrounding the telltale signs of naturality you will be discovering in *Peak Evolution.*

I also noticed that leaders, creatives, and entrepreneurs tended to experience "information coincidences" with greater frequency than the norm. This makes sense since these individuals generally operated further along the evolutionary continuum in the expression of their naturality.

Leaders need to know who they are and what they stand for in order to lead. Most successful entrepreneurs choose the companies they start based on what they love . . . therefore in alignment with their naturality. Creativity spontaneously emerges for creatives based on their natural *art*, the expression of their naturality. Also, creatives tend to experience *flow* with greater frequency.

With 20/20 hindsight, you should be able to verify that you experienced spontaneous knowledge when you were doing the things most meaningful to you, or that you were most passionate about, or when you were trying to do your *art*, or when you had slipped into *flow* state. If not, you could test the formula out on future projects which reflect your naturality. See if the magic happens. See for yourself if there are not a multitude of information coincidences and spontaneous knowledge events to assist your progress.

Cultivating Knowledge Technology Beliefs

A change in beliefs is equally as important as naturality for accessing information instantaneously. Changing your beliefs about your ability to access information is my challenge in this chapter. Taking action is key. Experiential learning is important for building new beliefs and know-how. The more you experience spontaneous knowledge, the faster you will be developing beliefs that you have access to it.

The stronger your beliefs, the more often you will create realities of spontaneous knowledge events and, thus, the more rapidly your capabilities will develop. With experience, not only does the frequency of spontaneous knowledge increase, but so too does the magnitude of the information "systems" that emerge complete in your consciousness.

Here's an example to help to change your beliefs. One of my clients, Charles, was the newly hired president of an advertising and public relations enterprise. The presidency opportunity had coincidentally appeared in his life when we had brought Charles to living in alignment with his naturality. He was a born leader and loved the creativity and mass impact of the business he was in. Every day was strengthening and expanding his expression of the person he authentically was.

Among his company's clients was one of the largest automotive companies. He had never had clients in this industry before. He was invited to a meeting with the president, top executives, and technical people of this client company to deal with a major corporate problem. With no technical knowledge whatsoever, he found himself presenting a highly innovative technical solution – complete with relevant jargon. The client executives and technical gurus were amazed. Charles was more amazed.

Visibly shaken by this experience and several similar ones that had recently begun to occur, he asked me when we next spoke, "What have we done to me?" He found his new power a little unnerving. I explained that spontaneous knowledge is one of the enhanced capabilities all of us will experience as we begin to operate the way we were designed to.

Picture having all of the components of a car. Picture how well these components would function if you put them in display cases around your home. Picture using them in your rock garden. Now picture how well they would function if they were perfectly integrated as a well-tuned automobile to be used for transportation. There would be a quantum leap in functionality in the last situation.

This is what had happened to Charles. His system was now operating the way it was designed to. There is a naturality . . . . a highest functionality . . . . an optimal performance . . . . an integrity . . . . for which it makes sense for the components of any system to be linked together in any given context. And this is the case for each of us as well in our personal system. There is a synergy whereby the whole has a greater functionality than the sum of the parts.

I then retraced our steps with Charles to demonstrate how we had taken him from being externally referenced to internally referenced. We had shifted him from allowing himself to be determined and controlled by others and the "things" in his life to choosing each moment to operate in compliance with his inner voice. He was now choosing to do what he resonated with. He was operating naturally and authentically.

When a person does this, a quantum leap in performance occurs just as would happen with the car components. Individuals will have new powers which the technologies in this book are designed to cultivate and channel advantageously. Charles was experiencing more passion and excitement about what he was doing . . . the telltale signs of naturality. Coincidences, including information coincidences were increasing daily. I suggested he could proactively support this metamorphosis that was occurring in him by just internalizing the identity and beliefs of a person who could access information spontaneously simply by focusing consciousness on the pertinent subject.

The next day, Charles was meeting with the Chief Financial Officer (CFO) of his new company to review quarter-end results. While the CFO was a most able man, Charles sensed the numbers were out by about $102,000. Trusting what we had done the previous day, he took a chance by telling the CFO what he thought. It took a couple of days of Charles holding firm on his "spontaneous knowledge" for the CFO to identify the problem. During that time, Charles was gradually able to define in greater detail the category of the problem he was sensing, leading the CFO to the place to look. The CFO discovered the $102,000 error and a deference for the rare capabilities of his new boss.

In the weeks that followed, the flow of information coincidences accelerated and intensified. Had Charles not expected them from our work together, he might have dismissed them as isolated incidents. Instead he was able to see them for what they were . . . evidence of a new level of functionality for him. He proactively used this observation to strengthen his beliefs even further that he had the ability to spontaneously access information at will. These stronger beliefs did, in fact, increasingly create that desired reality. His people are adjusting to not questioning what Charles is sensing to be true. In fact, as he leads by example how to operate in alignment with one's naturality, more and more of his employees are experiencing spontaneous knowledge. With win after win after win, his competitors are wondering why they had never seen Charles' company as a threat before.

Children who have perhaps not yet absorbed our limiting beliefs about what we can know, often present information their parents know their children have not learned anywhere. Or the information may be too wise for the maturity level of the child. Some children are even able to access the memory of someone who has already died. To some, this suggests reincarnation. Perhaps our innate capacity for spontaneous knowledge is an alternate explanation.

Those who have had a near death experience (NDE) describe a state of "all-knowingness." In that state, they find that merely by defining what they want, they are able to *know* the relevant information. They *believe* they can and so they can. Accomplished out-of-body practitioners (OBEs) who have been trained to release their limiting beliefs report similar experiences of seeming omniscience. These kinds of *exception events* suggested the true capabilities of human beings to the anthropologist in me. Accessing information spontaneously – merely by focusing consciousness – would seem to be the future natural state for evolving human beings. It is an evolutionary trend for human beings that you can have now.

SOME SCIENCE TO BUILD SPONTANEOUS KNOWLEDGE BELIEFS

Because beliefs create reality, our beliefs will determine whether we are going to have the ability to ultimately access knowledge spontaneously. I'd like to continue now with my desire to help you gain the necessary beliefs for spontaneous knowledge. Let's look at some of the science that instilled in me the beliefs to start using what has now become the Knowledge Technology.

Think for a moment about individuals with Multiple Personality Disorder (MPD), or, as it is now called, Dissociative Identity Disorder (DID). They represent an excellent example of instantaneous information access based on beliefs. As they shift from personality to personality, Multiples spontaneously *know* new knowledge, new languages, and even complicated scientific information to which they have had no exposure.

Their bodies seem to *know* new information as well. Each personality may have its own physical abilities, IQ, voice characteristics, brainwave patterns, biochemistry, bloodflow patterns, heart rate, scars, left- and right-handedness, and visual acuity. Even eye color can change. With a personality shift, a Multiple who is drunk can instantly become sober. Allergies associated with one personality can disappear completely with another.

Each Multiple personality would obviously have a different belief infrastructure. Since beliefs create reality, each identity would have access to different spontaneous information with the shift of consciousness and beliefs. This would suggest that we just need to release the limiting beliefs many of us have absorbed from our cultures. Therefore, by simply changing our beliefs, we can spontaneously experience new knowledge. Again, the exceptions suggest the possible functionality for all of us.

All Information is Nonlocal and Interconnected

Early on in my research, my resonance prompted me to investigate some things in quantum physics. Quantum physics proposes that all information is "nonlocal." This suggested to me that all information is actually distributed throughout the universe. I reasoned that if that was the case, then we could not have "local" memories. Rather, if we were limited to accessing information stored in our memories that had come in through our five senses or rational thought, it must be because we *believed* that we were limited in that way.

> *"Whatever model of reality we wind up with in physics . . . it*
> *must be nonlocal . . . No local model of reality can explain the*
> *type of world we live in."13*   Larry Dossey, M.D

I learned about the work of Candace Pert through Bill Moyer's PBS television series called *Healing and the Mind*[14] and later in her book *Molecules of Emotions* (1997). Candace Pert was chief of brain biochemistry at the National Institute of Mental Health. She has significantly advanced our understanding of the biochemistry of emotions and the mind.

Pert discovered that the biochemical events associated with both are distributed throughout the body consistent with the premise from quantum physics that all information is nonlocal. If there was a biochemistry of memory, Candace Pert's findings were supporting my hypothesis that it was not being held in a "local memory" in our heads.

> *"In the end I find I can't separate brain from body.*
> *Consciousness isn't just in the head. Nor is it a*
> *question of mind over body . . . the body is the outward*
> *manifestation of the mind."15*   Dr. Candace Pert

The Part Reflects the Whole

With Michael Talbot's *Holographic Universe* in 1991 and other books and materials, I began to learn about a number of scientists who were hypothesizing that a hologram may give us the best understanding of how information is ordered in the universe. Specifically, the hologram provided an explanation of how information can be nonlocal and interconnected.

One of our earliest introductions to holograms was in 1977 through the movie *Star Wars*. Princess Leia presents the problem to be resolved in the movie by pleading for help through a hologram. The hologram is a three-dimensional image that appears to actually be there until you put your hand through it and feel absolutely nothing.

Holograms are created with lasers and mirrors and stored on special holographic plates. You can't look at the plate and see the image the way you can with the negative of a photograph. Rather, the information is stored in a series of interference patterns, much like the collisions of the concentric waves orbiting out from pebbles dropped into a pool of water. Holographic plates look cratered and marked like the surface of the moon. When you want to bring a three-dimensional holographic image to life again, a laser is directed at the holographic plate.

One of the most powerful characteristics of holograms is that each piece of the holographic plate contains the information required to reconstruct the entire hologram. Even if you were to break the plate into tiny pieces, you can shine the laser onto a small fragment and the holographic image will again appear. This theme of "the whole being contained in the part" can also be seen in our own bodies. Every cell in our bodies contains the genetic material required to recreate our bodies. This is the science behind cloning. Dr. Ian Wilmut of the Roslin Institute pioneered the technique for creating the now infamous sheep, Dolly, from a single mammary cell of an adult sheep.[16]

Dr. Terry Oleson is a psychobiologist at the Pain Management Clinic at the University of California at the Los Angeles School of Medicine. He learned that acupuncturists have found the acupuncture points in the ear form the outline of a miniature human being. As a result, Dr. Oleson developed the means to use the acupuncture points in the ear to diagnose pathological conditions in the corresponding area of the body.[17]

Dr. Ralph Alan Dale, the director of the Acupuncture Education Center in North Miami Beach, Florida has accumulated evidence of eighteen such acupuncture microsystems in the body.[18] These include microsystems in the hands, feet, arms, neck, tongue and even the gums.

Both Oleson and Dale believe these microsystems exist because the body is a hologram and each of its portions contains an image of the whole. It is not much of a stretch to propose that we, as part of the universe, could, in fact, contain all of the information for the whole universe. The hologram, as the model for storage of information in the universe, helps us to *believe* that it is possible for us to access information spontaneously.

> *"In some sense man is a microcosm of the universe; therefore what man is, is a clue to the universe. We are enfolded in the universe."*
> Einstein's protégé, quantum physicist, David Bohm

The iris in the eye is another mirror image. Iridology maps the health of the various parts of our body in our eyes and is gaining in notoriety as a diagnostic tool. Reflexology is a type of massage therapy that accesses all points of the body through a similar pressure-point map on our feet. Palmistry may also have the same type of validity – not the hand-reading practices by fortune tellers but rather the 4,500-year-old Indian version of science. Ten common genetic disabilities, including Down's syndrome, can be associated with various patterns in the hand.

In *The Holographic Universe*, Michael Talbot suggests, "When the consciousness operates at the level of the information picture, not only is it no longer bound by the confines of space or distance, but it is also no longer restricted by the one-way flow of time."[19] If the underlying order of the universe is holographic, then time and space could no longer be viewed as fundamentals. Past, present, and future would all be embedded in the hologram simultaneously.

This would explain why resonance is observably able to operate as if it has access to all information – including knowledge of the future. This is much like being able to know and access every frame of a reel of movie film simultaneously. If every particle of matter interconnects with every other particle in a hologram, then the brain itself must be viewed as infinitely interconnected with the rest of the universe. Once you are able to release the beliefs which limit this access, spontaneous knowledge is inevitable.

> *"If it is possible for every portion of a piece of holographic film to contain all of the information necessary to create a whole image then it seemed equally possible for every part of the brain to contain all of the information necessary to recall a whole memory."[20]* Michael Talbot

Remote Viewing

Perhaps the holographic interconnection of all information "particles" is an explanation for a capability called "remote viewing," speculated to be available to all human beings. Remote viewing is the ability to describe accurately what a distant test subject is seeing or will see in the future. It is the ability to view remote locations.

In 1977, two laser physicists named Harold Puthoff and Russell Targ of the Stanford Research Institute (SRI) in California reported their findings about this newly identified level of human functionality in their book called *Mind-Reach*.[21]

The authors have also published their results in scientific publications ranging from *Nature* to the *Proceedings of the Institute of Electrical and Electronics Engineers*. Their findings have been duplicated. Their experiments irrefutably prove the existence of a human capacity for describing what's going on in distant locations – *past, present and future* – merely by focusing consciousness.

Puthoff and Targ demonstrated that test subjects could view what a designated experimenter is viewing at a designated time at a distance. Amazingly, test subjects could also describe remote locations experimenters would be visiting *in the future*. Subjects were able to describe "targeted locations" thus eliminating the possibility of telepathy as the source. Also subjects were able to describe targeted locations *before* they were chosen. These capabilities were not limited to those with psychic abilities.

Puthoff and Targ conclude "that remote viewing is probably a latent and widely distributed perceptual ability."[22] Here is a scientifically proven ability that we likely all have – the ability to access information spontaneously, even about the future. This is consistent with all information being nonlocal and the interconnectedness of all information as suggested by the hologram hypothesis.

Is it that we are so thoroughly conditioned to believe that perceiving the future is not possible that our natural precognitive abilities have gone dormant? Is it that our cultural requirement for objectively observable rationality is impeding our ability to use all of our capabilities?

If we had been taught as children that we could access information of future events, would those beliefs have created that reality? Is that the only difference between those with psychic abilities, intuition and gut-feel and those without? A simple change of beliefs and human beings may well evolve to a new level of functionality, individually and collectively.

Animal Intelligence and Resonance

Many other species appear to have access to spontaneous knowledge. This suggests our spontaneous knowledge ability may be part of all consciousness. In the spring of 1983, the Smithsonian Institute held a symposium on animal intelligence at which a number of researchers reported evidence to suggest other species may have consciousness.

Princeton ethologist and internationally renowned expert on honeybee behavior, James L. Gould, suggested that current wisdom views most signs of animal intelligence as the result of innate or "prewired" behavior patterns. However, he had an experience which disagreed.

In a recent experiment, Gould's purpose was to investigate how bees locate new food sources. He provided honeybees with desirable food sources. Once they became accustomed to feeding at the stations he set up for them, Gould moved the feeding stations by a factor of 1.25 the distance of the previous move.

Then, unexpectedly, the honeybees no longer needed to search for the new location. After a few such moves, the honeybees *anticipated* Gould's behavior so accurately that he found the bees circling the new location and waiting for their food *before he had even arrived.*[23]

Doesn't remote viewing perfectly describe the behavior of Gould's honeybees? They knew ahead of time the precise location of the next feeding station. From similar examples in a multitude of species, it is beginning to appear that spontaneous knowledge is a characteristic of consciousness. Our cultural worship of reason has simply interfered with this connection.

If you were the president of the beehive or the general in charge of the honeybee reconnaissance troops, would you have issued such an illogical order to send your troops to the new location? Would you have had this level of accuracy of *knowing* rather than *guessing* about the future location of resources you wanted?

If you were operating in the outmoded *Age of Reason*, there would have been no business case for allocating your troops or employees in the way the honeybees did.

If you were a child of the *Knowledge Age*, your resonance, the blocks and flows, and spontaneous knowledge sources such as remote viewing would have indicated the new location, compensating for the absence of information upon which reason could act. This is the means to keep your personal system safe and optimized. This is your competitive advantage for the survival of the fittest.

In *Peak Evolution*, I want to take you into numerous unknown territories to invoke peak performance, peak experience and peak evolution. You will need a new level of knowledge access to achieve these and keep you safe in the process. This is why the knowledge technology is presented first.

Since the human race is evolving to add new knowledge sources to their reasoning capabilities, those who evolve first will be the leaders. Those whose information access is limited to rational thought will not be able to compete. Our volatile world is changing too quickly.

Just Begin, and your Experience will Evolve You

Resonance, remote viewing . . . honeybees or human beings. All living systems seem to be connected to the dynamic, holographic, information database of the universe. To restore your own superior functionality, start small. Take action based on your resonance and what feels natural moment by moment. Where it's safe, begin to release the requirement for there to be logical reasons for your actions.

Take the actions your resonance indicates and then look for nature's logic in 20/20 hindsight. This will allow you to move to new levels of performance by tapping into nature's intelligence and knowledge. In time, you will not only be accessing information instantly, but you will be evolving the other powers presented in this book.

THE SPONTANEOUS KNOWLEDGE CONTINUUM

Experiential learning is essential to the process of strengthening the beliefs and expertise necessary to experiencing spontaneous knowledge. As your beliefs increase and intensify, you will move through four levels to ultimately achieve the ability to access all knowledge instantly.

You will gradually evolve from having to go to information, to having it come to you, to being able to deduce it from patterns of events, to ultimately receiving it spontaneously through an evolved state of being that results from using the knowledge technology, the growth technology, and the reality creation technology. Here, then are descriptions of the four stages leading to spontaneous knowledge based on your evolving beliefs that this is possible.

Level I: You are Physically Directed to the Information

As we begin along the Spontaneous Knowledge Continuum, most of us believe we must physically go to the information we need, such as using the internet or opening a reference book. This belief creates a reality with that requirement. Change your beliefs and you can change that reality.

Most of us are also accustomed to operating in a very linear way, expecting to proceed systematically from the first piece of information we need to the next and the next. We may even have a linear project plan on how we are going to be moving from Point A to Point B. That's what we've been taught. If you believe information gathering must be a linear process, this belief will also create that reality.

Until your beliefs are transformed by your progress along the continuum, using the knowledge technology will result in your experiencing a string of related information coincidences, ultimately giving you the information you need.

Using the knowledge technology means you will be following the naturality flow signaled by the ten *Optimizers*. Blocks, flows, resonance, naturality, your natural growth path, and your passion will all be relevant. First, commit to evolving to a more powerful method of accessing information.

Begin with the belief that you can simply *know* information as soon as you want it . . . . in other words, Level IV. Gradually rewrite how you go about your day as if that belief was true. Take decisions as if you already have that capability. Allow yourself to free-flow a little to see if you are taken to the place you need to be to collide with information coincidences.

Determine what information you want and assume you will have it shortly. Take action moment by moment based on your resonance. Change directions when you have blocks and proactively go into directions where you have flow events. This will draw you to physical sources of information so the knowledge can be consciously absorbed.

This includes sensing when to open a book or magazine at a particular page as if you know that page will hold the information you need next. It may entail following your resonance to call a particular person or turning on the radio or TV at a particular moment on a particular station or channel when you feel the urge. Or it may mean moving physically at the right time to a location where something transpires to provide you with information. These information sources could be symbols, objects, experiences or things people say.

Continually experiment as you go through your day in order to stretch your capabilities. For example, when entering the crowded parking lot of a shopping mall, check with your resonance to determine when to make a right or left turn to take you to the parking spot nearest to where you need to be, even if you don't know where that is.

Delightful coincidences abound when you release yourself to follow your resonance and the blocks and flows in partnership with your reality. Align yourself with your naturality by using the methods presented in this book, and you will develop this skill considerably more rapidly. Remember, we are designed to have spontaneous knowledge. The technologies help to remove the interferences to you moving to full functionality.

Level II: The Information Physically Comes to You

As you continue with Level I, you will begin to notice increasingly that, rather than having to go to the information you want next, it physically comes to you. The information just physically pops into your life by unexpected means with increasing frequency and intensity.

As soon as you focus your consciousness on the piece of information you need next, the phone will ring, for example, and someone will give you the information. If someone calls you and gives you the information you need right when you have identified that need, this is an *information coincidence.*

You could also call it an *information quantum leap.* The information coincidences really begin to become quite amazing. Watch for them. Expect them. Believe in them. Observe the dynamic flow of nature in action and be transformed by it.

Here's a Level II example from my life. Developing technologies to take people to peak performance is definitely part of my naturality, my passion and my *art.* In 1995, I was coaching Frank, a senior vice president of a major international financial institution. He was not making the quantum leaps as quickly as others I had worked with, yet he was an intelligent, accomplished executive.

Because, in the naturality paradigm, everything going on inside of us is perfectly reflected outside of us in events in reality, I was accustomed to using reality as a diagnostic tool. At this time, struggle events abounded in Frank's reality.

Struggle events are caused by conflicting beliefs creating conflicting, colliding realities. I helped Frank make the belief changes necessary to fix the first struggle situation, the second one, the third one, etcetera, and the problem events disappeared from his reality as they did with my other clients. Later these would unexpectedly re-emerge. Frank would backslide.

In one session, I suddenly experienced the spontaneous knowledge that all Frank's problem beliefs were interlinked in one convoluted mass (coincidence 1 and spontaneous knowledge). When I finished this session, I committed to drawing the information to solve this problem, not just for Frank but because I suspected others were also suffering a similar fate. Within a half an hour, my friend, Jack, called me and, with no invitation, began to read me the structural conflict section of the Personal Mastery chapter in Peter Senge's *Fifth Discipline* (coincidence 2).

Jack and I had never discussed a subject of this nature before. It was out of character. This contributed to my *knowing* this information was important. This incident led me to the development of the intervention to eliminate a multitude of conflicting beliefs linked to powerlessness that you will read about in Chapter 9, *The Powerless Reflex*. This was a typical Level II situation where the information came to me. However, as it turned out, it was also an example of Level III. Read about Level III and then I'll finish the story.

Level III: Knowledge emerges from the Pattern of Coincidences

As you experience more and more coincidences in Level II where information is coming to you unexpectedly, your beliefs evolve. You *expect* to have the information you want when you need it. Your relationship with the universe begins to shift. You begin to glimpse its underlying order and your participation in it. You are able to experience firsthand the interconnectedness of all things.

Gradually, as you experience a series of information coincidences, you will be able to see their logical interconnection and deduce new information from their pattern and flow. This is Level III. The fact that coincidences will be interrelated is a given. Reality is one of the ten *Optimizers* connected with the naturality flow – the underlying, optimizing dynamic harmonizing all systems in the universe.

It will become easier to operate at Level III over time as your continual attempts to see the patterns stretch your consciousness. Expanded consciousness will become your new norm. The ability to deduce new information from patterns of events will eventually become spontaneous, unconscious, and aligned with your current focus and passion. Let's put

Level III into actionable terms. As you progress along the Spontaneous Knowledge Continuum through your use of the technologies in this book, you are going to have a history of coincidences.

The more dramatic the coincidence, the more significant it is in indicating your pathway to naturality, peak performance and optimization. While each coincidence is enjoyable in its own right, you will come to see that the coincidences are part of a pattern and, eventually, a series of interconnected patterns. For a novice, these patterns are usually about three to seven coincidences long. You'll just have a feeling that a particular coincidence isn't finished yet or it will somehow be important in a larger way in the future.

When the fifth or six coincidence arrives, what usually happens is the process of emergence – a synergy where the whole is greater than the sum of its parts. The sixth coincidence may add additional information suddenly interlinking the previous five units of information in a new way for you. The result is an "Aha!" experience. A quantum leap in knowledge or understanding. Spontaneous knowledge. Sometimes, even omniscience. You can have complete systems of information coming into your head involving knowledge of fields you know nothing about.

Let your resonance, blocks and flows, and indeed all *Optimizers*, take you to successive information coincidences. The information in the *Resonance* and *Pathfinding* chapters will help you to gain this expertise. As you move *with* nature's *Optimizers*, coincidences will catapult you forward at incredible speeds.

Very shortly, the information coincidences will improve in quantity and quality. Your life will become magical. As your "collisions" with information increase, help yourself advance along the Spontaneous Knowledge Continuum by consciously grouping the various coincidences together that feel right or fit logically. I use the image of 20 cylinders in my head as a filing system for storing related coincidences until a critical mass in one of the cylinders suddenly yields a quantum leap into spontaneous new knowledge.

With 20/20 hindsight, you will be able to prove in your own life, objectively and quantifiably, that the underlying order I am describing exists. You will observe that you have been taken along pathways to the new knowledge you require for the ongoing re-optimization and enhancement of your personal system. It will appear as if you have been following a well-constructed course or precise plan designed to advance you. Amazing things happen when you take your hands off the wheel and let nature drive.

There will be no false trails if you have followed the dictates of your resonance and the blocks and flows. All *Optimizers* are indicators of the same underlying dynamic order and flow. By projecting these patterns into the future, you can *know* which directions will be supported by natural forces. This is how you tap into nature's creativity and intelligence to increase your performance and functionality.

Now back to the story of Frank . . . . Frank was responsible for leadership development worldwide at the financial institution – about 100,000 people. He had just been to a conference about Peter Senge's systems work in *The Fifth Discipline* (coincidence 3). Before I knew anything about that book, I had picked it up at a book sale a few weeks previous to Jack's call but had not yet read it (coincidence 4).

Peter Senge had collaborated with Robert Fritz. I had just finished reading Robert Fritz' book *The Path of Least Resistance* which I enjoyed immensely (coincidence 5). *The Fifth Discipline* identified the problem as powerlessness which they felt, as I did, was probably something everyone has (coincidence 6).

Yet, as of the time of publication in 1990, Peter Senge and Robert Fritz did not really have a solution to the powerlessness problem, thereby telling me it would be significant if I solved it (coincidence 7). I always love a challenge. Jack had a history of giving me the right information at the right time without even knowing that I needed it (coincidence 8). This told me the coincidences were important. In fact, the very existence of multiple interlinked coincidences told me they were important. I was observing first-hand the dynamic order of the naturality flow.

Because this was a significant flow pattern, I knew that discovering this solution was going to be extremely important to my work. *Coincidences increase in size and number the closer you are to operating in alignment with your naturality*. By projecting the path of the coincidences into the future, I knew precisely in which direction to go to experience more coincidences and to be supported by all of nature's *Optimizers*.

As a result, in the next few months, a series of clients flowed to me (coincidences), who were ideal for me to test out the emerging intervention

I was developing for powerlessness. Spontaneous knowledge and information coincidences arose indicating how to deal with each of them. Finally, I had tested my intervention out on so many executives that I could see the universal solution for everyone (coincidences).

Consequently, I am able to cause dramatic change in individuals through this intervention within the first few weeks of working with them. Lifetime limitations can be eliminated. When applied across the board to organizations, the performance levels, creativity and morale improve dramatically, especially if I include the intervention to eliminate judgment described in Chapter 10, *The Judged-Judging Reflex*.

And, yes, Frank, is doing extremely well, thank you very much. We removed these interferences to his naturality while at the same time strengthening it in the ways described in *Peak Evolution*. As a result, he experienced a series of incidents of spontaneous knowledge which told him how to create an internationally linked virtual university for developing and supporting leaders . . . . which he runs in alignment with his authentic identity, art and purpose. Frank is now living a life of accelerating growth and creativity consistent with what you will learn about in the growth technology chapters.

Level IV: Spontaneous or Automatic Knowledge

As you gain experience with and are transformed by Level III, the continuous pattern of interlinked coincidences will convince you that you are tapping into some underlying order of the universe. Once your beliefs about your connection to all knowledge have achieved a certain strength, you will find that you can simply focus consciousness on the information you want and know it.

If you believe you can "quantum leap" to spontaneous knowledge, you can make the shift from Level I to Level IV instantaneously. Quantum leap expertise is provided in the Quantum Leap Living chapter.

Again, the *spontaneous knowledge formula* requires knowledge access beliefs and alignment with your naturality. All *Optimizers* will be conspiring to take you to increasing expressions of your naturality. This is the integrated orderliness of the naturality flow attempting to optimize your system, and indeed, all systems. Therefore, operating in alignment with the flow of nature as identified by these *Optimizers* will increase your experience of spontaneous knowledge.

Alignment with your naturality, even temporarily, can result in spontaneous knowledge. Think of the times you have had a creative solution simply pop into your head. Were you doing something you love? Or was the instant knowledge related to something you were passionate about? Had you been living by a sense of inner knowing or resonance defining what actions you should take?

Were you doing things that were most expressive of the natural you, that get you excited and give you highs? Were you trying to help someone you care about a great deal? Were you pursuing something meaningful? Were you in *flow* state? These are the circumstances you need to build into your modus operandi to make spontaneous knowledge a way of life. Your enthusiasm and your resonance tell you something is the authentic you. When you are doing what you love, then, you will increase the occurrence of spontaneous knowledge.

Flow state is a special case of pure naturality and thus automatic knowledge. It is both a cause and a result of living in alignment with your naturality. As you will read in *Chapter 14, Beyond Flow*, the formula for entering flow state is one of being stretched just beyond your capabilities, doing what you love, following your resonance to do the thing that feels most right for you each moment, or choosing activities expressive of who you are. It is a time of peak performance which can include the automatic knowledge to handle the task at hand with increasing proficiency.

The methods presented throughout this book will ultimately take you to living in *flow* state. Again, *flow* is pure naturality. Naturality promotes spontaneous knowledge. Notice how integrated nature is. We are designed for complete interconnection with the information foundation of the universe.

CAPTURING SPONTANEOUS KNOWLEDGE

There was a study done some years ago at a U.S. university where they had university students study for their exams with a given percent of blood-alcohol. When they wrote the exam without any alcohol in their system, they didn't do as well as when they had the same blood-alcohol level as they had had when they studied. *Knowledge appears to be state-*

bound. You have to revisit the state you were in when you acquired the knowledge in order to access it again.

The same situation is true of spontaneous knowledge or any periods of great learning or creativity. This is especially true if complete systems of new information are emerging in your consciousness. Some of them can be quite large and intricate.

As vivid as your understanding may be at the time spontaneous knowledge arrives, you may have no memory of the information the next day or even an hour later. You will, of course, remember the wonderfully exciting event but you may not be able to bring the information packet into your consciousness again. It's as if you are operating at a different frequency or in a different state of consciousness when the spontaneous information arrives and you have to return to that state or frequency to re-access.

This is extremely frustrating to novices. What I suggest you do is to adjust your life for the capture of the spontaneous knowledge when it emerges. That might mean having paper with you at all times or a dictaphone or a hand-held computer. Many of my clients use their cell phones to leave themselves a voicemail. When you are thus organized and have your life fairly aligned with your naturality, you may find that you never actually do *work* again. Rather you just capture the solutions as they emerge. What a concept!

> *"The man who produces an idea in any field of rational endeavor – the man who discovers new knowledge – is the permanent benefactor of humanity."*[24]   Ayn Rand

6

ACTIVE INTELLIGENCE

Pathfinding in the Unknown

"It's not because things are difficult that we dare not venture. It's because we dare not venture that they are difficult." Seneca

Change is not only a constant but it's accelerating. Consequently, we are all faced with the need to move into unknown territory on a regular basis. In the face of our fears of the unknown, most of us resist change. This resistance diminishes with expertise on how to master the unknown.

The pathfinding technology is designed to give you this mastery. There is a fascinating transformation awaiting those who acquire pathfinding skills. With expertise comes increased safety. With safety comes the desire for lives of continuous adventure. Freed of our fears, the unknown becomes the only place we want to be.

It is my contention that this passion for the unknown is the true modus operandi of evolved human beings. We all come equipped with drives for creativity, growth, and learning which actually cause us to crave moving into unknown territory. We are naturally curious. Nothing delights us more than new challenges, new achievements, new creations, new skills, and new advancements. This is why I offer a word of warning about the pathfinding technology. *Once you know how to conquer the unknown, it can be habit-forming!*

Fear of the unknown is one of our greatest impediments to relinquishing ourselves to our drives to naturality. Fear of the unknown keeps us from being who we are and operating to our fullest potential. Safety is essential to unleashing an individual's natural drives for growth, change, learning, pioneering, creativity, and venturing into new territory. Therefore, the pathfinding technology is an important tool in taking us to peak performance and peak evolution. More importantly, it is a catalyst to unbridled freedom.

The pathfinding technology makes safe and efficient a whole host of activities requisite to succeeding in today's volatile world. For example, let's look at the skills sought by corporations today as an indicator of the capabilities needed by the human race: entrepreneurship, leadership, rapid learning (the "learning organization"), responsive adaptation, informationless decision-making, pioneering, dealing with crises, creativity and the ability to bring "the new" into existence.

These skills reflect an ability to deal with ambiguity and operate in unknown territory. Pathfinding is the underlying survival skill for our world of accelerating change. It restores and enhances the creative adaptiveness of the human race.

WHAT IS THE PATHFINDING TECHNOLOGY?

The unknown is any area in which we do not know all of the answers. The unknown is the preferred home of leaders, entrepreneurs, and creatives. It will be your home too once you have the necessary skills. The pathfinding technology is a means for conquering all the forms of ambiguity inherent in today's volatile world. It is part of the knowledge technology because *pathfinding is about creating or accessing new knowledge.*

Pathfinding is the means to proceed proficiently and safely into the unknown – whether that unknown territory is a new physical location, a new reality, a new mental state, or the creativity of bringing something new into existence. Everything I have developed in *Peak Evolution* was done using the pathfinding technology. Nature's *Optimizers* directed each and every discovery. I simply began by operating with the hypothesis and belief that I had access to all information .... spontaneously .... merely by focusing consciousness.

Pathfinding is reality creation. As such, it is also part of the reality creation technology. Pathfinding means you are bringing a new reality into existence. You are exchanging an unknown territory for a known one. This may not become clear until you read the chapters in the reality creation technology section of the book. Since, beliefs will create reality, it is actually possible to go from an unknown territory to the desired new state of knowing by changing your beliefs.

We called this *spontaneous knowledge* in the previous chapter. *Pathfinding is a quantum leap.* In most cases, pathfinding in the naturality paradigm is a collection of information coincidences. Eventually, the information units combine to create new knowledge. There is an explosion or quantum leap when the last unit is added and suddenly all of the previous pieces creatively recombine through emergence.

Original knowledge results. You quantum leap from not knowing to knowing. Pathfinding then is ultimately a nonlinear process fuelled by information. You quantum leap from a reality where you "don't know" to a reality in which you "do know." *Pathfinding is often another word for growth.* It is therefore also fundamental to the growth technology.

> *"There comes a point where the mind takes a leap – call it intuition or what you will – and comes out on a higher plane of knowledge."*   Einstein

OPERATING THE PATHFINDING TECHNOLOGY

Now, let's get some practical knowledge about using the pathfinding technology to achieve your goals. In its simplest form, pathfinding in the naturality paradigm means you stay absolutely in the present in order to take action on the *Optimizer* messages. These will lead you to collide with the information coincidences that will make the unknown known.

Most commonly, the Optimizers used are your resonance and the block and flow events in your reality. Simply identify the goal and start taking action on the basis of activities you resonate with. Stop with the blocks and proceed in any direction which has flow events. Isn't this simple? It must be experienced to be believed.

Let's look at what's going on to make it work. If you resonate with pursuing an unknown territory, your resonance indicates this territory is consistent with your naturality and therefore, the naturality flow. The blocks and flows give you the same messages as your resonance since they too are signals of the naturality flow. All *Optimizers* point in the same direction. For novices, however, reality may be easier to read than your resonance.

You need to take action in order for there to be any block events or flow events for you to read. The pathfinding technology raises your "active intelligence" by capitalizing on nature's intelligence when you are taking action. Your resonance and the blocks and flows will lead you to collide with the information units you need to fuel the emergence process. The combining of existing information will create the new knowledge which will bring you to a state of knowing.

Coincidences increase in the naturality flow. With the pathfinding technology, you can proceed safely and efficiently, knowing your resonance is attached to all knowledge, yet not know any of that knowledge yourself. You can proceed as if you have access to all knowledge including knowing the goal territory that is currently unknown to you.

Choose the Path of Least Resistance

Choosing the right pathfinding projects can make all the difference between success and failure, ease and anxiety. In order to be supported by the mechanisms and forces of nature, choose your pathfinding projects in the direction of the naturality flow. The ten *Optimizers* identify this direction for us. Hitchhiking on the naturality flow will catapult us along by quantum leaps, coincidences and flow events to make the unknown known.

The path of least resistance is when we are moving with the flow of nature. We want to capitalize on nature's superior intelligence and knowledge to move us safely, quickly and effectively through the unknown to our next adaptive reality. If you think you want to pursue a pathfinding project that is not in alignment with the naturality flow . . . . think again. What is the logic in pursuing a reality which must, by definition, be maladaptive because it won't support your naturality?

The easiest *Optimizer* messages with which to identify pathfinding project options are those of reality. Reality can be used as if it's a gigantic computer to tell you, by its past and present patterns of blocks and flows, precisely the directions supported by the naturality flow.

Look at the pattern of flow events in your recent past. Choose a pathfinding project in alignment with what you've learned. Look at the pattern of block events in your recent past. It tells you which directions are not smart choices for pathfinding projects. It would be illogical, if not masochistic, to continue to pursue directions blocked by the naturality flow.

Resonance is another *Optimizer* you can use for pathfinding project selection. What pathfinding challenge are you resonating with? Why not do the Resonance-Rating Exercise in Chapter 4 to find out which projects nature will support? Your resonance has been consistently leading you into alignment with nature.

If you are well connected to your resonance, you can use the string of events you resonated with in the past as a means to identify which directions you will resonate with in the future. If you've been absolutely passionate about particular directions, these are the ones you'll want to pick for your pathfinding projects. This will garner you the most support from nature.

How about using naturality as the *Optimizer* for selecting your ideal pathfinding projects? Nature clearly supports this *Optimizer*. If you have already identified the route of your naturality from your past, then choose future pathfinding projects consistent with that naturality. What do you know about your natural growth path to this point?

This always flows you to the highest expression of your naturality. What do you want to learn? What growth do you want to have? What has been supported in the past? Choose your pathfinding projects accordingly. Just begin pathfinding and you will be transformed by the process. Experiential learning is a byproduct of using your active intelligence.

Another way to help you choose projects along your optimization pathway is to choose them consistent with your *art*. If you know your *art*, or what you love to do, or those activities that provide the greatest expression of your naturality, pathfinding goals in alignment with your *art* will be advantageous. If you know your purpose or what is meaningful to you, this is another way to identify pathfinding projects that will have a greater likelihood of being supported by nature's dynamic, creative flow. Meaning reflects naturality.

Start Small in Neutral Territory

The fastest way to develop your skill in pathfinding is to start with projects that are not risky. Choose areas where you can be dispassionate or in which you are not wrought with fears. Pursuing information for some of your work projects might be ideal. If you've had trouble making money in the past, this is not the place to begin to perfect your pathfinding skills.

If you haven't been able to create a desired reality, you likely have a number of interfering beliefs and emotions impeding you. There are too many other factors complicating things to build your pathfinding expertise and beliefs. Choose more neutral territory to start with.

When you develop the expertise, you can return to pathfinding in the more emotionally charged territories of your life. Become an expert at pathfinding exactly the information you need when you need it. Then you will have a whole new skill to apply to "finding" money, for example.

Making money is most often a matter of having the right information at the right time, in any event. Whenever clients approach me to help them amass a great deal of money, I may go weeks before I really get into the discussion of money. Rather, I am working to provide them with new skills, identities, beliefs and a partnership with nature that will allow them to not only make the money but keep it.

Learning the pathfinding technology will make you more powerful than having the money. It's the difference between giving people fish to feed them for today and teaching them to fish so they can feed themselves forever. Pathfinding will give you the ability to have or do what you want when you want – the definition of power, the definition of abundance, the definition of freedom and the definition of a master reality creator.

Eventually, you will be able to make monumental decisions with no information yet proceed ahead at full speed in safety. In the full knowledge of 20/20 hindsight, you'll be able to identify a trail of flow events to prove you took the perfect route to your goal at every step. In other words, you will have confirmation that you proceeded as accurately and as quickly as if you had had access to all of the information you ultimately knew at the completion of your project. I do invite you to consistently look back over your projects to prove to yourself that reality is a profoundly accurate computer. This will increase your expertise, confidence, and beliefs for the next time you face the unknown.

Choose Your Desired Reality with Unlimited Thinking

It is important to blueprint your new reality or the end state of pathfinding with unlimited thinking. What do you truly want as an ideal outcome of pathfinding, even if this is just an emotional feeling? Try not to let fears, limiting beliefs, habits, or someone else's opinions or rules or needs limit what you aspire to with your pathfinding.

As you begin to let nature lead you with blocks, flows and resonance, and, indeed, all of the *Optimizers*, you'll come to see the infinitely creative ways that a problem can be solved. This experiential learning will, in turn, assist you in using unlimited thinking to define future outcomes of pathfinding. *Believe* that you have the ability to bring any reality into existence, and your pathfinding prowess will continuously improve.

Choose Goals you are Passionate About

If you are passionate about a goal, this tells you the goal is consistent with your naturality and thus supported by the naturality flow. Passion signals naturality. This means that nature's *Optimizers* will assist your progress in directions you are passionate about. In addition, strong emotions create realities faster.

Therefore, pathfinding will proceed faster for a goal you are passionate about. You'll want to avoid picking projects to do out of fear or out of habit or because you think you have to. Choose the things you love in order to conscript natural mechanisms designed to bring you into naturality.

Hold the Goal but Release the Channel to that Goal

If you choose a pathfinding goal and insist on following a set route to that goal, you are limited by *your* knowledge and *your* intelligence. If you choose a goal but operate consistent with the messages from nature's *Optimizers*, then you have access to *nature's* intelligence and *nature's* knowledge, which is significantly greater than ours.

When you release the requirement to proceed by a specific channel, what you will discover is the tremendous creativity of nature. When you take your hands off the wheel, you will discover that nature is taking you to your goal in a way you never would have thought, but which, in 20/20 hindsight, was by far the most effective route.

After ten years of experimentation, here's what it looks like to me. It appears that from an expanded view of multiple systems, nature can identify a number of routes to your goal from where you are right this minute. It then makes the fastest most efficient route, the "route of least resistance." This is the route supported by flows and coincidences.

Internalize Four Ideal Pathfinding Identities

In the *Power of Identity* chapter, you will learn that identities are integrated sets of beliefs. Beliefs create reality. Consequently, assuming an adaptive identity can be a short-form for expressing a multitude of belief changes you want to use to send reality different instructions.

Therefore, we will want to get this power working for you whenever you are pathfinding. *"You cannot travel on the path until you become the path itself."* These words of Gantana Bouddha take on new meaning in the context of pathfinding and reality creation. Here then are four identities I recommend for creating adaptive realities to assist your pathfinding efforts:

Pathfinding Expert

First, you will want to internalize the identity, beliefs and emotional structure of someone who is an expert in pathfinding or mastering contexts of ambiguity. Just assume or pretend you have been a great pathfinder for years and there is no pathfinding project where you will not succeed. These beliefs will create that reality.

Spontaneous Knowledge and Coincidence Expert

Spontaneous knowledge is a coincidence inside of you. It occurs as part of the same process as coincidences that occur out in reality. Both reflect the underlying holographic information infrastructure of the universe. Both increase along the naturality flow where nature's *Optimizers* can put you in the right place at the right time or in the right frequency for the connection to the ideal existing systems.

The whole business of pathfinding becomes easier if you have mastered the Knowledge Technology. Therefore, just assume you can know any information as soon as you focus your consciousness on it. Assume you can either know information spontaneously or create a series of information coincidences that will give you the piece of information you need when you need it.

Can you *feel* how it would feel to be a person with this expertise? Can you imagine having the ability to miraculously create coincidence after coincidence after coincidence to accelerate your progress? Can you *feel* how it would feel to bypass all the tedium of having to proceed linearly to your goal? Can you *feel* how it would feel if you could pathfind by quantum leaps at will?

Assume you can have information systems emerge complete in your consciousness or your reality. If you can feel it, you will begin to strengthen that identity so that all of its integrated beliefs are directing your reality creation.

Reality Creation Expert

As you will discover in the reality creation chapters, pathfinding is really the business of exchanging a current reality for a preferred reality. If we didn't believe we had to proceed linearly, we would allow ourselves to simply quantum leap to the new reality without having to go through all of the interim steps. Therefore, you will want to have the emotions and beliefs of a person who can create any reality at will.

The Person with the Desired Reality

How will you feel when you have succeeded with your pathfinding project? What will it feel like to have the new reality? Operate throughout the project as if you have already successfully completed this project and several more like it.

Alternatively, think of people who already have the reality you are attempting to pathfind. Can you absorb their emotional structure and beliefs? Can you *feel* what it would be like to be them? If so, you'll be sending out the right instructions for reality creation. *Wear* the identity to create the reality.

Take Any Action to Use Reality like a Computer

Now it's time for the real fun to begin. Simply take action in order for nature's *Optimizers* to tell you whether you're going in the right direction or not. In effect, by taking action and looking for the signals, you can use reality as if it's a computer. Sound too fantastic? Only your own experience will convince you of this underlying dynamic order in the universe. Here's what you need to do to convince yourself.

First, if we're going to use reality as a computer, we should have some questions to ask the computer. I'm going to call these hypotheses since we are trying to speculate on which way nature is trying to flow your system. *The Resonance-Rating Exercise* presented in the Resonance chapter is an ideal way to generate hypotheses.

List ideas for taking action. Use your resonance to rate these ideas out of ten in order to prioritize them. With practice, your resonance will be so accurate that you will automatically pick the best route. Take any action to test out each of the higher-rated hypotheses. If reality responds positively with flow events, you are going in the right direction. If reality blocks your progress, take that hypothesis off your list.

To help you get back in touch with your resonance, remember that the blocks and flows in reality are tied to the same optimizing flow and therefore usually agree with your resonance. In fact, all past patterns of *Optimizers* can be used to help you think up hypotheses to test in the future. This is the same process as discussed for choosing your pathfinding projects in the first place.

Try to operate strictly in the present taking action by the dictates of your resonance, block events and flow events. Take actions you are enthusiastic about or that are energizing or that feel natural to you. Don't take any action that is draining. This is your resonance "off" button.

Just because you are de-energized by an activity, does not mean it's a wrong action but perhaps just not an action to take right now. Blocks can mean "wrong direction" or "delay." As a corollary, activities you normally would never have enthusiasm to do, will feel right to do when it is the most advantageous time to do them. Here's a very important rule for novices: action all flow events to see if they lead to where you want to go. Just because you can't see how a flow event relates to your pathfinding project right now does not mean that it doesn't.

Something generated the flow event. As you move into greater alignment with your authentic core, all events will be relevant to the flow to increased naturality, optimization and your emotional goals. This means there will come a time when you cannot generate a flow event that is not relevant to your optimization.

Here's something else to consider. If you will make a commitment to action all the positive messages telling you in which direction to go, there will be no need to create as many negative events to help with the steering.

Coincidences are simply more significant flow events. Prioritize your action accordingly. You are likely leaving something substantial on the table if you do not proceed in the direction of a coincidence. One coincidence can save you hundreds of steps. And where there's one, there are likely more.

Coincidences are quantum leaps than can catapult you holographically to your goal, bypassing time and space. Remember, the more in alignment you are with the naturality flow, the more coincidences you will experience. They tell you your most ideal pathway. Nature likes to progress by quantum leaps. Therefore, the more integrated you are into nature's flow, the more coincidences and quantum leaps you will experience.

Here's another pathfinding challenge that is common with novices. It is imperative that you honor all block events. Stop! Cease and desist! Many of us have been brought up to fight to prevail over every block and challenge in our lives.

Sometimes it's difficult to believe life can be anything but a struggle. Let yourself partner with nature and reality and you will experience firsthand that things can indeed be different. When you hit a block, try some other directions and channels until you find one that has flow events, coincidences and/or emotional highs to support you on your way.

There's an old Chinese Proverb that says *"There are many paths to the top of the mountain but the view is always the same."* Release the need to fight to make a particular channel work. The key to the pathfinding technology and using reality like a computer is to keep taking action in new directions whenever there is a block. That's the only way you will get the additional information you need.

Blocks have just as much to tell us as flows. They are all benevolent signals pointing us to a better way. Do the Resonance-Rating Exercise again. Determine new hypotheses. Poll for new channels where there are flows by simply taking action to see whether reality responds with a block or a flow. This is business as usual for the pathfinder.

Amateur pathfinders tend to let seemingly negative messages from reality erode their intentions. They think that blocks are signals to give up their goal. Blocks mean "change directions" not "change goals." This is very important. If you had passion for your goal when you started, that tells you it is an expression of your naturality and should be pursued.

Another check you can make to see if you should continue with a goal is to look at the pattern of flow events. If you have had a series of flow events in your pursuit of this goal, you know it must be right. That's the only way flow events could have happened in the naturality flow.

Now let me remind you of the difference between blocks and struggle events. Blocks simply impede your progress but they rarely have a negative emotional charge – other than the frustration of confronting an impediment, of course. Struggle events, on the other hand, are the result of two conflicting beliefs creating two colliding and conflicting realities. They usually engender significant emotional turmoil.

Common conflicting beliefs include believing yourself to be valued and not valued, capable and not capable, and powerful and powerless. If you encounter struggle events in your pathfinding, you will want to clear these according to the methods in the *De-creating Undesirable Realities* chapters of the reality creation technology section.

Keep Taking Action

Again, keep taking action. The process of pathfinding will ultimately become your safety in the future. Safety in the naturality paradigm is dynamic. Gradually, you will learn to trust the process of optimization around your naturality that nature is orchestrating. We fear moving ahead into the unknown, but we aren't any safer staying where we are. Things can happen to take away that safety. Better to learn a methodology for handling the unknown and how to achieve dynamic or active safety.

Get moving on the project. *The solution to the unknown is information.* You must take action to get information from nature's Optimizers. Avoid dwelling on the future where things might seem scary. Get out of your head. Stay precisely in the present taking action consistent with blocks, flows and resonance. This is the simple pathfinding formula. Trust nature's *Optimizers* to flow you in the right direction and to keep you safe.

The more you turn yourself over to this formula, the more you will experience positive results. This knowledge will make your pathfinding easier and more efficient the next time. Let yourself gain this experiential learning. It will build your pathfinding beliefs.

The faster you get into the project, the sooner you will begin experiencing flow state and the emotional rewards of satisfying your drives for pioneering new territory. These are very addicting and they can make fears of the unknown disappear. They also entice further positive action. Move as quickly as you can to obtain your next "fix."

Try to get yourself to a state of being magnetized and propelled forward by natural irresistible drives for achievement, growth, learning, and the safety of the new territory. Every time you consciously follow this process makes it easier for you to hook into this state the next time.

Eventually, you will find yourself at home in the unknown. You will find yourself seeking out situations with frontiering tension and excitement. Adrenalin will flow at the prospect. You'll want this biochemical "fix" more often. You will have become a pathfinding addict . . . . or more accurately, a growth addict. Eventually, your "addiction" will have you residing in the gap between the known and the unknown.

In this place, your drives for learning, growth and achievement will perpetually mobilize you, de-energizing any anxiety you used to experience about the unknown. As a result, you will find yourself on an accelerated growth path. You will find yourself thrilling to the endless cycle of growth that is the process of living.

Learn to Operate Nonlinearly

Nature operates nonlinearly. Therefore, if the pathfinding technology pairs you with the naturality flow, then you too are going to have to operate nonlinearly. This means that often you will have no idea what you are to do next. There is just a black void between you and your goal. Most people want a perfect linear plan that will get them from point A to point B.

However, how often have you actually experienced a linear plan working perfectly? All sorts of unexpected events crop up. It is better to have mastered the process of pathfinding and creative adaptiveness in order to get where you need to be by the fastest route no matter what unexpected events occur.

Trust the process of pathfinding in partnership with the naturality flow. Over time, you will not only adjust to operating in the unknown, but, believe it or not, as you gain proficiency, you will come to crave it. You will go from hating it, to fearing it, to mastering it, and then loving it. The new, the different, the unknown . . . . This is the only place you'll want to be.

And if you love being in this territory, you will likely become the leader. This is the territory most people fear. If you are happy in this territory and good at operating there, people are going to be comfortable around you and seek you out. You will have followers.

As a civilization, our ability to adapt to change has trailed our ability to generate that change. Pathfinding releases the creative adaptiveness requisite to addressing this shortfall. Once you master the unknown, anything else will be too tame, too mundane. We are designed to frontier. Embrace the adventure of life! Set yourself free!

> *"Do not follow where the path may lead. Go instead where*
> *there is no path and leave a trail."*   (Unknown)

THE REALITY CREATION TECHNOLOGY

"What we achieve inwardly will change outer reality." Otto Rank

Each of the three major technologies presented in *Peak Evolution* is based on an uncommon belief – the hypothesis from which the rest of the technology evolved. For the reality creation technology, this uncommon belief is that *beliefs create reality*. Believing is seeing. Our realities are thus 100% self-created.

This means it is within our power to change them. While the knowledge technology is about sourcing information from your reality, the reality creation technology is concerned with emitting information to your reality and thus changing it.

The seven the reality creation technology chapters that follow extend how the pathfinding technology reintegrates us with the naturality flow. Chapter 7 provides an overview of the reality creation technology so it becomes evident how all of the subsequent pieces will fit together.

The following six chapters will then highlight key elements of the technology to help us to improve the precision with which we create reality. The first three of these chapters help us to stop inadvertently creating realities we don't want through unconsciously issuing toxic instructions. The remaining three chapters provide the expertise for proactively issuing more precise instructions.

Our instructions to reality are contained in nicely integrated packets of information called beliefs. Change your beliefs to change your reality. Hence, the expertise most in demand as we evolve will be belief engineering. As our expertise increases, we will gain the ability to control our destiny not only as individuals but as a global civilization.

The within is ceaselessly becoming the without. From the state of a person's heart proceeds the conditions of his or her life; thoughts blossom into deeds, and deeds bear the fruitage of character and destiny.   James Allen

7

REALITY CREATION

"The best way to predict the future is to create it."   Peter Drucker

Some of the greatest advances in human evolution in the decades to come will arise through our perfecting of the art and science of reality creation. The context of human existence will be irrevocably transformed.

Contemplation of this metamorphosis is so astounding, that, even if we were provided with irrefutable scientific proof we are indeed capable of reality creation, many of us would remain unconvinced. Those who did believe this to be the direction of human evolution would immediately want to gain expertise in this new level of human functionality.

I believe the needs of both the convinced and not-convinced can be met by simply providing instruction in the use of the reality creation technology. The only real proof that would satisfy non-believers is experiential evidence – their own first- hand experience. Therefore, let's begin to develop the expertise needed to gain that experiential learning and proof. Let's explore this new vista of human potential and peak performance.

I invite you to do the same experiment I did. The entire Reality Creation Technology you will be reading about in these seven chapters resulted from my strict adherence to a profoundly simple hypothesis. I kept pursuing this hypothesis day after day and month after month until I am now able to write these chapters for you with ten years of experience.

"What is this simple hypothesis?" you ask. *Beliefs create reality.* I systematically revised my life on the basis of assuming beliefs create reality. I then watched for confirmation as to whether it was true or not. If you do the same, you will end up discovering the reality creation technology. You'll end up proving the hypothesis.

For those who cannot invest as much time and effort as I did, the reality creation technology chapters will offer a number of shortcuts. If beliefs create reality then reality is 100% self-created by our beliefs. Therefore, if we wanted to change reality, we would need to simply change our beliefs. Rather than seeing is believing, we would have to adjust to *believing is seeing*. Instead of running around outside in the world to change what we would experience, we would have to shift our focus to what is inside of us.

Obviously, we'd have to change a great many of our beliefs in order for us to fully determine if our hypothesis is true. If we didn't believe that beliefs create reality then how could we experience a reality where they did?

If our hypothesis was true, we should be able to cause predictable changes in reality. We should also be able to look back at our respective lives and know our beliefs by the pattern of events in our realities created by these beliefs. You will discover that our hypothesis passes each of these tests.

To accelerate your process of absorbing the new beliefs necessary for reality creation, I'll briefly discuss the science that led me to experiment with the hypothesis in the first place. In addition, I'll provide some tests of your own you can do to begin accumulating first-hand knowledge of this phenomenon.

Then I'm going to speak to you as if you have accepted this worldview change and help you gain the expertise to improve the precision with which you create your own reality. As you become more expert, you will have numerous proofs of your own. These will develop and strengthen the beliefs that will accelerate your development as the architect of your reality.

The purpose of all of the technologies presented in this book is to restore our natural functioning so we can move to peak performance and peak experience. They help us to bypass cultural interferences to reintegrate with the naturality flow. Specifically, the objective of the reality creation technology is to enable us to bring desired and adaptive realities into existence quickly and with predictability.

We are already unconsciously providing the instructions to create our current reality. The reality creation technology provides techniques for reclaiming conscious control of those instructions so that, with great precision and reliability, more desirable realities can be created in the future. Proficiency in using the reality creation technology results in rapid evolution by quantum leaps.

CULTIVATING IDEAL REALITY CREATION BELIEFS

Believing is Seeing

Beliefs create reality. We have all heard of this concept before. We may even have the belief already that it's true. But how many of us consciously live our lives in accordance with this belief. We would need proof on a consistent basis before considering replacing our life-long belief that we are victims of circumstance in an "objective" reality.

The proof, however, will come from re-writing your life in accordance with the proposed new belief. And you and your reality will be forever transformed as a result. Simply operate as if there is not one thing that occurs or exists in your reality that is not created by your beliefs. Think of it as a one-to-one relationship. *Not one emotion, not one thought, not one symbol, nor one event occurs in your internal reality or your external physical reality without you having the necessary belief.*

Figure 7.1 represents this visually to try to emphasize the point. I find it effective to think in terms of each individual having a *belief blueprint* which contains all of one's beliefs. I arrived at the term based on the concept of our *genetic blueprint* comprised of the DNA in our cells. In fact, both blueprints simply reflect the single integrated information structure or database of our system. Beliefs and genes are simply biochemical and electromagnetic information storage units comprising the unique formula which instructs the total system for each of us.

Notice the arrows coming from your belief blueprint to your emotions, thoughts, the symbols in your life, and the events you experience. One of the key purposes of the reality creation technology is to help you get hold of those instructions you are sending to create your reality so you can control more precisely and predictably exactly what you will experience.

Since beliefs create reality, if you want to change what you will experience, you have only to change your beliefs. Why not try this? Choose a belief to change and see if your reality changes. This is very powerful! YOU are very powerful! This is another belief you will need to change as you become a reality creation expert. The intervention in *The Powerless Reflex* chapter is designed to help you embrace this important new belief.

Knowing that your reality is 100% self-created can cause some changes in who you are and your modus operandi. But, experiencing it as true totally rewrites your existence going forward. Your level of functionality increases exponentially. The upper limit of your possible peak performance shoots up. Who you have been in the past quickly becomes irrelevant for who you want to become in the future.

You step out of the confines of being a linear extension of the person you used to be. Rather, you simply redesign yourself and your reality and begin operating as that new person. Reality will restructure accordingly. Try rewriting your day and your life as if you are totally controlling your reality with your beliefs. The experience of reality responding in ways you never imaged possible will trigger dramatic transformation.

Quantum Mechanics

Quantum physics and Einstein's theory of relativity have demonstrated the world is subjective and, in fact, created by the observer. In the early part of the twentieth century, experimenters looking at light saw a particle of light, if that is what they expected to see, but a wave of light, if that is what they were looking for.

They concluded that the observer determines the reality that is observed and that observing changes what is observed. In other words, reality is participatory. The beliefs, expectations and goals of the observer determine the reality that will be observed. The reality creation technology extends this same subjective view of reality to new levels of understanding.

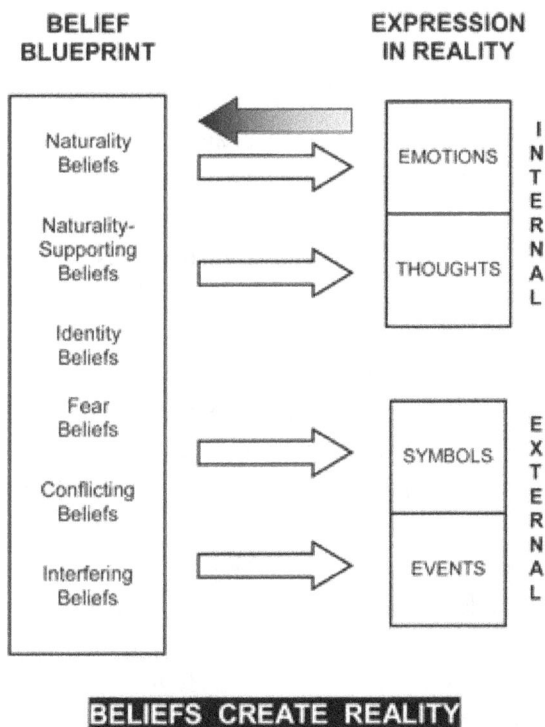

Figure 7.1

The Part Reflects the Whole

In the *Spontaneous Knowledge* chapter, the recurring universal theme of "the part reflecting the whole" was introduced. This theme was used to suggest it would not be too far-fetched for us to contain or have access from within us to the entire holographic information database of the universe.

Since we are a part of the universe, we can reflect the whole. Each piece of a hologram contains the information to reconstruct the entire holographic image. Every cell in our bodies contains the genetic blueprint for the entire individual. There are at least eighteen acupuncture microsystems in various parts of the body which mirror the various components, systems and organs of the body.

This is also the logic behind assuming that reality is a mirror image of us. It is only logical there would be a "blueprint" for the creation of the reality experienced by each of us. Just as our genes map the human body, so beliefs and "systems of beliefs" map our realities. This is our belief blueprint or information database. We can know what is in our belief blueprint by the events in our reality that reflect it. Change our beliefs and we change what we will experience in reality. Change the beliefs of human consciousness and the shared experience of all humanity can change.

Our bodies contain a multitude of self-correcting feedback systems constantly interacting and rebalancing us. The respiratory system, the circulatory system, the immunological system, and the nervous system, for example. Assume each of our bodies is the part perfectly reflecting the whole. We would know how the universe operates by the way our bodies operate. Just as there are "systems within systems" within our body, it would only make sense that the hierarchy of symbiotic systems would extend outside of us into reality.

Think of any biological ecosystem, for example. It is teeming with integrated and interacting species, forces and systems, all optimizing and re-optimizing to each other as change occurs. Systems are interacting with systems contained within hierarchies of systems within the system of the universe. Therefore, it seems unlikely our reality is separate from either us or this system of systems. Rather, it would be more logical to assume reality is another self-correcting feedback system that is part of balancing and optimizing our bodies and our beings.

Hypnosis

Hypnotists regularly prove that our beliefs create our reality. By accepting the beliefs suggested by the hypnotist, subjects are able to perform physical feats that would be considered impossible normally. They are given different beliefs about how reality operates and they come true. Deeply hypnotized persons can also control near-sightedness, bloodflow patterns, allergic reactions, heart rate, pain, and body temperature. In other words, the *reality* of their physical bodies.

If subjects are told they are holding a hot poker, blisters can appear on their hands. Experiments using formal scientific method have demonstrated that changing our beliefs through hypnotic suggestion can even override our genetic makeup. Hypnosis demonstrates, with great precision, the one-to-one relationship between beliefs and reality. It clearly shows, in concentrated form, the latent capabilities of all human beings to shape the reality they experience.

I am not a hypnotist but occasionally I have the opportunity to rewrite a client's belief systems so he or she will experience an entirely new reality. Normally, my clients are already fairly successful executives who have a lot to lose if they risk changing too much too fast.

Once in a while, I will come across a client who is so eager to change his reality that he will automatically relinquish his current belief system in favor of the new belief system I am offering him. I relish these situations. They are opportunities to see just how powerful the reality creation technology is.

So, let me tell you about George . . . . With personal and corporate bankruptcies in 1992, George had lost everything. In the past, George had often been quite wealthy. But here he was, at age 53, destitute and living with his brother's family. He had not been able to get a job or start a business again in almost 4 years. Even though George had been president of substantial companies more than once, he really was just an old-style salesman who had risen to the top of his selected industry.

An energetic man, George was already doing all the right things according to popular theory on how one makes money. Every day he was expending tremendous energy to try to turn things around. However, if beliefs create reality, he had the wrong identity and the wrong beliefs. He had the identity and beliefs of someone who could not make money, who believed himself to be someone people did not want to do business with, who was not valued, who was needy, and who lived in a world of scarcity.

Because George had nothing to lose, he readily absorbed the new identity and beliefs I gave him to realign him with his naturality. I imbedded a new set of beliefs in a vision of the ideal future for George. I strengthened his beliefs that he was an incredible dealmaker and businessman with clients lined up to do business with him. Instead of going to customers hat in hand as he had done in the past, I said they would court him.

In the vision, numerous service and supplier organizations flowed in to create a large virtual organization around him in short order. We re-created him with the beliefs that he was no longer the lone businessman he had been for four years but rather, a successful chief executive officer of a substantial organization.

I painted a vision of the ideal company for him as if he had been running it successfully for ten years. He became convinced that it would be an entity that customers would want to be a part of. While I was describing this ideal company for George, his identity was visibly expanding and he was feeling the emotions and passions he would feel if he ran such a company.

Because beliefs create reality, you can't feel the emotions if you don't have the beliefs. Therefore, we were causing major belief changes in George via this key belief engineering technique that will be discussed in greater detail in *The Power of Emotion* chapter.

I made certain that George was sending very precise instructions to create his reality. In short order, George drew investors to back his plan for a new company. If you hadn't known that the technologies in this book will create flow events and coincidences, the cluster of coincidences that occurred to make this happen might have been dismissed as unrelated to the work we did in changing George's beliefs. I pointed out the connection so that George would persist in strengthening his beliefs in order to continue to drive the generation of coincidences and flow events.

George next scheduled a one-week trip to Chicago to talk with the same customers he had been speaking to over the previous four years without success. The new beliefs and identity were precisely instructing reality as to what to create. When George arrived in Chicago, these customers did, in fact, court him, taking him out to lunch and dinner and asking him to do business with them.

After one week in Chicago, George came back with contracts in hand for $8 million dollars of business. So a four-year drought was now over for George. The changes in George's reality then helped him to reinforce his new identity and belief changes. This ensured he would continue to send the new instructions to reality which would sustain and even enhance his new life.

The Placebo Effect[25]

If beliefs create reality, then illness and healing are both created by our beliefs. The placebo effect is a medical phenomenon where something with no curative powers effects a cure simply because it is believed that it will. Sugar pills are often used as placebos in drug studies, but any non-traditional remedies or cultural rituals could produce the same effect.

According to Michael Talbot's research in *The Holographic Universe*, "on average 35% of all people who receive a given placebo will experience a given effect."[26] Double-blind studies have shown that placebos were 54% as effective as aspirin in producing the desired result and 56% as effective as morphine in relieving pain.

The placebo effect demonstrates the profound power of beliefs to control the reality experienced. The basic phenomenon appears to be akin to the power of suggestion experienced in hypnosis. The illnesses and deaths associated with voodoo result from the same reflection of beliefs into reality. The body's ultimate inability to distinguish between an imagined reality and a real one is pivotal.

Years of blind and double-blind experiments following strict scientific procedure to test the use of placebos have proven that beliefs create reality. If you believe a pill will heal, it will – even if it is only a sugar pill. There are documented cases of even those terminally ill with cancer who have been "cured" by placebos. It would not be logical to assume that only some realities are created by our beliefs. The proof in one territory must be extended to all reality.

Human Capabilities in an Emergency

Our extreme focus in a precise moment in the present during emergency situations suspends our normally limited beliefs about our capabilities and reality, often resulting in superhuman powers being exhibited. A mother faced with her child pinned under an object significantly heavier than she can normally lift, raises it with ease.

Science has not adequately explained this phenomenon. It was, however, one of the key instigations for my exploration of the hypothesis that we control all of the reality we experience with our beliefs. If we can manipulate reality under hypnosis or in an emergency, then we must be able to do it all of the time. We must have specific limiting beliefs that are preventing us from operating with these "superhuman powers" normally.

Multiple Personality Disorder

In Multiple Personality Disorder (MPD) or Dissociative Identity Disorder (DID), two or more distinct personalities inhabit a single body or consciousness. Most Multiples average between 8 and 13 personalities. Studies of the victims of MPD suggest not only the power of beliefs to affect reality but that our access to knowledge is also created by our beliefs.

Each personality often has its own set of physical abilities, interpersonal skills, and intellectual subject areas as well as foreign language fluency and IQ. Alternate personalities may vary as to speech and thought patterns, voice characteristics, physiognomy, posture and movement patterns, style of handwriting, announced gender, cultural and racial background, artistic talents, accessible memories, reported age and life history, and other individual and personality characteristics.

A major breakthrough in the study of MPD came with the ability to measure the physiological and biochemical changes resulting from a personality shift. Alternate personalities could thus be proved to exist. Each personality may have its own brainwave patterns, chemical composition of bodily fluids, bloodflow patterns, muscle tone, heart rate, scars, burn marks, cysts and left-and right-handedness, visual acuity, posture, skin electrical responses, and so on. Extensive physiological change would be required for the different voice patterns exhibited by the various personalities of Multiples, yet many Multiples achieve it. Even eye color can change.

With a personality shift, a Multiple who is drunk can instantly become sober. Allergies associated with one personality can disappear completely with another. An overdose can result when a child subpersonality takes over from an adult subpersonality that has been given an adult dosage. Subpersonalities resistant to anaesthetic may alarm surgeons when a personality shift has the patient waking up on the operating table.

One compelling explanation for how patients with MPD transform their bodies with each personality change is that each personality holds a different set of beliefs which then create a different physical reality. If we didn't believe in the inevitability of the continuation of bad vision or diabetes, for example, could we change our physical bodies as easily as a

Multiple does?

Gain the Ideal Reality Creation Beliefs First-Hand

During my experimental phase of developing the reality creation technology, I spent most of my time working one-on-one with executives. I believed consistent proof and reinforcement would be required to cause the leap necessary for them to believe in and operate in a belief-created reality. Basically, I used whatever situations existed within the client's life to demonstrate that beliefs create reality. I sought to repeatedly prove the relationship between the client's beliefs and the events he or she was experiencing.

As such, all of the events in a client's current experience serve as neutral feedback reflecting his or her beliefs. Once this is pointed out, the client can clearly see which beliefs should be kept and which need to be changed from the negative and positive events in his or her life. If a belief is changed, a client should expect to see immediate concrete change in reality. Because my clients instantly know that I have been accurate about their beliefs, the process of proving to the client that beliefs create reality has begun.

Since I'm not there to link your beliefs to the events in your life for you, can you do it yourself? It is critical to mobilizing all of the peak evolution science that you are able to do this. And it is essential to your being able to experience the resulting quantum leaps that are capable of not only taking you to peak performance but to greatness. Let me suggest some personal experiments to help you to strengthen your beliefs with respect to how reality is created.

One approach to proving to yourself that reality is self-created is to determine the beliefs that must have existed to create events in your recent past with a negative emotional charge. If beliefs create reality, then you should be able to figure out the dysfunctional beliefs you would have had to have in order to create negative events in your reality.

If you can't do this, maybe you could ask someone else to look at the events with objective detachment to determine the beliefs you must have had to have caused them. Quite often the negative events are created by the same two or three maladaptive beliefs. There's a reason for this as you will discover in the *Reclaim Your Reality* chapter.

Now try changing these interfering beliefs using some of the belief engineering techniques listed in this book or in others. At minimum, begin operating in your life as if you had replaced the dysfunctional belief. Let's say you have some events reflecting the belief that you are not valued or valuable. Walk around as if everyone values you. Does your reality start to change? Do people who never valued you in the past change before your eyes?

Experiment a little. Expect people who didn't value you to be different. Suspend your opinion of how you "know" them to be and let them behave differently towards you. Forget you have a past with them. Maybe you can only hold the new belief and the new reality for a week the first time. Gradually, as your belief that reality is controlled by your beliefs increases, you will find it easier and easier to change and sustain different beliefs and different realities.

You'll become increasingly more flexible over time. You'll want to become so proficient at this that you can make extensive changes to reality quickly. In Chapter 8, *Reclaim Your Reality*, there is a discussion on how to identify and change the unconscious instructions that have been creating your reality to this point. We don't want these interfering with the very precise instructions you are going to want to send to reality as you assume conscious control of reality creation.

Sometimes my clients think I have some supernatural powers because I seem to know them so well instantly or I know what things must be happening in their lives or what things will happen. However, I assure you (and them) that I am just reading the events, or more accurately, the patterns of events in their lives. From the events, I know their beliefs and from their beliefs I know what kinds of events they will be creating in the future. It is an entirely left-brain or "logical" brain capability.

This is a methodical and logical assessment of someone's beliefs that anyone can develop expertise in. You can predict future events for any person based on the beliefs in their belief blueprint. You will know what's in their belief blueprint because of past events that occurred in their life that were created by that belief blueprint. Because, again, you can't have an emotion, thought, symbol or event in your reality without having the necessary beliefs.

As you begin altering one belief after another, watch for the effect on your reality. Pay attention to your success in manipulating reality. As you do, you will be internalizing some very powerful beliefs that you can control your reality through your beliefs. These will then make it easier to do this in the future. Beliefs create reality. As a result, all events become neutral information events from which you can determine future adjustments you would like to make to your internal belief structure.

As proficiency and experience increase, the "corrections" in response to "environmental stimuli" become as automatic as those done unconsciously while driving a car. Be persistent in your experimentation with identifying and changing your beliefs. In no time at all, you will have proven to yourself that we are indeed designed to create our realities.

Your ultimate evolution then will be in mastering the precision of the instructions to reality. This will involve not only issuing precise instructions to reality but also eliminating any instructions you have been inadvertently sending out which are creating undesirable realities you have been experiencing. This is the work of the reality creation technology.

OPERATING THE REALITY CREATION TECHNOLOGY

I think it's time to give you a glimpse of how to operate this optimizing system we call reality. You will want to become very proficient at reading its messages in order to grow and create at your full potential. The operation of the reality creation technology is simple since it is a return to the natural way humans were designed to function.

The challenging part, however, is unlearning the ways we have been trained to operate since childhood. Hopefully, we will soon be in a position to help our children learn correctly the first time how to achieve peak performance in partnership with their self-created reality.

When you are in alignment with your authentic core, all of your beliefs support that naturality. They become one cohesive, integrated force which sends laser-sharp instructions to reality. In alignment with your naturality, you emit instructions to reality with your greatest strength, precision and speed. Trying to be someone other than the natural you can pollute or nullify your instructions to reality.

Inconsistency activates multiple beliefs that send out multiple instructions for reality creation that may interfere with each other. This interference dilutes the power of your instructions. Therefore, if you are trying to take action based on rules or the expectations of others, or in response to multiple identities you've picked up from your parents, your employers, your friends, etcetera, these are sets of beliefs that may be in conflict.

If all of our beliefs support our naturality, we cannot help but create adaptive realities which support the increasing expression of our naturality. We are at full power. At this point, you will no longer need the reality creation technology. You'll have reintegrated into the naturality flow. Nature will always be flowing your system in the direction of naturality expansion and optimization. Therefore, just as with the pathfinding technology, you will want to design future realities in the direction of nature's flow.

Second, it is critical to own your reality. We can't change what we don't own. If reality is 100% self-created by our beliefs then we and our realities are a single system created by the same belief blueprint. We must expand our identities to include not only what's inside of our skin but everything that occurs in our reality as well. Our personal system then includes everything inside of us and everything we experience in our reality.

As a sidebar, we evolve tremendously at the moment we own our reality in this way. Separation ceases to exist. We automatically move to oneness with our world. Oneness results from seeing everyone as a reflection of ourselves. Since many religions and spiritual doctrines favor the move to oneness, the use of the peak evolution science offers an alternate route. There will be an evolution in consciousness inherent in this process that will have a far-reaching impact on society.

Thirdly, you can start to make the paradigm shift to a world where we create our own realities by simply assuming a one-to-one relationship between an event in your reality and a belief you might have. The orderliness of the reflection in your seemingly chaotic reality will astound you. Because reality is just a reflection of your belief blueprint, you can know your beliefs by what is going on in your reality.

If there are beliefs you don't like, you can change them. Become familiar with your own belief blueprint by thinking about what beliefs you would have to have had to create the events you have experienced in your reality. If there are some pairings of beliefs and events that you can't figure out, don't worry. They are likely events being created by "systems" of interrelated beliefs. We'll be taking a look at how to deal with these in Chapter 9, *The Powerless Reflex.*

The fourth step is to determine your "true" reality creation goals from the symbols you are pursuing. Changing how you feel is the motivation behind all behavior. It is the pursuit of a different emotional state that propels us to action. All goals then are emotional goals. Believe it or not, the simple essence of human existence is the pursuit of desired emotion states, one after the other.

"How can this be?" you may well ask. I want money. I want to be President. I want the perfect romantic relationship. With a slight adjustment to your thinking, you will realize all of the symbols and situations you have been pursuing in your life are a desire to achieve the specific emotional states you associate with them.

In terms of the reality creation technology, the only purpose you want to assign to these symbols is to help you identify the emotional states you are seeking – in other words, your true goals. Figure out what you really want from the symbols you have been pursuing and then pursue your emotional goals directly. In addition, you can use the physical symbols as tools for generating emotionally charged instructions to change your reality. Reality responds well to passion.

Pursuing the symbols directly you want to have – the money or the job title, for example – is usually not the fastest route to your emotional goals. Some people spend a lifetime pursuing money and are sorely disappointed when they don't enjoy it when they get it. When people pursue money, they are often pursuing one or more of the following powerful emotional states: freedom, safety, feeling valued or valuable, status or respect, inclusion, self-esteem, achievement, meaning, contribution, success, and/or power.

How many people do you know who pursued money in order to experience safety who have never found the amount of money where they feel safe? Even though they would be considered wealthy by many standards, they continue to frantically pursue money while spending it unnecessarily frugally.

Do you know any people who spend their lives working at things they don't like in order to accumulate enough money to have the freedom to do what they want to do? How many of these do you know who actually found the cutoff point when they had enough money to be free?

Freedom and safety are states of mind. Money is not the only route to these emotional goals. Therefore, the fifth reality creation instruction is to hold the emotional goal but release the channel through which the desired emotion must come.

What you really want is to feel the desired emotional state as quickly as possible. We really don't care which channel it arrives by. Therefore, you want to become very adept at holding the entire emotional harmonic of a desired reality. If you can't feel it emotionally you cannot create it.

As you begin to partner with nature to use the Pathfinding and Reality Creation Technologies, you will quickly discover there are an infinite number of routes to your emotional goal. Where the human mind can think of only one route to a powerful emotional goal, nature, you will learn, is infinitely creative.

The *Optimizers* and the naturality flow can get you there faster. With expertise and experience, you will evolve to pursuing the powerful emotional states you are seeking directly by the fastest route rather than demanding they come through specific symbols or channels you have identified.

Do you really care if you actually have money if you are experiencing the security or the freedom you associate with having money? Do you really care if you have a particular parent's love and acceptance if you are receiving all of the love and acceptance you could ever imagine wanting from a multitude of other sources? Once a cup is filled, there isn't a need for more.

The reality creation technology provides methodologies for translating your pursuit of symbols into the desired emotional states and then materializing those emotional goals by the most expedient routes. When you're experiencing all the freedom or love or feelings of being valued you're craving, do you really care what channel brought you to that wonderful emotional state? Another way to say the fifth instruction is "to pursue the emotions not the symbols."

This is important because if we don't have the emotional state we want, it's because we don't have the necessary beliefs, not that we don't have the necessary symbols. Remember, both the emotion and the symbols of that emotion are created by the same beliefs.

Therefore, rather than focusing on how we can get the symbols, we need to focus on how to get the requisite beliefs. The sixth instruction then is to internalize the new beliefs requisite for the new emotional states you want next.

Reality, it would seem, is simply a tapestry of symbols of our emotions. Unfortunately, the same reality over time loses its power to evoke the same emotional highs. This is the same process of habituation that incites drug addicts to pursue greater dosages. Our propensity for adapting to stimuli compels us to continuously pursue stronger intensities of the stimuli to induce the same levels of our desired emotional states, never mind to provide greater intensities.

Consequently, there can be no arrival at a blissful state and then the maintenance of that state by clinging to the stimuli or symbols that invoked it. This is a false dream that must be replaced by a more insightful understanding of the nature of the human being. As creative beings, we are designed to be perpetually creating. Continuous bliss comes from flowing with the dynamic creativity of the universe. Accept this and then master the process.

As you are able to release the pursuit of the symbols you've identified in favor of your true goals, you will want to measure your progress against these true goals: "Are you experiencing your desired emotions?" The seventh step, then, is to measure your progress against your true goals, not your accumulation of symbols.

If your goal was money because it meant you were valued, the question you want to keep asking yourself is, "Did I experience the emotion of being valued today?" By concentrating on manifesting the desired emotional states directly, we create realities which include the very symbols we have been pursuing consistent with those states – money, for example.

Remember, if you don't have the symbols and events you want in your life, then you likely don't yet have the beliefs. Concentrate on generating and intensifying the beliefs rather than chasing after the symbols and events. These will come into your life when the necessary beliefs get strong enough.

Step number eight is a belief engineering trick. Feeling the emotion first in *virtual reality* can strengthen the belief so it will create the physical reality with the desired emotion. That is why we come equipped with the ability to visualize, imagine and dream. In fact, I would like to take a stand by stating that if you cannot feel the emotion *virtually*, you will never create it in reality.

Step eight then is to experience the desired emotion in virtual reality first. Visualization can change multiple beliefs simultaneously. Therefore, you want to become very adept at holding the entire emotional tapestry or harmonic of a desired reality. Pre-experience your desired reality frequently to speed its creation. If you can't feel it emotionally you can't create it.

To know why this is the case, we will need to go back to *Figure 7.1*. Notice the top arrow going from emotions to your belief blueprint? This is to indicate that, while beliefs create emotions, human beings have also been designed to use emotions to change their beliefs. We came equipped with imaginations and the ability to not only visualize what we want but to "feel" it, to "pre-experience" it, in exactly the same way we would in physical reality.

Therefore, if we can practise feeling the desired emotions on a regular basis through visualization, daydreams, affirmations or prayer, we will automatically be strengthening the relevant beliefs. And, as we know, these beliefs will eventually be strong enough to send the instructions to reality necessary to create in reality what we have visualized.

This is why many top athletes now have visualization coaches. I foresee a time when the reality creation process is understood and we all have visualization coaches.

Instruction nine takes a little adjustment in your usual modus operandi. It is to accept that all events in reality are neutral information messages. Detachment is necessary in order to clearly read what message events in your reality mean for both the knowledge technology and the reality creation technology. This means that all messages are benevolent . . . . blocks just as much as flows.

As you begin to examine the connection between your beliefs and their expression in reality, it is important to accept that all the events you experience are simply neutral information messages reflecting back to you what is in your belief blueprint. You can then make the necessary adjustments to the instructions you are sending to create reality.

While it is important to view both "positive" and "negative" events as benevolent information events, I use the term "negative" to describe some events only to assist beginners. All events help you to identify what's in your belief blueprint so you can adjust it as required. Therefore, may I suggest you refrain from "shooting the messengers" – those who are used to communicate "negative" realities to you as a reflection of less desirable beliefs in your belief blueprint.

Rather, you will want to thank them for communicating where your instructions are off-course for you to achieve your emotional goals. This is the state of "detachment" that so many religions and philosophies talk about. In a self-created reality, you cannot be a victim. There is just a cast of thousands in your reality reflecting your inner state to you.

Now that you know how reality operates, you may have to re-think and re-write your modus operandi. For example, a job-seeker believing in an objective world constantly refines his personal marketing skills of prospecting and persuasion to find hiring employers more easily and to sell them when he does find them.

A job-seeker who has mastered reality creation simply materializes a reality with an employer who hires him. If you believe you are needy with respect to money, that money is difficult to get, or that you must work at things you don't like to earn money, then that is the reality you will experience. Rather than running around doing a plethora of activities to bring money into your life, revise your beliefs and your identity with respect to money. The reality experienced will change.

People you had decided to dislike because they mistreated you, turn out to be benevolent in that they are messengers for dysfunctional beliefs you have. And rather than telling them to be different, you need only make the necessary adjustments in your belief blueprint and they will either change or disappear from your life.

Without your maladaptive beliefs, they cannot exist in their current form in your life. As you become more fluid in changing your beliefs, be prepared to let those dysfunctional people go from your life either physically or in spirit. Who knew life could be so easy?

Fully Expressing our Creativity

Successful systems adapt or re-optimize to any changes in their contexts. Creativity is used to resolve challenges to optimization. Systems grow and evolve as a result of these adaptive acts. Human beings are systems collectively and individually driven to re-optimize by natural forces. Human beings, as a successful species, are, by nature, creative. We are designed for creativity.

Our creativity is on the rise. Our increasing interconnectedness through technological advances is one reason for this. This is due to the requirement for more adaptations to changes in interacting systems. Another reason is a growing need to express our naturality. This is evidenced by the growing number of entrepreneurs in the world.

Over the next few decades, we will take our innate creativity to new levels of sophistication. We will conquer a new frontier of creativity. We will learn to consciously create our realities by design. As this happens, the Knowledge Age will give way to the Age of Creativity.

Creativity will become the mark of personal evolution. The most evolved human beings will be those fully engaged in the creative expression of their naturality – the objective of *Peak Evolution*.

These creators will be optimized, maximized, and operating at peak performance and peak evolution in alignment with their naturality. They will be the individuals with the greatest power and precision to create their realities. Individually and collectively, they will consciously assume responsibility for designing our future worlds and the course of evolution for humanity. These will be our new leaders.

8

RECLAIM YOUR REALITY

*"None of us can help the things life has done to us. They're
done before you realize it, and once they're done, they make
you do other things until at last everything comes between you
and what you'd like to be, and you have lost your true self
forever."*　　Eugene O'Neill

If beliefs create reality, who or what has been mucking up our lives? It's time to take control of the instructions we've inadvertently been sending out to stop creating what we don't want and to start creating what we do want. Nature is actually trying to help us to create adaptive realities. By partnering with the naturality flow, we can work *with* nature to purge undesirable elements from ourselves and our realities . . . . permanently!

Because most of us didn't know we create our realities with our beliefs, we didn't realize we have been constantly giving instructions to reality. If these instructions are creating "negative" realities, we need to gain control of them as quickly as possible. The next three chapters will deal with how to *de-create* undesirable realities by doing just this.

The subsequent three reality creation technology chapters will then present how to proactively create the realities you want. My objective is to install in you a permanent mechanism for ongoing self-correction and self-clearing as a way of life rather than a periodic tool. Nature is always trying to optimize your system. Therefore, by tapping into this optimizing flow of nature, we can access powerful mechanisms to clear disruptive elements from our personal systems continuously.

A Two-Pronged Approach

We will be using a two-pronged approach to deal with the problem of de-creating negative realities. First, I want to give you some new belief engineering interventions for *directly* addressing specific types of problem realities and beliefs. The fact that reality is a reflection of what is going on inside of us makes possible new tools for personal transformation. There are new ways to clear interferences such as conflicting, limiting and fear beliefs that are keeping us from peak experience. Natural forces try to help us clear these interferences . . . . if you know what to look for. The objective is to master the continuous creation of adaptive realities.

The second approach is *indirect*. As we click into naturality, many of our problem beliefs will change naturally or become deactivated. Interfering beliefs can be overruled by optimized beliefs supportive of our naturality. Pursuing our naturality and our *art* will cure many of the maladaptive beliefs creating disruptive realities for us. Naturality-supporting beliefs automatically create realities which support and strengthen our naturality. Our strategy will be to promote your naturality so your system evolves to a new iteration which does not have the interferences.

The intent of the interventions presented in these three chapters is not to clear this problem or that belief. Rather, I want you to evolve to a new level of being. I want you to reintegrate into the naturality flow and take action based on the Optimizers for both directions of growth – the ongoing removal of interferences to naturality and the increasing expression of naturality.

The process then for reclaiming reality interleaves both approaches. Individual growth to peak performance can be accelerated by alternating your efforts between the direct clearing of problem beliefs and the indirect approach of strengthening your naturality.

CLEARING TOXIC BELIEFS

The Contamination of our Belief Blueprints

The naturality flow is always trying to pressure us to have only those beliefs that support our naturality. If our belief blueprint is in alignment with our naturality, then we should automatically be creating adaptive realities that support our natural growth path. Not the case for you? Then you'll no doubt want to know how your belief blueprint got contaminated in the first place, how to detoxify it for optimization and precise reality creation, and how to keep it in its most powerful form on an ongoing basis.

It would be wonderful if I could teach you how to create reality with a clean slate, but this is not possible. Our belief blueprints are full of beliefs that are already creating our realities. It's time for some housecleaning. It's time to consciously choose what is in your belief blueprint.

Learning to choose our beliefs and hence, the realities we will experience, is a rite of passage for each human being. It is part of the natural maturation process for each of us to evolve from absorbing the beliefs of our families, teachers, bosses, culture and society in general to choosing, as an adult, what beliefs we will have in the belief blueprint creating our reality.

Because most of us didn't know this, we didn't realize the consequences of *not choosing* our beliefs. Thus, we have absorbed a lot of maladaptive beliefs that are creating negative realities for us individually and as a species. Belief blueprints which should have supported our evolution to the full expression of our naturality instead became corrupted. Our cultural indoctrination process has interfered with our natural maturation progression.

It was the cyclical nature of self-fulfilling prophesy that installed and reinforced beliefs in our belief blueprint. If, for example, your parents said, "You can't trust people," you, as an innocent child, might have simply absorbed this belief into your blueprint. What would be the consequence? You would unconsciously begin sending instructions to reality that would create events in which people let you down or misused/abused you or took advantage of you.

As you saw evidence of untrustworthy people in your reality, you couldn't help but think, "My parents were right. I can't trust people." You would have thereby strengthened that belief more, causing a commensurate increase in the strength of the instructions to reality and their consequences. The cycle of self-fulfilling prophesies would have been launched. You're caught in the first maladaptive loop. You have begun to create an unsafe world.

By the time we grow up, it would be hard to avoid having dysfunctional instructions creating our realities. Ideally, we would like to create a belief blueprint around our core identities which is 100% supportive of our naturality and doing our art. This is the direction in which nature will be pressuring us.

So how do we begin to do the cleanup? This is where we can use reality, the optimizing system. Once we know how to read its signals, reality can tell us everything we need to know to be optimized at any point in time. Reality can be used like a gigantic computer. It is a benevolent partner for moving beyond peak performance to peak evolution.

Detoxify Your Instructions to Reality

Since our realities are created by our beliefs, the events in our reality will tell us precisely what is in our belief blueprint. Reality can be used as a diagnostic tool. Because beliefs create the emotions, thoughts, symbols and events in our reality, we can know what needs to be cleared out of our belief blueprints whenever we have a negative experience. For those who never mastered the art of introspection, you can now *see* what's going on inside of you by the events in your reality.

The Initial Cleanup Period

If we want to de-create negative things in our realities, we must change the beliefs that are generating those events. I'd like you to commit to setting aside a period of time for the cleanup – anywhere from two weeks to two months depending on your schedule and how active your life is.

The reason for the time range is because the faster events are appearing in your life, the faster you can clear the beliefs that are creating problems. If you are not a person who takes a lot of action or who has a great deal going on in your reality, you will be seeing message events in your reality at a slower pace and therefore won't know what has to be changed as quickly as someone whose life is moving faster.

The trick for clearing your system on an ongoing basis is to assume that reality is your friend, partner, and optimizer and it is trying to help you move to maximum performance. Understand that, *with total neutrality*, reality will generate events reflective of all our beliefs – good and bad, right and wrong. Therefore, all we have to do is identify what beliefs we would have had to have to create the recent negative events in our realities and then change those beliefs.

Only Active Problem Beliefs need be Cleared

Fortunately, the whole belief blueprint is not actively creating reality at any point in time. Only the beliefs relevant to your system's current needs and goals are activated. So you only have to clean up the parts that are pertinent to your life *right now*.

There is no need to revisit past traumas in order to deal with them. It would be better not to relive past negative experiences because we don't want you to reabsorb and strengthen the emotions and beliefs of those unpleasant times. Whatever problems need to be solved can be solved with creativity *right now*.

You may have had a terrible childhood leaving you with all sorts of emotional scars. Growth in the naturality paradigm is not about going back and making right all of the damage we received from childhood traumas or unfortunate events in our lives. There is no need to relive those experiences in order to clear your system.

Doing that will re-vitalize all sorts of old dysfunctional channels, responses, and toxic beliefs and emotions. These, in turn, will create unpleasant events in your reality by reflection. To use these channels again is to strengthen them thus creating more unpleasant events in reality which will re-traumatize your system.

How much better it would be to allow those channels to atrophy from disuse. This is what nature does and nature knows better than we do how to re-optimize systems.

For example, nature has some of us repress traumatic memories so we don't re-damage our system. If we were to keep reliving negative events in our mind, we would be strengthening negative beliefs, and those beliefs would create the feared realities which would then re-traumatize us.

You can see how this could become an endless cycle throughout your life. Just because there is a defect in your system does not mean it has to be corrected.

You only need to clear what is interfering with the expression of your naturality right this moment as flagged by the ten *Optimizers*. If there are no negative events occurring, then assume your imperfect self is optimized. Optimization is just the ideal balance of the needs of all systems at any point in time. It may not be maximization or perfection.

Your system can be dysfunctional in many ways that are not called for by your current context. As long as your current circumstance does not invoke these dysfunctional pathways, you can operate at peak performance.

Your objective, then, as you learn this new way of being is to stay totally in the present to clear only what is creating negative events *right now* . . . . as a way of life. Eventually you'll have an eye for catching events hinting you have negative beliefs to be cleared before these beliefs create events big enough to be a problem to you.

And, as you become more fluid and more adept at belief engineering, you'll be able to make the belief changes more rapidly so that problems disappear as quickly as you identify them. This is the way to keep your system in top form for the rest of your life.

Toxic knowledge is state-bound in the same way that other knowledge is state-bound. Remember the experiment in the *Spontaneous Knowledge* chapter in which university students remembered best with the same blood-alcohol level as when they had studied? If you don't revisit the same state, you can't access toxic memories. The toxic knowledge within your system won't be reactivated.

Therefore, how quickly can you evolve your system to the next level whereby you can no longer access the state-bound toxicity? You will be able to objectively remember the events occurred, of course, but it's as if they happened to someone else. It's as if you are no longer vibrating at that frequency and can therefore not access the events experientially or emotionally. You are emotionally neutral. Your system then has been detoxified. This is the level of attainment I wish for you.

Inventory Recent Negative Events

For our belief blueprint cleanup, begin by making a list of events in the last three to six months that you would consider negative events. If beliefs create reality, what beliefs would you have had to have to create these events? Are you able to group these negative events by the beliefs that generated them? What do you know as a result of the pattern? What are the preferred beliefs you'd rather have, from here on in, to prevent the negative events from recurring or to stop these negative situations from persisting?

Nature Systematically Clears Interferences to Optimization

The first *Optimizer* identified in Chapter 3 is our natural growth path. This concept captures nature's perpetual attempts to optimize and adapt us as systems to our contexts. Progress is always toward the increasing expression of the naturality of the system. Nature seeks maximization of the system, as much as is possible within every context, based on the reason for all of the components of the system to have been bound together into a system in the first place.

Growth then can be defined as the continuous amplification of an individual's authentic core or naturality within changing contexts. Having studied the problem events in hundreds of people's lives, I have discovered that nature systematically clears one interfering belief after the next *based on its priority as an interference to naturality.* Take another look at your inventory of negative events in your reality. Is one belief the consistent culprit for all of the problem events?

However, as soon as the necessary belief change is made, you can see the events getting smaller and sparser until they disappear. As this happens, the next problem belief begins to generate message events in reality. Amid what appears to be a chaotic existence, nature moves in a very systematic fashion to clear each of the interferences from our systems in priority order!

If we know that nature is meticulously systematic about eliminating problem beliefs, we can begin to facilitate this natural process. We can look for the clusters of events signaling the next belief to be changed and simply quantum leap to an identity without the offending belief. (You'll know how to quantum leap by the last chapter.) After moving through several cycles of beliefs to be cleared, actioning nature's signals will be as natural to you as actioning the multitude of stimuli required for driving a car.

Begin Making the Indicated Changes Earlier

Because we know nature is always trying to optimize us, we can begin to read the signals for change earlier. Take a look at some significant negative events in your life. What beliefs would you have had to have in order to create those events? Which cluster of events associated with a belief is the largest? Can you trace the pattern of smaller events created by this belief as they gradually became more frequent and more intense over time?

What is the first small event you can find in the pattern of events attached to this dysfunctional belief? Could you retrain yourself to make the necessary belief changes when nature's signals are this small? This is the objective. Once you make the belief change, know the next belief to be changed will be starting to create small events in your reality. Watch for a cluster of small events to start. Make the changes before the events become too large. Why have struggle events when they are preventable? Protect your system from damage.

Accept the perpetual changes of the optimization process. Keep experimenting with this clearing process and the messages of events in reality until you have the experiential learning to make you proficient. Since life is an ongoing process, you can use the events in your life to trigger your experimentation. Every negative event in your reality can become a "learning" and "clearing" exercise for you.

Use every significant negative event in your life to determine the next belief to be cleared for you to move to naturality. Again, trace the pattern of events created by that belief to see how long ago you could have responded in order to have avoided your current pain. Keep improving your speed of recognition of what has to be changed.

As you continue to clear maladaptive beliefs in response to reality's events, you will eventually eliminate the majority of beliefs that interfere with you becoming the "authentic, natural you." You will increase the percentage of times you create realities that are conducive to your achieving your emotional goals. Accelerate your growth to this desired end by using this natural evolutionary clearing mechanism. Get hold of the instructions you are sending out to create the reality you will experience.

Every living thing is trying to optimize within its environment. For human beings, this actually means *creating* the optimal environment. Nature is trying to help you with this. Our goal is to get to a point where our lives are only about the creative expression of our naturality with no negative emotions, interferences or struggle events. From this perspective, we will be in a position to truly explore our full potential as creative beings.

Event Patterns are more Pronounced with Naturality

If you can't see this dynamic clearing pattern operating in your inventory of events, there is a possible explanation. Most of my research was done with leaders who are further along the evolutionary continuum in expressing their naturality. The better the leader, the easier it is for me to see this cyclical clearing process going on in their realities.

If there is no event pattern in your reality, check that you are not externally referenced and living your life totally to please others or in response to external stimuli. Are you one of those people who never do anything you would like to do or feels natural to you?

The truer we are to our naturalness, the more orderly is the pattern of events in our reality, and hence the more useful the pattern is to help us grow to peak performance. Naturality means that you are more integrated and congruent. Therefore, you will be sending more integrated and congruent instructions to reality.

If you are trying to be someone you are not − or several people you are not − these other personas will be sending instructions that together create a lot of noise events and mixed messages in your reality. It will be more difficult to identify patterns.

Reality helps you Clear Toxic Beliefs

Let's say the next item you need to clear for optimization is a belief you are not valued or valuable. Little whispered events will begin to appear in your reality identifying the fact that a belief change is required. If you do nothing, those messages will get larger and more numerous.

Mixed in with these increasing negative messages will also be some messages on how to solve the problem, such as a friend going through the exact same situation and solving it, for example. Or you are channel hopping and come across a television show on the same theme. Next, you might see a newspaper or magazine article about a real event or how to handle it.

Or . . . . and this part is really spooky in its prevalence . . . . you give enlightened advice to someone else on how to solve the exact same problem. This is so common that, as you move into alignment, you will want to begin tracking any advice you give to anyone. In all likelihood, it will be optimal for you to take your own advice.

Look for the models in your reality for identifying and solving the next interferences to the expression of your naturality. Remember, reality is your partner for optimizing. Know what it is trying to do and use it as a tool. Science is about understanding new levels of order. You are in the process of discovering new levels of order in your reality.

When you make the indicated belief change, there is no belief to continue generating those negative events and the events get smaller and less frequent until they disappear. As they get smaller, the next belief change required for your optimization begins to generate small whispers of events. This cycle repeats again and again. Therefore, it would only make sense to develop some prowess at dealing with this growth process – even to proactively speed it up.

Value Your Key Messengers

I find there are usually one or two people in your life who are the key messengers as to what beliefs you need to change. You *know* who these problem people are . . . . a parent, your mother-in-law, your boss, a co-worker, a sibling, your significant other . . . . They are often giving you messages you'd rather not hear. Messages that you are not accessing internally are simply being reflected into your self-created reality through messengers.

Instead of resisting them, *use these messengers to clear your belief blueprint*. In the big-picture view of your system, they are actually benevolent. They are reflecting back to you toxic beliefs you need to clear to move to full authentic expression. Believe it or not, as you gain expertise in the reality creation technology, you will come to feel gratitude toward your messengers. Let them be your stimuli and your report cards for growth.

Figure out what beliefs you would have to have to create them or the things they say or do in your life. Change those beliefs and one of two things will happen. Without the interfering beliefs, they will change before your eyes to someone who belongs in your new adaptive reality. Alternatively, they will leave your life with no toxic beliefs to hold them in it. This is one of the reasons why it is very important, as your growth accelerates, to let people leave your life who are not reflective of the latest iteration of you.

One of my clients, Thomas, had a real problem with one of his peers, Katherine. They were both executive vice presidents of a substantial international consulting firm. Katherine apparently was a bully. She bullied not only her people but also his. Thomas had unfortunately been traumatized as a child by bullies.

As an adult, he could not abide this kind of behavior. As an accomplished, capable, powerful and successful man, Thomas had a strong belief in the world being a safe place. Yet there was a part of him that believed the world was unsafe requiring him to protect himself and others. It was this belief which was creating a bully in the next office to him.

In our first reality creation session together, I asked Thomas for a list of things he would like to change in his reality. With some difficulty in disguising his outrage, Thomas emphatically blueprinted that he wanted Katherine fired and gone from the company.

I then explained to Thomas how we create reality to emotional goals rather than having control over the specific channels and symbols and events through which those emotional goals must come. He heard me but I could almost feel him reiterating under his breath that he still wanted Katherine fired. Despite this, I continued to explain the true emotional goals of his blueprint – safety for himself and the people he cared about.

In addition, I forewarned Thomas that, with strong emotion, positive or negative, reality would be created more quickly and more precisely. Thomas definitely had strong emotions around his Katherine blueprint. This was on Tuesday. Thomas and I were going to see each other again on Thursday.

He was quite shaken when we met next. I'd seen this before when people discover how truly powerful they actually are, yet aren't quite ready to cope with it. I had told Thomas that emotional goals can come through different channels than the ones specified and that's exactly what had happened in the case of Katherine.

On Wednesday, Katherine had come into Thomas' office for the first time since she had joined the company a year ago. The two rarely talked. She said, "I don't believe I fit into this company culturally as well as I would like. Would you mentor me?" The coaching session that ensued made it clear that safety had been returned to Thomas' world. Katherine was no longer a threat. So, there we have it . . . . the goal was met through an entirely unexpected means. When Thomas changed, Katherine changed.

When partnering with nature, you can expect coincidences and quantum leaps to your true emotional goals and that is precisely what Thomas experienced. Just clearing his belief that there were bullies in his world, that his world was unsafe, removed the bully from his life. She transformed within 24 hours of his belief change. He believed she would be gone and she, in effect, was gone by her transformation. Who is it that you would like to transform in your life? Make the transformations inside of you to see their reflections out in your world.

Let Go of the Old

Often we feel we have to persist with individuals and circumstances no longer supportive of our development. Normal evolution would suggest that things no longer aligned with our naturality should be allowed to flow out of our lives to make space for new, more aligned things to flow in. It is important not to block the natural optimizing process. You and your reality are one complete system created by your beliefs. If your belief blueprint shifts, it's important not to block reality from shifting with it by reflection.

It is adaptive to let people and circumstances flow into and out of your life as they support or don't support your growth process. You may want to re-evaluate your rules about keeping people and things in your life at all costs. If you made a belief change and you try to keep people in your life that are part of your old beliefs, they will reinforce your old belief and undo your new belief change.

Letting go of the old to keep your personal system clear of toxicity is even more important as your alignment with your naturality increases. As your instructions to reality are more purely aligned with your naturality, you can create realities much more quickly and powerfully. Therefore, if you have a toxic belief or a fear belief in this more advanced state, you are going to create negative realities faster. In this sense, naturality is a double-edged sword.

You'll want to keep your system clear of toxicity as you move along the naturality continuum to the full expression of your core identity. This is the reason these next three chapters are presented first in the discussion of reality creation. It is important to master the techniques for the continuous clearing that will be demanded by the optimizing process for the rest of your life. Again, what I am attempting to present is a new modus operandi for evolution in partnership with nature's ten *Optimizers* rather than a one-time fix-it technique.

New-Goal Syndrome

Every time you set up a new goal or blueprint a new reality you want to bring into existence, those parts of your belief blueprint that are relevant become activated. These beliefs then neutrally begin sending instructions to reality. As a result, some beliefs that may not have been active before and therefore have not been cleaned up yet, may start to create problem events in your reality. You may suddenly find yourself facing a number of struggle events interfering with you achieving your new goal.

As a novice at reality creation, you might assume these problem events mean you are not going to get the new reality you want. However, remember that reality is an *Optimizer*. You just didn't know what it was trying to communicate before. You may be tempted to think you are a victim of these new circumstances but remind yourself you now know better.

As a perfect reflection of your beliefs, reality operates as a tool – a self-correcting feedback system – telling you precisely the beliefs you need to change to experience both your emotional goals and optimization. Therefore, setting new goals allows you to accelerate the cleanup of your belief blueprint.

Assume this belief cleanup is part of achieving every new goal so that negative events immediately after goal-setting are seen as "business as usual." As you set each new goal, the relevant beliefs will be activated to emit instructions neutrally into reality. The bigger the goal the larger the cleanup is likely to be.

FEAR BELIEFS

"Once men are caught up in an event they cease to be afraid. Only the unknown frightens men."[27] Saint-Exupery

Let's continue with the process of clearing dysfunctional beliefs by looking at an especially powerful category of these . . . . your fears. In a paradigm where beliefs create reality, it is critical to deal with your fears. Fears are beliefs. Therefore, if left unchecked, they will become self-fulfilling prophecies by creating the feared realities.

One of the belief engineering techniques I mentioned in Chapter 7 relates to the single arrow going from the "emotions" box to the belief blueprint in *Figure 7.1*. If you want to change the beliefs in your belief blueprint to change the instructions creating your reality, you have only to visualize to the point of experiencing the desired emotion. Since you cannot experience the emotion without the belief, you will be strengthening the precise beliefs necessary to create your emotional goals.

Now, imagine you have a fear – let's say you're afraid you'll be fired. You visualize that distasteful reality. You feel all of the emotions associated with being fired with excruciating clarity. You relive the imagined eventuality over and over again. What you have done is use perfect belief engineering techniques to reinforce your fear beliefs that you'll be fired so that they are in a better position to send those instructions to reality. Perish the thought! Or, more correctly, perish the belief! Visualizing feared events to the point of experiencing the associated emotions is perfect belief engineering to create the feared reality.

Now that you know how reality operates, it becomes imperative to clear your fears on a regular basis. You don't want to inadvertently create your worst nightmare. By the end of your reading *Peak Evolution*, you will have a holistic methodology for keeping yourself safe and in safe realities. However, if this is just your first time through the book, you should consider yourself a novice at managing your self-created reality. Therefore, make clearing your fears a regular priority.

Disarm Your Fears Regularly

Fears undermine the precision with which you can create desired realities and interfere with your ability to read your resonance. They interfere with you moving to peak performance. Therefore, it's a priority to be continually disarming your fears. In many cases, this can be accomplished by simply becoming aware of the fear. In other situations, it may be necessary to "live" through the feared circumstances in your mind, observing yourself successfully dealing with each step in the process.

Whenever you feel the need to clear fears out of your system, make a list of 40 or 50 fears you have. Rate their significance out of 10 (10 is high) based on your resonance as discussed in the Resonance-Rating Exercise in Chapter 4. Disarm those fears you have rated 10 with the visualization of you successfully handling them.

Move step by step through each feared situation to give yourself time to creatively solve each of its challenges. Re-rate this list periodically to confirm previous "10" fears have been dissipated. Also, determine the next set of fears to be cleared that emerge as 10's, now that the first ones have been dealt with. Again, assume each of them has actually happened and imagine yourself successfully negotiating each stage of dealing with them.

Methods of Mitigating Fear

When you have done this fear clearing exercise a few times, you will have measurable proof that simply identifying a fear starts to reduce its impact. So many people seem to freeze up at the mere thought of the feared situation. The only question they focus on is how to avoid the feared event.

As soon as I get them to imagine that the feared situation has already happened and ask them how they are going to solve each of the issues associated with it, they no longer fear it. They find they are tremendously creative and resourceful when they begin to take action, even in their minds. Refuse to ever be a prisoner of your fear again. Below are some other ways you can detoxify your belief blueprint of fears. Some of the techniques have not been presented yet but you will learn about later in the book.

First, here is another belief engineering trick to enable you to push your own buttons for peak performance. Whenever you imagine a feared event, use this imagined negative reality to trigger a conditioned reflex to blueprint a positive reality. I will be talking about conditioned reflexes in the next chapter when we will be eradicating your "powerless" belief complex. With practice, you can become very good at installing conditioned reflexes in partnership with reality.

Think of how entrepreneurs have a conditioned reflex to use negative events in their realities to inspire new levels of creativity. Think of how an ant will continually try another route, and another, and another when encountering interferences to bringing food home to the anthill. As a new reality creator, your proficiency with creating conditioned reflexes to clear fears will increase as you gain the ability to define what you *do* want, not just what you don't want.

In the face of a fear, switch gears. Concentrate on visualizing the reality you would prefer. Ignore all messages and realities to the contrary of what you are blueprinting. Commit to having what you want and let nothing interfere with you sending instructions to reality that are precise, pure, integrated and consistent. The three chapters on *Creating Desirable Realities* will provide you with more details on how to do this.

If the fear is getting in the way of you defining what it is you actually want, here's a tip. In order to release yourself to think in an unlimited way, internalize the identity of a person who never fails. Let your emotions shift as you become that "superperson." Now, what would you do if you couldn't fail? Blueprint this reality and visualize it until you can feel the emotions.

You'll learn how to "reincarnate" yourself wrapped in a more adaptive identity in Chapter 13, the *Power of Identity*. Once you've read this chapter and have this skill, why not also reincarnate yourself with the identity of a person who is so creative and so innovative you can find the solution to any problem. Whenever you are blocked or up against a situation you fear, you can successfully innovate.

Another way to avoid inadvertently sending instructions to create reality through your fears is to stay in the present. It is our remembrance of past fears and the possibility of future problem situations that cause us to experience fear in the present . . . . even though we are in no imminent danger. As you will learn, much of the power of the peak evolution science comes from tools used in the present.

*"Whoever builds a house for future happiness builds a prison
for the present."* Octavio Paz

Almost universally, everyone who begins moving with the naturality flow eventually becomes a growth addict. As such, they gradually become experts in reading their natural growth process in the flow. Once you know what nature is up to, you will begin to understand and expect the perpetual cycles of growth. This enables you to avoid viewing every situation as new and threatening. Recognizing and clearing your fears will become a natural part of your growth cycles.

Clearing the next interferences to your naturality will also become business as usual. Growth expertise will allow you to eliminate many of your fears since you know what has to be done next. As you rid your belief blueprint of interfering beliefs, and especially conflicting beliefs, you will find the number of fear-inspiring struggle events created in your reality will gradually decline. This would be the ultimate solution to eliminating your fear.

In addition, as you increase your ability to control the realities you experience – in other words, to increase your power – *your habit of fear will dissipate*. Again, in *The Powerless Reflex* chapter, an intervention is presented that should help to remove or at least diminish the "powerlessness" belief I have found in everyone I have worked with. Powerlessness is a major cause of fear. If you believe you are powerful, many of your fears will disappear.

Further, as people begin to operate in alignment with their naturality, they begin to work on projects and creations that are very meaningful to them. Each creation works to strengthen his/her identity. It is amazing how fearless we can become in the face of a cause we believe in.

Think of a mother protecting her child. Fears for personal danger become subservient to the task of protecting one's child. The peak evolution science aligns you with your natural purpose or what is meaningful to you. It is a process which empowers you.

Therefore, embarking on a road to naturality will automatically increase your power while correspondingly reducing your experience of fear. Power of purpose and power of identity result in a quantum leap in the strength of an individual. The formula for eliminating the fear habit is one of increasing your power and diminishing your powerlessness through your partnership with the naturality flow.

Here's another way fear is eliminated as you become proficient with the peak evolution science. There is an expanded consciousness that emerges as you move with the naturality flow. It will happen to you without you even intending it. With this expanded consciousness you will look at reality very differently. You will not perceive as many fearful events. Think of a child and an adult looking at identical realities. The perception of fear will likely be entirely different.

Also, as your ability to create realities with precision increases, your fears will decrease. The reality creation technology then is also a solution to fear. In the face of a feared situation, use your new reality creation expertise to create a preferred reality to replace the feared reality.

Information can usually fix any problem. It can also dissipate your fears. Assume the feared situation has transpired and do the research necessary to solve the problem. If you do this in time, your fears may be allayed fast enough to prevent them from creating the feared event. The knowledge technology lets you operate as if you have access to all knowledge. In Chapter 6, you learned how to use the pathfinding technology to proceed rapidly to solve any problem moment by moment – even if you don't know the ultimate solution.

Although this is an oversimplification of pathfinding, you can basically take any action with the intent to solve a problem situation and reality will block you when you're going in the wrong direction and facilitate your progress when you're going in the right direction. Your resonance is key to the success of the pathfinding technology since it is the vehicle for colliding with pivotal information coincidences.

The knowledge technology allows you to use reality like a giant computer to solve any problem. Once you've developed a fair degree of expertise with it, your fear quotient will decline substantially. You will no longer be paralyzed by fear since any action will begin to tell you the route to eluding or correcting the feared situation. Any action will generate block events or flow events to tell you which route is safe.

One of the quantum leaps you can expect to have by using the reality creation technology happens as a result of owning your reality. When you truly internalize this paradigm shift, you will begin living your life very differently. You will experience everything that happens to you as simply a message about your optimization.

Rather than fearing situations, you will simply assume that everything that is happening to you is adaptive and trying to take you to your highest emotional states. All events, then, become benevolent messages. You will have to relinquish, once and for all, your identity of victim. You can't be a victim in a self-created reality. Everything that happens is reflective of your instructions. When you truly get this, fear toward anything but imminent physical danger will become illogical.

One of the most insidious causes of fear I have encountered is the fear of judgment by others. Being judged negatively can lead to some of our most powerful fears, such as abandonment, exclusion, rejection, failure, loss of freedom, and loss of love. A great deal of my work in large hierarchical corporations is to reverse the damage of institutionalized judgment. Judgment so impedes optimization and reality creation that I have created a separate chapter in which to discuss it.

By releasing self-judgment, you can free yourself from a judging reality. When you release self-judgment, what remains is self-love. As each individual releases the habit of judgment, our societies will be transformed. We will have created a world where each of us can take the chance to move to our highest creativity and our greatest expression of our true naturality. The absence of judgment brings with it new levels of freedom and safety, and new echelons of creativity and peak performance.

While all of these means for eradicating your fear beliefs from your belief blueprint may not be entirely understandable at this point in your knowledge of the peak evolution science, you are at least getting a sample of the power of these technologies to totally transform your way of life and your power to positively contribute to the world.

Going with the naturality flow offers a two-pronged approach to keeping our systems optimized. By clearing what nature is signaling to be cleared, we free ourselves from the interferences to expressing our naturality. By proactively doing our art – the highest expression of our naturality – we can move to full power as the truly creative beings we are.

Evolved human beings exist in a state of continuous creative expression of naturality. Every fiber of their beings, every belief, supports this optimized state. As the "noise" disappears from their lives, all that remains is pure authentic force. Adaptive realities are created automatically. When there is only the pure, concise, integrated communication of naturality, it cannot be otherwise. Reclaim this power as your birthright.

9

THE POWERLESS REFLEX

"A person and the cause of their problems are part of a single system." (Oshry, 1995)

Almost universally, our cultures have installed in each of us a whole system of conflicting beliefs linked to powerlessness. This belief complex is one of the greatest inhibitors to naturality and peak performance we face as a race and as individuals. Let's continue the process we began in the last chapter of removing interferences to our naturality and reclaiming control of the instructions creating our realities. I'd like to introduce a single intervention designed to eliminate the entire "powerless belief complex" . . . . permanently!

While we have been culturally inflicted with a powerless belief system, many of us are also blessed with a coexisting belief system that we are powerful. In a paradigm in which beliefs create reality, any pair of conflicting beliefs will create struggle events. Here, we are dealing with whole systems of beliefs around "powerless" and "powerful" that are in conflict.

This results in a reality riddled with struggle events that impede our growth and our achievements. The *power reflex* intervention uses the "powerless" side we all have to create a conditioned reflex to trigger our "powerful" side. In the process, numerous connected conflicting belief pairs are released . . . . extinguishing a multitude of struggle events from our lives. Sound good? Read on . . . .

The Prevalence of Powerlessness

In discussing the work of Robert Fritz in his *Personal Mastery* chapter in *The Fifth Discipline* (1990), Peter Senge reveals the prevalence of the beliefs in powerlessness and unworthiness in executives. He defines these terms, respectively, as "we can't have what we want" and "we don't deserve to have what we want." In *The Path of Least Resistance* (1989), Robert Fritz reveals he has met only a handful of individuals who do not have one or the other of these two contradictory beliefs.

So far, I have not met anyone who is not disabled in some way by these two sets of conflicting beliefs: powerful versus powerless and *valued/valuable* versus *not valued/not valuable*. I've stopped using the term "unworthy" with my clients because I've never found an executive who would accept it. However, they universally related to the terms of "not valued" or "not valuable." "Unworthy" means "lacking in value." The executives I encountered consistently felt the value was there but it wasn't recognized. Consequently, they rejected the term "unworthy."

PURGING YOUR POWERLESS REFLEX

Once I learned of the existence of something so prevalent and so pernicious in universally obstructing reality creation, I felt compelled to develop an intervention to eradicate it in my clients. You may recall the story of my developing the *power reflex* intervention in the discussions of Level II and Level III of the knowledge technology in the *Spontaneous Knowledge* chapter.

I wondered if dealing with the problem in the naturality paradigm and a world of self-created realities could release an individual from this insidious powerlessness. It turns out that partnering with our self-created realities does indeed provide a means to actually cure the problem. The quantum leap approach preferred by nature is also key.

What I developed is a way to quantum leap to a new state of being rather than a means to evolve gradually from "powerless" to "powerful." Basically, a whole portion of our belief blueprint is replaced in one intervention while partnering with reality for support.

Here, then, are the steps for you to make this all-important, life-changing quantum leap which uses our *powerless reflex* to install a *powerful reflex*. Let's start with a quick review of the process for eliminating the struggle events created by conflicting beliefs. A struggle event is an event in your reality with a negative emotional charge. It is created by conflicting beliefs creating conflicting realities. Struggle events are the result of mixed messages "fighting" in your reality.

If you believe you are both "valued" and "not valued," you will experience some upsetting emotions when these two opposing beliefs create juxtaposed events in your reality. The prescription for eliminating struggle events is to choose the positive side of the conflicting belief pair and to release the negative belief.

Thus, the answer – if you are using a simple belief engineering approach – is to discipline yourself to operate as if you were only "valued" until you begin creating a reality reflecting this belief.

Take decisions as if only the positive belief existed. Be the person who is always valued. Since beliefs create reality, your reality would gradually begin to contain events demonstrating that you are "valued." These would then help to reinforce and strengthen your "valued" belief until you would eventually cease to have the belief that you are "not valued." Without the "not valued" belief, you could not generate any negative events reflective of that belief. Simple, right? All you need is practice.

Now, beliefs like to travel with their friends. Beliefs automatically interlink into clusters to give you an adaptive and consistent view of reality. This is designed to keep the body in balance. Picture your beliefs as a cluster of green grapes where each grape is interconnected in the bunch.

Let's say that one of those interconnected green grapes represents the "powerless" belief. If you try to replace this green grape with a red "powerful" grape, the brain will see it doesn't interlink coherently with the other green grapes.

To get the integrated, consistent picture that is healthy and adaptive, the brain will automatically "write over" the red grape to make it a green grape. In other words, the "powerless" green grape would be reinstated. We'd be right back where we started.

The brain is in the habit of doing this on a number of fronts. For example, we actually physically see only about 50 percent of the picture finally perceived. The brain will fill in the blanks to complete the picture. An intuitive inspiration is based on your knowing, say, 20 per cent of the information required. The brain will "top up" this information to give you a completed solution or picture.

Therefore, the only way to eliminate a "powerless" belief is to replace the whole interlinked "powerless" belief cluster with a "powerful" belief system. Using our metaphor, we would need to replace the entire bunch of green grapes containing the green "powerless" grape with a cluster of red grapes logically interlinked around a red "powerful" grape.

In *Figure 9.1*, I have provided a partial list of the conflicting belief pairs I generally find attached to the powerless-powerful conflicting belief complex. Red grapes are on the left because we want your eye to see these first in order to reinforce them.

Once you've learned the green grapes on the right to start the intervention, you can fold the page in half vertically so you won't see them again. Normally, I present a list which is much longer and personalized for each client.

Here are a few suggestions for how you could personalize your list. First, look back over your recent history. Make a list of all recent struggle events or negative events. Figure out what conflicting belief pairs you would have had to have to create those events. If they are not in *Figure 9.1*, add them.

Second, once you start the intervention I am about to describe, look at what negative events immediately occur that are not created by the conflicting belief pairs on the list. When you figure out what conflicting beliefs you would have to have to cause them, add these to your personalized list as well.

As a third suggestion, you could also try a bit of a right-brain approach by trying to intuit what beliefs are in your "powerless" belief complex. What other feelings do you experience whenever you feel powerless? What are the beliefs behind those negative emotions? Add these to your personalized list of conflicting beliefs hooked to powerlessness.

A COMMON CONFLICTING BELIEF COMPLEX

Red Grapes   *Green Grapes*

POWERFUL: *Can have what you want*		POWERLESS: *Can't have what you want*
Work / Life has meaning	vs	No power to do meaningful things.
Valuable Contribution		No power to achieve significantly
Safe	vs	Not Safe
- *World is benevolent*	vs	- *World is malevolent*
Effortlessness		Struggle / Force
	vs	- *Expect conflict or resistance*
		- *World blocks your progress*
Supported		Not Supported
- *By everyone / world*	vs	- *Alone*
Free to be you		Controlled by Others
- *Internally referenced*	vs	- *Externally referenced*
Free to do what you want		Controlled by others or rules
Worthy:	vs	**Unworthy:**
Deserve to have what	vs	***Don't deserve to have what***
you want		***you want***
Valued / Valuable		**Not Valued / Not Valuable**
Respected	vs	Not Respected
Capable	vs	Not Capable
Successful	vs	Not Successful
Included / Accepted	vs	Excluded / Isolated / Judged
Trusting	vs	Not Trusting
Abundance	vs	Scarcity - *Time, money, friends,*
	vs	*opportunities, etc.*

Conflicting beliefs make naturality difficult to achieve.

Figure 9.1

Let's now look at the critical factor in this intervention. When an event occurs in your reality which had to be created by any belief interlinked to powerlessness, you will eventually experience powerlessness and probably most of the other "green grapes." This is your "powerless reflex."

If an event occurs which makes you feel "not valued," "not capable," or "not respected," for example, and you do nothing, the whole cluster of "green grapes" will likely be activated through a conditioned reflex. Whatever you have listed on the right side of Figure 9.1 will be activated and thus begin to create events in your reality.

The beliefs in the complex are interlinked and therefore activate each other. If you don't take preventative action, the interlinkage between the system of beliefs around "powerlessness" will cause the whole cluster to be activated. You will experience all sorts of negative emotions as a result.

More importantly, however, these activated, maladaptive beliefs will create an undesirable reality by reflection. You will not only find yourself feeling "powerless" but will be experiencing a pattern of events in your reality to reflect that powerlessness. The activation of the cluster is a conditioned reflex. It happens automatically. You can see how your instructions to reality can get away from you.

A conditioned reflex is exemplified by Pavlov's dogs salivating automatically to a bell ringing because the bell used to ring whenever they were brought food. Here is the simple but pervasive law of learning through conditioning: if an unconditioned stimulus (example: a bowl of meat) that normally causes an unconditioned response (example: the dog salivates) is repeatedly associated with a conditioned stimulus (example: a bell), the conditioned stimulus (the bell) will eventually cause the unconditioned response (the dog salivating) without any need for the unconditioned stimulus (the bowl of meat). Behaviorists came to believe that all forms of learning could be reduced to conditioning phenomena.

This is how we became conditioned to respond to events created by any of the beliefs in the right-hand column of *Figure 9.1* by shifting into any and all elements of the powerlessness belief complex. A negative event in your reality caused by a powerlessness-linked belief becomes the stimulus. The stimulus triggers your conditioned reflex which automatically invokes your whole "powerless" complex.

The negative event stimulates a negative emotion which invokes all of the other negative emotions on the right side of *Figure 9.1*. These negative emotions reinforce all of the negative beliefs surrounding "powerlessness." The result is an endless loop of creating negative events, which reinforce the negative beliefs, which create more negative events, and so on.

It will therefore be important for us to take remedial action as soon as the "stimulus" negative event occurs in our reality. We have to block the impending reflex to powerlessness. What I am proposing is using every negative event in your reality over a two-week period to help install a replacement conditioned reflex to our "powerful" belief complex in the left-hand column.

When even a small event occurs reflective of your not believing yourself "valued," or "capable," or "free," etcetera, immediately invoke all of the feelings and beliefs in the "powerful" belief cluster . . . . the positive emotions you could be feeling if you had all of the beliefs in your "powerful" list on the left side of *Figure 9.1.*

Before beginning, take a moment to experience how you would feel if you were "powerful," "free to be you," "valued and valuable," "respected," "supported," etcetera, until you can be the person with only the "powerful" belief complex on the left-hand side of *Figure 9.1.*

Create an emotional blueprint of this tapestry of positive feelings. You want to be able to experience those emotions at a moment's notice upon encountering a negative event in your reality over the next two weeks.

We want this emotional experience to become a conditioned response equivalent to Pavlov's dogs salivating. Our bell will be any negative event in your reality that had to be created by one of the beliefs in your "powerlessness" belief complex in the right-hand column of *Figure 9.1.* At every event causing a negative emotional charge, take a moment to visualize and experience the positive emotions associated with the "powerful" belief complex on the left-hand side of *Figure 9.1.*

Use this approach to install your power reflex over a two-week period. Set yourself free from your powerless reflex. Let every negative event invoke your power reflex . . . . for the rest of your life. Make every negative event in your reality a means to make you stronger . . . . stronger in the face of negative events, but also stronger in your ability to create positive realities with precision.

As your "powerless" belief complex gets weaker and weaker, its component beliefs will not even be strong enough to create events in your reality any more. Your "powerful" belief complex, in the meantime, is getting stronger and stronger. Gradually, you will find that your world only "values you," "respects you," "supports you," and so on. You will not only have stopped creating negative events in your reality. You will be proactively creating positive events.

With a little effort from you to partner with reality in this way, a significant block of the conflicting beliefs, that took a lifetime to build up and are playing havoc with your life, can be eliminated. You will know you have been successful with the exchange of your powerless reflex for a power reflex by the events now occurring in your reality. You should no longer be creating negative events based on the beliefs in your "powerless" belief complex. Your life will be working better. You'll be feeling more positive emotions and fewer negative ones.

Limitations that have incapacitated even the most accomplished individuals simply fall away with this intervention. Once you know about the powerless-powerful conflicting belief complex, it becomes illogical and certainly masochistic to let it exist a moment longer in your life. As a result of switching to the "powerful-and-valued complex," some individuals who have not felt "valued," "respected," and "included," for example, by their current employers or groups in their life, may choose to leave. Let me suggest an alternative.

By creating the power reflex, you have removed the negative side of a whole series of conflicting beliefs. Therefore, there will be no negative beliefs to create negative events in your life. As a result, those people who were messengers of the problem beliefs will either transform positively or disappear from your life.

Once you change to believing you are valuable and that the world values you, reality will reflect this. Here's your challenge. Can you release your former understanding of who these messengers were in order to allow them to become reflections of the new you? Experiment a little. Do they, in fact, transform or disappear from your life?

Here's an example. Ron worked for a manager, Dan, whom he did not relate to. The feelings were reciprocated. Ron was not valued by Dan. In fact, Dan had indicated that Ron better change or he was out. Through a number of interventions including the release of the powerless reflex, Ron and I had managed to shift him to valuing himself and expecting to be valued by his reality. I forewarned, Ron, that all those who did not value him would either transform or leave his life, and that included Dan.

At a climax point in Ron's progress in strengthening his "valued/valuable" beliefs, Dan was immediately moved out of the slot as Ron's boss. Dan was moved sideways to run a new startup subsidiary on his way to being moved out of the company two months later. During the two months before Dan was fired, he actually courted Ron's friendship and, in asking for Ron's input on many things, indicated how much he valued Ron.

Therefore, Dan both transformed and left Ron's life in response to Ron's new valued/valuable beliefs. About half a year later, Ron received an unsolicited job offer. He became the president of a company where he says he's being "overvalued" on a regular basis and loving it. Finally, at age 50, he ends a lifetime of "devaluing" contexts.

Growth by Quantum Leaps

There is no possibility of gradually evolving from powerless to powerful. The brain will reject the "red grape" introduced to the cluster of green grapes. Rather, the only possible solution is a quantum leap. The change had to be a "rewriting" or a "replacement" rather than a gradual evolution. A reincarnation into another form was required. It is easy to see why nature favors the use of quantum leaps. Some changes just can't be achieved gradually by a linear transition.

The installation of the *power reflex* is a concrete example of how we can quantum leap along our natural growth path. In one leap, a plethora of interferences to the expression of our naturality are removed. This quantum leap operating style is a new modus operandi for change, growth, and optimization which will be referenced again and again in *Peak Evolution*, culminating in the *Quantum Leap Living* chapter.

Any partnership with natural processes will increase our experience of quantum leaps. To re-integrate into the naturality flow, then, we will need to become proficient at the art and science of the quantum leap. This will enable us to work proactively with nature rather than fighting nature, even when nature incites quantum leaps.

If you've had an opportunity to experience the effects of replacing your "powerless" belief complex, you can now imagine how whole segments of your belief blueprint can be quickly changed. What you will experience in reality is commensurately altered as a result. Sweeping transformations are possible in short order to accelerate evolution. Rather than simply one belief change like "powerless" to "powerful," several belief changes can occur simultaneously.

As a civilization, we are going to need the ability for this magnitude of transformation in order to keep pace with the accelerating change of our world. Specific interventions like installing the *power reflex* demonstrate how we can make substantial growth a way of life through mastering the quantum leap technology gradually being introduced throughout this book.

Over time, we can become increasingly fluid, easily expanding and redesigning ourselves around our naturality in order to move to our next level of impact on the world. The intervention in this chapter is just the beginning of identifying the process of peak evolution.

The Power of Unconflicted Beliefs

How much more energy, passion, life force and power would you have without having to deal with struggle events? Act on struggle events when they are very small and just beginning to appear and there will be no need to ever experience ongoing struggle events again. If, every time you encounter a struggle event, you make the indicated belief change(s), before long, you will have freed yourself to shift from wasting time fire-fighting problems to doing your art – the pure creative expression of your naturality. This is the ultimate purpose of your system – to grow yourself and then your creations.

Removing disempowering beliefs would free you to apply your special talents to major contributions to the world. By having only beliefs in your belief blueprint that were singularly supportive of your natural authentic core, you would achieve congruence.

You would be able to move to new levels of performance. Your ability to create precise realities would increase as you were able to emit a single integrated, authentic message. Pure naturality automatically creates perfectly adapted realities.

If you had only those beliefs that defined and supported your naturality, the automatic creation of adaptive realities reflective of that naturality is the only possible outcome. What you would have is the ability to create what you want when you want it – *the ultimate definition of power, freedom, abundance and reality creation expertise.*

The Sandcastle Syndrome

Before moving on to discuss power in the naturality paradigm, let me identify one disabling reality creation outcome of conflicting beliefs. I call it the *sandcastle syndrome.* Conflicting beliefs perpetually create a cycle of creating and then de-creating desired realities . . . . much like a sandcastle built too close to the water where tides can quickly dissolve a day's work.

Check back over significant events in your life. Can you recall when things were humming along on projects with lots of flow events and coincidences and then, suddenly, disaster struck? The target reality you had wanted and had come to assume would be yours suddenly disappeared. This is the work of conflicting beliefs.

Let's say your goal had been the closing of a deal whereby you would receive a particular sum of money. Let's say the goal symbolized you were valued and valuable. The "valued" side of your conflicting belief pair was operating very well in the first part of the project to create positive supportive events in your reality. Then somehow the "not valued" part of the conflicting belief pair got activated.

Was it that you crossed some threshold for how much valuing you could experience or deserved to have? Did you suddenly realize the valuing at the end of the project would be much bigger than you had imaged and you choked at the thought having that much valuing? You could no longer perform effectively on the project. Or perhaps you found yourself actively in the grips of your not-valued belief, sabotaging the project to ensure that a not-valued reality reflective of that belief was created?

You may have thought that the de-railings of a multitude of projects after they initially looked promising were random events in your life. Check again. Look for the pattern of conflicting beliefs in operation causing an approach-avoidance alternating cycle in the achievement of your goals. In fact, look more closely to see if it isn't the same conflicting belief pair causing your setbacks.

Take a look at the symbols you were pursuing with each project. Were your emotional goals in each case actually the same? Could reality indeed be this orderly? If you've had a project turn sour recently, try it again after you eliminate a plethora of conflicting beliefs by doing the power reflex intervention.

EXPANDING YOUR PERSONAL POWER STRUCTURE

What if you succeed in eliminating your conflicting beliefs and are able to create realities with greater speed, impact and precision? Are you ready to have that much power? Initially, I find reality creation novices are lost in the moment, just enjoying the thrill of spontaneously creating. Then, with a series of successes under their belt, the magnitude of their power hits them. It can give you quite a scare. Some will begin to sabotage their progress to keep their performance in line with their identity as far as power is concerned.

This is similar to people who win the lottery but who don't have the belief and identity structure to support having a lot of money. They will sabotage themselves by rapidly spending all the money until reality shrinks down to the level of their identity. This would be a shame if it happened to you. I'd rather prepare you to expand your ability to hold and manage more power so the initial reality creation momentum is not interrupted.

It is important to expand your identity and your physical power structure to accommodate the power surge associated with the technologies presented throughout Peak Evolution. This is discussed in the Power of Identity chapter. Without an expanding structure to manage your increased capabilities, you will be taken off balance – de-optimized.

Therefore, even if it is not your goal to become powerful, it will happen automatically and it is advisable to be prepared for this growth byproduct. Let me begin to assist you with this issue by introducing you to a different comprehension of power in the naturality paradigm than is commonly assumed by our society. Your relationship with power will need to be revised in a paradigm in which realities are self-created.

A New Definition of Power

Power invokes a conflicted response in our society. A great deal of energy is expended to get it – especially in the pursuit of the trappings of power – money, position, influence, and freedom. Yet, at the same time, many have been brought up to believe that people who have power and its trappings are corrupt, almost by definition. Many of us have been damaged by authority figures in our lives and hence are very discriminatory in our views of people with power. We are power bigots.

As you will discover in the next chapter, if you are judging others with power as abusive, spiritually bankrupt, corrupted or other such negative categorizations, you will also judge yourself harshly if you become powerful.

Consequently, while you are pursuing expertise in the peak evolution science and gaining inevitable personal power, you will become conflicted internally as your prejudices are directed against yourself. You will create new conflicting belief pairs to disempower yourself thus undoing your work with the *power reflex* intervention. Let me begin to address this culturally induced problem by redefining power in the naturality paradigm.

In a self-created reality, dominion over others does not exist since separation does not exist. There is no power over anyone else because everyone in your reality is created by you and is a reflection of you. They are all *one* with you. You and your reality are one and the same thing, created by the same consciousness and the same belief blueprint.

As your awareness of your consciousness expands, separation and fragmentation will cease to exist. Your worldview will shift to the singular perception of the interconnectivity of all things in a dynamic universal system creatively flowing to perpetual re-optimization.

In a self-created reality, power is determined solely by whether you are creating the reality you want to create. The *competition*, so to speak, is with yourself to better your previous skills and to improve and refine the reality you are experiencing or will experience in the future. Again, the ultimate definition of power, abundance, freedom and success is the ability to have what you want when you want it and to do what you want when you want to do it.

Internal Power versus Reflected Power

Let me oversimplify for a moment to extend our investigation of power in the naturality paradigm. Think of power in our old worldview as being *externally referenced* and conferred from outside of us by our positions, possessions, and associations with people or things. We receive *reflected power* based on things or events *external* to us.

In the self-created realities of the naturality paradigm, we have 100% *internally referenced* power. This is power based on our ability to create what we want when we want it by the reflection of our beliefs out into reality. This is a new distinction for many in our understanding of power.

Yet, in the naturality paradigm, it is a power so great it needs only a whisper to express itself. The technologies of *Peak Evolution* will induce internally referenced power in you even if power is not your goal. It is built-in.

The Powerlessness of Externally Referenced Power

What we are really seeking is *the power and freedom to be who we truly are*. This is healthy. As a society, however, we have been taught to pursue this power by specific channels. We are incited to pursue reflected power – titles, possessions or associations with people or things that will give us power over others. The peak evolution science offers an alternate route to our goal.

To most people, the pursuit of externally referenced power is a recipe for powerlessness. As we pursue reflected power, we will actually become drained of our personal power, making us feel powerless. Think of yourself trying for the next job title up the hierarchy. Think about asking for a raise. Think about trying to get your superiors to like you so they will give you a promotion or a raise without you having to ask for it. Do you feel the powerlessness?

Now think of a situation where someone threatens your child. Your power quotient can go off the scale as you do whatever it takes to protect your child. You will move mountains, fight incredible demons, and take action with internal stores of power you never knew you had. In emergencies, we get a glimpse of our true power. The challenge is how to release yourself to full power and peak performance at all times. How do we make our emergency power structure available to us in our everyday living?

> *"Courage is not the absence of fear, but rather the judgment that something else is more important than fear."*
> Ambrose Redmoon

Releasing Internal Power

Now think for a moment of times when power emerged spontaneously from inside of you. Imagine a time, for example, when you have found a critical solution to a problem. You *know* in every fiber of your being you have discovered something truly of benefit to others. You would then feel totally empowered, for example, to bring onside those same superiors who would invoke powerlessness if you had to approach for a raise or promotion. *Power of purpose empowers.*

Benjamin Disraeli once said, *"Nothing can resist the human will that will stake even its existence on its stated purpose."* We are rallied to peak engagement around causes that seem to be driven from our deepest authentic core.

Let's look at what else invokes our full power. *Doing your art empowers. Creativity and creation empowers.* Wouldn't you work nights and weekends, go without food and sleep and money, endure whatever it took, to be able to do your *art*? We have great power when we are passionately pursuing our *art*. The musician will find the courage, tenacity and strength to do whatever is necessary to play his music.

The same can be said of artists and actors willing to starve for the opportunity to creatively express their naturality. How many of us have worked overtime without pay to finish a work assignment we loved? Doing one's *art* leads one to shift into *flow* which, by definition, incites one to peak performance and power.

Identity empowers. If individuals view themselves with a particular identity, they will again be highly empowered to sustain that identity. A person with the identity of leader will lead in any territory. A doctor who views himself as a healer will seek to cause healing no matter what the circumstance . . . whether paid or not. A teacher will seek to teach. A coach will seek to coach.

What I am defining as the source of internal power is, in fact, the expression of our naturality – the interlinkage of our true identity, meaning, and *art*. The very foundation of the peak evolution science, the natural flow of our system to its optimization around naturality, is the means of moving to our greatest power. *Naturality empowers.*

The natural growth path to the increasing expression of our naturality is the route to maximum power and peak performance. This is the reason I discovered that the most successful leaders were the furthest along the growth continuum towards living their naturality. The Emerson quote from "Power," *the Conduct of Life* (1860) is so appropriate: *"All power is of one kind, a sharing of the nature of the world. The mind that is parallel with the laws of nature will be in the current of events, and strong with their strength."*

The *power reflex* intervention, then, will achieve its best results when done in conjunction with the other techniques in this book for hooking us to our naturality and the natural flow of nature. This is a repetition of the two-pronged approach presented in the previous chapter for reclaiming your reality: removing interferences to our naturality and increasing the expression of our naturality.

With circular logic then, this is also the reason why I feel compelled to prepare you to cope with the increased power you inevitably will have as a result of both the *power reflex* intervention and the increasing alignment with your naturality resulting from using the peak evolution science. Your personal power draws directly from naturality. There is no other means to sustain true power. Power conferred from the outside is just a temporary facade.

Unexpected Power

Now here is the exciting thing. Pursuing the expression of our naturality is not only the fastest route to internally based power but to externally based power. For most people, the direct pursuit of externally based power makes us feel powerless. This powerlessness is reflected into the symbols and events of our reality. These serve to strengthen our belief in our powerlessness.

The stronger our belief in our powerlessness, the faster and more effectively we will create a reality perfectly reflective of that powerlessness. As a result, we will not have the externally based power we are seeking but we may even have eroded our internal power.

Alignment with our naturality and the naturality flow is the only possible foundation for moving to our greatest personal power. A self-created reality would automatically reflect internally based power. Symbols of power would spontaneously materialize once internally referenced power emerges. These, of course, would include the symbols of externally based power position, associations, and possessions.

For those who are specifically seeking power, you now have the formula. The pursuit of internal power is the means to attain the external trappings of power. With both, you are in a position to stretch your being to the fullest. What is the maximum expression of your naturality possible? What is the ultimate peak performance of your system? What are the greatest contributions you can make to the world? What will be your legacy? Enjoy your new-found freedom.

10

THE JUDGED-JUDGING REFLEX

"No one can make you feel inferior without your consent."   Eleanor Roosevelt

Institutionalized judging may be one of the most disabling and disempowering facets of our cultures today. Fear of judgment is the number one reason people don't express their true identity, *art* and purpose. It's one of the greatest inhibitors of creativity, pioneering, growth and change – the very skills needed in today's fast-changing world. Judging prohibits peak performance, optimization, naturality, and precise reality creation. For these reasons, it's got to go.

Experiencing judging events can damage our systems. As with powerlessness, judgment is central to another complex of interlinked negative and conflicting beliefs inadvertently creating undesirable experiences for us. As budding reality creators, we will want to quickly regain control of the instructions our judgment-linked beliefs are sending to reality. In a paradigm in which beliefs create reality, we need to jettison judgment for entirely selfish reasons.

What I am prescribing is another quantum leap. In the last chapter, we replaced a disadvantageous conditioned reflex with an enhancing one. A *powerless reflex* was replaced by a *power reflex*. With one intervention, a number of maladaptive beliefs were removed from your system. You were able to de-create undesirable realities dependent on those toxic beliefs. Naturality was freed.

The intent this time will be the complete eradication of our *judged-judging reflex* and the toxic events associated with your judgment-related beliefs. The ideal result of this intervention would be the removal of any beliefs in our belief blueprints which could create judging events out in our realities.

> *"Too many people overvalue what they're not and undervalue what they are."*   Malcolm Forbes (1919-1990)

What is Judgment

Dictionaries tend to define judgment as the process of forming an opinion by discerning and comparing. This seems too mild for what most of us associate with our experience. The judgment I'd like to address in this chapter is emotionally-charged – an emotion of judgment which defines judgment beyond the intellectual description of dictionaries. Judgment is a separation disease in our civilization today.

Judgment, by its very nature, is an act of exclusion and separation. To judge or be judged, one must separate oneself from another. There must be a separation between the person judging you and the person you are judging. Without separation between the judge and judged, judgment cannot occur. Defined this way, the solution to our culturally-induced judging problem becomes readily apparent: non-separation or oneness. Judgment is a habit we have absorbed from our cultures. It is the habit of separation.

Judgment, as it is commonly understood, assesses something as good or bad, right or wrong rather than simply "what is" with dispassionate detachment. In the naturality paradigm, reality is self-created based on our beliefs. Therefore, each of us and our reality compose a single system derived from the same belief blueprint.

Judgment, then, is really a division of the oneness of our system into pieces or subsystems which are operating in opposition. One part of our system is judging another part of us as good or bad, right or wrong. This is illogical, divisive, masochistic and counter to the unification direction of our evolution as individuals and a race.

As with all systems, all parts of our system want to work in harmony in alignment with our naturality. We want wholeness and oneness inside of us and out. Individual evolution and the evolution of the human race are always towards increasing oneness, congruence, interdependence, and integration.

This is evident from the creative direction of our technological enhancements to interlink us: the internet, for example, or the interdependence and interlinkages of our global economy resulting in multi-country trade agreements. Therefore, to advance, we will inevitably eliminate the separation necessary for judgment. We can wait and struggle against this trend or we can proactively do it now.

The elimination of judgment is most frequently promoted in the realms of religion, philosophy and spiritual growth in the context of being good to our fellow man. That is not my primary purpose here, although that will certainly be the outcome. Many religions attempt to teach you not to judge for unselfish reasons. My interest is in motivating you to not judge in order to selfishly protect your system.

I am promoting self-care. I want to free your system to peak performance and sustained success around your naturality. In other words, the elimination of judgment – given, received or perceived – is a very selfish act for our own personal gain and the health and well-being of our personal system.

> *"When we hate someone, we hate in him or her something which resides in us ourselves. What is not in us does not move us."*
> Hermann Hesse - Demian

All judgment is self-judgment. The elimination of self-judgment results in self-acceptance and oneness inside and, by reflection, outside of you. Is the elimination of self-judgment a backdoor to self-love? Yes! We've all heard the entreaties of well-wishers for us to love ourselves, but most of us have no idea how to accomplish that. The formula for releasing judgment presented here may provide us with a way.

Think about this. If we hadn't been damaged as children through judgment or separation disease, how many of us would have self-love? Releasing judging from our systems can lead to a whole series of cascading quantum leaps that can transform and evolve us. It can lead to peak performance, peak contribution and peak rewards. It is essential to optimization.

Our List of Judgeable Offences

If judgment by others cannot be experienced without self-judgment, how did we develop the criteria for self-judgment? The only reason we do anything is to change our emotional state. As children, we learned by experience what to do to avoid pain and attain pleasure. We determined the actions necessary to avoid negative states such as abandonment, exclusion, isolation, hate, rejection, loneliness, failure, discrimination, and not being valued or needed.

In general, these are routes to separation and loss of love or oneness. Or, we identified the actions necessary to ensure positive emotional experiences such as love, self-love, self-esteem, valuing, acclaim, affection, success, respect, inclusion, intimacy, achievement, contribution, and safety. These emotions are routes to oneness inside and outside. The resulting activity prescription we each developed is what I call our *List of Judgeable Offences*.

Think of events that happened in your childhood that might have added rules to your List of Judgeable Offences to prevent you from experiencing pain. We tend to develop almost ritualized activities and rules to avoid these feared states. At the same time, we developed a whole other category of activities to add to the list which prescribed how we should pursue pleasure or positive emotional states.

We gradually begin to attach very powerful emotional goals to these activities and we judged ourselves against these activities accordingly. We also begin judging others against them as well. In effect, certain situations came to trigger conditioned reflexes in us in the same way Pavlov's dogs salivated the second they heard the bell ring they associated with food being brought. We developed a *self-judging reflex* based on the items in our list.

As we grew up, we developed the habit of doing these activities without realizing there were faster, easier and more direct ways for achieving our emotional goals. The peak evolution science is a more effective means for achieving our emotional goals than self-judgment against our List of Judgeable Offences.

Accordingly, in this chapter, I want to give you the formula for eliminating judgment from your reality, thereby freeing you to become all you are capable of becoming.

Catching the Judging Virus

Most of us catch the judging virus as children through institutionalized judgment. We catch it first-hand in our schools and churches and through our cultural indoctrination process. We catch it first-hand and second-hand from our parents and our teachers who caught it in their childhoods. Judging is institutionalized in our society through a multitude of memes or thought viruses. As a result, judging is a habit and skill we all begin developing at an early age.

"Meme" is a word coined from a Greek root for "memory," and is purposefully similar to "gene." A meme is an information pattern held in an individual's memory which is capable of being copied to another individual's memory. Memes, like genes, pass on information. "Beliefs," especially organized and promoted beliefs, are memes. Judging is not only a meme but is fast evolving to a sophisticated art-form in our society today. The media, for example, is helping to train us to be professional judges.

Institutionalized Judging

I developed this judgment intervention because I was continually encountering executives suffering the effects of decades of institutionalized judgment in our corporations. There would be no opportunity for me to take them to full power around their naturality without first freeing them from their judged-judging reflex – judgment given, received and perceived.

In the corporate world, they must give and receive annual performance reviews, including, for many executives, the use of 360-degree feedback instruments whereby key people they interact with are invited to judge their performance. Their compensation is often based on the subjective judgment of others.

Many are so inhibited by the prospect of being judged, they have ceased to risk action. They have ceased to even set personal goals or dreams. In this context of increasingly more sophisticated institutionalized judging, corporate employees are pressured to increase creativity, pioneering the unknown, and implementing change. These require taking risks.

Since fear of judgment stifles risk, people become paralyzed. It's too dangerous to take action in a territory of professional judges. As a result, corporations do not reap the benefits of the full performance of their human assets. Nor do these individuals experience the benefits of being fully self-actualized around their creativity and naturality. Since the demand for creativity and change is not going to diminish, institutionalized judgment will inevitably have to be released. Management science will eventually deal with this problem. Why wait?

Judging creates Judging in a Self-Created Reality

For entirely selfish reasons, judgment needs to be eliminated in the naturality paradigm. The four types of judging are equally the problem: *you judging you, you judging others, others judging you, and others judging others.* In a belief-created reality, they all create a reality of you being judged . . . . the least desirable state.

. . . the state we tried to avoid by constructing our List of Judgeable Offences in the first place. To create a reality with any form of judging events in it means we have to have the beliefs necessary to do that. We not only believe in a judging world of judging people but we have a List of Judgeable Offences – a set of beliefs against which we judge ourselves and others.

How does judging create judging in a belief-created reality? Let me answer entirely from the perspective of the naturality paradigm to assist you in making the translation from your current worldview paradigm. If beliefs create reality, the same judging-related beliefs will create all four types of judging events in our realities. Consequently, if any of the four types of judging events are occurring in your life, you must have judging-related beliefs. These beliefs will eventually create a reality in which you are judged either by yourself or others.

Having judging beliefs interferes with our ability to send precise instructions to quickly and effectively create the realities we prefer. We will want to clear our system of judging beliefs to, first, become more effective with the reality creation technology and, second, to free ourselves to move to our highest potential around our naturality. These are the two primary goals of this chapter. Let's look more closely at why judging creates judging in a self-created, belief-created reality.

If you judge yourself, reality will perfectly reflect your beliefs about yourself and create others who will judge you in the same way you do. Judgment by others, then, is the outcome. Note that it is your personal List of Judgeable Offences which determines when you will experience the emotion of being judged.

If you believe yourself not very attractive, for example, or not very capable or valuable or intelligent, events will occur in your reality which perfectly reflect your belief you are not very attractive, capable, valuable, or intelligent. These events will usually be in the form of other people judging you as you have judged yourself.

If you judge others, you will also create a reality in which you will be judged, but it's a little more complex to explain the connection. In order to judge others, you must have a set of rules by which to judge them. If you've got a set of rules then you are undoubtedly applying them to yourself. This is your List of Judgeable Offences.

You may simply not have been aware you were regularly judging yourself against your List. As above, judging yourself will mean others will judge you by the same criteria. These criteria are the only ones meaningful to you and hence these are the ones for which you have judging-related beliefs creating your reality.

You and your reality are a single system created by the same beliefs. Since your reality is a 100% reflection of what is going on inside of you, *judging others you have created in your reality means you are indirectly judging yourself.*

If you *own* your reality, to judge parts of it as negative is to make a negative judgment of yourself. You are separating from parts of yourself you disapprove of. This will become more obvious as you actually experience your ability to change your reality by changing your beliefs. This experiential learning will transform you and change your relationship with your reality.

Judgment by others is also created by judgment of yourself. If a stranger judges you on something you are very comfortable is not true of you, there is a great possibility you won't give it another thought. You will not "experience" the emotion of judgment. If the same stranger judges you on something you judge negatively about yourself, then negative emotions will likely be invoked by the incident.

If someone judges us for something we don't have on our List of Judgeable Offences, then it is likely we won't experience the emotion of being judged. It will roll right off of us. But if we are judged negatively about something on our List, we will experience the emotion of being judged. All judgment is based on our judgment of ourselves. It all began back in childhood as we accumulated the prescription for what we had to do to avoid pain and experience pleasure.

Let me give you another perspective on how the act of judging others creates self-judgment. If you judge someone as not working very hard, watch how you suddenly start to judge yourself with respect to not working hard enough. You will want to be "perfect" in this regard, so the person whom you judged could never turn around and accuse you of what you accused him or her of.

Every time you judge someone, you are seeing evidence of another item on your judgment list for you to release. You are seeing how you have become your own jailer. You are seeing another opportunity to free yourself!

Often what we judge negatively in others are the things we fear are true about ourselves. This is called projection. Fears are beliefs which will create the feared events in our reality. These fears along with fear of judgment will create what we fear. Fear of judgment can increase with the lack of naturality.

By the same token, an increase in naturality can reduce fear of judgment. If, in not accepting ourselves, we have put up a facade, we will have created new areas where we may fear being judged or found out. Our fear beliefs around judgment are then intensified, increasing the likelihood of their sending instructions to create a reality of our being judged.

Every time we experience the emotion of judgment, we are activating and strengthening the "judging-related beliefs" which can create new judging events in our reality. This is the judging loop. Experiencing the emotion of judgment reinforces the beliefs which created that emotion in the first place.

The stronger our judging-related beliefs, the stronger are our instructions to reality to create incidents that generate the emotion of judgment. It will be necessary to eliminate these beliefs in order to prevent this cycle of toxicity in our systems and to issue pure, precise instructions for reality creation.

With the reality creation technology, we can now directly create a reality with our preferred emotional state. This is more effective than conforming to a List of Judgeable Offences as the means to achieve a desired emotion. An artist in looking at the sky he has painted may decide he prefers it to be different. The sky is not good or bad, right or wrong, just not what he prefers at this moment. With the reality creation technology, we can begin to look at our reality in this way. It is a neutral messaging system rather than something separate from you to be judged good or bad, right or wrong.

As the artist of our reality, we can simply redefine what we want at the moment of discontentment and/or inspiration. If we don't like what is in our realities, we can make an adjustment inside of us in order to create what we would prefer outside in reality. The partnership with nature promoted through the peak evolution science will systematically remove interferences to the optimization of your system such as judgment. Look for the signals and help nature to align your system with your naturality.

How to Kick Your Judged-Judging Habit

There is a perpetual evolutionary flow to oneness in all systems. The evolution of the individual and race is to oneness, wholeness and non-fragmentation. Our most powerful state emerges through oneness and congruence and harmony inside and outside. This is the innate dynamic evolutionary path of every individual and, indeed, every system, including the system of the human race.

Since judgment is a separation disease, its removal is an inevitable step en route to optimization and our most evolved state. Oneness is the solution to eliminating judgment.

> *"We were born to unite with our fellow men, and to join in community with the human race."*   Marcus Tullius Cicero (106-43 BC)

Quantum physics has delved into the deeper reality beneath what to our physical senses appears to be a material world of separation. What it has discovered is the powerful interconnection of all life. Physicist Fritjof Capra, in his book, *The Tao of Physics* (1975), observes:

"The basic oneness of the universe is not only the central characteristic of the mystical experience, but is also one of the most important revelations of modern physics. It becomes apparent at the atomic level and manifests itself more and more as one penetrates deeper into matter, down into the realm of subatomic particles."[30]

The elimination of our judging reflex, then, is a return to the state of oneness we had at birth before we were separated from the naturality flow. For those who'd like to kick the judging habit, the strategy is simple. *The elimination of separation removes separation disease.* Let's see how the naturality paradigm helps you to accomplish this simple but daunting task. Here are some tactics for oneness and the elimination of judging from your world.

THE 'ONENESS' ARSENAL FOR
CURING SEPARATION DISEASE

The Abstention Weapon

Cease and desist judging! Experiencing judging events strengthens our judging-related beliefs and reflexes only to create more judging events. Stop the vicious cycle of creating realities in which judgment occurs. Give up your addiction to judgment of any kind -given, received or perceived. *Go cold turkey! Cease and desist separation*!

Do it for entirely selfish and self-protective reasons. You don't want any more attacks on your system. If you give up your "judging-related beliefs" and your List of Judgeable Offences, you cannot create a reality where judging or judgeable events impact you. You can entirely eliminate the *emotion of judgment* from your life!

This is another instance where the key to major change is not best accomplished gradually but, rather, through a quantum leap – a reincarnation to someone without "judging-related beliefs" or "judging realities." Free yourself from the cycle! Abstention from separation results in oneness. Consequently, this is the first weapon in *the Oneness Arsenal for Curing Separation Disease.*

"Look for strength in people not weakness, for good, not evil.
Most of us find what we search for."   J. Wilbur Chapman

The Oneness Weapon

We all crave oneness inside and out. We want wholeness. This is the optimized evolutionary path for each of us. Oneness is not only our natural evolutionary direction, it is the solution to any separation disease. Oneness is coherence. Cohesion. Consistency. Congruence. "Oneness" dissolves judgment. If we are experiencing "oneness," we can't experience separation. Consequently, we can't experience judgment. It is that simple! *Judging and "oneness" are mutually exclusive.*

Therefore, every time you generate a judging event in your life, just "will yourself to oneness" – with the judge, the judged, yourself and/or the world. Make it a habit to unify with anyone who is attempting to judge. See them as an extension of yourself, a neutral feedback mechanism in your system in the same way all the systems in the body are self-correcting feedback systems.

Allow judging events in your reality to trigger a conditioned reflex to oneness in the same way we used powerlessness-related events in the last chapter to trigger the power belief complex. Once you have internalized reality as a part of your system – a reflection of your beliefs – you can use any events in reality as the trigger to correct your system.

Weaken the judging beliefs in your belief blueprint whenever a judging event occurs in your reality. Simply experience the emotion of oneness every time judging occurs until every judging event functions like the bell stimulating Pavlov's dogs to salivate.

Let this conditioned reflex strengthen the oneness belief in your belief blueprint in the process. Judging-related beliefs will automatically be replaced. You will automatically be creating a reality of oneness by reflection.

This weapon could also be called the **No-Separation Weapon**, the **Non-Fragmentation Weapon**, or the **Nonduality Weapon**. Nonduality means no separation between the observer and the observed, the judge and the judged. No mind-body-spirit split. No him and me. No them and us.

With nonduality, our bipolar understanding of the world ceases. We harmonize together with nature into a single creative force. Oneness is optimization. We can therefore also call this the **Optimization Weapon**. Our systems are always trying to move to optimization around the authentic core. *Optimization includes non-separation.* The release of judgment then is an imperative for our peak performance.

The Detachment Weapon

How do we begin to give up judgment? Judgment is labeling something good or bad, right or wrong. We, therefore, need merely to replace judgment with *neutral and detached assessment or discernment* of ourselves, other people, things and events in our realities. The detachment weapon seeks to replace emotionally-charged judgment with neutral discernment and assessment.

Events are neither good nor bad, right nor wrong. Reality just *IS*. Accept reality neutrally and unconditionally *as it is. Assess* without labeling right or wrong, good or bad. Accept yourself and your state of evolution neutrally and unconditionally as you are.

Detachment becomes easier when you see reality as simply a neutral feedback system reflecting your belief blueprint. In a self-created reality, all events – including judgment events – are neutral messages. Why not use those messages to correct and enhance your system?

Think of the painter metaphor. It might have been a perfect sky at the time it was first painted. Now a different sky is preferred. Again, the current sky is not good or bad, just "not preferred."

Because you create reality, I want you to envisage it as consisting of a cast of thousands forming a flat organization underneath you. There is no one over you to judge you. So release the possibility of that perspective. Everything that happens to you becomes a reflection of what is going on inside of you. Therefore, so-called "negative" events in your reality will tell you precisely what you will want to change.

In a 100% self-created reality, judging events are only a message or reflection of an area in which you are judging yourself. The trick is to use all of reality's messages to optimize yourself. View reality with detachment and clarity of perception. Like the Buddhists, strive to achieve the state of "pure observation." Only with this knowledge and understanding will you have the perspective to effect the changes in yourself and in your reality to accelerate your progress, your growth, your optimization, and your success.

"It is fair to judge people and stained-glass windows only in their best light."   William Arthur Ward 1921

The "Unconditional Acceptance" Weapon

Eliminating judgment does not mean you need to eliminate your ability to assess people and events in your reality. Rather, it means to give you and them unconditional acceptance. To accept *what is*. To accept all the elements of your reality precisely the way they are and give them unconditional acceptance.

Unconditional acceptance means "no reason for separation." Giving unconditional acceptance to yourself and others is another powerful strategy for *oneness*. Again, my interest is in the health and performance of *your* system not others, although others will, of course, benefit. Unconditional acceptance protects our systems!

Again, set up a conditioned reflex. Make unconditional acceptance another conditioned reflex you use to respond to any judgment "bells" in your reality. As you build up your ability to give others unconditional acceptance, you'll discover you are increasingly able to give it to yourself. The habit of self-judgment begins to fall away.

When you or others are judging you, let this trigger an immediate feeling of unconditional acceptance if not love for yourself and others. This is the ideal self-care for protecting and freeing your system. Alternately, if it's easier, you can simply make the conditioned reflex to oneness.

As part of our quantum leap to oneness, we will need to replace judgment with *unconditional acceptance for ourselves and for others* to create a supportive reality. Love of self is really non-judgment of self. By eliminating the block to self-love – judgment – we may actually have found a backdoor to having exactly that. Self-love is the absence of internal separation.

"The ultimate lesson all of us have to learn is unconditional love, which includes not only others but ourselves as well."   Elisabeth Kubler-Ross

The "Protective Compassion" Weapon

Compassion eliminates judging because it is another trick for achieving *oneness*. You unite with the judge or judged. Developing compassion will also eradicate your need to judge. To avoid the harmful effects of judging events in your reality, you will want to give unconditional acceptance to everyone in your reality including yourself. In many circumstances, this is no easy task. The fastest way I know to replace the judging habit with the unconditional acceptance habit is through compassion.

If you have to make an assessment, a discernment, a distinction to someone whom you would rather judge, but you don't want the negative side-effects impacting your system, compassion is your secret weapon.

Think of someone with whom you feel great animosity. Do they deserve compassion? Probably not. Now, think of something of a potentially explosive nature you have to tell this person to correct their behavior. Shift yourself over to having great compassion for this person. Before approaching the individual, think of suffering they might have had in their life or current problems they might have.

If that doesn't work to internalize the feeling of compassion, think of the compassion you might feel for one of your children who has suffered. Now, shift that feeling of compassion over to the person you have to correct. Hold that feeling and quickly connect with the individual. Retain that feeling of compassion for them and yourself during the interaction. Then quickly leave.

Over time you will be able to *hold* this protective compassion for longer and longer periods of time but, for now, let's not push it. With practice you'll also become more fluid so you can easily morph in and out of protective compassion at will.

Now, I'm actually being a little strategic here. I'm giving you unconditional acceptance this moment to not be a compassionate person in general. If all of the religions in the world cannot make you feel compassion then who am I to convince you. However, what I'm suggesting is you do an entirely selfish act of fluidly reincarnating yourself as a compassionate person in order to avoid doing judgmental acts that might damage your belief blueprint thus creating toxic realities for yourself.

I'm not talking about putting on a facade here and hypocritically becoming a compassionate person. Reincarnation is a way of repackaging your core identity to speed reality creation and growth. Naturality is still the foundation. You are just going to shift that authentic identity to include compassion and exclude judgment.

Feel how it would feel if you had been this newly defined person for at least 10 years. This is the time to meet with the person to be corrected or when you feel judgment. You will find out more about the belief engineering technique called reincarnation in later chapters.

Believe it or not, compassion can become habit-forming once you've had good emotional results from it. As you "wear" protective compassion more and more in order to selfishly avoid judgment realities, it can become addicting. Inadvertently, you will evolve in the direction you are being optimized towards by nature anyway.

Optimization is always towards oneness of the human race and compassion is, of course, en route. So, just as judgment experienced in your self-created reality will have negative effects on your system, compassion, given or received in your self-created reality, will have positive effects.

Giving compassion to someone else will be the same as giving it to yourself if you have been successful in expanding your identity to include all of your self-created reality. *What a concept! Whatever emotions you give out to people in your reality, you are simultaneously giving to yourself. Here's a whole new route to self-love.*

Again to our theme – "selfishly" looking after your growth and optimization can be beneficial to everyone around you. It can result in your expanded capability to unselfishly contribute to the world in the ways you can give the most.

> *"All people are endowed with the faculty of compassion, and for this reason can develop the humanitarian spirit."* Albert Einstein

The Naturality Weapon

We develop more reasons to incur judgment when we try to be someone we are not. You may have heard of the imposter phenomenon. If you can be the person you truly are and accept that person yourself, no one can invoke the emotion of judgment in you. This then is our goal. Naturality is a very powerful weapon against judgment.

Naturality is oneness with our pure essence, our authentic core, the true theme of our personal system. It is congruence around our true being. It is compliance and integration with the integrity of our system. It is oneness within. Therefore, use of the peak evolution science proposed in this book will automatically increase oneness and congruence inside of you and, by reflection out into the world. Naturality then is another oneness weapon to eradicate the separation disease, judgment.

For most of us, we began as children to judge particular facets of ourselves to be inadequate. We begin to live in fear of discovery or of being "found out." What is it we are really afraid of? Isn't the real fear that if somebody knows who we truly are, they will not love us, respect us or value us?

So, as we go through life and experience invalidation, rejection, betrayal, humiliation, and abandonment, the walls we build to hide our naturality behind, become larger, more impervious, and more durable. Gradually, we become progressively more defensive until even tiny threats of judgment can invoke all of our stored pain from every similar incident in our past. We overreact. This is the emotion of judgment this chapter is seeking to correct.

As we begin to live authentically moment by moment with our resonance, and experience the safety of this way of life, the walls will come down. As you feel more comfortable in your own skin, you will create others in your reality who will reflect the *true you*.

Those people from your past who don't reflect you will transform or gradually leave your life since you have no beliefs to keep them in your reality. Begin by letting down your defenses and saying: "This is who I am." Give yourself unconditional acceptance to be that person.

When somebody attacks you and you spontaneously defend, figure out what you are frightened of, what you are defending. What are you hiding? In time, you will unearth precisely what you have been hiding from so you can purge it from your system. Whatever emotions you need that you are being inauthentic to get, give them to yourself. Become a completely self-nourishing system.

Naturality and self-acceptance prevent feared events from occurring in your reality. If you are totally comfortable with the authentic you, and are being re-charged regularly by operating in alignment with your naturality, then judgment cannot touch you, even if it is accidentally created. All events of judging in your reality will be just neutral messages with no emotional charge. You will not experience the emotion of judgment.

The next two points are part of the naturality solution to judgment. For emphasis, I have broken them into separate elements:

(a) The "Internally Referenced" Weapon

One of the fastest routes to naturality is to become internally referenced and to choose the activity that feels most natural to you each moment. As the moments accumulate, you will discover, to your surprise, you are living in alignment with your naturality. This approach is also another means to achieve non-separation and a non-judging world. *One must be externally referenced in order to experience the judgment of others.*

Being internally referenced, then, is a weapon against being externally referenced. Being internally referenced means if something feels right according to your resonance, you do it. As the intensity of your naturality increases as a result, only what feels right and natural will matter. You come to trust that feeling entirely. If you resonated with every step you have taken, you will not fear someone's judgment of your actions.

Once you've had a taste of alignment with your naturality, you won't have to discipline yourself to eliminate giving, receiving or perceiving judgment. You will be addicted to living in alignment with your own internal messages not the external judges. They will become irrelevant. You will be moving with your internal drum. You will be following your heart. You will have evolved a new modus operandi and state of being.

Your judging reflex will disappear naturally. Reliance on the voice of resonance inside of you to determine your identity, your actions and your emotions will increase. The impact of external voices and demands will decline. Events where you are judged will no longer be experienced.

In a self-created reality, if you are externally referenced – taking your identity and beliefs and emotions from events, people and things in your reality – you are being driven by events created by the beliefs of a previous iteration of yourself. You are being created by your previous creations and thus become locked into an endless chicken-and-egg cycle.

Becoming internally referenced then is a key tool to becoming detached and impervious to the judgment of others. Nature's optimizing systems support us in moving in this direction as they take us to increasing expression of our naturality.

(b)   The *Flow* Weapon

Flow state precludes separation. *Flow* is pure naturality. *Flow* is oneness inside and outside with the world. It is an egoless state in which we experience wholeness. It is *activity fusion* in which you and what you are doing become one. We are pure *being* in *flow*. There are only positive emotions in *flow*. Experiencing the emotion of being judged is therefore not possible.

In addition, the separation required for judgment does not exist. Therefore, the more time we can spend in *flow*, the less time we will judge or be judged or experience the emotion of judgment. And since *flow* is an addictive process, the more we turn ourselves over to this state, the more we will be drawn to experience *flow*.

One way to increase *flow* in our lives is to spend more time living authentically and pursuing, moment by moment, things we love to do. Doing our *art* can put us in *flow*. *Flow* is our highest measured psychobiological state. It represents our system optimized for peak performance. Hence, all the peak evolution science techniques will be taking us to *flow*, and for that matter, oneness. All *Optimizers* point us to *flow*.

Consequently, as we evolve with these technologies, the emotion of judgment will subside or even disappear. Living the pathfinding technology – operating in the present and using resonance, blocks and flows – will increase our experience of *flow* and oneness. These *Optimizers* strengthen our naturality. The more we operate in alignment with our naturality the more often we experience *flow*. The process is circular or, more precisely, holographic, rather than linear.

The "Expanded Consciousness" Weapon

Using the peak evolution science automatically causes consciousness to expand. The causes will be identified throughout the book. As you might expect, the gradual ownership of your reality through the reality creation technology and the reading of the patterns of events and messages in reality for the knowledge technology and the growth technology will be continuously expanding your span of perception. As your consciousness evolves, the separation requisite for judging will be eliminated.

Think about your changed perspective as you look back at earth from a spacecraft launched slowly into outer space. Things that on earth appear fragmented and separate are in fact understood to be part of something larger. The separation of individuals and the boundaries of countries disappear as you rise. Everything begins to fold into the oneness of the earth . . . . and then the oneness of the universe. Where you used to see only individual events, you will now be able to "aerial view" patterns of events. You will see reality for the messaging system it is and no longer get caught up in single events or separation from the whole.

You will eventually achieve the state of nonduality exalted by many spiritual, philosophical and psychological teachings as our most evolved state. Nonduality is also an egoless state where any sense of being the observer vanishes altogether. You don't look at the sky, you are the sky. Awareness is no longer split into a seeing subject in here and a seen object out there.

Nonduality is nonfragmentation or oneness. You become one with everything. You observe the world from a perspective of total integration within whatever you are observing. Separation diseases disappear. You are one with all. *You are home.* You have successfully used expanded consciousness as a weapon against judgment.

You can take the slow route to evolve expanded consciousness or you can quantum leap. The quantum leap technology is described in Chapter 17. For example, you could start by reincarnating yourself as a person having the "identity" of someone who has a nondual state of consciousness. Leaps to oneness, naturality, or being a person who no longer has judgment in his or her world are other routes.

Expanded consciousness arises naturally from more evolved states of *flow* where self-awareness and ego cease. Oneness and expanded consciousness increase in *flow*. The more time you spend in *flow*, the faster you evolve. It stimulates reintegration at a higher form. Evolving through *flow* will be discussed in the *Beyond Flow* chapter.

The Leader Weapon

Leaders unify. Judgment separates. We can't judge or be judged without separation. Judgment, by its very nature, is an act of *exclusion* and *separation*. To judge, one must separate oneself from another. Leaders unify people to achieve some goal. Leadership is about taking people whose hearts and minds are somewhere else and bringing them to the same purpose, direction or perspective. Leadership is about "oneness" and unification not separation. Leadership and judgment then are mutually exclusive.

Consequently, we can use leadership as another weapon in the oneness arsenal for curing judgment. Can you don the identity of leader in all the territories where you expect to be judged? If you never allow people to separate from you, judgment cannot occur. As leadership prowess increases, your success in unifying people to a goal will also increase.

Consequently, the number of judges you will encounter will decline. As you become stronger, try extending your leadership to leaders and authority figures in your world. Lead the leaders. Reincarnate yourself as a leader or unifier and then be true to that identity in all territories.

If you are in a situation requiring leadership, the hearts and minds of potential followers will be different than yours initially. It will be your job as a leader to unify others to your beliefs, vision or goals. This is how the Leader Weapon can defuse your experience of the emotion of judgment.

Dissension is an implicit phase of the leadership cycle. Further, leaders, by definition, lead people into new territory. When people fear change, and almost everybody does, they tend to attack the person instigating that change. They may judge harshly as a result. *Know* this ahead of time. No need to absorb this judgment. It isn't about anything being wrong with you.

Deal with fears of change directly with assessment, discernment, detachment, compassion, and unconditional acceptance. Come to accept this as another characteristic of the leadership cycle without experiencing the emotion of judgment.

The peak evolution science automatically fosters leadership since leadership develops and increases as one moves along the evolutionary continuum to naturality. Capitalize on this as you evolve in the naturality paradigm.

The Coach Weapon

For some, being a coach or a counselor may be a better weapon against separation than reincarnating as a leader. The effect is the same. Through empathy, unconditional acceptance, compassion and partnering with someone for their well-being and advancement, you can again achieve the oneness that precludes judgment.

If coaching is more your style, try this effective strategy. Instruct others on releasing judgment. As you do, you will be causing the same beneficial changes in yourself. Take your own advice. Working to change someone else's beliefs around judgment will help to reinforce the change of your own beliefs.

The Growth Technology Weapon

The growth technology is designed to hook us into our natural growth path so we will experience accelerated growth as a way of life. If we become growth experts then, with each of nature's signals of a problem through the *Optimizers*, we will quickly clear interferences to our optimization from our system. Through the partnership with natural creative processes as prescribed by the peak evolution science, we will constantly be clearing undesirable elements from our system and adding preferred ones.

Any events which trigger the emotion of judgment will simply be part of a whole category of signals for growth. These interferences will be cleared as part of the growth technology "business as usual" in the life of a growth expert. Responding to nature's clearing messages will be a standard the growth technology conditioned reflex in the same way Pavlov's dogs salivate at the sound of a bell.

The Reality Creation Technology Weapon

With reality creation expertise, if reality is not to our liking, we can change it. There is no need to endure judging or any other negative realities. As we master the reality creation technology, any negative situations we experience will simply serve as stimuli for us to clarify our preferences and create a preferred reality.

The reality creation technology gives us new ways to deal with judging events in our reality as well as ultimately removing them from our experience. As you become more powerful in your use of the reality creation technology, the effect of judgment will ultimately become nil.

The "Emotional Satisfaction" Weapon

We feel the impact of judgment events most when we are in a weakened or needy state. Satisfying your emotional goals is another weapon against judgment. An emotionally satisfied individual can weather judgment much more effectively. If you are emotionally replete, judgment will roll right off of you.

The emotion of judgment is not even invoked. In the next chapter, we are going to take an in-depth look at how emotions fit into the peak evolution science and our optimization. The achievement of your emotional goals on a regular basis is part of the balancing and optimization of your system and is fully supported by nature's creative flow and *Optimizers*.

The Power-Abundance Weapon

Abundance, power, freedom, and reality creation expertise have the same definition – the ability to create what we want when we want it. We tend to experience the emotion of judgment more acutely when we are operating out of "powerlessness" and "scarcity." You will want to avoid these states as you transition or quantum leap to judgment-free living.

Use the intervention in the previous chapter to install your power reflex to rid you of powerlessness. Create a safe place away from your key judges to allow yourself to eliminate your judging reflex. Wait until the number of judgment events disappear from the other parts of your life before interacting with your primary judges once more.

Listen to your self-talk. Are you assuming people will attack you or prevent you from doing what you want? This is scarcity thinking and the beliefs behind it need to go. Use belief engineering techniques to clear your system. Use the reality creation technology chapters to develop the ability to create what you want when you want it – the state of abundance and power. Operate in alignment with your naturality so you are at full power. This strategy also increases your experience of *flow* which is your most powerful state.

Judgment is often a two-way street with judgment given and received through the same interconnecting channel. I find a great deal of judging occurs when someone is standing in your way to some very powerful emotional goals – being valued, powerful, safe, free, loved, respected, and successful, for example. Judging derives from our requirement that these emotional goals be met through a specific emotional channel. This is a prescription for powerlessness, scarcity and judging.

As you will learn in the *Designing Future Worlds* chapter about blueprinting your desired realities, it is pivotal to avoid blueprinting the channel. That limits you to the thinking of the human mind. What you want is to conscript nature's creativity to get you to your emotional goals by the fastest route. The pathfinding technology will partner you with the naturality flow.

Between the reality creation technology and the knowledge technology, you can avoid the emotional quagmire which raises the *judging quotient*. As you will discover with the peak evolution science, there is an infinite number of ways for achieving your emotional goals when you partner with nature . . . . ways that might never have occurred to you.

The No-Victim Weapon

Release your "victim mentality." If you own your self-created reality, you cannot be a victim to anyone or anything. You are the only creator. Reality is just a flat organization with a cast of thousands reporting to you. You certainly cannot be a victim of judgment, except your own self-judging. Reality is simply a dump of symbols and events created by your beliefs at any point in time.

Judging events generating the emotion of judgment are only reflections of self-judgment based on your List of Judgeable Offences. Separation is required to be a victim. Releasing your "victim mentality" is another way of approaching your commitment to oneness.

The Fear-Clearing Weapon

Fear of judgment may well be the greatest oppressor of the creative expression of the human spirit – the very vehicle for human survival and optimization. Any fear is a belief that will create your reality. If you fear judgment, you will create it.

The emotion of judgment cannot be experienced without self-judgment. Judgment is surrounded by a number of conflicting beliefs in the same way we discussed for powerlessness in the previous chapter. Our List of Judgeable Offences was developed in the first place to deal with a multitude of fears about love – ways to get it and ways to avoid losing it.

We developed a list of behaviors we should avoid to prevent negative outcomes such as abandonment, exclusion, rejection and failure. Or we identified behaviors we should do to ensure we achieved positive emotional goals like valuing, affection, success, achievement, contribution, and safety. The list of activities is linked to various fears we have. And, in a world where beliefs create reality, those fears *will* create the very realities we fear.

Since fears are beliefs, our judging fears need to be cleared as part of our program to de-create undesired realities. Check back to the *Reclaim Your Reality* chapter to review what is required to clear fears. In addition, why not use your new reality creation expertise to create a more desirable reality. First, blueprint your unconditional acceptance by the world. Second, *feel* how that would feel in order to energize your blueprint. Third, expect to have it. And finally, operate as if it's already true.

This completes the list of weapons in our *oneness arsenal for curing the separation disease of judgment*. Ladies and gentlemen, *choose your weapons!*

A Release from Judgment

Martin is a highly intelligent and highly educated head of a major international consulting firm. As he became managing partner, his anxiety increased substantially. Martin often felt helpless or powerless because he feared judgment by others which, in his mind, was linked to abandonment. As a result of events in his childhood, this had always been one of Martin's greatest fears. He wanted to avoid rejection and critical judgment by others at all costs.

To protect himself, Martin had set the highest standards for himself and judged himself rigorously against those standards. Consequently, his List of Judgeable Offences was longer and more strict than most. His extreme intelligence afforded him greater knowledge of what *could* be done for performance beyond reproach and he therefore kept adding rules to his list.

Now as head of the firm, he was going to be judged by the

performance of the other consultants in the firm. This was a new source of judgment, rejection and abandonment. He immediately set about to make the firm as "perfect" as he tried to make himself. He became obsessed with this despite his dislike for wasting so much time doing it. When he could control himself, he was the best possible coach, nurturing and teaching constantly in order to upgrade the skills of his subordinates. Martin even won a company award for being the partner who contributed most to the employees. People loved it, but it was depleting him.

When his dislike of the task got the better of him, his powerful self-judging reflex was somewhat harshly and frankly turned on his unsuspecting consultants. There was a Jekyll and Hyde situation going on here which was destructive to the firm and to Martin's system. As a result, a long-time partner, who had been a peer before Martin's promotion, left the firm. Some consultants Martin had so meticulously been training, resigned and set up shop in competition. This abandonment was exactly what Martin had sought to avoid.

His fear beliefs created the feared reality. Martin was now even further from his goal of creating reliable resources within the firm so he could feel confident taking on any consulting assignment. In fact, Martin loves to market and he had been holding back for some time his desire to pursue various business opportunities he was "resonating" with in order to ready the firm.

Here are the key interventions I used for this scenario. Ignoring one's resonance is verboten for any of my clients, so that was the first imperative change. I can't keep someone optimized without it. It is a direct optimizing signal from the naturality flow. Next, I sought to install in Martin new approaches for resolving his life-long fear of judgment. I had Martin immediately release judging – given, received or perceived – so those same beliefs would not create events in his reality whereby he would be judged.

Just identifying a number of the fears surrounding his judging reflex helped to weaken them. This meant there would be fewer of the events he'd like to avoid created in his reality. Toxicity in his system could be reduced. Martin was trying to avoid some powerful negative realities he felt threatened his very survival. Yet he had given himself just one single channel through which to prevent their occurrence – incredibly perfect performance by his consultants – performance that would be continually beyond reproach. What are the chances of that unconscious goal succeeding?

I suggested a new approach – a new vision, if you will. What if we used the reality creation technology to blueprint a reality where the clients were always extremely happy and impressed with his firm's work? What if we could trust nature's signals to take us to the end goal by the fastest and easiest route – including by incredible coincidences?

Then we blueprinted the creation of a spectacular consulting team underneath Martin that could respond to any client demands better than any other firm. They did not need to know everything because they were very entrepreneurial and creative and easily mastered new territories. What if we could create the ultimate adaptive consulting firm?

To make this more credible, I walked Martin through the reality creation technology and the knowledge technology. Between the two technologies, I demonstrated how he could *create* or *find* whatever resource or piece of information he needed when he needed it. This meant he didn't have to spend his time creating it before he needed it or trying to create perfect readiness for any circumstance. He could take any assignment that excited him and *know* the firm could figure out how to complete it.

I then gave Martin some incentive to change. I reminded him he had been in this precise situation before, just before he was fired from his last firm where he had been managing partner for only a short time. In other words, his attempts there and here to avoid judgment, rejection and abandonment were resulting in precisely what he feared. I did some other things such as rewriting the organization's identity to be the same as Martin's so he could operate strictly authentically and therefore at full power. This is a critical strategy for the success of any leader. Aligning him with his naturality signature meant his progress would be easier since coincidences and flow events would help him and, thus, the company, proceed. Peak performance became possible.

It also meant he could follow his urges to new learning and new challenges while meeting the firm's goals at the same time. In fact, we set up another blueprint whereby each client would take him to the next step of his learning in his area of expertise. As he became a world authority in his particular field, the most exciting projects would always come to him. This was quite a change from believing in a world of scarcity which was motivating him to keep clients he didn't want and forcing his firm to try to be all things to those few clients.

While we are on the subject of clients, we also blueprinted there would be blocks to signing up clients who would ultimately give him trouble or judge, reject, or abandon him. Where, in the past, Martin might have fought to overcome these challenges, now he agreed to honor these messages from reality and let those clients go. If a client was right for his firm now, he would not only have resonance but coming together with that client would be an effortless and positive experience with lots of flow events.

Within a couple of months, this firm was one of the most sought after consulting firms in North America. They were constantly developing leading-edge interventions and there seemed to be no situation in which they did not come up with a creative solution. There were some new faces on Martin's consulting team who energized the new culture. Camaraderie was strong.

And the consultants were unified in thinking they worked for absolutely the most exciting boss in their industry. They had never learned so much, done so much, or grown so much in their entire careers. In a few short months, the culture had shifted from stifling rules and rigidity to creativity and an entrepreneurial spirit. Could the creativity sought by so many organizations be spontaneously released with the removal of judgment from their leaders and their modus operandi? I speak from experience when I say, "Yes!"

Judge Selection

Beliefs create reality. Since most of us have judged-judging reflex beliefs, we can therefore expect to have people in our realities reflecting back that judgment. In most people's lives, I find they have one to three key judges. It could be you are the only judge but normally there is an individual – a boss, a peer, a spouse, a mother-in-law, a parent – who serves to reflect back the status of your judging reflex. In remote cases, it could be some objective measure like scores or ratings or the like.

I invite you to look at your key judges with complete detachment. They are part of a feedback process helping you to optimize your system. They can be viewed simply as messengers indicating how strong your self-judgment is at any point in time so you can take corrective action.

Rather than thinking ill of these people, I want you to feel gratitude towards them in providing the information you need to correct your system. They serve as a "report card" on how well you're doing vis-à-vis eliminating your judging reflex. View them as totally neutral, or, better yet, benevolent. If there is an interference to naturality inside of you, it will neutrally be reflected into reality. No need to engage your emotion of judgment.

If you can, think of them affectionately for their serving as the messenger or reflector of your self-judgment and thus identifying for you what has to be cleared out of your system for optimization. Even if you were to leave and go to a whole new territory where none of those people existed – move to another city or country – new messengers will emerge if you have not cleared out your self-judgment beliefs.

It is therefore more expedient to clear disruptive judging beliefs where you are with your current messengers. Once you have cleared judgment, then decide where you want to be. I've seen executives change jobs year after year only to recreate the same paradigm based on beliefs they haven't cleared. Change yourself first to change what you experience.

If you don't like having the feedback coming from the person it currently is, use the reality creation technology to change it to someone else. Alternatively, commit to reading very small messages so they don't have to become large before you clear interferences from your system. You could choose to read the status of your judging reflex from strangers and acquaintances thereby creating no judges within the people who are commonly in your life. However, accept that there must be some reflection from your adaptive feedback system, reality, of judging beliefs that must be cleared.

Another option could be to receive no feedback from reality directly to you. Instead, you'll read the status of your judging reflex from events in your life – whether it's something that happens in the life of a friend, a co-worker, an article you read in the newspaper or a television show. Simply assume any judging event in your reality pertains to your status as far as clearing judging from your belief blueprint and take action accordingly to finish the job.

Understand, however, if you don't deal with judging and it is interfering with your optimization, your expression of your true identity, the reflected messages will get louder and more frequent until you make the necessary changes. With experience, you'll learn to react to the tiniest of messages in your reality and make the required changes on an ongoing basis. This process may seem daunting as you begin because you have a backlog of messages to act on to clear and optimize your system. Honor your "reality feedback system." It is trying to evolve your existence to its highest form.

Vision of a Non-Judging World

"Judgment" is as pernicious as "powerlessness" in de-optimizing us and oppressing the human spirit. Within the first two years of encountering the institutionalized judging of our school systems, statistics show we abandon the innate creativity we need to normalize and re-balance ourselves.

Without creations expressing our naturality, we lose sight of who we are and what is adaptive for us to do. In a world in which beliefs create reality, it is impossible to achieve any kind of precision in our instructions to reality if we are prisoner to conditioned reflexes and toxic beliefs commonly linked with fear of judgment.

Humanity is now reaching a state of evolution where it is appropriate to begin to project the vision of an end to separation disease. It is time to proactively remove "judging-related beliefs" from the world belief pool. We want to stop perpetually creating toxic waste in our realities that can inflict harm on both our personal system and that of the global community.

It is time for our infrastructures of corporations and institutions to comprehend that it is more profitable and effective for them to eradicate judgment. People of all ages will be freed for enhanced performance. When societal infrastructures release the requirement for institutionalized judgment, a wave of freedom will permeate to all parts of society. We will stop harming ourselves and each other. We will unleash our full creative potential to evolve the kind of world in which each one of us may flourish.

> *"We must build a new world, a far better world – one in which the eternal dignity of man is respected."*   Harry S. Truman

11

THE POWER OF EMOTION

"For human beings the reality that ultimately matters is the reality of their feelings."[28]   Jauregui Jose

Emotional drives are one of the ten *Optimizers* signaling the naturality flow. The only reason we do anything is to change our emotional state. We pursue one desired emotional state after the next, after the next. This is the basic simplicity of human motivation. This is our purpose at the most fundamental level.

Emotions are biochemical and electromagnetic processes in our system. Our emotional goals are triggered by the re-optimizing requirements of our systems in response to changes in our context. Since re-optimizing through the pursuit of emotional goals will be a perpetual process for all of us, we will want to become skillful at it. We will want to become experts at satisfying our emotional goals consistently and expediently as the most fundamental purpose of our lives.

Emotions are power tools for optimization and achieving our full potential. They give us the power to push our levers for peak performance and achievement. Indeed, emotional engineering is key to accruing the enhanced human functionality possible through the use of *Peak Evolution*. Emotions are levers for precise reality creation in the naturality paradigm. They are intrinsic to both selecting and creating preferred realities.

All Goals are Emotional Goals

With this reality creation technology chapter, we transition from our three-chapter examination of how to stop inadvertently creating *undesirable realities* to a three-chapter exploration of how to proactively create *desired realities* with precision. Specifically, we are going to look at the role of emotions in reality creation.

All human motivation is based on our desire to change our emotional state. Since emotional change is our only goal, all goals are emotional in nature. *Therefore, anything we wish to create in our realities is only a symbol of our current preferred emotional state.* The outcome of any successful reality creation effort, then, is a preferred emotional state.

In a belief-created reality, everything in our reality – whether it's an event, a symbol, an emotion or a thought – exists because we have the requisite beliefs. Therefore, whether we want to experience our emotional goal directly or to create the symbols representing that emotional goal, the procedure will be the same. We must acquire the underlying beliefs.

Furthermore, emotions are not only our goals, they can also be the means to achieve those goals. They can help us to internalize the new beliefs that will generate our revised reality. In other words, emotions can be a belief engineering tool. Emotions can be levers for driving belief changes and, hence, reality changes.

Emotions are Information

Emotions are one of our adaptive survival mechanisms. They are part of our information access system which provides us with information about our internal and external environments. They are biochemical and electromagnetic events in our system designed to help us achieve and maintain optimization within our changing contexts.

Until recently, the concept of matter and energy was thought to be the basis for understanding all phenomena. Today, the concept of information is replacing energy and matter as the common denominator for understanding all biological life. Our emotions are linked to the underlying information infrastructure of the universe.

Emotion is a key component in the behavior of conscious beings. It may not, in fact, be possible for us to be emotionless. We are either happy or sad or afraid or something else all the time. Emotion is requisite to recollection, thinking, and planning. Emotions are key to "rational" decision-making. In *Emotional Intelligence*, Daniel Goleman presents the case of an individual who had lost the functioning of the parts of the brain affecting emotion who was then unable to make decisions:

"In work with far-reaching implications for understanding mental life, Dr. Antonio Damasio, a neurologist at the University of Iowa College of Medicine, has made careful studies of just what is impaired in patients with damage to the prefrontal-amygdala circuit. Their decision-making is terribly flawed – and yet they show no deterioration at all in IQ or any cognitive ability.

Despite their intact intelligence, they make disastrous choices in business and their personal lives, and can even obsess endlessly over a decision so simple as when to make an appointment. . . . . Dr. Damasio argues that their decisions are so bad because they have lost access to their *emotional* learning."[29]

Emotions allow us to make fast decisions in crucial situations. Before we have time to think, we can access an *emotional memory or data base* that can look at external situations, compare them to things in the past, and know whether we are in danger or not. Emotions help us to survive.

All Information is Distributed

As we learned in investigating the Knowledge Technology, quantum physics proposes that all information is distributed or nonlocal. There is no local information or localized memory. It is a law of information theory that information transcends time and space, placing it beyond the confining limits of matter and energy. I thus hypothesized a holographic interconnection of all information. A universal information hologram into which we, as information systems, are integrated.

> *"Time and space are modes by which we think, not conditions in which we live."*   Albert Einstein

Consistent with this, scientists have demonstrated that the biochemistry of both the mind and the emotions appear to take place throughout the body. It would therefore not be too much of a stretch to assume that the distribution of the information of our minds and emotions extends throughout our personal system to include all of reality as well. I will be telling you how to operate as if this assumption is true. You will then have the means to prove it to yourself with first-hand experience.

Candace Pert, Ph.D. was a Research Professor in the Department of Physiology and Biophysics at Georgetown University Medical Center in Washington, D.C. when she discovered the biochemical mechanism of emotion and the links between consciousness, mind and body. She has documented the story of her discovery and her nomination for a Nobel prize in her book entitled *Molecules of Emotion* (1997). Candace Pert found that chemicals, transmitters and receptors associated with how the mind works are actually distributed throughout our bodies. She not only determined that emotions are biochemical events but speculated at the time they may also be electromagnetic events.

According to Candace Pert,

"If information exists outside of the confines of time and space, matter and energy, then it must belong to a very different realm from the concrete, tangible realm we think of as 'reality.' And since information in the form of the biochemicals of emotion is running every system of the body, then our emotions must also come from some realm beyond the physical. Information theory seems to be converging with Eastern philosophy to suggest that the mind, the consciousness, consisting of information, exists first, prior to the physical realm, which is secondary, merely an out-picturing of consciousness." [31]

Emotions are Information Distributed throughout our Realities

If emotions are information and all information is distributed, it is improbable that our emotions end at our skin. It is improbable that our emotions would be localized. It is more probable they would continue out into the symbols and events in our self-created reality. Whatever is going on inside of us is extended out into our reality in a single continuum. The themes of our emotions would exist throughout everything in our conscious system. *Smile and the world smiles with you.*

Accordingly, when we are trying to create something in reality using the reality creation technology, we are, in fact, attempting to materialize the symbols associated with the emotional theme we next want to experience throughout our system. If we pursue a new goal, it is either that our emotional goal has changed or we have changed the symbol by which we hope to achieve the previously pursued emotional state. Unfortunately, the human body adapts to stimuli fairly quickly and therefore constantly needs new stimuli to sustain emotional highs. Proactive reality creation then will be a continuing necessity.

The hypothetical continuum between what is inside of us and what occurs in reality is further supported by other evidence. All of nature's *Optimizers* provide consistent messages throughout our personal system, inside and out. They are all part of the same system messaging continuum.

You will discover this as you begin to apply *Peak Evolution* concepts in partnership with nature. Emotions, you will learn, are an extension of the block-and-flow messaging continuum in reality which we use for the pathfinding technology. Positive emotions are flow events and negative emotions are block events.

Every thought, emotion, event and symbol, everything inside and outside of us, is based on our beliefs. Therefore, everything inside of us and outside into our realities derive from the same belief blueprint. Perhaps what is materialized is based on the strength of the underlying belief. Perhaps thoughts and emotions can be created with less belief intensity than matter. This would suggest our realities are filled with meaningful symbols as expressions of a *belief-emotion-matter continuum* or, more simply, a *belief-matter continuum*.

There is one further proof of this emotional consistency inside and outside of us. We experience emotions identically in our imaginations or imagined realities as we do in reaction to actual physical events in our reality. Who has not had a nightmare where events were just as fear-inspiring as any real life situations? The emotions invoked are identical in dream reality as in physical reality. When this fact is viewed from the naturality paradigm, a reason for the evolution of our imaginations begins to emerge.

Why have We Evolved Imaginations?

We evolve new functionality for survival and adaptive reasons due to changes in our environments. From this perspective, then, why have we evolved imaginations and dreams? In a world where our reality is 100% self-created, it would make sense for us to evolve imaginations as a safe place to plan our reality creation – to design what we want to experience in physical reality. Since all goals are emotional in nature, we would need emotions to be consistent between our safe laboratory and our physical reality. Our experience of emotions in our imagined realities must therefore be identical to that of our physical reality.

Imagination is the place to experiment with our reality creation. We can try new realities on for size. See how they feel. Pre-experience them. Make refinements. Determine if our emotional goals can be met. Our imagined reality assists us in gaining clarity about our preferred physical realities. This suggests not only why visualization works but also why we all need to do it.

Imagination is also a tool for reinforcing the beliefs that will be necessary for creating our new preferred realities. If we can visualize to the point of experiencing the new emotions we are seeking to have with a goal reality, we will be strengthening the beliefs behind those emotions. Those beliefs will eventually be strong enough to bring a reality consistent with our emotional goals into existence. I call this belief engineering technique *visualization to the point of emotion* . . . . pre-experiencing with every fiber of your being.

Further, imaginations allow us to balance our emotional needs more quickly without having to wait until we can actually materialize the desired physical reality. We can visualize to the point of emotion in seconds. It may take months or years to create physical realities supportive of our emotional needs. Isn't it interesting that nature appears to use the same technique?

When we fail to experience the desired emotions in physical reality or in our imaginations, we will automatically experience this re-balancing in our dream realities while we sleep. That is why we become dysfunctional if we are prevented from dreaming. We need the biochemical and electromagnetic re-balancing inherent in our experience of various emotions in order to re-optimize. It would seem that physical reality, imagined reality, and dream reality are all part of the same continuum to enable us to re-optimize biochemically and electromagnetically.

Accept Continuous Re-Optimization

Let's say you have created the perfect reality. You feel fantastic. As a novice reality creator, your success will suggest you have figured out the reality creation technology and can now sustain perpetually good realities. Let me introduce you to the problem.

Because we are an adaptive species with the ability to successfully adapt to changing environments, the same stimuli cannot perpetually sustain the same positive effect. Over time we'll adapt to their stimulation. This habituation is advantageous in helping us adjust to pain or negative environments.

This is not good news with respect to experiencing pleasure. We'll need to continuously create new realities with stimuli that are new or more intense to sustain the same positive emotional states. This also means we will perpetually encounter negative emotional states as the previously positive stimuli lose their power.

Negative emotional states are therefore built into our existence and our re-optimization cycle. We can use this predictable state to create a conditioned reflex to trigger us to immediately blueprint our next desired reality. Every negative emotional state can become a trigger for us to quickly define our next emotional goals and preferred reality. As your proficiency with reality creation increases, dreaded emotional states can actually become exciting opportunities for dramatically enhancing your world.

Here are some belief engineering basics for your next cyclical negative emotional experience. Immediately choose your preferred emotional state. Next, use imagined reality to *experience* your emotional goals. To visualize to emotion. This will change your beliefs to instruct the next iteration of your reality. Enjoy the positive emotions associated with the new physical reality generated by those new beliefs until your system again adapts to the positive stimuli.

When the negative emotions set in once more, install and reinforce a conditioned reflex to start the cycle again. This is a belief engineering process that can now be incorporated into your modus operandi for living. It is part of the larger process presented in *Peak Evolution* of perpetually using negative signals in your reality to clear and re-optimize your system.

Human beings are built to adapt to stimuli – whether pain or pleasure. Accordingly, it is not easily possible to arrive at some peaceful nirvana. We are going to have to perpetually create new stimuli to sustain our positive emotional states. It is best to accept this as the continuous emotional cycle. It is business as usual and therefore can be prepared for and handled cyclically.

Negative emotions are a call to create your next preferred reality. If you don't proactively do this, the negative emotions can create negative imagined realities – *visualization to negative emotion* – which will create and reinforce negative beliefs. Negative realities will come into existence as a result of those beliefs. Do yourself a favor. Proactively handle your negative emotions as soon as they begin.

> *"There can be no transforming of darkness into light and of apathy into movement without emotion."*   Carl Jung

Let's take another look at the reality creation process introduced in Chapter 7 with an emphasis this time on the role of emotions rather than beliefs. New or intensified emotions are the true goals of reality creation. This dramatically affects both our understanding of our goals and how we can achieve them.

SELECTING REALITY CREATION GOALS

Focus on Emotional goals

The single motivation for all human activity is the pursuit of ever-changing desired emotional states. The emotional states pursued reflect the needs for biochemical and electromagnetic re-optimization. The things we seek to create in physical reality, then, are just symbols of emotional states we wish or need to have. Therefore, our true goals are the emotional states, not the symbols we associate with those emotional states.

Reality creation success, then, is based on the achievement of our preferred emotional goals, not specific realities. If you are trying to measure your reality creation progress, you will need to measure against your experience of increasing intensities of the emotion you are pursuing, *not* the symbols or events which represent that emotion to you.

Beliefs create emotions, thoughts, symbols and events. Both the emotion and the symbols associated with that emotion are created by the same beliefs. They are part of the same reality creation continuum generated by differing intensities of the same beliefs. It takes less power for a belief to materialize an emotion than it does to materialize matter.

Therefore, we *know* the symbols will be coming shortly once we have begun to experience the emotion. The emotion is the goal. The subsequent symbols are a bonus. This requires a dramatic reversal in our modus operandi from the way most of us operate. In our commercialized culture, many of us have assumed we had to have the symbols first in order to experience the desired emotions.

To gain the reality creation technology expertise, focus on increasing the intensity of your experience of your goal emotions. That will tell you how strong the requisite beliefs behind those emotions are getting. It is those beliefs that will eventually create events and symbols that you associate with your preferred emotion. When the underlying beliefs are strong enough, physical materialization will occur.

This requires a quantum leap in our thinking. Instead of concentrating on changing things outside of us, our focus must instead be on changing things inside of us. We need to focus on creating the goal emotional state not the symbols. The challenge then is to *shift from chasing to creating* – from chasing after symbols in our reality to changing beliefs inside that will automatically change reality outside.

> *"Every phenomenon on earth is symbolic, and each symbol is an open gate through which the soul, if it is ready, can enter into the inner part of the world, where you and I and day and night are all one."*   Hermann Hesse

Determine your True Goals from the Symbols

Take a look at all of the things you are trying to bring into existence. Can you figure out what emotional states you expect to have when you get them? For example, are you seeking to feel valued by getting a raise, powerful with a desired new job title, loved and lovable by finding the right "significant other," and safe by having a certain amount of money?

The emotional states, not the symbols, are your true goals. They are what you want to create with the reality creation technology. These are the states you must measure your progress against during the process of reality creation, rather than the materialization of the symbols. These are just possible channels to your emotional goals.

Perhaps you aren't able to identify precisely the emotion you want. For example, perhaps all you know is that you want your boss to praise you. You may not realize that what you really want is valuing of your work from someone with the credentials to understand its value. Praise from your boss is just a symbol of the biochemical state you are craving. You can use this symbol to visualize to the point of feeling your desired emotional goal so beliefs are changed and reality is restructured accordingly.

What you really want is for the desired emotion to come by the fastest route. If it feels exactly the same, do you really care where it came from? Do you care that you gained industry recognition rather than your boss' praise as a source of valuing? There are an infinite number of routes to your emotional goals if you'll let there be.

Developing faster more advantageous routes to your goals is a matter of *tolerating creativity*. Would it make sense for a stockbroker to say, "I want to make a lot of money this week," and then require all of it to come through one particular client and one particular stock? Why would he want to ignore all of the other infinite possibilities? Why would you? You will not want to restrict your reality design to a specific channel to satisfy your emotional cravings.

Align your Goals with your Naturality

Reality creation improves when you choose your goals in alignment with your naturality, *the emotion of naturalness*. This is the ultimate emotional goal of all of our systems. You are choosing goals in the direction of your evolution to increased authentic expression if you are passionate about a goal, have resonance with it, or move into *flow* whenever you are working towards it.

Passion

The more powerfully the emotional goals associated with a desired reality are experienced internally, the faster a desired reality will come into existence. Therefore, you will want to concentrate on choosing goals for which you are passionate. Since passion is a sign of naturality, you can begin to see why following your passion will lead to realities in alignment with your naturality.

Resonance

If you don't have resonance, energy, enthusiasm, or at least an inner "knowing" that a goal is right for you, you are likely wanting a reality that is not adaptive for you. Could it be you are forcing yourself to create a particular reality because of habit, fear, or someone else's rules or goals? If you choose realities that make you "leap for joy" at the thought of them coming into existence, then you will find yourself more successful at reality creation.

Flow

Flow is included in this chapter on reality creation with emotion because it is our highest psychobiological state. As such, it is often filled with the best emotional experiences and always devoid of negative emotions. As a result, being in *flow* will automatically create adaptive realities. Pure positive emotion will create pure positive realities. *Flow* is a state of pure naturality and naturalness. *Flow* is the state of optimization.

CREATING EMOTIONAL BLUEPRINTS

No Emotion, No Creation

We've been indoctrinated to believe that if we can get the symbols, we will have the emotions we want. What I am saying is the exact reverse. *In the naturality paradigm, if we aren't able to experience the "feel" of the desired reality, we won't be able to create it.* Both the emotion and the reality are created by the same underlying beliefs. No emotion, no creation.

If we want to create the symbols, we have to create the emotions first. In other words, we need to achieve our emotional goals in order to create in our reality the symbols that reflect those emotional goals. As you evolve as a result of your use of the reality creation technology, the symbols will inevitably become redundant.

If you are pursuing a symbol but can't experience the feelings and emotions of being a person with that symbol in your reality, then you will not create that reality. Period! If you can't feel the emotion, you don't have the beliefs and there is nothing to send instructions to reality to create what you are seeking. I don't care how much you passionately "will" the desired reality into existence or intellectually define it, it won't happen.

Or, if by some chance it does happen, it will very shortly disappear again. Or, it will appear to be a confirmed event and then at the last minute it will fall through. It is important to concentrate our efforts on increasing our experience of the goal emotions in order to create the necessary beliefs.

> *"We are what and where we are because we have first*
> *imagined it."*   Donald Curtis

Emotionally Blueprint your Preferred Reality

Many find it too complex to figure out precisely which emotions they are pursuing or which beliefs are needed to create a specific reality. Emotions equip us with a shortcut. If we can experience the desired emotions internally – in other words, *visualize to the point of experiencing our emotional goals* – then we can create the symbols and events representative of those emotions externally.

And this shortcut works both ways. If you find yourself desiring specific symbols or events in your reality, use them to tell you precisely what your emotional goals are so you can pursue those emotional goals directly.

Alternatively, we can simply imagine we already have the pursued symbols or events in our life. Experience the "feel" of having them, and voilà – we just created the emotional blueprint of our preferred reality. Beliefs are changed. By experiencing our goal emotions internally, we open up the possibility of creating faster routes to them than the logical approaches we might conceive of for acquiring the symbol.

In many cases, knowing how to collide with the right coincidence can save us hundreds of steps and may even take us to a whole new form of the goal reality than we could ever have experienced. We often are so intent on acquiring a specific symbol that we don't realize the goal emotion feels exactly the same no matter how we achieve it.

It is the absence of creative thinking that has narrowed our focus to so few channels for satisfaction . . . . money, for example. Nature, however, is infinitely more creative. We can tap into this creativity if we are open to merging with the naturality flow by complying with the ten Optimizers.

Our proficiency at reality design depends on our ability to effectively blueprint the "end" emotional states we expect to experience so that the fastest reality symbolizing those emotional goals comes into existence. Basically, constructing a reality blueprint is our means for communicating directly with nature.

It is an infrastructure of beliefs that will issue instructions to create a new emotional reality. Let's take a look at two techniques to help us to emotionally blueprint the realities we are trying to create more effectively: "Emotionally-charged Visualization" and "Borrowed Emotional Blueprints."

Emotionally-Charged Visualization

"I noticed an almost universal trait among Super Achievers, and it was what I call Sensory Goal Vision. These people knew what they wanted out of life, and they could sense it multidimensionally before they ever had it. They could not only see it, but also taste it, smell it, and imagine the sounds and emotions associated with it. They pre-lived it before they had it. And the sharp, sensory vision became a powerful driving force in their lives." Stephen Devore

Let's look more closely at the *visualization-to-emotion* belief engineering tool. It simply means visualize until you can actually experience the emotions you expect to have if you had created your goal reality. If you can experience the emotions, your beliefs will automatically change to the ones that will be necessary for instructing the required changes in reality. It is my contention that visualization will not work if the *emotional blueprint* of your goal has not been activated.

Each visualization of a preferred reality carries with it an integrated tapestry of emotions. And each emotion is triggered by a belief or a set of beliefs. Therefore, if you are feeling the emotion, you are strengthening the underlying beliefs. And each visualization can strengthen a large number of beliefs in a very short period of time. As you become more experienced with this and more fluid in your belief structure, even 30 seconds might be enough. Whole sets of integrated beliefs can quickly be restructured by each visualization.

Borrow Emotional Blueprints

Are you having trouble figuring out what your beliefs and emotions should be for creating a specific reality? Are you having trouble visualizing to the point of creating the necessary emotional blueprint? Here's a quick blueprinting trick. Assimilate the emotional structure of someone with the reality you want to create by using clairsentience.

You can quickly absorb the emotional power of others in order to cause the belief changes for changing your reality. Clairsentience is "clear feeling" in the same way that clairvoyance is "clear seeing." As we move into alignment with naturality, we evolve an increasing empathic or telepathic capability which allows us to absorb the emotions of others. This is part of the knowledge technology's information sourcing capabilities.

Find the model. Identify people with the reality you want to have. Use clairsentience to absorb their emotional structure as your own. Because of the link Goleman presented between emotions and decision-making, *if you have a person's emotional structure, you will have their decision-making and motivational capabilities.*

This technique is especially useful when you have difficulty visualizing yourself with the desired reality. As long as you know the emotions you are trying to achieve, the body seems to know what beliefs need to be changed to create the symbols in your reality of those emotions.

If you want to improve your golf game, for example, find a golf pro or exceptional player that you relate to. As you go around the course, absorb, through clairsentience, his/her emotional structure and hence the history of his/her positive experiences, beliefs about ability, love of the game, skill, and decision-making ability. Experience the emotions in the same way you did with visualization. Without emotion, there will be no change in beliefs, and, hence, no change in your reality.

The emotional blueprint you absorb allows you to change all the beliefs that need to be changed to improve your golf game without even knowing specifically what those beliefs are. And, oh, by the way, the more you do this, the more you will find yourself drawing the perfect models by coincidence to help you create your next reality preference.

Hold the "Feel" of the Emotional Goal until Reality Restructures

Whenever you have accurately determined the right reality

blueprint, you will experience a "resonance click" or an internal "knowing" that it is right for you or that you've got it right. Once you have experienced the "click," hold onto the blueprint until reality restructures to reflect it.

Mentally, visually, and emotionally lock in the emotional "feel" of having the symbol or events in your life. Hold that "end" complex of feelings. That is your true reality design. Remember it. Revisit it frequently. Commit to having it! Expect to have it by the fastest route! The more you re-experience internally your emotionally charged reality design, the stronger you make the beliefs creating your experience of those emotions and, thus, the stronger will be the instructions from those beliefs to reality.

One of the hardest parts of the reality creation process for novices is holding the emotional blueprint until materialization occurs. Often beginners are deterred from energizing the emotional blueprint because of negative events in their realities created by old instructions from maladaptive beliefs.

If you stop holding the new messages in the face of old message events in your reality, you are locking yourself into a cycle of perpetually creating the same reality over and over again. If you absorb any part of the old messages, you are dissipating the power and clarity of the new instructions you are trying to issue.

Let's say the symbol representing your emotional goals is money. Through visualization you are experiencing your desired emotions by visualizing yourself wealthy. Yet, in your life, you are concentrating on the bills that aren't paid or the client that won't pay you or the client that got away . . . . in other words, things that suggest you are not wealthy or not on your way to wealth.

Or you have conflicting beliefs about becoming wealthy where you think you both deserve it and don't deserve it; or that you can make money and can't make money; or that having money will make you a spiritually bankrupt person. What you are doing is sending mixed messages to reality which first build the desired reality but, just before you actually experience it, wipe it out.

I have introduced this previously as the *sandcastle syndrome*. If you'll recall, the positive side of conflicting belief pairs issues instructions that begin building the perfect sandcastle. When counter-instructions are sent, it is just like having water sweep up and wash the sandcastle away.

Holding your emotional blueprint is another way to overcome this syndrome. Concentrate on sending consistent instructions to reality for achieving your emotional goals, despite the messages coming back from reality. Recognize that everything you are doing is sending instructions. Ignore what is already out there. Reality is simply a work in progress. With clarity and consistency, keep issuing your instructions for a new reality.

Gradually, you will notice the message events reflective of the old less desirable reality are getting weaker and weaker while events reflecting the new reality are getting stronger and more numerous. The risky point is when the beliefs for the old reality and the desired reality are of equal strength. It is important at that point to really become passionate to push through to the new reality.

Every time you see events in your reality reflective of your emotional goals, even in a small way, you want to grab onto them and say, "Yes! I did it!" Enjoy even small achievements of your emotional goals. Just as with visualization, you will be experiencing the emotions which will strengthen the beliefs that will speed reality creation.

Remember, the measurement is not, "Did I create the goal symbols today?" but, "Did I increase my experience of my goal emotions today?" If you did, internalize this to let it strengthen your beliefs even more. Your only focus is to intensify your experience of emotions in order to change the beliefs that will change your reality.

Pursue the Emotions not the Symbols

We impede our progress by chasing the symbols and events which signify our goal emotions to us rather than pursuing our emotional goals directly. If we can achieve the desired emotions, the symbols will not be long to follow. Here's an example from the experience of one of my clients.

As the new executive hire in the company, John wanted desperately to be accepted and valued by his peers. His selected measure of this would be his receiving the highest bonus, since peer ratings were included in bonus decisions. The bonus, then, was the symbol of his emotional goal.

We defined this goal as a level ten intensity of being "valued." We assumed John's belief that he was valued and valuable was currently only at a level one intensity. We began in April and bonus time was the following January.

John's assignment from me was to create events in his reality that demonstrated increasing levels of being valued. As the events occurred, John was required to pay attention to them and absorb them into his system to strengthen his belief that he was valued and valuable. He was to "feel" what it is like to be valued. He was to visualize until he could comfortably hold in his system what it was like to be valued at a level ten intensity. This is a challenge for people like John who have never believed they are valuable and valued.

I often found myself having to point out the valuing events in John's reality because he just wasn't accustomed to taking notice of them. It's almost as if they took place in some foreign language not understood or translatable by John's system. He was so convinced that no one valued him that he could not even detect valuing when it was happening.

Our strategy was for John to *BE* the person inside first who was valued at a level ten for his performance, so he would be able to reflect that state into reality. As the resented outsider of this promote-from-within company, John was not experiencing many valuing events in his work environment.

Consequently, we looked for some new territories outside the company where John could feel valued much more quickly. Our focus was singularly on having him experience being valued more frequently anywhere in his life. This is because, once his valuing belief was strengthened to a level ten, John would be able to be valued in every context – including work. The same belief blueprint creates all aspects of our reality.

We found John both a charity board and a business board to sit on using the pathfinding technology. Both groups found his contribution exceptional. He was continually told how valuable he was. In addition, John began working with a premier consulting firm to accelerate the work he was doing with his employer.

The partners of this firm were incredibly impressed with John's ideas and energy and found him to be a breath of fresh air compared to his peer group at his Fortune 500 employer. Every time they valued him, John quickly worked to absorb this valuing to drive the strength of his belief from level one to two to three to four, and so on to level ten.

The leading partners of this consulting firm began to tell the top executives of John's employer how impressed they were with John's performance. Their valuing did not stop there. They also nominated John for the industry award of *Man of the Year* for his breakthrough achievements. He won in December. With this outside recognition, John moved over the top on his perception of himself as a valued and valuable executive. He was well past the level ten intensity that had been his target.

All of his peers at work began valuing him daily in perfect reflection of how he now valued himself. Another outside board position rolled in that carried with it lots of options. An unexpected takeover resulted in some rather astounding financial returns that far exceeded what would be possible through his bonus.

But, right when he no longer needed the top bonus, when his emotional states were so far beyond what he had set out to achieve, he also received the largest bonus ever issued by his employer. The symbol of the original emotional goal materialized.

In the naturality paradigm, the trick is to keep your focus on increasing the intensity of the emotional state you want to achieve. The symbols will take care of themselves. If John had focused on being valued by his peers every day, he would have had confirmation that he was indeed not valued and neither his belief nor his reality would have been enhanced. In fact, there's a good chance they would have deteriorated.

SPEEDING CREATION

There are a few ways to use emotion to accelerate your reality creation process and the achievement of your emotional goals.

The Clearer and Stronger the Instructions, the Faster the Creation

A stronger, clearer and more passionate message will create the desired reality more quickly. Choosing reality creation goals you are passionate about means you are moving with nature towards the full expression of your naturality. You will have the support of coincidences, flow events and *flow*.

Passion is a telltale sign of naturality. Consequently, your instructions to reality will be stronger and clearer, thus creating adaptive realities more quickly. Also, the more passionate your emotional blueprinting, the more effective the reality creation. Fears, conflicting beliefs, limiting beliefs, and conflicting requests will decrease the strength and speed of reality creation. Toxic emotions and beliefs need to be cleared regularly.

Use Virtual Realities for Quantum Leaps

We have evolved imaginations to help with the reality creation process. We can use imagined realities to quantum leap over the interim physical realities we think must occur for us to progress linearly to our goal reality creations. Rather than concentrating strictly on strengthening his "valued" belief from level one intensity to level ten intensity, John could simply hold the emotional feel of being valued by his peers without doing the work he assumed was necessary to earn their respect.

He didn't actually need progressive valuing events in his reality if he could have experienced those events emotionally through visualization. Use whatever it takes to change the underlying beliefs. It is much faster to create an imagined reality to change beliefs than to wait to create a physical reality.

John could have visualized several times a day to accelerate the strengthening of his "valued belief." Use your imagination to short-circuit the time it takes to get to your emotional goals. How many iterations of reality can you experience emotionally through visualization rather than having to physically create those realities to lock in the belief changes? Visualize, to the point of emotion, your end emotional goal to speed the creation of physical reality. If you think this is reminiscent of what coaches do for Olympic athletes, you're right. It works.

Let's say in physical reality it would take ten steps to go from Reality 1 to Reality 10. If I can create Reality 2 through 9 in my head by visualization and then go directly to Reality 10 in physical reality, you can see that productivity is possible. These interim imagined realities are highly adaptive. They are a key tool for growth.

Emotions are expressions of beliefs, but they are also the means to lay down those beliefs. A basketball team that visualizes perfect performance to the point of vividly experiencing the accompanying emotions can actually outperform a team that physically practised.

This is because the positive beliefs of the team that practised are eroded by their mistakes or limited to their actual performance during practice. The team that visualized made no mistakes. Perhaps it was not just that the visualizers made all of the right moves, but they made no wrong moves in their imagined realities to interfere with the internalization of their success.

Visualization coaches have now become commonplace among athletes because there is a great deal of data demonstrating that visualization works in the way I have described. As we realize how realities are created, the demand for those who can help us visualize to the point of emotion will increase. The demand for visualization coaches and emotional engineering coaches will rise dramatically. Whose performance has not improved bathed in the unconditional love and belief in us of our lovers or our children?

Release the Need for Linear Progression

It is advantageous not to insist that your progression to creating desired realities proceed in a linear, logical way. This is not an instruction you want to send reality. Wouldn't you rather create a coincidence that will let you quantum leap to your desired reality? Release your demand that your desired realities must come into existence by a string of logically connected events. If you require "linearity," that is the reality you're going to experience. Believe in a nonlinear world full of coincidences and that is what you will experience.

Pathfind your Desired Reality

In the Pathfinding chapter, I had suggested that reality creation and pathfinding are really the same thing. In pathfinding, we define a goal and then partner with the blocks, flows, and our resonance to *find* the desired reality by the fastest route. It's a matter of moving through the unknown to our goal reality. For reality creation, we do the same thing.

You know the reality you want to create but likely have no idea how you are going to create it. Once you have the "feel" of your goal reality, you can use the pathfinding technology to poll various channels to identify which ones your desired reality is trying to come through. You want to look for which pathways you resonate with and/or which ones have flow events to help your progress.

Both pathfinding and reality creation bring a new reality into your life. The reality creation technology, then, is an enhancement to the pathfinding technology. It is a more sophisticated pathfinding process which uses beliefs and emotions to improve accuracy in exchanging current realities for goal realities, or a known reality for an unknown one.

Increase Fluidity

The more we use the reality creation technology to change our beliefs to change our reality, the more fluid we will become. Consequently, we will be able to change our beliefs and our reality more quickly in the future. We will learn how to flick in and out of emotions very quickly so that visualizations for a new reality can have their impact in seconds. As a result, quantum leaps will become more prevalent in our lives.

Hold the Emotional Goal, Release the Channel

Unfortunately, all too often, we require our emotional goals to be met through a specific channel – a specific event or symbol. Once you're experiencing your emotional goal, do you really care how you got there? Remember the old Chinese proverb? *"There are many paths to the top of the mountain but the view is always the same."* As you gain experience with the reality creation technology, you will discover that nature's ten signals are always directing you to your emotional goals by the fastest route.

Nature doesn't seem to care about the symbols, only the optimization of your system as quickly as possible. And, nature has infinite creativity and minimal patience for how you achieve the emotions necessary to bring you into balance.

The insistence that emotional goals be met through a single possible reality is the number one reason why people think they have no control over their realities. They think that because they failed to create a specified symbol, they could not create reality. They were measuring their performance against the wrong goal. The test is whether they created the desired emotion through any channel.

Minimize Creation Anxiety

We've all experienced it. The second we commit to a new goal which we don't know how to achieve, we are bombarded by negative emotions – fear of failure, fear of judgment, generalized fear, hopelessness, worry, discouragement, and depression.

If our ultimate evolution is to the full creative expression of our naturality, then we are always evolving to increasingly more creative lives. Accordingly, it is advantageous for us to not only accept creation anxiety as part of our existence but minimize its interference. Let's look at how that might be accomplished.

If you're holding emotionally the reality of your satisfied emotional goals, you will not simultaneously be able to experience creation anxiety. It can't be done. Further, if you've been through several successful reality creation cycles, your knowledge of what you are capable of creating will begin to outweigh the illogic of creation anxiety.

Also, creation is about going into the unknown. As your expertise with the pathfinding technology increases, your creation anxiety will diminish. Pathfinding in new frontiers and colliding with coincidences which at any moment may catapult us to our desired reality are thrilling. The addiction to getting thrill after thrill tends to eradicate performance anxiety.

As we gain expertise in conquering the unknown territory between current reality and the reality we'd prefer to have, we will actually begin to crave only being in this creative gap. We become addicted to the growth and creativity possible in this unknown territory between where we are and where we want to be. When you feel the fears and powerlessness of the gap, take creative action, particularly around your *art*. This will not only strengthen and optimize you but will addict you to taking more steps.

At some point, while doing what you love, *flow* state will kick in, and flow events and coincidences will start to occur, and then, all of a sudden, you are through the gap and experiencing the new reality. This is much like the car when all of the components are assembled correctly and the car *system* is applied to the transportation function for which it was designed.

A quantum leap in performance occurs. And it is a quantum leap to a level of performance that cannot be linearly projected from our start point. Performance anxiety disappears when you are performing at levels beyond all previous experience. What remains is pure exhilaration

We had it Right as Children

Anyone who has watched children has observed the way they openly seek to gratify their emotional goals. They show us how we are designed to respond to the natural *optimizing emotional requests* from within us. Our cultures interfere with these natural drives. If the optimizing requests are not satisfied, the biochemical-electromagnetic imbalance persists. Toxicity is introduced into our systems as a result. The continuous process of our re-optimization breaks down.

Our cultures teach us to pursue *symbols* of our internal emotional requests through prescribed channels rather than responding to nature's directions. Our cultures give us rational, intellectual prescriptions for meeting our emotional goals. What our cultures do is prevent us from satisfying the optimization requests of our systems by the fastest route in partnership with the naturality flow. We need to evolve our cultures to allow our children to retain and enhance their connection to internal stimuli rather than teaching them to ignore them or to make them wrong for following them.

As reality creation techniques become common knowledge, we will be able to pull together as a world civilization to collectively choose the realities we want to bring into existence. We will effectively learn how to manage the world belief pool to create a world in which each one of us may thrive.

"Civilization is the intelligent management of human emotions." Jim Rohn

12

DESIGNING FUTURE WORLDS

"There is a deep longing to create that resides within the soul of humanity. Beyond our natural instinct for survival. . . . we also have a natural instinct for building, organizing, forming, and creating."[32]   Robert Fritz

World design was once reserved for the rich and powerful. As our reality creation capabilities evolve, we will each have the ability to design future worlds. Napoleon Bonaparte once said, "Imagination rules the world." This will never be more true than in a world where we'll all have the power to create our realities.

In this future paradigm, our imaginations will determine what we will experience. Imagination will decide the *haves* from the *have nots*. The quality of our lives will depend on the strength of what we imagine for ourselves. We will evolve the power to interrupt history and "quantum leap" to future realities which are not linear extensions of our past. Let's find out more about the art and science of the reality design process which will make such cataclysmic change so effortlessly possible.

VISION VERSUS REALITY DESIGN

Achievers know the value of a vision for helping us to attain our goals. Visions provide clarity, focus and motivation. Visions are conceptualizations. They are impressions, abstractions and mental images of a possible and desirable future state. They represent our ideals. Visions articulate a more attractive future than now exists. Just as architects make drawings and engineers build models, a vision is a way of giving expression to our hopes for the future.

However, are visions enough in a paradigm where beliefs create reality? If reality is 100 percent self-created, are we not going to want a clear blueprint for our *total reality*, not just visions for a project here and there? It will be quite a challenge for many of us to evolve the expanded consciousness necessary to think in terms of designing the totality of our experience.

And, here's another interesting thought. If we had mastered the art of creating reality, how would we spend our day? I suspect we'd become very dedicated to designing what we want to experience next, and next, and next. Reality design would become a pivotal part of human existence.

Given that beliefs create reality, a reality design is a simple way to package up all of the beliefs we need to have to create our next desired reality. Reality design is a more active blueprint than a vision in that it defines the changes that must occur in our belief blueprint to send changed instructions to our reality.

Reality design is the process of selecting and internalizing new beliefs in order to change the instructions we emit to reality. It is about choosing our next belief blueprint and thus our next reality. Reality design is, in effect, belief engineering.

Think of reality as if it was a painting that can never be finished. We can continuously customize it by adding new preferences. Everything is changeable. We can change colors here and there as our preferences change. Reality is a perpetual work-in-progress. We seek to continuously co-evolve our reality and ourselves in order to optimize the synergy between them at all times.

As you will learn in the growth technology chapters, the underlying theme of human existence is perpetual iterations of self-creation and creation. We grow ourselves to grow our creations and are then grown by those creations. Growth is the process of internalizing the beliefs necessary to increase the power of the realities we create.

A vision may be conceived of once and then remain fixed until we achieve, revise or abandon it. Reality design, by comparison, is a very organic and interactive process. It is continuously adjusted and adapted in response to information from nature's *Optimizers*. The one constant, as we discovered in the previous chapter, is the emotional *feel* of the next reality we are wanting to create.

Both visioning and reality design generate pictures of the future we seek to bring into being. The difference between them, then, is one of degree. If we're going to change our reality, it will be necessary for us to first *own* that reality.

It will be necessary to conceive of ourselves and our reality as a single system created by the same belief blueprint. The difference between vision and reality design is therefore also one of ownership. How all-encompassing is your vision? How much of your reality are you ready to own?

Own Your Reality

In a paradigm in which beliefs create reality, everything is created by our beliefs. Therefore, we have one single system which includes everything in our realities. We are automatically creating that reality.

Once we become aware of this, the next obvious evolution is to consciously design the realities we will experience. We will want to proactively determine what we will experience. We will want to evolve to new levels of sophistication with respect to designing and creating ourselves and our realities.

The speed with which we excel in reality creation depends on how quickly we can take ownership of our entire reality. Are you ready to assume responsibility for what is in your reality? Are you ready to stop blaming others as if they are somehow separate from you? Will you allow yourself to escape the confines of your linear heritage? Can you dream dreams of futures which are not an extension of your past?

Could you envision yourself in a future reality in no way associated with your previous reality and hold that vision long enough for your beliefs to change? Would you be comfortable regularly interrupting your linear progression with quantum leaps in unpredictable directions? Your answers will determine the speed with which you will reach your personal peak potential and speed of evolution.

Increase your Ownership Gradually

Precise reality design requires owning all of the beliefs that are sending instructions out to create reality. This is too big a challenge for most of us to embrace day one. Try developing visions one at a time for each segment of your reality as your passion, creativity, and resonance are ignited to do so. All the visions will eventually link up into a completely integrated reality design . . . . for some, within months, for others, it may take years. This must be the case if you are always following the whispers of your naturality. The key is to begin the ownership process.

As you align your life around your naturality, the process will become simpler, more orderly and more manageable. Over time, you will find yourself weeding interfering, maladaptive, beliefs out of your belief blueprint. As a result, dysfunctional realities will start to disappear. You'll be ridding your life of "the noise."

At the same time, your consciousness will be expanding as you work to manage the progress and precision of your reality creation efforts. Eventually, you will find yourself tracking every nook and cranny of your reality. You will have evolved to an organic interactive oneness with your reality. Reality design and reality creation will no longer be separate conscious acts but automatic reflections of your naturality.

DESIGN IN THE DIRECTION OF THE NATURALITY FLOW

Ask yourself, "Where is nature trying to direct my system? Is my reality design consistent with that natural flow?" If you think you want a goal which conflicts with the naturality flow, you don't. Why fight nature when we can harness powerful natural forces to support our reality creation efforts? When we partner with the underlying dynamic of nature, an enhanced functionality is possible.

Going with the naturality flow is the secret to powerful reality design and creation. It is also the route to the benefits of the knowledge technology, the reality creation technology, the growth technology, and pathfinding; accelerating progress by quantum leaps and coincidences; achieving your emotional goals; and clearing toxicity from your system.

Nature's *Optimizers* are the arrows that will identify the directions we should pursue with our reality design efforts in order to bring new realities into existence much more quickly. You will find the *Optimizer* signals surprisingly consistent with each other, thus reflecting the underlying orderliness of nature's intent. Our lives will eventually become an organic conversation with nature.

The direction of the naturality flow is singularly consistent. It is perpetually toward the increasing expression of our naturality within the changing context of a multitude of co-evolving systems. Our natural growth path proceeds toward the expansion of our authentic core by concentric circles.

Align with Naturality

We will therefore want to design in the direction of increasing the expression of our naturality. If your reality creation efforts have failed in the past, try moving with nature rather than fighting the flow to naturality. Naturality is a fluid and changeable state. It is not some fixed term that can be stamped on your forehead to identify yourself as a "something" – a "this" or a "that."

Rather, it is the attractor holding the components of your system in balance vis-à-vis your current context. It is the reason the components were combined in the first place and continue to stay connected. *Naturality* is experienced as *an emotion of naturalness*. This feeling of naturalness is the only real constant associated with naturality.

Alignment with our naturality is the natural outcome of taking one action after the next in harmony with this emotion of naturalness. Therefore, we will want to select our reality designs based on how natural they feel to us. We might have a tendency to choose unnatural realities for our creation activities based on the identities conferred on us by authority figures such as parents, teachers, and bosses.

We could also be led astray in our reality design by the norms of groups to which we have chosen to belong. Over the years, we have all absorbed habits and beliefs from our cultures which interfere with *naturality-focused reality design*.

We all have a number of distractions interfering with our ability to connect with our emotion of naturality. How can we ensure we are choosing the best reality designs for ourselves? If you have passion for a vision of reality . . . I mean genuine passion . . . that tells you a reality design is consistent with your natural growth path to naturality.

If you have no energy for a goal reality or are creating it out of fear, for example, then it's not adaptive for your system. It won't be supported by nature. Proceed at your own peril. Blocks and problem events will riddle your path when you're heading in the wrong direction. Coincidences and flow events will support you when you are attempting to create adaptive realities. As a novice, it's always best to choose reality designs for which you have great excitement.

Our *art* is another indicator of naturality that, if honored in our designs, will lead to greater reality creation success. Our *art* is the expression of our naturality. It includes the things we love to do, that we do well naturally, and which, to everyone else would be work. To us our *art* is an effortless effort.

When we are living in alignment with our naturality and doing our *art,* all of the events in our reality become perfect messages from nature as to how to proceed quickly and effectively. The instructions of the *Optimizers* become obvious. The direction for future reality design supported by nature becomes evident.

Design towards your Passions and Positive Emotions

Much of what was described in the previous chapter for using emotions and our emotional drives for reality creation was, in fact, advice to be used for reality design. As such, only a few brief points will be repeated here.

Our positive emotions and passions are like neon signs steering us in the direction of our natural growth path to naturality and optimization. Ideal reality designs, then, will always target positive emotions rather than the avoidance of negative emotions. Therefore, rather than trying to eliminate negative realities, proactively pursue your preferences.

Our only motivation for doing anything is to change our emotional state. Therefore, all goals – or goal realities – are emotional goals. If we design any specific realities we want to bring into existence, they are only symbols of emotional goals we would like to experience. The only way to experience a new emotional state is to change our beliefs.

For most of us, it would be much too tedious to work out the specific beliefs required for each new reality. Therefore, human beings have evolved a shortcut. Our emotions. If we can visualize to the point of "feeling" the desired goal emotions internally, we are already causing the necessary belief changes to lock in the desired reality change. We will be creating the requisite reality design.

A reality design, then, is ultimately just an infrastructure of beliefs that will issue instructions to create a new emotional reality. It is a belief engineering technique. Passionate emotional blueprints will speed the change in beliefs necessary to bring our desired new realities into existence.

Constructing an emotionally charged reality design is our most effective means for communicating our instructions to nature. If we can *feel* how it will *feel* to have the reality we are seeking, then we have completed our reality design process. Our reality designs then can be no more specific than an emotional blueprint. Knowing what our next preferred reality will *feel* like is enough to change our beliefs.

Hold the "feel" of your goal reality until reality restructures. This is your true reality design. Remember it. Revisit it frequently. Commit to having it! Expect to have it by the fastest route! The more you re-experience internally your emotionally charged reality design, the stronger you make the beliefs creating your experience of those emotions and, thus, the stronger will be the instructions from those beliefs to reality.

Design in the Direction of your Resonance

Our resonance is another telltale signal of the direction of the naturality flow. Choose reality designs based on your resonance. Resonance tells us we are choosing a reality design that is natural for us. It signifies that a reality design is aligned with our naturality.

There will be no point developing reality designs we don't resonate with or we have reservations about. They will be taking us off-path. Proceed at your own risk. You are choosing a reality design for the wrong reason. When you are fighting the naturality flow, you can expect blocks and negative events.

If your resonance, energy, enthusiasm, your internal "knowing" and emotions don't increase or, ideally, "leap for joy" at the thought of the new reality you want to bring into existence, you haven't picked a nature-supported reality design. Rather, you've selected a reality that's not right for you at this moment. Could it be you are forcing yourself to create a particular reality because of habit, fear, or someone else's goals?

Is your reality design requiring your emotional goals to come through the wrong channel? Are you trying to comply with someone else's rules about what you want or how specific goals can be achieved? Are you trying to please someone else rather than following your heart? Listen to the voice of nature instead. Choose reality designs that are consistent with your present resonance and the pattern of your resonance events in your past.

Design Consistent with your Historical Pattern of Blocks and Flows

Block events and flow events in our realities are also *Optimizers* to be heeded in our reality designs. An ideal reality design would be one that is consistent with every block and flow we have ever experienced. It would not include any pathways which have previously been blocked in our life. It would proactively pursue directions of categories of events in our life that have flowed.

Ideal reality design presumes nature has been consistent and correct in its signals from all of its *Optimizers* as to the routes to your naturality and optimization. Assume there is a level of order in our chaotic lives we have not yet been trained to see. Look for it and honor it in your reality designs.

I can tell you that reality is orderly, but it is so contrary to how many of us have come to understand life. You will, therefore, likely need to prove it to yourself. I recommend making a written inventory of recent events, perhaps surveying the last six months. Look at what's been flowing and what hasn't. Assume there are themes and look for them. When you find consistent patterns of flow events, project these themes out into the future so you can know the paths and goals supported by nature. Choose your reality designs accordingly.

Block and flow events are direct instructions from nature as to the direction of the flow of optimization for your system. Move with this flow and you will encounter more flow events and coincidences and quantum leaps to accelerate your progress. *Always reality design with your flows.*

Avoid reality designs in the directions of your blocks. These blocks are telling you to find another route. Heed their benevolent message. It is illogical, never mind masochistic, to continue down pathways you already know will be blocked by nature. Find another route to your goal. As you improve your reality designs, you will become less accustomed to experiencing blocks. You will therefore become sensitized to them. As a result, you will honor them more quickly and when they are smaller.

If you can't identify a pattern of blocks or flows in your life, take action in multiple directions towards a goal until a pattern starts to emerge. Experiment until you can read with great rapidity precisely the pathways that are optimal for you at any point in time.

Once you have worked with patterns of events for awhile, you'll become familiar with your personal patterns and know that the messages are very consistent, orderly and benevolent. Until your consciousness expands sufficiently to keep track of the pattern of events in your head, keep a written record of events to help you identify the patterns.

There could be another explanation for your inability to read the pattern of blocks and flows in your life. The more we are out of alignment with our naturality, the more difficult it is to see the patterns. The more we're living in alignment with our naturality, the clearer and more orderly the themes of our blocks and flows will be.

If you know you haven't been living in alignment, start by honoring your resonance moment after moment for a week or so. Then take a look at the blocks and flows. Is the order starting to appear?

Also, the more we heed nature's signals, the faster we'll move into alignment with our naturality and the more precise the *Optimizer* messages will become. Withhold your evaluation of the accuracy of reality's patterns of events in the beginning until you can get some alignment with the consistent direction of nature's *Optimizers*.

Resonance, natural creative and growth drives, passions, the pattern of blocks and flows, your natural art, the knowledge you are passionate about pursuing, the pattern of your *flow* states . . . . these will all be moving you along the same natural growth path.

As you comply with that flow, the order will increase and so will your ability to predictably create reality. The patterns become easier to identify the more you take action in compliance with them. Keep experimenting. You will become proficient in understanding nature's communications.

Follow the Optimizing Trends for the Human Race

Nature's consistency derives from the integrative creative flow of every system in the universe. The universe, as we know it, is just another system flowing to its optimization and naturality. What are these natural trends of the larger universal system? We will want to choose our reality designs consistent with the creative flow of this larger system. This will increase our chances of creating our desired realities and increase nature's support of our progress.

The human race is also a system. It too has its naturality and it too is always trying to move to optimization. Therefore, we will be supported in reality designs that are moving with nature's optimizing flow for the entire human population. Our reality creation, then, will improve with reality designs that are integrated into the optimizing processes that are shaping the human system. Here are some current evolutionary trends for humanity that you might want to take into consideration for your reality design work:

1. The flow of the human system is towards oneness, wholeness, unification, interconnectedness, integration and cohesiveness. The terms "clustering," "convergence," "alliance," "networks," "networking," "internet," "internetworking," and "community" are increasingly used in business.
2. There is a continuous flow to optimization through creativity, the creative expression of naturality, and quantum leaps.
3. Individuality is increasing.
4. Creativity is increasing.
5. The race is evolving towards expanded consciousness, nondual or unity consciousness, and higher frequency consciousness. We are progressing from egocentric to worldcentric and beyond.

If you're setting up a business, choosing one on the basis of providing increased interconnectivity or the unification of the human race, for example, will help to ensure your success. This should be your reality design. The demand for interconnection in the human race is driving the creativity on the technological front rather than, as some have suggested, the other way around. We have always sought to link up for unification. At the same time, as we are seeking unification, our need for expressing our individuality is also increasing.

In *Global Paradox* (1994), John Naisbitt proposes that, as the world becomes interconnected into a single marketplace, the importance of the individual will increase. The key paradox he identifies is that "the bigger the world economy, the more powerful its smallest players." Technology is bringing the individual to global interaction and power. Although people will want to unify to *trade* more freely, they will want to be independent politically and culturally.

Naisbitt forecasted that the more people are bound together economically, the more they want to be *free* in other contexts to assert their own distinctiveness. We will gravitate to tribes and communities of like-minded people . . . . another direction of unification. This is consistent with my proposal in Chapter 1 of the Age of the Individual.

The trend to individuality and creativity is also demonstrated by the dramatic increase in entrepreneurial companies worldwide. In many Western countries, for example, at least 80% of companies have under fifty employees. In 1999, twenty-five percent of the Harvard MBA class went to work for companies with fewer than fifty people, while the same percentage of Stanford MBA graduates joined companies with fewer than twenty-five employees.

While new companies are being set up to allow individuals to express their naturality, large multinationals continue to preside as part of the trend in humanity towards unification. The two trends will unify as corporations learn how to honor the natural growth path of individuals to the full expression of their naturality while harvesting the peak performance and creativity that will be the byproduct.

In addition, unity and individuality will thrive through the extension of corporations to an increase in alliances, business webs, and internetworking of companies. Boundaries around corporations and nation states will dissolve as part of this movement to meaningful communities and tribes. This trend will be supported by the evolving expansion of human consciousness.

The natural growth path for individuals proposed through the peak evolution science includes the same trends happening in the larger human system. Specifically, each individual will be supported in moving to oneness, especially since individual cohesiveness will contribute to the ability of the race to move to oneness.

Individuals will be supported in moving to their full potential around the creative expression of their authentic *art*, especially since this will allow the total human race system to move to its full optimization and peak performance. The creativity of each individual determines the creative adaptiveness for the survival of the total human system and therefore will be supported. These, then, are trends that we will want to capitalize on when we are constructing our reality designs.

Automatic Reality Design and Creation

In *Peak Evolution*, we are artificially dissecting a totally integrated process so we can develop the skills for each of its components. Again, the process of perfecting a tennis serve is an effective metaphor. An instructor will work to correct each part of what will ultimately be one automatic sweep.

The peak evolution science is designed to free us from cultural interferences as well as teach new techniques for transitioning to full functionality. However, once the transition is made and we have reintegrated into the naturality flow, we will no longer need it. We can operate on our natural automatic pilot that is guided by internal drives and external forces. Therefore, let me describe what will ultimately be automatic reality design and creation to assist you in achieving your full potential.

Assume you've advanced in your use of the peak evolution science. You've reintegrated into the naturality flow. You've aligned your life with your naturality. In other words, you have *naturalized*. You would be operating with an *emotion of naturalness* at all times.

Over time, you'd become hooked by the *Optimizer* drives into significant goals and projects which would give voice to your natural *art* and what is meaningful to you. Coincidences and flow events would pull you along your natural growth and creation paths. Your life would revolve around simple integrated themes. Most of your day would be spent in *flow* state.

As you used the reality creation technology to continuously perfect your reality, eventually everything in your life would be personally selected by you and therefore meaningful. Your belief blueprint would have been detoxified leaving only those beliefs supportive of your naturality.

As a result, you would automatically be emitting instructions to create realities reflective of your naturality. It could not be otherwise. If you are totally integrated into alignment with what is natural to you, then your instructions to reality for reality creation will also be consistent with that naturality. You will therefore automatically create realities that are adaptive to your system's optimization. Your true nature will be instructing reality.

We have all visited this magical harmony when the world miraculously seems to support our projects at every turn. Everything seems to be provided by a multitude of coincidences and flow events. This is truly peak performance. The peak evolution science provides the formula to help us to make this modus operandi a way of life.

Ultimately, as we evolve and optimize around our naturality signature, no conscious reality design will be required to create adaptive realities. They will emerge automatically. We will be able to take our hands off the wheel and shift into *automatic pilot.*

Again, the peak evolution science will not be required once we reintegrate back into the naturality flow. We will do everything automatically . . . . naturally. The technology will be there if you fall out of the flow or need to fix a problem.

A partnership with any of the *Optimizers* will automatically lead you back into the naturality flow. Select the *Optimizers* you have resonance with. You will automatically end up in sync with all of them. They are all moving together based on the same underlying dynamic of the universe.

> *"Man is so made that when anything fires his soul, impossibilities vanish."*　　　Jean de la Fontaine

Unrestricted Asking

Between our cultural baggage and our personal baggage, we each have a number of interferences restricting the quality of our reality designs. Most of them limit what we ask for. We are not accustomed to getting what we want so we don't even bother to ask. Notice how our children don't have this problem. Are you expecting to fill a small metal cup with your reality design or several Mack trucks? We'll want to make sure we're not asking for only what we think we can get. We will only create what we expect to create. We therefore want to cultivate the art of unlimited thinking whenever we develop our reality designs.

There is a widespread tendency to choose our next reality based on what we think is possible given our current reality. This is often because our rational brain can only identify one or two channels in our current reality through which the new reality might come. We tend to make our reality design "fit" those channels.

There is a tendency to forget that nature is infinitely more creative than we are and that nature has an infinite number of channels already in existence that we are not even aware of. Through the peak evolution science, we are re-integrating back into the naturality flow because we want to access intelligence and resources far beyond what we personally possess. We'll want to design our realities more expansively as a result.

In our reality design process, it's also important to remember that our real goal is a new emotional state. Our intent is not to have that goal come through a specific channel. When we're experiencing the desired emotional states, do we really care how we got there?

Reality design is ideally done without consideration to the routes to the new reality. If the design is meaningful to you and it excites you or you have a strong "knowing" that it is precisely right for you, then nature is telling you that it is consistent with your naturality signature at this moment in time. Try not to let old thinking and old beliefs get in the way of your believing you can have what you want.

The reality design process is one of conceiving of the goal reality, experiencing it emotionally, and then holding this emotional blueprint until the goal reality comes into existence. Nature's creativity can formulate the fastest route for you. The route is usually nonlinear and accessible by the pathfinding technology.

If you make the "process" the goal, the requirement for "process" will be the reality you'll experience. There'll be no chance for coincidences and quantum leaps to accelerate your progress. There'll be no chance to capitalize on channels unbeknownst to you that already exist in the underlying fabric of the universe. You'll limit your performance to *your* capabilities rather than harnessing *nature's* creativity to your cause.

I can't stress enough that good reality design doesn't require your desired realities to come in a specific form or through a specific single channel. When you are integrated into nature, there are an infinite number of channels through which your desired emotional states could come. If you're experiencing any emotional goal – love, oneness, success, being valued and valuable, respected, desired, contributing – that's more important than the route by which it arrived. Let nature's optimizing systems and creativity take you by the fastest route.

Assume reality is fluid. I like to use a metaphor of a glacier melting into icebergs to liberate reality design efforts. In the beginning, we see reality as immutable, much like a glacier. As we move along the continuum to owning our reality, various parts of our reality will come under our control as reality creators.

We will increasingly experience these reality segments as fluid and changeable. We will be able to let some parts of the reality glacier break off into floating icebergs. Eventually we will achieve totally unrestricted reality design as if reality is water waiting to be poured into the images we construct.

Keep a continuous watch for the territories in your reality you assume are immutable. These are the territories in which to focus your belief engineering efforts. Some people might start by assuming they have control over their reality at work. They will not, however, extend this control to family members whom they think have always been a certain way and cannot change. Others may want to be valued yet think their employer will never recognize their value because it has never happened to this point.

It's only logical to assume that, if we are able to control reality creation in one territory of our life, then we can do it throughout our reality. The process is identical. The same belief blueprint is involved. All that needs to happen is to jettison our limiting beliefs. Watch for them, and help nature clear them away en route to the full expression of your naturality.

As you become familiar with nature's ways, you'll build into the design your expectation for coincidences and quantum leaps. You'll stop requiring your creations to proceed in a linear fashion and this will be reflected in your designs.

Scarcity thinking is another interference to the magnitude of our designs and hence our creations. Cultivate a belief in abundance and hold that belief until reality conforms. Develop abundance consciousness. If we have limiting beliefs, our blueprints will be limited and therefore our progress will be limited. If we don't have the beliefs we can design and create reality, then our reality design will not work. Also, check to see if you have any fears about having the reality you are designing. You'll want to go through a fear-clearing exercise to ensure you do not inadvertently interfere with the reality creation process.

Powerlessness. This is another "enemy" capable of interfering with our ability to hold our reality design long enough for reality to restructure. We don't want to let an unexpected block to our progress invoke our old feelings of powerlessness. Powerlessness will cause us to settle on a restricted version of our blueprint . . . . or perhaps to abandon it altogether.

Remember, only the route to our emotional goals is expressed by the blocks and flows. Hold your original reality design in the face of blocks and poll for the route riddled with flow events trying to take you to your goal. Let yourself evolve to owning everything in your reality and having total power over it.

If you've been damaged and bruised in the past to the point of feeling no control over your reality and powerlessness, then it's time to clear this toxicity out of your system. Set a specified time of two weeks or so to accomplish this and commit to make it happen.

All of us have heard of some young superstars who, in their early twenties or younger, moved into immediate success. Much of this success was simply because they didn't know what they were attempting to do was considered difficult or impossible. They had unlimited thinking. They didn't know any better. They simply began pursuing their emotional goals and they experienced incredible success.

Once they are informed through the media or public acclaim of the risks they were taking, they lose their unlimited thinking. They have fears. They have doubts whether they can do it again. Many at this time lose everything they have gained and might take years to release their spirit and enthusiasm again for a project . . . . if ever.

Unlimited thinking works. See if you can't get it working for you in your reality design process. The expansiveness of your reality design will determine the extent of your creations in reality. So, avoid letting your anxieties about your ability to bridge the gap between your current and future realities to limit, in any way, the future reality you design.

Also, we learned that as your beliefs that you can create any reality increase, the substance and power of your reality designs will also change. In fact, as you gain experience with all of nature's optimizing systems and the peak evolution science, your reality design focus and capability will change. As you get more experience connecting with the order behind many of nature's processes, the way you do reality blueprinting will change to capitalize on your experience.

INCREASING YOUR SPEED AND PROFICIENCY

As creative beings fully capable of creating our realities, we will want to become fast and proficient with the process. How can we accelerate our rate of achievement and evolution? I'd like to highlight a series of tips for the use of the peak evolution science which are particularly relevant to reality design.

My challenge in writing this chapter is to find a snapshot of the reality design process which will instruct beginners while at the same time provide the progressive information required by those who revisit the chapter time and again as their skills, experiential learning and naturality increase. If this is your first time through, feel free to just absorb what you can and reread the chapter when you've had some practice.

Design Interactively with Nature

While I've stressed the importance of holding the feeling of the end reality we want to create, it's critical to accustom ourselves to leaving everything fluid between our current and desired realities. This creative gap is where we can organically partner with nature.

Reality design does not yield a fixed result. It is a continuous process. Try to allow the details of your ongoing reality design to emerge through the reaction of the *Optimizers* to your taking action towards your goal. Take any action to source new information from the *Optimizer* reactions. Then modify your reality design accordingly.

To see if you've identified an adaptive reality design for the evolution of your system, take action on it. If your reality design is advantageous for you, taking action will be greeted by flow events, coincidences, strong resonance, positive emotions, *flow* state, and/or spontaneous knowledge. Reality design is a perpetual creative process in partnership with nature.

Through the *Optimizers,* we can determine the best channels through which to proceed at any moment in time within a universe of continuous change. Peak performance will not be achieved by defining a detailed vision, locking on to it and then proceeding linearly towards it. Things might have changed in relevant co-evolving systems. Without the *Optimizer* information, we'll miss the access to coincidences and quantum leaps which can take us nonlinearly and even spontaneously to our desired reality.

Link Reality Design to Growth

The quantum leap and growth technologies presented in the growth technology chapters are integral to both reality design and creation in the naturality paradigm. To be effective, each reality design needs to be a commitment to become the person who would have the desired goal reality. It is a commitment to reincarnating yourself as that person.

Since we are usually asking for a reality which is beyond the person we are now, effective reality design is therefore a commitment to growth. You conceive of yourself in a more evolved form and then become that person. Reality transforms accordingly.

Growth is the increasing expression of our authentic core. Growth locks into our system new, more adaptive, beliefs supportive of a more expanded expression of our naturality. Beliefs are the storage units for information in our system. Growth is the progressive change of beliefs.

Growth is about changing the information infrastructure of our system. There is no growth without a change in beliefs. Reality creation also requires a change in beliefs. New beliefs mean you will be creating your reality differently. Reality design, then, is the process of generating a new set of beliefs in order to create a more adaptive reality.

Reincarnation is a belief engineering technique designed to trigger a quantum leap in growth and creation. You can design your next preferred reality and then reincarnate yourself as the person with that reality. You then begin operating as that person until reality reflects that new identity.

Simply redesign yourself now, this moment, and begin to walk around as this person. Cease and desist all linear connection to the person you were before. Try it. Identity is really just a packet of integrated beliefs which can quickly instruct reality creation. As you will learn in the next chapter, choosing a new identity is an effective reality design technique. Reincarnation is the ultimate reality design / reality creation / growth tool.

To increase creation speed, reincarnate yourself first as a reality design and creation expert. If we don't have the beliefs we can design and create reality, then we won't have that capability. Next, reincarnate as the person with your goal reality. To accelerate this process, find someone who already has the reality you want and use clairsentience to absorb his or her emotional blueprint. This is a fast way to internalize your ideal next reality design.

Rather than just modeling others, assimilate. Wear their identity in order to internalize their emotion and belief structures. Quantum leap to recreate yourself without the flaws, limitations, or toxicity interfering with your new reality creation.

Decide on who you want to be and with what reality, and simply become that person. Operate as if it's true until it is true. In fact, assume you've had the desired reality for ten successful years. That way you can handle any new situations inherent in the new reality with the ease of experience.

Emotional blueprinting and reincarnation are two techniques for rapidly designing new realities without having to worry about the details. If you can *feel* the goal reality, you are already on the road to creating it. You will get better at these with practice until eventually you are able to do them both within minutes. As you become more fluid in re-conceiving yourself and your reality, the desired realities will be created with increasing speed and precision.

> *"Your past is not your potential. In any hour you can choose to liberate the future."*
> Marilyn Ferguson

Think Nonlinear

Focusing on process in your reality design creates a reality requiring process. If you make the process the goal, the process will be what you experience. If you don't believe you can quantum leap directly to having the desired reality, guess what? You can't! If you believe every new reality must come by a set linear pattern of activities and events, guess what? All of those activities will be required.

And, what if your intelligence, as impressive as it is, did not even conceive of the fastest linear path to bring your desired reality into existence? You have limited the speed and perhaps the magnitude of your reality creation.

What if nature has a series of creative channels already in existence that you don't even know about which would bring your reality into existence much more quickly? Had you followed the *Optimizers* to collide with these pathways, you would have experienced coincidences that catapulted you to your goal in its currently imagined form or an even better re-conception of it.

In any form of reality design, you have the choice of using just your intelligence or capitalizing on nature's intelligence. Requiring process is just as restrictive to reality creation as requiring your reality to come through a single channel. As you experience successes and failures with reality creation, you will improve your reality design capabilities.

Again, the knowledge must be gained through experiential learning. There is unfortunately a limit to what I'm able to communicate to you as you start out. You must learn by doing and have your beliefs altered by that experience.

Let go of the concept that you and your reality must be linear extensions of the past. I think you'll be pleasantly surprised at what unrestricted reality design can create for you. With experience, you'll learn how to reality design in a way that capitalizes on the creative channels already in existence in nature and the inherent coincidences and quantum leaps that are possible.

The result will be quantum leap living – quantum growth with commensurate quantum changes in your reality. Chapter 17, *Quantum Leap Living*, will reveal more about "quantum leaping" as a way of life.

Use Your Blocks

Amateur materializers tend to let seemingly negative message events from reality erode their intention to have the emotional goals inherent in their reality design. The blocks are just as important as the flows in helping us to refine our emerging reality vision. They are a call to innovate, create, and experiment to try to find new and better channels to our goals. Trust your original emotional blueprint. This is pure communication from nature uncorrupted by the human mind. If you were passionate about it, the goal reality reflects your naturality.

Try not to let blocks deter you from your emotional goal. Any blocks or negative messages that might occur are merely to signify you are attempting to go down the wrong channel to achieve your emotional goals. Nature is saying there is a better or faster route. "Poll" with your resonance until you find it. If the blocks are "emotionally charged", then they are not "blocks" but "struggle events" created by conflicting beliefs. These are simply beliefs to be cleared in order to experience your new goal reality.

In the face of blocks, let yourself be the creative being you were born to be. If you have experienced a series of positive *Optimizers* in the pursuit of a goal reality in the past, trust them as confirmation you are on the right path. Don't dismiss all those flow events with the sudden appearance of a block. Nature is very consistent. Trust that nature is trying to help you to achieve your emotional goals. Change your route not your goal.

Ensure Clarity

Doubts, fears and conflicting beliefs can interfere with the clarity of our reality design and what it communicates to reality. You will also want to take stock that you have cleared all limiting beliefs and fear beliefs that might be invoked by the proposed new reality. You'll want to make certain your powerless reflex and judged-judging reflex are also in check when you sit down to design your next reality. These will erode any vision by sending mixed messages to reality.

Blueprinting and emotion-based visualization need to be done with full power and consistency for effective reality design. Every time we doubt we can have the desired reality, it's as if a part of the instructions we have been giving reality have been rubbed out. Vacillation is the enemy of effective reality creation. Emotion is the catalyst. Expert reality creators are excellent emotional engineers. They can quickly energize reality designs with the emotional harmonic that will change their beliefs to change their reality.

If there are people in your reality who fear your goal or are afraid for you, they are simply reflections of your own fears. Use the information to clear those fear beliefs. Further, if you encounter individuals who are hostile, check to see if you are conflicted about your goal. Resolve your conflicting beliefs to remove the conflict from your reality. Reality is your friend. It is a benevolent *Optimizer*. Listen to its event messages and adjust your system. Reality is a perfect feedback system so you know precisely what is in your belief blueprint. You can then quickly change it to adjust reality.

Clear "New Goal" Struggle Events

I've mentioned the problem of *new-goal syndrome* before. But, since every reality design is, in effect, a new goal, it belongs in a discussion of design speed and proficiency. Each time we commit to a new reality design, all relevant beliefs in our belief blueprints are activated and neutrally begin to send instructions to reality.

All of a sudden, we may find ourselves facing a number of struggle events getting in the way of our creating our goal reality. This is because new goals may activate beliefs you haven't used for awhile and therefore may not know are maladaptive for you. Or maybe they only become maladaptive as you commit to a new goal reality . . .

Struggle events are caused by conflicting beliefs creating conflicting forces in reality. Problem events in our realities immediately after committing to a new reality design simply tell us what beliefs need to be cleaned up in order to have the desired new reality. As with blocks, it's important not to abandon your reality design in the face of struggle events. Rather, take the time to resolve the conflicting beliefs impeding your progress. Accept this as part of the reality design process.

Over time, the gradual elimination of conflicting beliefs in your belief blueprint will remove struggle events from your experience. You may not yet be fluid enough to do this overnight. However, if you don't begin the process, you'll definitely never create a struggle-free life.

Simply keep determining what conflicting belief pairs had to exist to create each struggle event that occurs in your reality and then just will yourself to believe the most adaptive side of the conflict. When your new belief is clear and strong enough, the struggle event will simply disappear. Problem people who are created by the conflicting beliefs will simply restructure before your eyes or disappear from your life.

Expand your Consciousness

Expanded consciousness is the natural outcome of using the peak evolution science. However, it is also the means to enhance reality design speed and efficiency. Expanded vision allows us to see many more of nature's patterns and themes. This gives us the opportunity to better align our reality designs with the naturality flow. As a result, adaptive realities will come into existence much more quickly and powerfully.

Establish Standing Reality Designs

What are the permanent changes you want in all your realities? What beliefs would you have to have to bring them into existence? As you start to own your reality and systematically design the various parts of your life, you can short-form reality creation by having standing *rules* or reality designs as the consistent foundation of your reality design process. Then you only have to concentrate on the new territories of endeavor or new areas you are *renovating.*

Even though reality may continually take new forms, you'll gradually have developed some standing instructions for much of it. What your family life will feel like. What your work life will feel like. How your world will treat you. How fast you will grow. How fast your financial excess will increase. What emotions you expect to feel generally. What kind of clients you want. Your relationship with your significant other. Your health.

As a result, the portions requiring reality design on an ongoing basis will diminish. The "canvas" holding your reality will become more stable. I encourage you to define these standing beliefs as soon as you're ready to allow yourself to move to a simpler life around your naturality.

Improve Reality Design through Reality Creation Expertise

All aspects of the naturality paradigm are integrated because nature and indeed the universe are integrated. Therefore, as you learn each part of the paradigm, you will be able to deduce or extrapolate the other parts. They will always make sense. Learning in one area of the paradigm will always contribute to the enhancement of your knowledge of other parts of the paradigm.

As you gain experience with the reality creation technology, the way in which you will do reality design will change to capitalize on that experience. Mastering the reality creation technology, for example, changes your beliefs about how reality can be created and therefore how you can instruct reality through the reality design process. Because you experience reality responding in a certain way, you will know you can design differently.

Experimentation to see how reality responds to various designs is required to develop reality design expertise. The result will be greater speed and accuracy in reality creation. Eventually, with experience and expertise, reality design, reality creation, and growth will become inseparable. They will merge. I can't tell you all of the ways this will occur just yet because they must be absorbed experientially. In addition, you would need the growth technology knowledge and experience from the final four chapters to see how it all comes together.

Reality design will coincide with reality creation once you have internalized the requisite new beliefs about your personal ability to create realities. What does this mean? Let's say there is a specific reality you want to bring into existence. When your expertise increases, as soon as you conceive of the desired reality, your beliefs that you can create any reality are activated and a reality of you being able to create realities emerges. Your specific goal reality can then come into existence within this context.

If you have enough experience of being able to create reality at will to have internalized very strong beliefs about your capabilities, you'll find very little separation in time between the conception of the new reality and your experiencing of it. Reality design and reality creation will become a single action.

If you reread this chapter a year from now, it would convey very different information since you would have been transformed by seeing reality creation in action. For example, as you see the prevalence of coincidences, you can start to take the nonlinear advances of quantum leaps into consideration. With experience, you can get a feel for when they will occur and factor them into your reality designs.

Not only do you improve, then, as a reality designer, but the whole process of reality design shifts as you become an evolved reality creator. Consequently, what you read in this chapter as a novice will be very different from what you will read after a year of experimenting with the reality creation technology. You don't just get better at the design process, the design process actually changes as you evolve.

Master your Creation Anxiety

Every time we generate a new reality design, we create a gap between current reality and our preferred future reality. Until we become the creative beings we were designed to be, this reality gap is a quagmire of creation anxiety ready to sabotage any new reality design. The reality gap is where we will find our anxieties and fears associated with change, ambiguity, and dealing with the unknowable and the unknown.

However, this gap is actually the center of our greatest power as we master reality creation as a way of life. Human beings are designed for creation and creativity, growth, change and learning. Some of our most significant emotional highs are associated with these kinds of activities. As a result, they are designed to become beneficially addicting. These innate drives are the reason for man's successful adaptation to his environment. Embracing them is pivotal to our optimization and peak evolution.

Therefore, to ensure uncompromised reality design, reincarnate as an expert in creativity, growth and change. Become a person who can traverse any reality gap effortlessly – a person who actually thrives on reality gaps. Reincarnate as a person who loves the highs of creativity, growth and learning.

This is highly adaptive since our individual and collective evolution is towards creativity around our naturality and *art*. Why not consciously and proactively align with nature and redefine yourself in a way that optimizes? *Know* that you are developing numerous new capabilities through the peak evolution science which will allow you to traverse the reality gap effortlessly.

Creativity expertise makes an excellent solution since it also eliminates fear and powerlessness. One of the fastest ways I know to take an individual out of a tailspin is through having them take immediate action to creatively express their identity – in other words, to do their *art*. When you feel the fears and powerlessness of the reality gap interfering with what you're willing to incorporate into your reality design, take creative action, particularly around your *art*. It'll not only strengthen and optimize you but will addict you to taking more steps.

At some point, while doing what you love, *flow* state will emerge, and flow events and coincidences will catapult you forward, and then, all of a sudden, you're through the gap and experiencing the new reality.

Since the peak evolution science is designed to take you to your highest creative expression, you're likely already beginning to make creativity a habit. Creation and creativity, growth, change and learning are all inherent in the expansion of your authentic core. Each new gap can be set up to trigger a conditioned reflex to stimulate the enervating biochemical changes of excitement. Therefore, over time, creation anxiety challenges to reality design speed and effectiveness will diminish.

Reality Design Progression

Reality design is an interactive visioning process in partnership with the information from nature's *Optimizers*. For a peak evolution science novice, reality design is usually just a commitment to create a symbol or an event – a certain amount of money, a coveted job title, or a specific goal, for example. These are symbols for emotional goals. Reality design for the novice is the creation of an emotional harmonic in order to cause the necessary belief changes for bringing a desired new reality into existence.

As we "visit" every part of our reality to identify our goals, the separate goals will become interlinked into a complete design for our total reality. If each goal reflects our naturality and our naturality is the natural integrated core of our system, then our separate reality designs cannot help but ultimately merge. Our reality will merge to alignment with our naturality. A new theme of simplicity prevails.

It's impossible to use the reality creation technology or, indeed, any part of the peak evolution science, without the *Optimizers* drawing us into alignment with our natural core. Once into alignment, adaptive realities are created automatically. We won't even need to know the details of a reality design in order to bring it into existence expeditiously. We need only stay in the present to take action on the *Optimizer* messages as they occur.

Our natural growth path is not linear. Rather, it is our continual expansion, by concentric circles, around our authentic core. The result is an increase in our creations – our impact on the world. As we come into alignment with our naturality, our natural growth path itself becomes our direction and draws the ideal contexts for our continued development. Our natural growth path automatically becomes our reality design.

Naturality automatically creates a reality supportive of naturality. We enter *flow* within the naturality flow. We achieve naturality within the naturality flow. Our natural drives align with nature's drives. We shift into overdrive. In this state of congruence inside and outside of us, we are accelerated to peak evolution.

For peak evolution science experts, the ultimate goal reality is dynamic without end. It is a state of being – an active state of peak performance, peak growth, peak creation, peak rewards, peak experience, and peak evolution. It is a state of pure creative expression of increasing naturality. It is pure creativity. The dynamic goal reality requires no specific form or outcome since the desired emotional blueprint can be achieved creatively in an infinite number of ways as determined by the naturality flow.

All that exists is the altered consciousness of our deepest *flow* states resulting from operating precisely in the present to action the signals from the naturality flow. It is personal *flow* embedded within universal flow. It is nondual consciousness in which the observer and the observed are no longer separate. Our separate identity ceases to exist. Reality design ceases to be a conscious act and merges into the dynamic of universal unity consciousness.

> *"Your real self is identical to the ultimate Energy of which all things in the universe are a manifestation."*   Ken Wilber

13

THE POWER OF IDENTITY

"I have often thought that the best way to define a man's character would be to seek out the particular mental or moral attitude in which, when it came upon him, he felt himself most deeply and intensively active and alive. At such moments, there is voice inside that speaks and says, This is the real me." [33]   William James

True power is the ability to create what you want when you want it. This is also the definition of abundance, freedom, and reality creation expertise. The reality creation technology empowers us to become laser-sharp instruments for emitting precise instructions for creating realities.

Identity is a reality creation power tool for quickly transforming massive parts of our belief blueprint, and hence our reality. Identity is essentially a belief engineering tool because it's a shorthand vehicle for conveying a large system of integrated beliefs. Beliefs themselves are storage units for locking information into our system. An identity, then, simply aggregates synergistic information for internalization into our system.

Three Kinds of Identity Power

There are three categories of identity power in the naturality paradigm: *extended identity, natural identity,* and *expressed identity.* Each has a contribution to make in enhancing our expertise as a reality creator.

Our *natural identity* is, of course, dictated by nature. It is the result of generations of information which emerged in our systems over time as creative solutions to optimization challenges. This is our naturality – a set of stable information storage beliefs at our core which glue the components of our system together. Naturality is the shared information database of our system. As beliefs, our natural identities are always instructing reality creation.

While nature determines our natural identity, we choose our *expressed identities*. When used adaptively, they are the channels we select at any point in time for expressing our natural identity. In a paradigm in which beliefs create reality, an expressed identity is a belief engineering technique for causing massive changes to ourselves and, hence, our realities. For peak performance, the trick is to choose your expressed identities in sync with your natural identity. This will give us incredible power and precision in our reality creation endeavors. Our realities can then change by quantum leaps rather than by a gradual evolution.

EXTENDED IDENTITY

The fundamental belief of the reality creation technology is that beliefs create reality. Our realities then are 100% self-created by us and therefore can be changed by us. Our bodies are also a materialization of our beliefs. There is no difference between our body and our reality. Both are created by our belief blueprints. Both are therefore part of the same system. Our identities then, either natural or expressed, extend throughout our entire system, including reality. They are not just contained within our bodies. This is our *extended identity*.

Most of us have been brought up to believe we are separate from the people and things in our realities. As children, we are actually born at one with everything in our consciousness. We must be systematically taught separation.

The reality creation technology and, indeed, all of the peak evolution science are designed to restore us to our natural state. They will give you a way to demonstrate to yourself that we and our realities are one and then enable you to capitalize on this. Internalizing this extended identity gives us the basis to transform the human experience.

NATURAL IDENTITY OR NATURALITY

Every system has an "attractor" of some sort which holds the components of the system together. This uniqueness or "identity" is what distinguishes a system from its environment and other systems. From an evolutionary perspective, variations among members of a species or within a category of systems are beneficial. In the event of an environmental change, there's a greater chance that at least some members might be suited to the new environment. Distinctness of a system may also improve its competitiveness for resources.

Our natural identity is the attractor holding the components of our system together. It is based on the application, function or purpose that caused our system to emerge in the first place as a solution to optimization challenges for other systems. Naturality is the fundamental glue for our personal system. The attractor evolves as the rest of the system evolves or as new parts are added.

Our authentic natural identity is a set of beliefs representing the historical evolution of our system at any point in time. It is an evolving set of rules, a formula, or an algorithm defining the center of our system at a given moment. Our personal system is dynamic and fluid. Therefore, so is our natural identity.

Our natural identity is the sum total of thousands of creative adaptations to changing environments we and our ancestors have generated in order for our system to optimize, survive and thrive. Through the transmission of genetic, cultural and probably electromagnetic information, our personal system represents a long history of multi-generation creative solutions to resolve optimization challenges in the changing contexts of our existence.

Unless we've been cloned, each of us has our own unique genetic makeup and hence our own unique natural identity. Between beliefs and genes, we each contain unique information. Sometimes our natural identity can be described in words. More often than not, it is just a natural "feeling" when you are behaving in a certain way that causes your whole "system" to harmonize and feel right.

Emotions convey information to our consciousness. Our natural identity is a feeling state – an emotion of naturalness or naturality at the center of our being. It is an inner knowing that we are being true to the person we are with each action we take.

Our authentic identity is about the truth of our being. Our essence. Our original concept. Our current information structure. Our natural identity is an "inner knowing" that something is "you." We all know when we are being natural. We know when we're doing our *art* – the thing we do best and which is the highest creative expression of who we truly are. We know when something is meaningful to us. Meaning and passion. These are elements that help us to recognize our natural identity or naturality.

Our natural identity is not a static state in the normal sense. However, the feeling state of naturalness is the same and consistent even though our personal system is evolving at a rapid pace. This is similar to the constancy of being in the eye of a tornado where everything is perpetually calm despite horrific swirling winds surrounding the center.

Our intellects are not developed enough to keep us aligned with a naturality that must continuously adjust to changing contexts. We need nature's *Optimizers* to reintegrate us with the naturality flow. Only the naturality flow can lock us into the calm bull's-eye constancy possible at the center of our system as it perpetually re-optimizes.

As you release yourself to being natural and following your resonance, you may be able to begin to put some words around that naturality based on the historical pattern of your experiences of it.

For others, your essence may be difficult to capture in language. Let that be alright. Some part of you always knows what is and isn't "you." No need to wait until you have a word identifier before you express the "real you." Alignment with our naturality emerges by choosing moment by moment the natural expression of yourself.

THE POWER OF YOUR NATURAL IDENTITY

It might be advantageous to take stock of some of the power and benefits of our natural identities. Naturality is the only foundation on which to build for growth to our highest potential. This is because natural forces support the natural expression of each person's system. Increasing the expression of our natural identity is our fundamental life purpose. Our naturality engine drives the creative adaptiveness of our re-optimization process that is responsible for the survival of our system.

Naturality is the vehicle for having a number of powerful natural forces accelerate our progress to creating desired and adaptive realities. As our naturality expands, so does what we create to express that naturality.

Those creations then reinforce and expand our naturality further. There is an endless conversation between naturality and its expression that demonstrates why our most evolved state is pure creativity. Naturality is only known by its expression. Authentic expression strengthens naturality. This iterative process perpetually expands the envelope of the potential of our system. This leads to peak evolution.

The creative expressions of our naturality provide the healthy contexts that make it possible for our system to evolve to new potential. The underlying theme of human existence presented in the growth technology chapters is an iterative process of self-creation then creation, or self-growth then creation-growth. We expand our naturality and then create at that new level of strength.

Those creations in turn strengthen our naturality so we can increase our impact on the realities we will experience. When our lives are aligned with this simple theme, we have the formula for peak evolution. Our internal drives and the drives of the naturality flow merge to pull us beyond peak performance to new states of being.

Automatic Creation of Adaptive Realities

Beliefs are the information storage units of our system. Like all beliefs, our authentic identity beliefs drive reality creation. The automatic creation of adaptive realities was discussed in the previous chapter as the ultimate goal. When we live in alignment with our naturality, we can only emit the pure instructions for reality creation based on that authentic core. There are no conflicting identities or beliefs to interfere with it. This is the power of our natural identity for reality creation.

If only naturality is instructing reality creation, then reality will perfectly reflect, support and reinforce that naturality. Reality will be adaptive. This is part of the increased functionality that is possible for human beings.

If we can align with the naturality flow and our naturality, we will ultimately no longer need to consciously design and create our realities.

They will automatically be adaptive for increasing expressions of our naturality. Once the peak evolution science has enabled the transition back to the naturality flow, it will no longer be necessary.

Getting to this state, however, is the challenge addressed in *Peak Evolution*. How do we stop interfering with the pure instructions from our natural identity? How do we move into alignment with our naturality? In the reality creation technology chapters, we have examined the elimination of conflicting beliefs, fear beliefs, maladaptive beliefs, toxic beliefs, and both the powerlessness and judgment belief complexes. Now, we are going to look at not only eliminating interfering complexes of identity beliefs, but proactively amplifying the instructions from our natural identity through increased alignment.

To be someone other than your authentic self creates conflicting instructions to reality. Identities, as systems of beliefs, can also be in conflict. Conflicting beliefs create struggle events. Struggle events interfere with the precision and strength of reality creation, especially when they result in the *sandcastle syndrome* of creating, demolishing, creating, and so on, based on the alternating emissions from opposing beliefs.

Personal power is dissipated by having conflicting beliefs since the power invested in one belief is undermined by power invested in the equal and opposite belief. Therefore, the only logical foundation on which to move to peak performance, peak experience and peak evolution is our authentic identity. Nature's *Optimizers* will help us achieve that state if we will let them.

New Peak Performance Levels

Individuals move to a new realm of performance when they are aligned with their naturality in the naturality paradigm. A metaphor that depicts this is the use of a car for something other than transportation as compared to being well tuned and used for transportation.

When the car system is used for the function for which it was designed, there is a leap in performance. You will know when you hit your "naturality groove." The same leap in performance occurs when we achieve alignment and are suddenly sending pure adaptive instructions to reality.

Adaptive realities are created automatically. Coincidences and flow events increase promoting growth, creation, learning and progress. Creativity increases. Spontaneous knowledge increases. Naturality is the formula for experiencing whole systems of new knowledge entering into our thought processes.

An individual's active intelligence is observably augmented. Growth accelerates. Emotional highs increase. Humanitarian urges to service emerge. The magnitude, complexity, importance, and contribution of creations increase. Consciousness expands enhancing our perspectives on everything.

More Meaningful Messages from Reality

Not only does our naturality increase our power to create a desired reality quickly, but the resulting adaptive reality will reinforce and strengthen our naturality. The increased order of a reality reflective of our naturality will also be more useful to us for creating better future realities.

The purity of instructions from our naturality signature results in every event in our reality becoming a meaningful message for when and how to grow and in which direction to move. All events in our reality become meaningful messages to facilitate our progress.

In alignment, the patterns and themes of adaptive messages indicating the naturality flow are much easier to identify. As a result, we can grow or progress to our emotional goals much more quickly. With the help of the peak evolution science, a series of quantum leaps will stimulate alignment which will transform and evolve us and our capabilities. These are discussed in the quantum leap chapter.

Greater Contribution to Humanity

As we come into alignment with our naturality, we will automatically become very humanitarian. Very philanthropic. Very oriented to service. Very interested in helping the human race evolve. It just happens. It doesn't need to be pursued. Discipline is not required. It seems to be inherent in the human system as part of the optimization instincts in individuals and the race.

Our seemingly selfish needs for pursuing our creative expression begin to focus on serving mankind. Simultaneously, our ability to contribute to the world increases significantly. Monumental contributions to mankind may suddenly be possible for individuals who would have been considered ordinary in the past.

If everyone is doing their art and is supported by nature in doing it, it follows they would be doing their best work. Therefore, they are making their greatest contribution to the world. When the benefits to all of us of this approach are understood, civilization as we know it will be transformed. It will be based on supporting the highest authentic expression of its constituents. There will be world freedom based on individual freedom.

Surprisingly, it seems that human beings are intrinsically good. Misalignment with our naturality seems to be a prominent factor in our appearing otherwise. Perhaps it is the balance that comes from meeting our emotional goals regularly when in alignment that is the key. Another factor could be the oneness with the world and humanity that spontaneously emerges through expanded consciousness. As you master the peak evolution science, you will automatically be moving down a path to which many religions and spiritual disciplines have been trying to direct us.

> *"Too many of us hope and work in a vague sort of way for a better world without first coming to terms with ourselves. And yet what is most deeply wrong with the world is often but a reflection of what is most inwardly wrong with each of us."*
> Source Unknown

AMPLIFYING YOUR NATURALITY

With all these benefits available from expressing our natural identity, we'll want to learn how to amplify it. We can start by linking into the naturality flow. Nature is always trying to optimize us to increasing naturality. Therefore, proactively assisting this process is advantageous. This is the intent of the peak evolution science and thus is the subject of the entire book. Accordingly, I will overview briefly some of the ways for amplifying our naturality here.

Identify your Naturality

While naturality is "the emotion of naturalness," there are some things we can do to increase our familiarity with it. Inventory what you know about your naturality and where it has been evolving. Here are some exercises to help you learn more about your natural identity and to detect the direction in which it is progressing.

Total Gratification Exercise

Most people have some goals they have been pursuing for some time . . . money, a job title, contribution, or success in some form. Imagine you've already achieved your goals and achieved them a hundredfold beyond what you were striving for. If your goal was money, for example, assume you have a guaranteed income of a million dollars a year for the rest of your life.

As a result, picture yourself doing all of the things you would do immediately upon learning this. Perhaps you would take some time off and take your family around the world. Perhaps you would spend time buying everything you've always wanted to own . . . . a certain kind of house, recreational property, cars and other vehicles, electronic gadgetry . . . . If your goal was contribution, picture you have already done monumental things to change the world which would satisfy most people with respect to their lifetime achievement.

Now picture yourself relaxing on a beach for a couple of months with nothing to do, having gratified whatever goals you have had in the past. In that state of satiation, abundance, and relaxation, what do you then choose to do? When you get the answer to that question, what you are likely looking at is your naturality and its expression, your *art*. These are actually the same thing since naturality is an active state known by its expression.

The Amnesia Test

Assume you have lost your memory and are dropped into a foreign country. What is it that you want to do? Assume you have more money than you know what to do with, so it is not an issue. What would you choose to do? Consider a number of possible catch-phrases for you to "wear" to describe your identity. "Wear" them for a week or two to see which ones fit. Try them out on your friends or family. By trial and error, you could discover some words to give form to the ambiguity of naturality. This exercise again will give you insight into your natural identity.

Childhood Talents

You can also look back to your childhood before your identity had been interfered with. You were probably more authentic and natural as a child. Think about the categories of things you liked to do as a child. Extrapolate those categories or themes into your adult world.

Things You Love to Do

Is there a recurring theme or common pattern that exists in all of the things you love to do? Your *"art"* is the natural creative expression of your naturality. It is that thing or category of things you love to do and are naturally good at. Other people might think of your *art* as work if they had to do it, but for you, doing your *art* is its own reward. You would put in long hours of work for no pay in order to do it. It is something you would describe as *"the effortless effort."*

You continually seek opportunities to do it. You have undoubtedly enjoyed doing your *art* since you were a small child. If you can't determine what it is, think back to your childhood and look for the common themes among the things you enjoyed doing.

Even though I call it your *"art,"* it is not necessarily artistic. For some people, their *art* might be their gift for parenting or building relationships or teaching. These are not occupations but rather natural talents and desires which can then be applied to creating what is meaningful to your system.

Your creations are a form of self-expression. You know who you are by your creations. Your creations also reinforce who you are. Your creations serve to facilitate self-expression, self-knowledge, and self-Creation. What you choose to create also tells you what is meaningful to you.

> *"The truth is that all of us attain the greatest success and happiness possible in this life whenever we use our native capacities to their greatest extent."* Smiley Blanton, psychiatrist

Fantasies

Take your fantasies and day dreams seriously. They likely hold clues to the "true you" as well. They are telling you your passions – a sure sign of your naturality. Look for consistent themes in your passions. Wherever you experience or think about doing things that generate positive emotional states, you are likely being shown your naturality.

Patterns of Blocks and Flows

You'll be surprised by the tremendous orderliness of nature continuously trying to optimize your system. The swirl of *Optimizer* messages attempting to align you over a lifetime with your naturality is unmistakable when you know what to look for. Are there common themes that suggest the direction that optimizing forces are attempting to take you to increase the expression of your natural identity?

Review the high points in your life right back to childhood. Look at the pattern of blocks and flows over your lifetime. You'll find strong flow events around activities representing your naturality. You can know your naturality by this pattern of flow events. You can therefore have some reasoned foundation from which to select categories of activities for the future. As you do those activities, they will reinforce your naturality.

What is Meaningful

If you have some overriding purpose you've been pursuing in your life, you can deduce your identity from that. Alternatively, you may see patterns and themes in the meaningful events and activities of your life. What you choose to create can tell you what is meaningful to you. You would not be excited about a creation that isn't meaningful to you. And what you are excited about reflects your naturality.

If you simply begin to operate with your resonance moment by moment, in no time at all you'll find yourself only doing things that are meaningful and natural to you. The resulting patterns and themes will define your natural identity.

Meaning is a reflection of the authentic core of each human system. Naturality is an active state. There is no evidence of naturality without expression. It is an expression that changes your world in some way. Our naturality can therefore be detected by our primal drives to take action. I often give executives, not yet in alignment with their naturality, noble causes to pursue with which they resonate in order to trigger that alignment. The cause generates creations reflective of their authentic identity which, in turn, strengthen it.

Whenever I ascribe the right core identity to individuals, they will almost blossom before my eyes. It's as if they are receiving nourishment they have been deprived of. It is reminiscent of the revival of a wilted plant suddenly watered. The feeling is definitely one of "aha!" But it's also a feeling of being home again . . . . at last.

This will happen at each stage of the unfolding of your naturality throughout your growth. The common thread remains the same but the nuances and distinctions and dimensions that enfold the thread transform.

As you commit to going forward as the "authentic you," look for events in your reality which reinforce and confirm. At the same time, you'll want to protect your new naturality from events in reality that contradict your identity. These may be leftovers from previous instructions the "old you" sent reality.

> *"To do good things in the world, first you must know who you are and what gives meaning in your life."*
> Paula P. Brownlee

Naturality Increases Naturality

Each time we do activities consistent with our naturality, we strengthen it. The more we use our naturality, the stronger it gets. Accordingly, it's a good idea to check in with your resonance periodically through the day to determine if you're doing activities in sync with the natural you. Are you doing things you are enthusiastic about or that you have an inner knowing are the right things for you right now?

Naturality results from being, every moment, the person you truly are. The "true you." That core set of beliefs that is "you." That information database that is "you." This is the only foundation on which to achieve your full potential. This is the only way to turn yourself up to your full possible volume – your full strength of character. In order to become authentic, you simply need to begin. This moment. Then the next moment and the next. All of a sudden, you'll find you're not only living authentically but have become addicted to it. Before long, you won't be able to do "unnatural" things even if they are things you've tolerated for years. Ask yourself periodically, "Does this activity feel natural or not?"

Identity-Affirming Creation

Identity grows with its expression and shrinks with disuse. Naturality must be expressed to increase. Creations that are the product of your naturality will strengthen your naturality. The more you use the reality creation technology to create adaptive realities, the more those realities will reinforce your naturality. The more actions you take to do your *art*, the stronger your natural identity will become. And, the stronger your natural identity, the larger or more significant your creations in reality.

Let's say you're at identity level 1 and generate a level 1 creation in your reality. If you're really proud of your performance, that creation will reinforce your identity. Looking at a creation you are passionate about is the same as looking at your naturality. Naturality is only known by its expression.

That strengthened identity will then be available to generate a more powerful creation than the first one. Identity level 2 will enable a level 2 creation. And so on, back and forth. This is an iterative process where creation and identity feed off of each other. Simply by strengthening your identity – growing – you can enhance what you create. Growth and creation are linked. The theme of human existence in the naturality paradigm is self-creation/creation or self-growth/creation-growth.

When I have clients who are very restricted in the expression of their naturality, I try to find some way, in their current context, for them to do their *art*. I can begin to normalize and then optimize each person's system if I can get it doing activities for which it was designed. This may take some creativity since many feel they have no freedom to do anything differently.

Find charity work if you have to in order to begin to express your naturality. Try to find a way to do your *art* from where you are in your life right now rather than having the disruption of starting all over in a new context.

We want to kick-start this iterative process of strengthening your naturality signature by creations reflective of it. We want to start a cycle of creation, identity reinforcement, creation, identity reinforcement, and so on. When your naturality is strong enough, it will automatically create a more adaptive reality for you through coincidences and flow events.

As you change, reality will change. One more word of advice as you set out to increase your naturality through your creations . . . . Give yourself permission to be "you" at all times. To help you do this, give yourself and others *unconditional acceptance*. Release judgment in all its forms. This will disarm fears you may have about taking action.

Resonance

By far the most powerful tool for amplifying our naturality is to operate strictly in the present with our resonance. To develop this new habit, start by checking in with your resonance at each decision point of your day to choose your next activity. If you find you are operating in sync with your resonance each moment, you are in alignment. Over time, your life will align with your naturality and all of the benefits of living in the naturality paradigm will accrue.

Release "Un-Naturality"

Another approach to amplifying your naturality is to cease and desist doing unnatural acts. Give yourself permission. Often we adopt inauthentic behavior in order to avoid states which we fear; or that have negative emotions attached; or to achieve positive emotional states.

For example, we might become the person someone else wants us to be because we are afraid they will abandon us if we don't. We want to "please" in order to avoid loss or separation. Or we might do it because we hope to get the positive emotional states of being loved, valued, admired, respected, and so on. Avoid those people who believe you to be someone else until you are on firm ground in your transition to naturality. It's time to choose naturality.

The Leap from Externally Referenced to Internally Referenced

If we are internally referenced, *we* create our realities. If we are externally referenced, our realities create us. Most of us are trained from childhood to be externally referenced – to take our identities and our other beliefs from outside of us. Rather, to achieve the full power of identity, we will want to move inside to listen to our own resonance and naturality.

To be externally referenced, we would decide who we were, or what to think of ourselves, or how to feel, or what actions to take based on the opinions of others or based on symbols or events external to us. Letting your identity be determined by how much money you have or by what others call you are examples of being externally referenced.

An externally referenced identity is a "borrowed identity" based on the people, things and events in your reality. Externally referenced power is "borrowed power." If your power is given to you by something or someone outside of you, it is transient. If power is based on money or possessions or position, these things can be lost. Your identity and power will also be lost as a result.

Internally referenced means you are expressing the "true you," from the inside out, regardless of reality's reaction. It is your true authentic identity. It is about listening to your inner voice or your own drum. Alignment with your naturality happens at the moment you become internally referenced. Therefore, becoming internally referenced moment after moment after moment is the formula for living a life in alignment with naturality.

If you're externally referenced, you are simply whatever reality creates you to be at any moment in time. You won't have the power of a clear identity emitting pure instructions to reality. Here's a way to look at the problem. Imagine you're emitting a single beam of light with instructions to reality.

Now imagine you're a leaf being swirled around endlessly by rapids on a river and try to emit the beam-of-light instructions. This light stream of instructions is now being emitted in all different directions as a result of your being buffeted about. Chunks of all sorts of realities are springing up all over the place and, just as rapidly, disappearing. In other words, *sandcastle syndrome.*

If multiple identities and conflicting beliefs are creating your reality, then your power will be dissipated by its division. You won't have your full force working to create your new desired reality. The moment you become internally referenced is the moment your power over what you'll experience increases dramatically. It "quantum leaps." When you become internally referenced, you allow your well-ordered and integrated core identity beliefs to send clear, concise instructions to your reality to create what is absolutely reflective of the true you. As a result, you'll find that physical materialization of your goals becomes rapid and effortless.

Flow is Pure Naturality

A life of endless *flow* state is the ultimate goal for every human. *Flow* is the "effortless effort of excellence." It is not only a state of pure naturality but also of peak performance. It is an egoless state of oneness with the activity at hand. In the naturality paradigm, the formula for partnering with the *Optimizers* to align with naturality is also the formula for living your life in *flow*.

Each time we experience *flow*, we strengthen our natural identity and increase our chances of experiencing *flow* more often. Again, *flow* increases *flow*, in the same way that naturality increases naturality. Our natural state is highly addictive. Spend a few weeks in your "naturality groove" and you may not be able to tolerate life any other way.

Growth Addiction

Growth, by definition, means amplification of naturality. Our natural growth path is best represented by ever-enlarging concentric circles expanding out around our authentic core. We are designed for growth. If the growth technology chapters provide you with enough information to make you a growth expert, it won't be long until you are also a growth addict. Succumbing to your innate growth addiction is an effortless way to increase your naturality.

A Word of Caution

While you go through this amplification process, you'll want to be a little protective of yourself since you know how reality operates. You'll want to avoid those circumstances where you often feel powerless. Or you might have people who want to hold you in other identities than this natural authentic person you are trying to nurture.

Therefore, you may also want to avoid them for awhile. The body is so at home when you hit your "naturality groove" you won't want to come out of it. You will become addicted to this natural state. Once this happens, you can move into problem territories with less fear. Take the time to build up your resistance strength.

An Example of Reality Creation with Natural Identity

Paul is a tremendously creative individual with a talent for synthesizing large amounts of market information into corporate identities and brands. His mind tends to think expansively, holistically and strategically. He loves business. He has an intuitive ability to embrace the preferences of the masses. What Paul liked to do was to create identities and brands for significant corporations and to design how these would be expressed out into the marketplace. Paul had an incredible gift for this.

When I started to work with him, he was running a consulting firm. This was not ideal for Paul's talents. Since the firm also had financial problems, he was spending only a minute fraction of his time on his actual *art*. When we figured out what his identity and *art* were, Paul said, "If this is my *art*, then I want to work on the most significant and challenging projects in the world in which I can do my *art*." And I want to begin doing these projects now. I don't want to progress linearly to gradually build a reputation so I can get this kind of work."

We spent some time making a list of companies he would like to develop new identities for. One of the largest companies in the world caught his attention. Creativity and spontaneous knowledge bubbled up inside of him. This was a significant flow event telling us we were on nature's optimizing path to his naturality.

Within a week, Paul was on a plane to see the company to tell them his ideas. The company's president was enthralled with both the ideas and the creative mind that had generated them. Over the next few months the president persuaded his executives, the board of directors, and subsidiaries they should contract Paul and implement his ideas.

While this was proceeding internally within the potential client company, the market opportunity Paul had created leaked out into the marketplace. The top consulting firms in the world began to arrive to compete against Paul. A New York consulting firm seemed to come up with the ideal solution. They decided to buy Paul's firm for a few million dollars paid over a few years. Within a short time an even larger firm bought the New York firm that had bought Paul. Paul had not even closed the deal yet with the client and he was already a wealthy man. In addition, the big company had all of the connections to keep him in exactly the kind of projects he wanted without him having to build up a reputation.

Despite a terrible case of nerves and self-esteem issues in the face of massive competition and a reality more successful than he was ready for, Paul did eventually close the pieces of the business that he particularly wanted. When the job was completed, he set about to repeat the process with a slight change to his wish list.

This time he wanted the projects to come from particular countries to allow him to travel to the places in the world he always wanted to see. One after the next, corporate identity projects arose in order of priority for the countries he wanted to visit. The adaptive realities were created automatically in response to someone who now, with good reason, believed he was a reality creation expert.

THE POWER OF EXPRESSED IDENTITIES

"We must be the change we wish to see in the world." Gandhi

Expressed identities are the specific packaging we choose to "wear" at any point in time surrounding our natural identity. If we choose an expressed identity correctly, it is the ideal channel for expressing our natural identity for a specific project or territory of our life. Each expressed identity represents an integrated set of beliefs.

There are two types of expressed identities – current and desired. If we *consciously* choose a desired identity, we can communicate specific changes to our reality. This is an effective belief engineering technique for causing extensive changes to our realities simply and easily. I call it *reincarnation*. Reincarnation is effectively a quantum leap from one identity-reality combination to another.

As the channel to express your natural identity and do your *art*, you may currently be a lawyer. However, your next desired reality for the expansion of your naturality (growth) may better be served by becoming a community leader through politics. You can use reincarnation to speed the change in your reality.

Consider another example. You may be both a mother and the president of a dot com company. These are both *current* expressions of your natural identity. If you internalize expressed identities of "Super Mom" and "President of the fastest-growing dotcom company in the next decade," you're using *desired* expressed identities to cause belief changes. Reality changes for these two segments of your life will result.

The "Natural Identity" - "Expressed Identity" Partnership

The historical evolution of our system and its components determines our natural identity. In other words, nature determines our natural identity. *We* determine our expressed identities. Since identities are packages of integrated beliefs and since beliefs create reality, both natural and expressed identities determine the instructions creating our realities. To go to full power, then, we will want to choose expressed identities that support our naturality identity.

Over time, you'll come to be able to read nature's *Optimizers* sufficiently to be able to predict, with a fair degree of accuracy, in which direction nature will be attempting to optimize you. Knowing the direction of the naturality flow for your system is advantageous for both choosing the realities you want to create and actually creating them. With practice, then, you'll be able to routinely benefit from the cumulative power of bonding adaptive expressed identities with your natural identity.

We are often pressured to be someone we are not. As a result, we may have one or more expressed identities which may or may not support our natural identity. Consequently, we may find ourselves with massive beliefs from multiple identities emitting conflicting instructions to create our realities. This results in a big mess in your reality.

It is difficult to see the patterns of nature's *Optimizers*. This is a key reason why it appears we don't have control over the realities we experience. Like a leaf in a pool of eddies, we are buffeted about in every direction. Your natural identity could be creating one reality and your expressed identities could completely wipe it out – a classic case of *sandcastle syndrome*.

The ideal situation for accurate materialization, then, is to choose expressed identities that work in harmony with our natural identity. Choosing a desired expressed identity is a reality design for massive changes to your reality. With a word or a brief epithet, numerous belief changes can be communicated to our belief blueprint and from there to our reality. Let me give you a feel for the power of identity for reality creation.

Expressed Identity Test Drive

Take a few moments to "wear" each of these expressed identities emotionally. While you're doing so, think about how many instructions or belief changes I've been able to communicate to you if I asked you to reincarnate as the following while still remaining true to your naturality.

1. *A world leader in your field for the last 10 years*
2. *A Nobel Prize winner - the peace prize, for example.* Notice how this expressed identity suddenly shapes how you behave and what you would be doing out in the world. It communicates, in a precise package, a plethora of beliefs, feelings, emotions, historical accomplishments, modi operandi, and the kind of people in your world. You are instantly wearing an entirely different life than you are used to. You are internalizing new beliefs and those beliefs are actually communicating all of those instructions to reality. This is the basic power of expressed identity. It is a short-form for communicating immense change to your reality. Try this one:
3. *A person with the Midas touch who can create money effortlessly for yourself, for others, for your company, or for any cause.* Assume that no matter what you did, you would generate wealth. Money will just roll in . . . . much too much to ever worry about money again. Notice how, just by using the identity of the Midas touch, I've communicated much more than the words I've given you. Notice the emotional tapestry that you experience and all of the secondary concepts associated with the identity. You can begin to see the power of an expressed identity as a short-form for communicating belief changes to transform yourself and then your reality.
4. *"Entrepreneur of the Year"* with your own successful company around your natural art. Notice how each "sub-identity" invokes whole systems of beliefs and emotions in a very concise way. Identity shorthand can provide an immense number of detailed instructions to rapidly change any reality. That's the kind of latent power we all have through the use of identity. The real challenge is whether you can release your linear connection to the past to

incorporate the new identity. Can you move to a future state that is not a linear extension of everything that you have experienced in your life to this point? Can you quantum leap? Then, can you hold that change for a period of time until reality restructures?

MPD - A Special Case of Reincarnation

Nature was again my teacher for developing the reincarnation technique. In the face of extreme distress or trauma, nature helps some individuals cope through dissociation. Accordingly, Multiple Personality Disorder (MPD) is now called Dissociative Identity Disorder (DID). Here is the intriguing thing. *The physical realities of multiples change as they flick from one identity to another.* This is what you would expect as they switch from one identity's belief blueprint to the next.

One identity might be allergic or inebriated while the next is not. Each personality may have its own physical abilities, IQ, voice characteristics, brainwave patterns, biochemistry, bloodflow patterns, heart rate, scars, left- and right-handedness, and visual acuity. Even eye color and prescriptions can change. While we think of MPD as an illness, it could well represent an example of how all human beings could evolve to more sophisticated reality creation. The success of the reincarnation tool for emergence, creation and growth is a powerful affirmation that this may, indeed, be the case.

As an aside, I was fascinated to discover websites on the internet where Multiples are protesting the discrimination against them by so-called Normals or Singles. They felt they were an oppressed minority. Some were fighting for the right to keep all of the adaptive personalities they had evolved.

In some instances, there was even the suggestion by some Multiples they might be more highly developed than Singles. Isn't this an interesting change in perspective! The Institute of Noetic Sciences has a research bulletin featuring an article entitled *"Multiple Personality – Mirrors of a New Model of Mind?"* They suggest that what has previously been treated as a disorder could possibly be the emergence of new order. Rather than splitting off, the mind is becoming more adept at manipulating consciousness; it has learned how to switch into different gears.[34]

How to Use Reincarnation

Identity is a shorthand way to bundle up hundreds of instructions to reality. Using identities eliminates the need to systematically select belief after belief to cause reality to change – an inefficient procedure that exposes one to the possibility of selecting beliefs that might be incompatible or maladaptive. Identities usually come equipped with integrated, compatible beliefs.

As we have specific projects we want to create or passions we want to pursue, we'll want to choose expressed identities that accelerate our progress. A person who loves to make business deals might use a corporate finance "expressed identity" to help create a channel for expressing that *art*. Once in a corporate finance department of a major financial institution, the individual might internalize the expressed identity of "leader" in order to shepherd an all-important deal to completion or to head the whole department. In this way, identity serves as an efficient form of reality design for more rapid reality creation.

It is a state of constant change that gives the water fountain its appearance of constancy. We too appear stable because of constantly replenishing ourselves to be the same as we were a moment ago. This continuity is not a requirement but a choice. The idea of reincarnation is to consciously choose your identity in one moment and *be* it in the next moment . . . . without the need for continuity with the previous moment. Pretend you are transformed and live it until it is indeed true.

Start your reincarnation process by using effective reality design techniques. Determine a clear and concise blueprint for your new reality that ignites your passion. Choose an identity supportive of moving in the direction of your natural growth path – the increasing expression of your natural identity. In other words, ensure both authentic and expressed identities are mutually supportive and integrated.

Define your new expressed identity. Commit to being that person. Internalize the identity's emotional signature. *Feel* it emotionally. If you can't *feel* how it would *feel* to have this reality, then you can't create it. Period! *Feel* how it would *feel* if you were this person until you have no discomfort with it at all.

Release your linear connection to the past. Visualize yourself going through your day as this person. Walk around as this person as if you have always been this person. Redesign yourself in one minute and then *be* that new person from then on. Take decisions and actions all day long as if you are now this new person until you have installed new habits. Ignore any evidence in your reality that you have any other identity than this selected one.

Hold that identity until reality adjusts to reflect it. *Hold* that identity, "emotional complex," and modus operandi until events occur in reality to reinforce that identity. *Expect* to see dramatic change in your reality. Take note of the events in your reality that reflect your new identity beliefs. Internalize each of those events in order to strengthen your new identity beliefs. The new reality will reinforce the "new you" to lock in the new identity that will perpetuate the new reality.

Expand your identity to *be* the person with the desired reality. You may feel "resistances" initially as you try to envisage yourself in the new reality. This means you don't yet have the identity beliefs to create the necessary reality. Imagine you have had the desired reality for ten years and have now gone on to even bigger realities than the one currently sought. This makes it much easier to "wear" the current reality without performance anxiety or other fears.

Install a conditioned reflex so every event in reality which suggests you are not the new identity instantly reinforces your belief that you are. We discussed the installation of conditioned reflexes in the powerlessness and judgment chapters. This is an effective trick for using current reality to help you better create your desired future reality.

In addition to internalizing the identity of the person with the next reality you want to create, why not also have a "standing identity" as a "master materializer." Internalize the identity of being a reality design expert and, of course, a reality creation expert. Just decide from here on in that this is who you are. This will speed your creation of any new reality. You deserve to have the beliefs to enable you to create what you want when you want.

Use clairsentience to absorb the identities and emotional structures of individuals who already have the realities we want to create. This will give you their confidence and decision-making capabilities. Assimilate existing models wherever you can. We want to internalize the ideal blueprint in any way possible in order to cause the necessary belief changes. If someone else has what we want, internalize what they have until the changes occur. No need to reality design from scratch every time.

How fluid are you? How fast can you switch identities to switch beliefs to switch realities? The more we use reincarnation, the more fluid we'll become and the faster we'll be able to change reality. Perhaps the first time you use it, it will take a few weeks to start to see changes. As your beliefs increase that you can cause changes, this time will reduce.

Eventually you'll be able to internalize your next expressed identity and see reality shift all within the hour. Feel free to borrow my beliefs that this is possible in the interim. As you become more fluid in re-conceiving of yourself and your reality in this way, the desired realities will be created with increasing speed and precision.

Release yourself from the need for continuity with your past. If you believe you must be an extension of your past, then that is the reality you'll create. If you believe it will take a long process to change your reality, then that will, in fact, be the case. If you believe you can fluidly re-conceive yourself on the parkway on the way to work, then *that* will be your reality. You will immediately begin to see events confirming your new identity.

Once you conceive of a new reality you want to have or the new person you want to be, release the need to gradually evolve. As an adept reality creator, simply become the person with this reality. Shorten, and then grow to eliminate, any transition periods. Do you think this is possible . . . . that this could be true . . . . that it could be this easy? If you never begin to practise it and develop the beliefs and experience necessary, you'll never find out that the answer is "Yes!"

Be prudent about nature's signals. Learn to crawl before you walk. *Don't take major risks.* Start with smaller, less risky projects at first till you gain proficiency and experiential learning. You'll still need to continue to honor your blocks and negative events for clearing and redirecting your system as prescribed by the naturality flow. You'll need to remove any interferences to your selected identity such as conflicting, limiting and fear beliefs as the message events occur in your reality.

Operate organically in partnership with *Optimizer* messages from nature and your reality. Free-flow with your resonance and the blocks and flows to collide with coincidences that will bring your emotional goals much more quickly.

Remember that the human mind is no match for nature's creativity and its partnership with an established and evolving underlying creative order in the universe. Assume there are a multitude of channels to your goal reality which you have no knowledge of.

Resist restricting your reality design to the limitations of the channels you think are available to take you to your goals. And, as you advance, perhaps you'll even learn to leave the final form of your goal open to nature's creativity as well. If your new reality meets all of your emotional needs, do you really care how you got there? Think about it! Experiment!

Examples of Reality Creation with Expressed Identities

Some years ago, I had a sense from a series of recent messages in my life that I was shortly going to have clients that were too advanced for my current capabilities. For example, two clients called me "kingmaker" in the same week. This was not an epithet I had heard before and I had not thought of myself in these terms. If I did draw clients more senior than I was ready for, this would throw me out of flow state in my interaction with them.

In *flow*, I have access to spontaneous knowledge, expanded consciousness and my full creativity. If I'm not in flow, I'd have to rely on just my own much more limited intelligence and capabilities. As a result, my capabilities would be even less for dealing with more senior people than I had now. Therefore, I was going to need to quickly grow to be the person with more advanced clients.

At this point in my life, I'd had six years of being able to fluidly redefine myself and hold the new identity to hold the new reality. Therefore, I simply redefined myself as someone who had been successfully creating world leaders for over ten years. I decided to overshoot the reality I was expecting to ensure I had lots of capacity to handle whatever I sensed was about to happen in my work. Within about twenty minutes, I felt as if I would be advanced enough for any client that would be coming down the pike shortly.

Within another twenty minutes a complete system of knowledge came into my head as to how I might adapt the peak evolution science to create world leaders. It came complete with diagrams I could use with my clients. As a result, my whole transformation was complete within an hour.

In the following few weeks, three new clients, operating on a more advanced scale than I had yet experienced, came into my life. In addition, I had two existing clients quantum leap to operating at the level of world impact. I would not have been ready for those events if I had not taken an hour for reincarnation. I would have been intimidated and would therefore have had too much anxiety to enter flow.

The speed and magnitude of the quantum leaps you can achieve through reincarnation will increase with practice, fluidity, experiential learning, and the internalizing of new beliefs about what is possible. Each time you reincarnate in this way you will become faster than the previous time. Eventually, you can make the change within minutes and see results in reality within the hour.

Allen had been overlooked at his blue-chip corporation where he had spent his entire career. He was four levels down from the CEO of the blue-chip company. He was forty-five yet only a vice president. But Allen was a natural leader. He was designed to be company president. The people reporting to him just loved him.

But he was a different person "up" the hierarchical organization. Allen would become subservient, approval-seeking, and ever vigilant to avoid criticism and judgment. He would become externally referenced. Leadership and being externally referenced are mutually exclusive. Allen was not a leader when working "up" the organization. As is the case with so many of us, he was not his best when dealing with authority figures or potential judges.

What we did was make Allen consistently authentic in all territories, whether with the charities he was working with, down the organization, operating with his peers or, more importantly, "up" the organization. He was to be a leader no matter what the context.

He moved from being externally referenced to internally referenced. Instead of being created by his context – wearing the identity of his job title and the person his fellow workers thought he was – he began operating from the bedrock within him. He gave his resonance free rein. He let go of all of the rules he thought were necessary to "win" within the corporation. We systematically removed all of his fears. We released Allen to naturality, all day, every day.

I encouraged Allen to borrow my beliefs that he did not need to be gradually promoted up the organization. He could release the need for linear progression and move directly to president. If he could internalize a new expressed identity and reality of president, reality would restructure by the fastest route.

He visualized this many times a day to the point of experiencing the accompanying emotions so the necessary beliefs would change. He internalized "president" with every breath. We worked to get him comfortable with changing his context in order to have his goal reality. We removed the natural tendency to insist that the presidency come through the single channel of this company, the only employer he had ever known.

We developed a number of projects he could do right in his current position which would allow him to do his *art* of leadership at more sophisticated levels. The resulting creativity and flow experiences transformed him and advanced his system. His creations strengthened both his naturality and his expressed identity so that he could perform at even higher levels in the next iteration of his system. We also worked to strengthen Allen's beliefs that he was valued and valuable in order to create events in his reality reflective of those beliefs.

Within four weeks of my supporting Allen in wearing this new identity, he began to call the chairman and CEO of the company to make recommendations on leadership tactics. He began to lead the leaders. He mentored other CEOs leading global organizations of the same stature that he encountered through charity work, golf and business associations.

As a result of his demonstrated leadership, within that same four weeks, Allen received a job offer from outside the company to become the president of one of North America's most exciting entrepreneurial companies. He received a multi-million dollar signing bonus – just because he was valued so much.

Needless to say, Allen continues to this day to use expressed identities to enhance his growth and creation. His career has been riddled with quantum leaps and coincidences as a result. Friends and colleagues are in awe of the change in his career from the slow methodical advancement of the first twenty-something years to the chain of visible successes he now enjoys.

Allen's original employer is now faced with competing with his new employer, which has become a significant adversary in his hands.

They have continuously attempted to woo him back, wondering why they never noticed his leadership strength before. Allen is delighted he is finally getting the valuing he was seeking from his original employer. When they are ready to offer him the CEO slot, he may consider their offer.

Shift from Chasing to Creating

The methodology I am suggesting is to simply change your identity to the person who would have the reality you are seeking and let reality bring you the reflected symbols and events by the fastest route. This change in modus operandi is one of shifting from "chasing" to "creating."

Creating allows you to experience new realities much more quickly by coincidences and quantum leaps. You change yourself to change your reality. Things you might have thought would take you months to achieve by linear progression can be achieved in a fraction of the time. Chasing is the old paradigm approach of establishing a linear project plan to get what you want and then working your plan. Try both and see which you prefer.

TROUBLESHOOTING IDENTITY-BASED REALITY CREATION

There are a few territories of identity-based reality creation that may cause problems that I wanted to alert you to. Once you are hooked into the naturality flow advancing you to increasing expressions of your naturality, you'll be perpetually growing and changing. It will be necessary to make it a habit to constantly let things flow out of your life in order to make room for the new.

Look for instructions from patterns of block events and your resonance trying to tell you when it's time for something or someone to be released from your life. Disobey those messages from nature at your peril. If you fight to keep something in your newly aligned life, the conflicting beliefs will begin generating struggle events.

Alignment with one's naturality will increase the speed of materialization. Unfortunately, the same process will also cause our fear beliefs to materialize faster. As we come into alignment, it will be increasingly important to clear fears as they crop up before they create major feared events in our realities.

Conflicting Identities

Earlier in the reality creation chapters, we focused on eliminating maladaptive beliefs, conflicting beliefs, and fear beliefs which interfere with the expression of our naturality. We looked at ways to remove whole belief complexes around powerlessness and judgment. This detoxification process can be accelerated through stripping away whole belief complexes associated with maladaptive identities as well. We picked these identities up from our parents, our schools, our employers, our peers, our life partners, and society at large.

Now it's time to consciously choose your expressed identities rather than being a pawn to the dictates of your past. By following nature's *Optimizers*, your authentic identity will gradually replace non-supportive expressed identities as it grows. They just won't fit any longer.

While multiple interfering identities exist, however, they can generate a mish- mash of message events in your reality. Because they are, in effect, conflicting belief complexes, they can create significant struggle events that interfere with reality creation and your quality of life. Removing toxicity from our belief blueprints is a life-long process as we pursue our true purpose, the greatest possible creations or creative acts that express our naturality. For human beings, optimized survival includes the iterative process of being nourished by our own creations.

> *"Men can starve from a lack of self-realization as much as*
> *they can from a lack of bread."*
> Richard Wright, Native Son (1940)

The Trauma of Transitioning to Naturality

At the point at which you are transitioning from un-naturality to naturality, you are, in effect, experiencing another instance of two identities in conflict. When your old and new identities attempt to coexist, struggle events are inevitable. An identity crisis occurs. As the transition has been proceeding, you've had a taste of what it's like to be in alignment. You have real passion for some major projects which allow you to do your art. You likely have been flicking in and out of alignment throughout your day. You've experienced moments of extreme elation or possibly even feelings of "coming home."

Your system knows where it wants to be. Your head, however, is still trying to have you do the activities your misaligned identity did. These activities become increasingly disagreeable as time goes on in comparison to the *flow* state associated with doing your art. Parts of your reality that used to work no longer do.

There eventually comes a point of no return where we can't put you back into the box, so to speak. There are just too many drives that hook us into naturality alignment that won't let go once they've been activated. Since you can't go back, the best strategy is to try to accelerate the process of going forward. Therefore, the obvious solution is to quantum leap or reincarnate, as quickly as possible, as a person in alignment with your naturality.

The Trauma of Coming out of Alignment

Here is a third scenario of conflicting identity problems. If you move into alignment with your natural identity for perhaps even just two weeks, you may find your system likes this natural state so much that it will put up great resistance to coming out of it.

This conflict inside of you is reflected out into events in your reality. You will notice all sorts of struggle events and blocks emerging when you slip off your natural growth path. You'll have major negative events because our systems rebel against coming out of alignment.

For a few weeks or a month, you may have experienced the bliss of moving with the naturality flow. Reality for that period has been entirely supportive with lots of flow events and coincidences. All of a sudden a traumatic problem suddenly appears in your life. Retrace your steps to see where you made a wrong turn.

Look at the history of your resonance, for example. Where did you ignore it and end up deviating from your natural growth path? Where did you do something you didn't want to do? When did you revert back to your old habits and modus operandi? When did you think you knew where nature was taking you and decide you knew better how to get there than following your resonance?

You will be "zapped" by problem events when you try to come out of living in alignment with your naturality. The longer you're in alignment, the greater the "zap events" when you try to come out. Go back to the basics of the peak evolution science until you have reintegrated into the naturality flow.

THE GROWTH TECHNOLOGY

"The living self has one purpose only: to come into its own
fullness of being, as a tree comes into full blossom, or a bird
into spring beauty, or a tiger into luster."
D. H. Lawrence, The Phoenix

Each technology is based on an uncommon belief. For the knowledge technology, this uncommon belief is that we have access to all knowledge – ultimately spontaneously – merely by focusing consciousness. For the reality creation technology, the uncommon belief is that beliefs create reality and therefore the reality we experience is 100% self-created.

For the growth technology, it is that natural forces perpetually pressure us along an evolutionary continuum to the full expression of our naturality – an expansion by concentric circles around our authentic core.

The growth technology and its quantum leap technology, integrate all other technologies to provide the final understanding of the process for moving to peak evolution. When all of our internal drives align with nature's drives in the naturality flow, we are locked into an accelerating growth process which pulls us perpetually beyond previous levels of peak performance. We shift into overdrive.

In the end, rather than simply raising the bar on human peak performance as we know it, we will quantum leap to functionality yet to be defined. We will achieve peak evolution, individually and for humanity.

The knowledge technology is about sourcing information from the universal hologram, the underlying information medium of the universe. The reality creation technology is concerned with sending new information out to reality to create what we will experience. Any product of creativity is new information. Therefore, using the reality creation technology actually changes the universal information structure.

The growth technology is about changing the information infrastructure of our personal system. The basic information of our personal system, held in information storage units called beliefs, is redefined. Growth changes the belief blueprint that creates us and our reality. For growth to have occurred, our beliefs must have changed.

If our beliefs have changed so too has our reality. And so too, then, has the universal information hologram. The growth technology is about recreating ourselves at higher levels of potential and creation power. Growth increases the impact of our natural expression on the world.

The growth technology adds dimension to the underlying theme of human existence – iterations of self-growth then creation-growth or, to say it another way, self-creation and then creation. We grow ourselves to grow our creations. Our creations then lock in that growth and increase it so that greater creations are possible in the future. Our creative expression is the ultimate simplicity of human purpose. We are creative beings.

"The job is, if we are willing to take it seriously, to help ourselves to be more perfectly what we are, to be more full, more actualizing, more realizing, in fact, what we are in potentiality." Abraham Maslow

14

BEYOND *FLOW*

"We have all experienced times when, instead of being buffeted by anonymous forces, we do feel in control of our actions, masters of our own fate. On the rare occasions that it happens, we feel a sense of exhilaration, a deep sense of enjoyment that is long cherished and that becomes a landmark in memory for what life should be like. This is what we mean by optimal experience."[35]
Mihaly Csikszentmihalyi

Since Csikszentmihalyi's ground-breaking book, *Flow*, came out in 1990, everyone seeking peak performance, from athletes to executives, has been pursuing flow. Professor Mihaly Csikszentmihalyi is a former chairman of the Department of Psychology at the University of Chicago, and a key researcher of *flow*. He calls it the "optimal experience."

Daniel Goleman, psychologist and author of *Emotional Intelligence* (1995), identifies *flow* as the "neurobiology of excellence." Athletes call it "the zone," or "being in the groove," or refer to times of having "supernatural intuition," or "spontaneous excellence."

Before I knew of Csikszentmihalyi's work, I called *flow* "active meditation," "the effortless effort," "activity fusion," and my secret weapon for accelerating individuals along their natural growth path. Dramatic growth is possible simply by increasing the time in *flow* . . . . whether it's on the golf course or in the boardroom. *Flow* accelerates our evolution to naturality and peak performance.

We have all experienced *flow*. Time, space, and all self-awareness can cease to exist in *flow*. It is an altered state of consciousness in which we are only aware of the activity and our masterful control over its execution. It is a state of "activity fusion" in which you and the activity you are doing are one. Every part of your being is recruited to the activity at hand. That is why, in *flow*, we achieve peak performance. We are operating at full power. It is a state of pure naturalness and pure naturality.

Changes in *flow* are physiological, psychological, emotional and spiritual. *Flow* re-optimizes our system during our active times in the same way that sleep does at night. Self-esteem improves. We are made whole. All emotional needs are met. In *flow*, negative emotions don't exist, even if we are accomplishing tasks we would normally consider unpleasant. *Flow* can also be filled with elation, spontaneous joy, safety, excitement and oneness with the universe. Self-transcendence and omnipotence are often experienced. Needless to say, *flow* is a highly gratifying state. It leaves us wanting more.

We are Born *Flow* Experts

Flow appears to be a phenomenon everyone experiences in the same way, regardless of age or gender, cultural background or social class. Children seem to operate in flow constantly, indicating this is a natural inborn trait of human beings. We are born *flow* experts. Unfortunately, our natural fluidity for shifting into *flow* is one of the casualties of our cultures and especially our institutions. These have interfered with and suppressed this natural adaptive mechanism and the pleasure it brings.

Western culture and modus operandi, in particular, neither promote nor accommodate individuals moving into *flow*. As we conform to various rules in an attempt to operate within restrictive cultural contexts, we lose the ability to slip into *flow* to re-optimize our system. The peak evolution science offers a means to restore this capability.

Flow within Nature's Flow

The naturality paradigm offers profound new ways for achieving and sustaining *flow* . . . . with evolutionary consequences. *Flow* is the means for our systems to re-optimize. *Flow is optimization.* It occurs when we slip into alignment with the naturality flow. Therefore, this entire book is designed to help you achieve a life of 100% *flow*. *Flow* is one of the ten *Optimizers*.

However, all *Optimizers* are attempting to integrate us into the universal optimizing flow acting on all systems. Therefore, using any and all *Optimizers* will direct us into *flow*. That is life in the naturality paradigm. When *flow* is fully mastered and exists in every part of your life, you are living in the naturality paradigm. This is *flow* within the naturality flow.

In the naturality paradigm, *flow* is pure naturality, naturalness, and optimization. Because we are in pure naturality in *flow*, our instructions to reality are precise and powerful. We can create adaptive realities automatically as discussed in the two previous chapters.

That is why, in *flow*, it can feel as if we can do no wrong. All of nature's processes and mechanisms are supporting us. Coincidences abound. Flow is a state of pure positive emotion. If the only reason we are motivated to do anything is to improve our emotional state, then *flow* is the ultimate emotional goal. Our objective in the naturality paradigm, then, is to live our lives entirely in *flow*.

Flow Accelerates Growth and Evolution

Flow is the highest scientifically documented psychobiological experience for human beings. It can be a state of peak growth and evolution if we know how to cultivate, sustain, and capitalize on it. This is because *flow* is an addicting process.

Yet, to enter *flow*, we must be stretched beyond our previous capabilities. Growth is built into *flow*. Consequently, we can establish a compelling cycle of repetitive self-transcendence in which the norm in our lives is that we continuously surpass ourselves. This is a state of peak evolution rather than just a spike of growth or high achievement. If we master the art of perpetual *flow*, we can continually raise the bar on what is peak performance for our system.

Flow is nature's ways of re-ordering, re-optimizing and evolving our personal system. It is an evolutionary mechanism built into each person. Each experience of *flow* reintegrates us at a more evolved and expanded state of consciousness.

The more time you spend in *flow*, the faster you evolve. Our speed for shifting into *flow*, our ability to sustain it, and the power and depth of the experience can all increase with practice.

Not all *flow* states are equivalent for the acceleration of our growth, though. Our evolutionary path is towards increasing expressions of our naturality – in other words, our *art*. *Flow* states in which we are specifically doing our *art* will, of course, evolve us more quickly. *Art*-based *flows* are more penetrating and powerful.

WHAT IS *FLOW*?

Naturality is the emotion of naturalness. There is no state in which we feel more natural and true to ourselves than *flow*. *Flow* is the highest neurobiological state identified for human beings. It is our optimal experience. It is free from emotional static. *Flow* is optimization. In *flow*, we are simply "one" with the task at hand.

Flow is Activity Fusion

In *flow*, awareness merges with action. "Csikszentmihalyi tells the story about a surgeon performing a difficult operation. When the procedure was done, the surgeon looked around and happened to notice a pile of debris in a corner of the operating room. When he asked what had happened, he was told that part of the ceiling had caved in during the operation. He was so fully absorbed in his work, he hadn't heard a thing."[36] *Flow* is an active state of extreme attention in the moment. It is characterized by complete absorption in the task at hand.

There is an externally visible state of "altered consciousness" in which some kind of exceptional productivity occurs. Execution of the activity is easy if not joyous. The activity is intrinsically rewarding: *doing the activity is its own reward*. The outcome is not what motivates our action in *flow*.

This altered state of consciousness becomes more intense with use and alignment to naturality. Dream state re-optimizes our consciousness when we are asleep. *Flow* state promotes the same type of re-optimization when we are awake and active. Activity fusion brings us to a rejuvenating orderliness in alignment with our original blueprint, our naturality.

The occurrence of *flow* state can be identified through neurological studies of the brain. Cortical activity in *flow* moves to efficiency, order and harmony. Only the precise parts of the brain required for the task at hand are active. Activity fusion or *flow* is evident by the focused activity of the brain. In periods of non-*flow* and especially during stress and fatigue, many areas of the brain are firing at once. No wonder *flow* is a time of superior performance. All of the body's resources are measurably recruited to a single focus.

Flow is a Quantum Leap to Re-Optimization

Nature likes quantum leaps for transforming, adapting and re-optimizing. Nature uses quantum leaps to quickly resolve optimization challenges. Some evolution is not possible through a gradual linear process. How could a human eye, for example, evolve gradually?

Flow offers a quantum leap to our naturality and to optimization. Clicking into *flow* is a quantum leap to sudden alignment with the naturality flow and all of the *Optimizers*. It is therefore a quantum leap to the naturality paradigm, the goal of all of the technologies presented in this book.

Flow is the state of being optimized for peak performance. It is pure naturality and naturalness. The challenge of *flow* is to hold onto the new order that it offers us. Honoring the *Optimizers* will help us to do this and will, over time, lock us into *flow* permanently.

Without Time and Space

As a quantum leap, *flow* is nonlinear and atemporal. We may arrive at end states which could not be predicted by projecting linearly from our starting state. Consequently, our relationship to time and space may change. If time is not relevant to the task at hand, we may lose all sense of it. We may re-emerge astounded that several hours have passed. Other times, we may lose all perception of time, yet re-emerge at the perfect time for our next appointment.

Here's an example. John arrived at the office with creative information bubbling up inside of him for a life-changing project he was passionately pursuing. He did not want anything to interfere with the *flow* of spontaneous knowledge. Yet there were five other critical items that also needed his attention in this time slot.

Using reality design techniques, John directed reality to invoke coincidences to delay or eliminate the issues. He then turned himself over to capturing the new information on his computer as it surfaced. Through phone messages and email received during his *flow* state, John learned that all was well with four of the five critical items. One disappeared entirely from the need to be on his radar. Another was resolved be someone else's creativity. The other two were delayed until later in the week.

The fifth item was tricky, however. He critically needed to meet with the corporate lawyer who had taken time off when his wife had a baby the preceding night. No one knew how to reach him and no one expected him in the office. As John was on his second hour of *flow*, he found himself suddenly getting up and walking to the lawyer's office on the next floor up. He arrived at the same time as the lawyer who was unshaven and dressed in sweats and obviously just stopping in to quickly pick something up.

Within fifteen minutes, John was back at his computer, mission accomplished, and his *flow* state still in full force. At 10:20 a.m. when John would have to leave his office for a meeting, the *flow* state spontaneously ended despite John having no awareness of what time it was. Some part of him was cognizant of time and knew when it was time to go.

Flow is a Series of Coincidences and Flow Events

John's experience points up another aspect of *flow*. Coincidences and flow events abound in *flow* state because our internal order is reflected out into our self-created reality. While each flow event is a quantum leap to order, the actual performance of an activity in *flow* is usually a series of coincidences and flow events.

This is to be expected since coincidences are really quantum leaps as well. Nature is shifting us into optimization through a series of quantum leaps in *flow*. This is what makes our performance in *flow* so exceptional.

In addition, because we are in pure naturality in *flow*, we emit the instructions to create an adaptive, naturality-based reality that supports us with the activity. The almost magical pattern of events contributes to the feelings of exhilaration and omnipotence characteristic of flow.

Since *flow* is natural alignment, we can expect all of nature's *Optimizers* to be working on our behalf. In the state of *flow*, we unconsciously pick up and action all of nature's signals as we are designed to. Everything clicks. Coincidence after coincidence.

When we are pursuing a goal which will help to expand our naturality and optimize us, we automatically generate an adaptive reality. In an adaptive reality perfectly reflecting our naturality, whatever is required at each point along the process is provided. Instructions from our belief blueprint or information database are actioned spontaneously and immediately in order to sustain the re-optimizing *flow* state.

Outside of the *flow* state, a project plan for completing an activity might require twenty steps. However, in *flow*, one coincidence or quantum leap might catapult you instantly to the end goal. A basketball player in *flow* might experience a series of information coincidences or spontaneous knowledge as to where the ball is going to be at each moment and therefore be able to be there ahead of time. As a result, he or she is more effective each moment.

As you live in *flow*, what you will experience is a series of similar events in which you are in the right place at the right time to "catch the ball," so to speak. String twenty or thirty such events in a row and you are going to feel as if you can do no wrong . . . . as if the universe is supporting your every move. Your naturality is creating adaptive realities at every step of the way. Adrenalin highs are not uncommon as you progress at speeds and levels of performance far beyond what is normal for you. This is life in the naturality paradigm.

Peak Performance, Surpassing Ourselves, and Self-Transcendence

Reporting on a study by his team at the University of Chicago, Csikszentmihalyi commented that, "The frequency of *flow*, more than objective measures of cognitive ability (such as the Scholastic Aptitude Test), and more than personality traits or parental status and income, was the best predictor of the development of talent."[37]

If we were freed from cultural inhibitions and toxicity, our natural drives would make us growth addicts and achievement junkies. If the world was a safe place, we would like nothing more than to continuously surpass ourselves. We would pursue new learning, and mastering new obstacles, and new levels of achievement.

Most of the best athletes rely on *flow* for exceptional performance and to extend their capabilities. Imagine what could happen to you in your field of endeavor if you did the same. Complying with nature's *Optimizers* to experience flow accelerates the quality and rate of our achievement. It leads to a state of accelerated evolution.

Flow is Active Meditation

I call *flow* "active meditation" because I believe all of the same benefits are achieved as experienced through meditation. The same states of alpha brainwaves are involved. Even hard work done in *flow* can seem to refresh and replenish in the ways experienced by accomplished meditators. This is good news for aspiring meditators with type A personalities who find inactivity and silence of the mind a challenge.

Even experienced meditators may find it difficult to meditate in the face of stressful situations. They *need* to meditate to calm themselves but can't get the problem out of their heads. If we can experience *flow* in some other way, the same goals may be achieved. An action-packed computer game, for example, can keep you enthralled and in *flow* state for respite from thinking about your problems. You'll emerge rejuvenated as if you just spent an hour in meditation.

Egolessness, Nonduality and Oneness

People stop being aware of themselves as separate from the actions they are performing in *flow*. They lose all self-consciousness and self-awareness. There is a quantum leap from duality to oneness. The doer and the action are no longer separate. Interconnectedness with all things replaces separation and fragmentation. This is reminiscent of the Zen idea of no-mind: a state of complete absorption in what one is doing. In Zen, the word for "mind" and "the consciousness of the universe" are the same. The mind of the individual and the mind of the universe are also perceived as one in *flow*.

In this egoless state of pure being, our concept of self – the information we use to identify to ourselves who we are – is realigned with our naturality. We return to our original optimized form. The challenge is to sustain this alignment after *flow*. The degree to which one is externally referenced and created by one's surroundings will determine how quickly alignment with naturality will dissipate after *flow*. Internally referenced individuals will hold their *flow* naturality longer.

Spontaneous Knowledge

Spontaneous knowledge increases with *flow* in both its frequency and in the magnitude of information that presents. Premonition and supernatural intuition are common. Complete systems of information can emerge in our thinking. This is what you would expect from the state of naturality we are in when experiencing *flow*. This is the *spontaneous knowledge formula* presented in Chapter Five.

Any alignment with naturality is a source of a connection with universal holographic information. *Flow* by definition is naturality. In the discussion of the knowledge technology, *flow* was one of the key ways to access information spontaneously. Information coincidences increase in *flow* in the same way that all coincidences increase in *flow* or in alignment with the naturality flow.

Since all knowledge is state-bound and our access to spontaneous knowledge increases in *flow*, we do not have the same all-knowingness when we have left *flow*. Information we had access to in *flow* may not be accessible when we are no longer in *flow*. Therefore, it's very important to record and consciously review new knowledge that emerges in *flow*. This experience of all-knowingness is a highly addicting state. It is disconcerting when it ends but this does not compare with the frustration of not being able to remember any of the information.

Increasing Depths of *Flow* – Is There a *Flow* Continuum?

Just as meditators achieve increasing depths of experience and altered consciousness with practice, so too do those who continue to pursue the naturality paradigm formula for experiencing *flow*. As naturality alignment increases and, in particular, we increase our time doing our *art*, or work that we are passionate about, our *flow* states increase in their intensity. Our functionality as human beings increases dramatically.

All *flow* states do not evolve us equally. There is a difference in the *flow* state that might occur when we are playing a video game versus one associated with doing our *art*. As you might imagine, the latter is much more integrated with our flow to optimization. It will therefore be supported by the naturality flow.

There are also likely more parts of your life associated with your *art* and you have a long history and a wealth of information that comes into play in doing your *art*. Hence, *flow* will be deeper and include more support by the ten *Optimizers* – more coincidences and flow events, more emotional highs, greater pull by our growth, creativity and naturality drives, and so on.

However, if you have had very little experience doing your *art* and very little history of slipping into *flow* naturally, then an all-absorbing video or computer game might help you to at least begin. *Flow* will increase with each daily game session. You will gradually find yourself in *flow* for other activities in your life.

As you increase your time in *flow* in doing your *art*, your consciousness will shift. An ever-expanding awareness can ultimately lead to a multidimensional perspective. At this point, whole systems of complex information may suddenly emerge complete in your awareness.

In the *Spontaneous Knowledge* chapter, we learned of the experience of a newly hired advertising and public relations firm CEO, Charles, who suddenly found himself resolving the technical challenges of a major automobile manufacturer. As a gifted advertising CEO, his *art* was basically running a creativity assembly line. As we shifted Charles into greater alignment and his *flow* states intensified, he suddenly found that creativity spilling over into every dimension of his life including the actual business of his clients.

Clairsentience is heightened with increasing depths of flow. This is the "clear feeling" of the emotional state of another person.   Absorbing the "information" contained in someone else's emotions is likely part of the enhanced access to spontaneous knowledge that occurs in alignment and in *flow*.

Coincidences and flow events increase in number and magnitude with augmented flow. They reflect the ordered state inside of you which emits laser-precise instructions from your naturality. Adaptive realities are automatically created by reflection. We are able to create reality changes almost as soon as we conceive of the change we want. This is a source of great delight in comparison to the primitive way we normally operate. We are creating instantaneously in advanced *flows* so that whatever is needed by the activity next appears by a series of coincidences. The reality creation technology and the knowledge technology are no longer required.

The bad news is that you lose your comprehension of time and space and even your own identity in the deeper *flows*. The good news is that you lose your comprehension of time and space and even your own identity.

In deep *flow*, we are very receptive to nonlinear processes and can fluidly quantum leap to new perspectives. Without the restrictions of time and space, we seem to be able to move to new levels of conception of the problem. As a result, creativity increases tremendously.

We also are free to re-conceive of ourselves in more significant ways in the deeper *flows*. We are free to re-wire ourselves. We evolve. We lock new information into our system. We quantum leap along the evolutionary continuum towards naturality alignment.

As your *flow* states increase in intensity and power, it may be necessary to allow for periods of acclimatization after *flow* for you to regain a sense of who you are and where you are in normal consciousness. You can tell when you are experiencing these greater depths of *flow* when you have been intensely focused for a long period of time and then try to deal with numbers, dates, geographical locations and even who you are. It may take a few moments to a few hours to reinstate those linear understandings, especially if you've been doing your *art*.

Near-Death Experience

Flow is the shift into the naturality paradigm and the quantum leap to integration with the naturality flow. As such, our *flow* experiences give us an idea of our true capabilities. Many of the advanced capabilities available to us in the deeper levels of *flow* are reminiscent of the anecdotal material from those who have had near-death experiences (NDEs).

If we could remove the physical trauma from the equation, could the advanced functionality of NDE represent a progression further along the same continuum as *flow*? *As flows become deeper and deeper, are we perhaps looking at an evolutionary continuum to our true nature?* Perhaps NDE is the ultimate *flow* consciousness and indicates the peak performance through increased functionality we could have when not restricted by the limited thinking of our cultures.

This evolutionary continuum also seems confirmed by the overlap between what NDEers experience and what happens in out-of-body experiences (OBEs). During the events, NDEers and OBEers experience all-knowingness or spontaneous knowledge as soon as they focus consciousness on a subject. NDEers and OBEers often say that during the vision of total knowledge, the information arrives in "chunks" that register instantaneously in one's thoughts.

This is similar to my observation of quantum leaps in knowledge and the experience of complete systems of information being absorbed by individuals, the closer they are to their naturality. Knowledge in *flow* is also state-bound in the same way that NDEers and OBEers have difficulty bringing it back with them into normal consciousness.

NDEers and OBEers frequently re-emerge with a firm understanding of the holographic interconnectedness of all things. This is the same understanding that I have observed emerging in individuals who move into pure naturality in the naturality paradigm. Their consciousness expands and alters, especially with the help of spontaneous knowledge. Those in deep *flow* often report the experience of oneness with universal consciousness. They too comprehend the interconnectedness.

Most NDEers and OBEers feel an exceptionally positive emotion for which they have difficulty finding a descriptor. Many settle, with a feeling of inadequacy, on the word "love." This could be a natural extension of the 100% positive emotions in *flow*.

Many NDEers come back perfectly aligned with who they are designed to be – the goal of the peak evolution science. Many know the work they want to do that is the expression of their naturality. As the depth of the *flow* states increase, I have seen this realignment occur in individuals who suddenly quantum leap into the naturality paradigm and an integration into the naturality flow.

Robert Monroe is the author of several books about his OBE experiences. In *Far Journeys*, Monroe confirms that beliefs create reality in the dimensions of OBE altered consciousness just as they do in the naturality paradigm: "These nonphysical senses are further hampered by the constraints our own self-limiting beliefs place upon them. For example, as they [OBEers] became more experienced, they found that they could 'see' in all directions at once without turning their heads. They had to eliminate their belief that they could see only through their eyes. They had to realize they possessed 360-degree vision."[38]

Many NDEers report being able to see in all directions like OBEers while in the disembodied state. Perhaps we already have perceptual capabilities for "eyeless sight" but our beliefs are limiting us. The scientifically documented remote-viewing capability discussed in the *Spontaneous Knowledge* chapter is an example. Imagine what other capabilities we might have if we changed our beliefs.

For both NDEers and OBEers, they no sooner conceive of what they want to create next and that appears in their reality. This is the same as occurs in flow state. Adaptive realities, coincidences and flow events are automatically created just as occurs for those in alignment with their naturality. Because beliefs create reality, would whatever one believes about death determine what one experienced at that time . . . . the next reality to be created?

Another characteristic of OBE's is the blurring of the division between past and future. Everything exists simultaneously. Most NDEers also report that time and space cease to exist. This is consistent with our experience in *flow*.

Questions

Could the near-death be an extension of the depth of *flow* as one advances along one's natural evolutionary continuum to alignment with extreme naturality? *Were near-death experiencers actually experiencing the true functionality and consciousness of human beings?* Is this the functionality we could all expect as we achieve peak optimization in the naturality paradigm?

Is there a reality continuum stretching from the physical reality through our imagined reality to a world of frequencies based on the fading strength of our commitment to our cultural beliefs and the world belief pool? The shared world beliefs are felt the strongest in our physical world where we conspire to co-create our shared reality.

In imagined reality, in our dreams, for example, the attachment to these shared beliefs weakens and we experience distortions of physical reality similar to reports from NDEers and OBEers. And finally, we move to pure naturality in a pre-belief world of frequencies, again as reported by some NDEers and OBEers. Is it possible that, as we distance ourselves from our culturally-based, world belief pool in the pursuit of natural alignment and optimization, we get a glimpse into our true natures?

Does the strength of whatever beliefs we bring from the physical world determine what is experienced all the way along this *flow* continuum? And, if this is the case, which is better for us? To stay in the physical world tapping into the shared beliefs of the culture to which we belong? Or, is it better to let go of those beliefs and flow along the continuum until we reach pre-belief frequencies? Are increasing depths of flow simply advances along a continuum to higher frequencies? Is there no death but merely a change in frequency?

Are We Evolving to Higher Frequencies?

In his 1980 book, *Life at Death*, Kenneth Ring reports the tendency of NDEers to describe a dimension of "light," "higher vibrations," or "frequencies." He suggests the act of dying involves a shift of consciousness away from the ordinary world of form and into a more holographic reality of pure frequency.[39] Medical science has long known that humans are electromagnetic beings. We have EKGs, EEGs, and EMGs to record electrical activity of the heart, brain and muscles, respectively. In the 1970s and 80s, Valerie Hunt, a physical therapist and professor of kinesiology at UCLA, developed a way to confirm experimentally the existence of the human energy field.

Hunt has discovered that an EMG or electromyogram can pick up the electrical presence of the human energy field. The normal frequency range of the electrical activity in the brain is between 0 and 100 cycles per second (cps) with most of the activity occurring between 0 and 30 cps. When people focus on the material world, their energy field is in the lower range. Hunt has found that psychics or those with healing abilities tend to vibrate at 400 to 800 cps. Those who go into a trance to channel other information sources through them are usually between 800 and 900 cps.

People with frequencies above 900 cps are not merely conduits of information as was the case for psychics and trance mediums. They also have the wisdom of knowing what to do with the information – a more advanced active intelligence. They have expanded consciousness and are aware of the interrelatedness of all things. They operate in the naturality paradigm. They access information spontaneously as predicted by the knowledge technology for those in alignment with their naturality and in *flow.*

Using a modified EMG, Hunt has recorded individuals possessing frequencies as high as 200,000 cps. There appears to be good reason for mystical traditions to have referred to highly evolved individuals as possessing a "higher vibration" than normal people.[40] The spontaneous knowledge that occurs when we are optimized and doing our *art* would make sense if we are operating at a higher frequency.

The higher the frequency, the more light we could hold and thus the more information our systems could contain or process. The peak evolution available through the peak evolution science may be due to its ability to raise our frequency thus augmenting our connection to the holographic information database of the universe.

In deep *flow*, we can experience the same quantum leap to the enhanced capability that NDEers experience. In a world unlimited by the beliefs of our current cultures, this may actually be the level of peak performance we can all aspire to. Could it be that NDEers simply move to a frequency beyond which our equipment is able to detect activity and therefore appear dead?

Flow is free of emotional static. Not only does it have no negative emotions, quite often extremely positive emotions are experienced. As we shed our "heavy" negative emotions, are we able to move to higher frequencies which permit the enhanced functionality observed?

ENTERING *FLOW*

Successful organisms continuously re-optimize to their environment. It would therefore be logical to assume human beings, as a successful species, come equipped with the means to quickly re-optimize. *Flow* is our means to do this. Unfortunately, our cultures often interfere with our ability to replenish our systems – psychologically, biologically, and spiritually – through *flow*. Let's explore the ways to help nature to keep us in the states of rapid growth, achievement, and optimization possible in *flow*.

All Optimizers Lead to Flow

Flow is one of the ten *Optimizers*. *Flow* is pure dynamic naturalness. It occurs when we merge with the naturality flow. *Flow* is therefore our modus operandi in the naturality paradigm. Just as the dynamic flow of the naturality paradigm is signaled by the ten *Optimizers*, so the other nine *Optimizers* can be used to identify our pathway into *flow*. We can use any and all of the *Optimizers* to guide us to reintegrate with the dynamic flow of the universe and to experience our peak performance in *flow*. In the naturality paradigm, all *Optimizers* lead to *flow*.

Not only do all of the *Optimizers* indicate how to enter the naturality paradigm and *flow*, they become much more powerful, identifiable, and enticing in *flow*. The result is that being in *flow* helps to lock us into the naturality flow. In turn, being in nature's flow ensures we will experience *flow*.

Therefore, all of the techniques and technologies presented in this book will lead us to enter *flow*. As we shift into *flow* as a way of life, we will no longer need the transitioning technologies of the peak evolution science. We will be home. We will be reintegrated into the dynamic *flow* of the universal optimization process acting on all systems. We will exist in the naturality paradigm.

When we're in *flow*, the nine other *Optimizers* are working for us in the most adaptive ways. The *Optimizer* drives intensify and begin to addict us to our natural growth path which is the fundamental dynamic in the naturality paradigm. The *Optimizer* drives again are to growth, naturality, meaning, creativity and creation, *flow*, resonance, positive emotional states, and knowledge.

In *flow*, we are pure naturality. Adaptive realities are created automatically as reflections of our naturality. Consequently, the patterns of block and flow events in reality become clearer, more concise and easier to follow. Coincidences and flow events energize our progress. Our resonance indicates we are doing exactly what we are meant to be doing at any particular moment. Spontaneous knowledge emerges.

Flow Generates *Flow*

In the *Power of Identity* chapter, we learned that naturality increases naturality. The pursuit of naturality, or the *emotion of naturalness*, is the formula for moving into *flow*. Since *flow* is pure naturality, *flow* breeds *flow*. The more we experience *flow*, the more fluidly we can slip into *flow* in the future. Each *flow* experience increases our alignment with our natural growth path to naturality.

Therefore, if we can shorten the elapsed time between *flow* states, we can hang onto the advances along our natural evolutionary path accomplished in *flow*. Not only will we increase our time in peak performance, we will raise the bar on that peak performance. We will experience peak evolution.

In addition, the more time we are in alignment with our naturality, the more instructions we are emitting to create adaptive realities by reflection. Realities supportive of our naturality will, in turn, reinforce our natural expression. This is part of the addictive loop that will tend to lock us into the naturality paradigm once the peak evolution science gets us there.

Also, the more time we spend in *flow*, the more addicting it becomes. If we can achieve tremendous throughput in this pleasant state of peak performance and the "effortless effort," who wants to go back to the tedium of having to do work again – and to a reduced capability for achieving our goals?

Resonance - Tapping into Nature's Intelligence

All *Optimizers* lead to *flow* but resonance is perhaps the simplest, most effective one to use. If you take action based on your resonance each moment, you can't help but end up in *flow*. It cannot be otherwise. Naturality each moment results in us operating in alignment with our naturality.

Both *flow* and resonance are pure naturality. Choose an activity that feels most natural to you, preferably one that excites you or that at least invokes an inner knowing that it is the most optimal activity for you this moment. Turn off that editor in your head so you can comply with nature's direct instructions to you through your resonance.

Anyone can use resonance to choose activities they resonate with. We don't need to be the peak evolution science experts to dramatically increase the percentage of time per day we spend in *flow*. This is one of the ways I knew the peak evolution science was correct.

If you do nothing but follow your resonance to increase your *flow* states, you will end up in the same place as if you did everything that the peak evolution science prescribes. In other words, you will end up in the naturality paradigm fully integrated into the naturality flow. The accuracy of the peak evolution science is confirmed because it takes people to the same place as nature's resonance-*flow* approach.

In *flow*, negative emotions don't exist, even if we are accomplishing tasks we would normally consider unpleasant. Resonance can lead us to be in the right place at the right time to do even unpleasant tasks in *flow*. Using your resonance moment by moment to allow the body to optimize itself vis-à-vis its context will dramatically increase the percentage of time per day you will spend in *flow* state.

Eliminate Judgment

Judgment interferes with hearing our resonance. It often keeps us following rules that interfere with slipping into *flow*. It keeps our focus on self-awareness rather than letting us fuse with the activity. Judgment separates. *Flow* is a judgment-free zone. It is a state of oneness. Eliminating judgment and thoughts of success and failure from your performance of an activity will promote your movement into *flow*.

Become Internally Referenced

Becoming internally referenced and following one's resonance are two ways to achieve the same thing. They are both means to listen to inner instructions for moving into alignment with your naturality. Focus on the activity rather than the outcome of the activity. The pursuit of fame, wealth and winning and other externally referenced outcomes interfere with the need to be totally in the present in activity fusion. They require ego-centered thinking while *flow* is an egoless state in which self-awareness and identity disappears.

Stay in the Present

Watching the clock interferes with *flow*. So does concentrating on future outcomes or past limitations. *Flow* is a period of extreme focus on the activity at hand. This is why I call it activity fusion. Obviously, to achieve this level of concentration, one must be totally in the present. We need to have a Zen-like immersion in the action.

Staying in the present, therefore, can also be used as a means to trigger activity fusion and *flow*. Focusing on the present and, in fact, living in the present, are also the means to sustain the *flow* experience in your life. When you are always where you want to be you are in the NOW. The corollary is a little more challenging: if you let wherever you are be where you want to be, you will live in the moment.

> *"The bliss of the animals lies in this, that, on their lower level, they shadow the bliss of those – few at any moment on the earth – who do not 'look before and after, and pine for what is not' but live in the holy carelessness of the eternal now'."* George Macdonald

Choosing *Flow*-Invoking Activities

Our goal is to spend 100% of our day in *flow* for peak performance, peak growth, and peak evolution. The *Optimizers* define a way of life which will automatically promote greater time in *flow*. However, if you're not there yet, you can choose activities which are likely to induce *flow*. Since *flow* generates *flow*, consciously increasing your *flow* experience will increase the chances of entering *flow* unconsciously for other activities that are part of your day. *Flow* from any source will evolve and optimize one's system.

Achieving *flow* becomes more inevitable when a person has clear goals to be reached, especially if those goals are taking you in the direction of optimization. Take a look at the pattern of positive *Optimizer* messages in your past and choose your goal as an extension of that pattern into the future.

Having a goal helps to create the focus necessary for activity fusion to take place. While a goal-directed task helps to provide the order, motivation and focus to induce *flow*, concentration on outcomes will impede *flow*. Anxiety is distracting. The best *flow*-invoking activities are intrinsically rewarding. Doing the activity is as rewarding – if not more rewarding – than the outcome. Stay in the present to fully focus every part of you on what you are doing.

In *flow* state, we are relaxed yet highly focused. It is a state of complete absorption and deep concentration. Therefore, choose activities in which you find it easy to intentionally focus sharp attention. With experience, *flow* expertise and addiction will induce *flow* spontaneously in other activities in your life. In the *Evolving Self* (1993), Csikszentmihalyi states that "*Flow* experiences are reported more frequently in the context of work, family interaction, and driving a car than in leisure activities, provided that these supply the necessary conditions, such as a balance of challenges and skills."[41] "... typical working adults in the United States experience *flow* on the job three times as often as in free time."[42] Novelty, variety, and excitement tend to provide *flow* on the job. Select *flow*-invoking activities in your life accordingly.

Flow seems to emerge when we are challenged to give more than usual or to develop new skills. We seem to enter *flow* while performing at our peak or stretching beyond former limits. Tasks too simple generate boredom. Tasks too challenging result in anxiety. *Flow* occurs somewhere between the two.

We'll want to find tasks which we are skilled at but where there is still room for our capabilities to grow. *Flow* emerges when we are challenged to the fullest capacity. Logically then, as our skills increase, we are going to require heightened challenges in order to re-enter *flow*. Consequently, growth is built into the pursuit of *flow*.

Because *flow* is such a pleasing state, the more we experience it, the more we want it, and the more we will grow. This is why *flow* is a key component of the growth technology. All *flow* states are not equal with respect to evolving one's system. Pursuing your *art* will stimulate *flow* events of a depth and transformative power that can exceed all other *flows*.

Doing what you love increases your chances of entering *flow*. This may be why it often results in taking people to their greatest achievements. In *flow*, they are operating at peak performance.

Creativity or creation is one of the fastest routes for transforming people and taking them to their highest emotional states. I often induce creativity in individuals to re-balance and optimize them. Creativity is also a key approach to entering *flow* state, especially when doing one's *art*. Bringing something new into existence is an excellent way to meet the *flow* entrance criteria for being stretched beyond our previous capabilities.

The partnership of creativity and *flow* is a key element of the creative adaptiveness that has made the species successful. In a few places in this book, the challenge of dealing with the creation anxiety associated with creativity has been discussed. It will be important to avoid this anxiety in order to stay in *flow*.

We are our most evolved when we are in *growth-creation flows* in which doing our *art* changes our world in some way. This is our most primal motivation. Key human drives and the direction of our evolution in a 100% self-created reality suggest this focus. We grow to create better realities and the resulting creations grow us more. We *know* ourselves by our creations. We *grow* ourselves by our creations. This continuous cycle of self-growth and creation-growth is the underlying dynamic of the human experience.

15

GROWTH ACCELERATION

"It takes a lot of courage to release the familiar and seemingly secure, to embrace the new. But there is no real security in what is no longer meaningful. There is more security in the adventurous and exciting, for in movement there is life, and in change there is power."　　　　　Alan Cohen

Growth is the success skill of the new millennium. Our world is changing at an accelerating pace. Those who wish to survive and thrive must excel at the art of growth. With growth expertise will come growth safety and proficiency. Because of our natural drives, if growth is safe, we will want to do it all the time.

If we commit to growth as a way of life, as a raison d'être, eventually there will come a point of no return where we will become benevolently addicted to growth. We are so designed for growth that once we become growth experts we will become growth addicts. Growth is exhilarating when you know how to do it.

Nature is the expert in growth and adapting to change. Rather than trying to duplicate nature's expertise, the smart strategy is to partner with nature. The Optimizers give us the means to do this. When we harness natural forces through the peak evolution science, we can achieve unforeseen rates of growth as a way of life. The growth technology promotes a powerful and profound way of being and becoming in partnership with nature.

It is my hope that by making you consciously aware of the naturality flow and enticing you to reintegrate into it, you will get to the point where no conscious effort is required for growth and peak performance.

The analogy I like to use is one of learning to drive. Initially, there seems to be all too many things to remember and too many stimuli competing for our attention. Over time, however, the whole process of driving becomes natural, automatic and unconscious. That is our goal for your future modus operandi – automatic growth and automatic creation in unconscious compliance with nature's *Optimizer* signals and your naturality.

My perception of the evolved human being is based on accelerated cycles of self-creation, creation, self-creation, creation, self-creation, and so on in perpetuity. Alternatively, you can think of this iterative process as self-growth, creation-growth, and so on. We grow ourselves and then our creations grow by reflection. The pursuit of more significant creations is the impetus for growth. The process of striving to create better realities grows us. Growth, then, has a single focus and that focus orders our lives.

Isn't the real focus of existing in the dimension we do to create at our maximum potential and evolve in the process? We want to achieve our greatest legacy through our greatest capability. More than this outcome, we want to sustain peak creation as the ultimate expression of ourselves.

The experience of *growth-creation flow*, with its built-in peak performance and peak evolution, is the ultimate state of human existence. The stretch required for the pursuit of meaningful creations invokes *flow* at the deepest levels and *flow* is a growth state. New growth is the byproduct of creation and new creation is the byproduct of growth.

Growth is a change in beliefs. Beliefs are information storage units in our system. Growth means the information held in our systems has changed. In a belief-created reality, our realities will change as our beliefs change. If our realities haven't changed, we could not have changed our beliefs and no growth has occurred. To grow our reality creations, we must grow ourselves. We must hold new information that sends different instructions to reality.

GROWTH IN THE NATURALITY PARADIGM

*"Mere change is not growth. Growth is the synthesis of
change and continuity, and where there is no continuity there
is no growth."*[43]   C. S. Lewis

*"All growth is a leap in the dark, a spontaneous,
unpremeditated act without benefit of
experience."*[44]   Henry Miller

Human growth is a process of developing, maturing, increasing, advancing, and strengthening. Physical and psychological growth is well documented. We also have good evidence of how we evolved to our current physical and cultural state.

Our understanding of future evolutionary growth of individuals, however, is still emerging. This perspective can instruct on a modus operandi for living that will generate our highest emotional states, our highest levels of performance, our greatest contributions, and our greatest rewards.

In the naturality paradigm, evolutionary growth is the process of continuous re-optimization that is required as a result of interacting with co-evolving systems in our context. Creativity in one system changes the environment of another system requiring it to re-optimize. As such, growth entails the creative resolution of optimization challenges.

Growth is advantageous, adaptive change where an improved level of functioning is sustained. It is the process of continuous adaptation to our changing world. Consequently, there is no arrival at a final end state. Our growth expertise is defined by the degree of adaptiveness of our personal system. The growth technology dramatically increases both the quality and speed of our adaptivity.

Science routinely discovers new hierarchies of order out of chaos. There is an underlying dynamic order that exists throughout the universe and, by token of us being part of nature, within every one of us.

The growth technology, as with all the peak evolution science technologies, capitalizes on this universal optimizing dynamic, the naturality flow. Nature is the expert for re-optimizing or growing us. Consequently, we don't have to go through a major learning curve to become growth experts. We just need to learn to partner with this optimizing dynamic as identified by the ten Optimizers.

Evolutionary growth in the naturality paradigm is achieved by aligning with the optimizing forces of nature. These forces are relentlessly re-adjusting interacting systems for optimal performance in reaction to changes within any or all of their co-evolving systems. Because we are designed for re-integration into the naturality flow, we can expect to be benevolently addicted to this flow. We come equipped with natural drives to draw us into this flow and emotional highs to keep us there. Our cultures have simply interfered with this process.

In the naturality paradigm, growth and re-optimization to environmental changes are always in the direction of naturality. Growth is towards increasing expressions of our naturality. Think of the expression of the "true you" expanding by concentric circles around your authentic core. This is our natural growth path. It is not linear.

Natural forces are perpetually acting on us to push us to intensify our expression. We do not need to have conscious control of it. We can simply action the messages of the ten *Optimizers*. Growth then can be defined as the amplification of an individual's true innate identity. Growth is measured by the creative expressions of that natural identity . . . . our reality creations.

Progression along our natural growth path is really a process of locking new and stronger beliefs into our system. Growth is about changing our belief structure. Beliefs are information storage units in our system. Growth, then, changes the information structure of our system.

Therefore, without belief changes, no growth has occurred. In a paradigm in which beliefs create reality, new beliefs mean reality will change. Therefore, if there is no corresponding change in reality, can we really say that growth has occurred? The degree of improvement of the adaptivity of the new reality over the old reality is the measure of our growth at any point in time.

The purpose of growth, then, is to enable us to create the next reality we want to bring into existence, the next expression of our natural identity. Growth is an iterative process of self-growth and creation-growth. If we are happy with our current reality, there would be no need for growth.

However, human beings are not designed to maintain the same

emotional highs from the same stimuli. Unfortunately, we adapt to them. We need new stimuli to sustain the same positive emotions. We are designed to grow, learn and create new things. Therefore, the requirement for growth is perpetual. In addition, because of the interaction of multiple creative systems, our capability for sustaining a reality over time isn't possible. Change is a constant.

The growth process then is really to define our next desired creation and become the person who has accomplished that creation. When the creation comes into existence, it will then reinforce our new state of evolution. Self-creation. Creation. Self-creation. Creation.

There is no growth without the expression of that growth out into reality. A change of beliefs creates a change in reality. We grow and create in the same direction, since growth and creation are two sides of the same coin. As you change your beliefs, reality is automatically changed.

GROWTH DIRECTION

Choosing the right growth direction can accelerate growth. The direction for every aspect of the technologies presented in this book is identical. Successful growth projects will move in the same direction as successful pathfinding and reality creation projects. The formulas for experiencing spontaneous knowledge, *flow*, and growth are not only consistent but identical. To maximize our potential, we must move with nature in the direction of the naturality flow.

The dissection of our ideal re-integration with nature's optimizing flow into the knowledge technology, the reality creation technology, the growth technology, the pathfinding technology, the reality design technology, and the quantum leap technology is artificial. It is just a means to perfect each of the components that will allow us to transition into the naturality paradigm to operate proficiently in the way we have evolved to function.

Growth is a continuous process of adaptation to our environment. The peak evolution science is a means to transition back to our highest form of creative adaptiveness for peak performance and peak evolution. Let's examine the direction of growth so we can remain focused and strategic in our efforts.

Move with the Naturality Flow

If we can grow in the direction nature is trying to evolve us, growth will be easier and more efficient. We will be moving with nature rather than fighting it. A multitude of natural processes and mechanisms will facilitate our progress rather than interfering with it. If we know nature's growth goals for us, we can go directly to them. This is more advantageous than meandering through disconnected growth events without getting their cumulative effect. Where possible, we would want to minimize disconcerting transition states and instead move from one stable state to the next. In other words, we would rather quantum leap than transition gradually. This becomes easier when we know where we are going.

If we want to accelerate our growth, all we need do is identify the naturality flow by the ten Optimizers indicating its direction and move with that flow rather than fighting it. In fact, it might be more strategic to become *proactive* in accelerating ourselves in the direction supported by nature.

Coincidences, flow events, quantum leaps, and spontaneous knowledge events will abound. We will experience the peak performance and peak experience of *flow*. Emotional highs will optimize and energize us. Because we exist in pure naturality in *flow*, adaptive realities will automatically be created by reflection. Whatever is needed next will appear by a series of coincidences reflective of the precision of our instructions to a belief-created reality.

Short term, systems want to operate at their peak efficiency to meet their needs. Long term, systems want to survive. You will notice, through the *Optimizers*, nature taking both aspects into consideration before supporting any changes to our system.

With 20/20 hindsight, it will become apparent that nature has much more information than we do from which to choose directions of growth. That information leads to additional options and creativity unavailable to us.

Until our consciousnesses are expanded enough to see how everything interconnects, we can rely on the ten *Optimizers* to flag our ideal growth direction based on nature's greater intelligence and knowledge.

Growth is about constantly adapting to a changing context. With pressure from nature, our system will be trying to re-optimize every time something changes. Interacting systems which are also constantly using creativity to resolve optimization challenges must constantly re-adapt to each other. All of the systems then are progressing. They are growing and changing.

Therefore, for our system to remain at its peak, we will always have to keep pace with systems relevant to our survival. Our system must co-evolve. Again, the ten *Optimizers* will reflect nature's greater knowledge of what's happening in all of our surrounding systems. They will point us in the ideal direction for growth.

With each creative resolution of an optimization challenge in any interacting system, the whole context advances. Re-optimization then has both a short-term aspect and a long-term aspect. Short term, your system might just adjust to come back into balance and optimal performance given a single change within your context. However, that short-term change is ideally made in such a way that the long-term fitness of your system is increased or maintained.

> *"We cannot remain consistent with the world save by growing inconsistent with our past selves."*[45]   Havelock Ellis

Let's think like nature for a moment. "Fitness" indicates a system's ability to keep as many options open as possible to adapt to future environmental changes. Fitness then is the means to ensure the long-term viability of a system. Therefore, fitness is the way we will keep our system safe and thriving. Whenever nature is resolving an optimization challenge to our system through growth, fitness will be a consideration.

When operating in a shared context, an improvement in the "fitness" of one system will lead to it having an advantage over competing systems. Therefore, continuing development is a must just to maintain a system's "fitness" relative to the rest of the systems it's co-evolving and competing with. This concept is called *The Red Queen Principle* and it was proposed by the evolutionary biologist L. van Valen (1973).

The Red Queen Principle is based on the observation to Alice by the Red Queen in Lewis Carroll's *"Through the Looking Glass"* that *"in this place it takes all the running you can do, to keep in the same place."*[3] Ideally then, we will want to keep pace with the rest of the human race.

Therefore, re-optimization is a never-ending process both short term and with respect to the long-term increase of the fitness of our systems which enable us to co-evolve with the supporting and competing systems within our context. Not only does our system have to adapt and adjust to each system we bump into, our system also has to progress with the rest of the systems in order to ensure our needs are met. If growth is re-optimization, then growth is with us forever and we will want to become expert at it.

Only Two Directions of Growth

Let's translate the direction of the naturality flow into practical, actionable terms. There are only two major directions we need to be concerned about with respect to growing in the direction of nature's flow. The first is the removal of interferences to naturality (Growth Direction I).

The second is the continuous augmentation of the expression of the authentic nature of our system (Growth Direction II). Everything needed to comply with these two directions is presented in this book.

Specifically, this includes the ten *Optimizers* and the peak evolution science: the knowledge technology, the reality creation technology, the growth technology, and their subsets, the pathfinding technology, the reality design technology, and, finally, the quantum leap technology you will learn about in the next chapter. The ten Optimizers help us identify the naturality flow for both the expansion of our naturality and the clearing of interferences.

Growth along our path of optimization around our authentic identity is a given. If nothing else, we have only to get out of nature's way and it will happen. That means we have to stop fighting nature – trying to go in a different direction than what the messages are indicating. In fact, by honoring nature's messages, we can accelerate this inevitable natural growth process.

GROWTH DIRECTION I: Clearing Interferences to Naturality

Our self-created reality is a phenomenal tool for helping us to clear the maladaptive beliefs interfering with our expanding naturality. In the Reclaim Your Reality chapter of the reality creation technology*'s De-*

Create Undesirable Realities section, we learned that nature is very systematic about clearing one disruptive belief after the next. This clearing is prioritized based on the threat each belief is to either being able to operate with naturality and/or to the achievement of our current emotional goals.

A cluster of events reflective of the dysfunctional belief will emerge in our reality with increasing strength and number until it is cleared. Take an inventory of past events to see this incredible orderliness in action in your own life. This needs to be seen to be believed. This is obviously a growth direction we want to not only comply with but to proactively assist. Toxic emotions are cleared in the same systematic way in partnership with reality.

We also learned how to clear struggle events which result from conflicting beliefs creating conflicting realities. In addition, we learned how to clear fear beliefs since fear beliefs can create realities in the same way that any other beliefs can. Reality design technology can also be used to create information coincidences for reality to act as your mentor; or to provide courses on the various territories of growth that you need to pursue; or toxic beliefs that need to be cleared.

In Chapters 9 and 10, we learned how to clear whole complexes of beliefs interfering with our naturality with respect to powerlessness and judgment, respectively. Both these belief complexes are unfortunately culturally induced and therefore inhibit many of us from being the people we were designed to be. The effects of removing these two belief complexes are so dramatic that the process for each should be considered a quantum leap.

We have another opportunity to clear a plethora of conflicting beliefs every time we set a new goal. I've mentioned the new-goal syndrome before, especially with respect to problems when setting new reality creation goals. However, it has advantages in the growth technology for accelerating growth. We can proactively use this phenomenon to address Growth Direction I challenges for growth.

With each new goal, all relevant beliefs are activated and begin neutrally sending instructions to reality. Some may yield positive events while others are negative. Pairs of beliefs may be in conflict creating struggle events. Consequently, right after setting a new goal, we may experience a number of struggle events.

Struggle events flag conflicting beliefs we need to change in order to achieve the new goal. The faster we change them, the faster we will achieve our goal and the faster we will grow. The bigger the goal, the greater the number of belief changes because more parts of our belief blueprint are activated. Proactively setting substantial goals, then, is a means to clean up our belief blueprint that much more quickly.

At first, the negative post-goal-setting events might seem to suggest we should not be pursuing that particular goal. Blocks have no negative emotions associated with them, other than perhaps a little frustration. Therefore, if your post-goal-setting events have a definite negative emotional charge, you are likely experiencing struggle events caused by conflicting beliefs.

As well, if you have passion for your new goal, then you know it's right for you. This is a clue as well that the problem events might simply require the removal of interfering beliefs activated by your new goal rather than abandonment of your goal. Once you know what nature is trying to accomplish, you can help it, accelerate it, and become proactive. Some of the common conflicting beliefs usually include valued/not valued, respected/not respected, powerful/powerless, abundance/scarcity, safe/not safe, free/not free, capable/not capable, and worthy/not worthy.

To grow, all you have to do is your normal procedures for clearing interferences to naturality presented in Chapters 8, 9 and 10. You will want to incorporate the cleanup of conflicting beliefs into every new reality design you make. As you become a growth expert, you will automatically be actioning any struggle events that come up in order to eliminate the conflicting beliefs that caused them. But as a "growth novice," this may not be business as usual for you yet.

By consistently setting significant goals, you will be able to identify maladaptive beliefs interfering with your naturality at a much faster rate. This means you can clear them faster thus freeing yourself to move along your natural growth path more quickly.

Whenever you set a new goal, all of the beliefs relevant to that goal are activated to create the necessary reality. We often can't identify problem beliefs through introspection. However, when they are dumped out as events in reality they become much easier to identify. Reality then becomes one of the many self-correcting feedback systems designed to keep us in optimal form.

When you make the necessary belief changes, events reflective of the old belief get smaller and less frequent until they fade away. At that point you have verification that growth has occurred. Reality has changed. Therefore, the information in your belief blueprint must have changed. Because reality is 100% self-created, you can use it to strengthen your naturality as well as clearing interferences. Using the new-goal cleanup process is an example of how you can proactively accelerate a process that nature is doing anyway. If we respond to the messages early enough, there is no need for growth to be painful.

You may have had a terrible childhood leaving you with all sorts of emotional scars. Because growth is re-optimization, it is not about going back and making right all of the damage we received from childhood traumas or unfortunate events in our lives. There is no need to relive those experiences in order to clear your system.

In fact, doing that will re-vitalize all sorts of old dysfunctional channels, responses, and toxic beliefs and emotions. These, in turn, will create unpleasant events in your reality by reflection. To use these channels again is to strengthen them and create events which will re-traumatize our system.

How much better it would be to have those channels atrophy from disuse. This is what nature does. Just because there is a defect in your system does not mean it has to be corrected. The way to enable these pathways to become dormant is to not keep irritating them or engaging them.

This could be accomplished by avoiding toxic territories. It can also be achieved by building a parallel replacement structure as we did when we exchanged the powerless and power reflexes. And, rather than evolving this replacement structure linearly, it can more quickly come into existence by reincarnation and a quantum leap, again as we did in the powerlessness intervention. Therefore, rather than developing a reality design which evolves you out of the previous toxic state, you need only re-conceive of yourself with new, more advantageous pathways.

Growth is re-optimization, not perfection. Your system can be dysfunctional in many ways that are not called for by your current context. As long as your current circumstance does not invoke those dysfunctional pathways, you can operate with peak performance.

If new goals require the activation of some of your dysfunctional beliefs, these beliefs will create problem events in your reality. Once the problem beliefs can be seen in the events in your reality, you know this is *new-goal syndrome* and can routinely clear them. Whenever you have negative emotions, this is the signal to select your preferred emotional goal or a reality that symbolizes your preferred emotional state and re-start the cycle of self-creation, creation, and so on.

It is only necessary to clear what is interfering with your naturality right this moment as flagged by the *Optimizers*. If there are no negative events occurring, then assume your imperfect self is optimized. The ten signals will tell us when there are changes to be made for the current needs of our system. Nature's focus is strictly in the present at resolving whatever the current optimization challenges are. Nature does not go back to correct historical flaws or previous evolutionary states of the system.

Our system, however, does store the record of past creativity used to solve problems. For example, your body can store antibodies which were developed to re-optimize from a smallpox immunization shot or worse, after the trauma of the disease. We can look at the blood serums of individuals and trace from what peoples and geographical locations their ancestors have derived. We can identify our physical evolutionary history through looking at the primitive states a human embryo passes through.

Nature didn't go back and correct this embryo for a more efficient version attuned to how we are in our current evolved state. It patches what is not working. Again, good or bad, the history of past creativity and evolution is captured in our system. What is not relevant to our present circumstance is not activated.

To help nature, we want to avoid territories that keep active or reactivate toxic channels. Move in the direction of nature's ten signals in order to attain peak performance and peak experience. Those signals will lead you to quantum leap to a life of pure creativity where you are experiencing your highest emotional states doing your *art* in *flow*. In no time at all, you won't even be able to access the old toxic emotions.

GROWTH DIRECTION II: Increasing Your Naturality

Growth or re-optimization is trying to happen to us all of the time.

Just as our various internal systems clear toxins out of our bodies every day, we have just reviewed elements of the naturality flow attempting to do this by purging interfering beliefs and emotions from our systems (Growth Direction I).

Simultaneously, the naturality flow is also trying to amplify, enlarge, and expand the expression of our authentic core, our true identity. Following here, then, are the elements identifying and supporting Growth Direction II. Compliance with these directions should greatly accelerate your growth process and your understanding of how nature is acting on your system to optimize and evolve you.

Follow your Natural Growth Path

For Growth Direction II growth, we will want to continuously expand our naturality or the strength of our naturality by concentric circles. This is the natural growth path. It is not linear. It is not the progression from one form to another. Rather, it is an enlargement or intensification around our central core. Naturality is *the emotion of naturalness* that results when we are in alignment with the state of optimization of our system – when all of the information inside and outside of us is in balance. This is our best functioning at any moment in time.

You have to feel the emotion of naturalness inside of you. You have to feel those drives trying to take you to naturality from inside of yourself – drives to self-knowledge, self-improvement, self-esteem, self-expression, self-creation, self-valuing; drives to creativity, creations, achievement, contribution, service, and to meaning; drives to being valued for who you are and what you contribute or achieve; drives to being free to be you, to belonging – with your uniqueness intact.

Naturality is not a static state but changes with our adjustment to our context. The only constant is the feel when you get it right. This natural feel is our continuous goal state. It is similar to moving from the noise and disorder of the outer swirl of a tornado to the order, calmness and power of the eye of the tornado. We want to remain in the eye by doing one natural act after the next, after the next. This will drive our expansion by concentric circles.

At each expansion of our naturality, we will be capable of a new level of power over our realities with respect to creation. If those creations are expressions of our naturality, they will reinforce our naturality and strengthen our authentic core even more. The process of expressing our naturality strengthens that naturality. As a result, our next creations will be an even more significant expression of our naturality. It will again reinforce us to even greater intensities of our naturality.

The basic dynamic for living soon becomes self-growth, creation-growth, self-growth, creation-growth, and so on. Therefore, the more you express your naturality, the faster you grow. If you are trying to be someone else in various territories of your life, you are interfering with this natural growth process. In every territory, you need to take action based on the same *feeling of naturality.*

As we come into alignment around our natural growth path, every seeming impediment in our reality becomes a call for growth along this path. As we clear the problem beliefs, or change directions with the block events, our lives will gradually move to an ordered simplicity. Everything will be about our progress to our next level of growth, no matter which area of our life we are dealing with.

Align your Life to your Naturality

You can be proceeding on your natural growth path before you have aligned your life with your authentic expression. However, as you do meaningful projects which are consistent with your naturality, you are transformed.

Once you've experienced operating at your peak in the *growth-creation flow* which emerges when you do your *art*, you become less tolerant of your less evolved functioning in other parts of your life. They seem to be digressive "noise" that has nothing to do with your true work and state of being.

Projects not aligned with your optimization path and thus not supported by *flow*, will seem to be too much work given your enhanced capabilities in *flow*. Also, your productivity is less than in *flow* where flows and coincidences support you and there is an absence of blocks and struggle events. Eventually, you will find yourself shifting every part of your life into alignment with your naturality and the naturality flow.

In alignment, quantum leaps can become daily occurrences. Growth accelerates dramatically. Functionality increases. Peak performance and peak experience come into play. There will be exponential changes. Amazing new powers. Because you are in alignment, you are sending very precise instructions to reality with the full force of who you are. No parts are in conflict. Every facet of your being is conscripted to a single focus.

Consequently, the accuracy, speed, and adaptiveness of your reality creation increases. In fact, realities supportive of your natural growth path appear with no conscious effort on your part. These supportive realities and creations further strengthen your naturality. The process spirals up to higher levels.

Alignment makes all Message Events Meaningful for directing Growth

The more you are in alignment with your naturality signature, the more accurate and valuable the messages in reality will be for your progress, your creations and your growth. These include all of the messages from the *Optimizers*: blocks and *flows*, coincidences, events that generated passions and emotional highs, flow states, toxic events, and struggle events.

Eventually you will align to the point where everything that happens to you is a significant message for your progress, for accelerating the growth-creation cycle even more. The number of extraneous events diminishes. This messaging phenomenon includes those clearing messages of the *Reclaim Your Reality* chapter. These systematically signal what interfering belief needs to be cleared next in Growth Direction I for growth acceleration. As a result of more meaningful message events, you can read the growth path easier which increases your speed of growth.

In alignment, the blocks and flows indicate the direction of growth and creation since these are expressions of the same naturality flow. If you are hitting block events, they are significant. Cease and desist. This is not the time to martyr yourself pursuing a particular channel to your goal that is generating block events in your life. No matter how sure you are that this is the only route, stop. *You are wrong!* You need to poll other possible routes. Or delay moving forward at this time.

And, if flow events are making it easy for you to go in a particular direction, go with them, even if you don't see how they are related to achieving your current goals. One thing I've found is that "growth novices" leave a lot of flow events on the table which might accelerate their progress. Again, experiment.

Do seemingly irrelevant flow events lead to beneficial results when you follow them? Test out whether nature is trying to facilitate your progress after all. New beliefs about reality, nature, the optimizing process and direction need to be gained experientially. May I suggest you honor all blocks and flows until you've acquired your own experiential truth?

All of the *Optimizers* leave a historical record of communications from nature which we can use to identify our ideal growth directions to intensified naturality. For example, you will have flow events in your life when you are moving in the direction of your optimization and nature's optimizing dynamic, and blocks when you are trying to go against it. Take an inventory of events in your past: blocks and flows, coincidences, events that generated passions and emotional highs, flow states, toxic events, and struggle events.

If you want to grow more quickly, you can simply analyze what the projections of those themes might look like in the future and proactively quantum leap to the indicated next level of expansion. If you are craving a faster growth rate, it is not necessary to wait for the signal events to appear in the present. Nature is very consistent so you can trust the historical record.

Take a look at the pattern of blocks in your past. It is telling you where not to go or grow in the future. There is no point in trying to grow in the direction of your blocks. Nature has already spoken. It is a mistaken cultural norm that has us constantly struggling against the blocks in our life.

Persistence is desirable in committing to have your goal. However, it is not advantageous if you are insisting on a particular channel and fighting all blocks to make that channel work. Innovate or change directions when blocks are encountered. However, persist to achieve your original emotional goal. If you are blocked in the pursuit of the symbol of that goal, find another symbol of the same emotional goal which is supported by flows.

If there is no pattern of block and flow events or other Optimizer message events in your life, it likely means that you have been externally referenced. External rather than internal events have been running your life. Use someone else's life to prove to yourself that the messaging patterns exist. This will at least build your beliefs that this is, in fact, how reality operates.

To investigate, choose the reality of a leader or someone who operates authentically or naturally or has strength of character. In the meantime, begin to follow your resonance and the other *Optimizers*. Within a very short time, you will have generated a pattern of accurate message events in your reality. They will shepherd you to your natural growth path and naturality and help to clear interferences to that naturality.

Resonance always leads to our natural growth path and hence naturality, optimization, *flow* and the naturality flow. This is also the perfect way to see all of the growth trends and optimizing systems presented in this book in action.

Unfortunately, we have habits, beliefs, rules and cultural norms which interfere with following our resonance. The peak evolution science is designed to get you back to what is natural. Natural drives will lock you into nature's flow so the science will no longer be needed once you are in alignment.

Resonance was one of my greatest clues that the naturality paradigm was correct. If you do nothing but follow your resonance, you will end up in the same place as if you did everything that the peak evolution science prescribes. In other words, you will end up in the naturality paradigm fully integrated with the creative optimizing flow of nature.

If you honor your resonance, you are automatically going to be slipping into *flow* state more frequently. *Flow* has growth built in. The entrance fee for entering *flow* is that you must be stretched beyond your current capabilities. Therefore, you can't help but grow.

Flow or activity fusion is a backdoor to growth. *Flow* is pure naturality. Flow increases flow. And *flow* increases naturality. *Flow* is a re-optimizing state bringing you back to your naturality. Flow automatically advances us on our evolutionary path. The trick is to hang onto your gains between flow states. Doing your *art* in *growth-creation flow* is the best activity for growth gains.

If all *Optimizers* lead to *flow*, and *flow* is a growth addicting state, then we are designed to be perpetually in growth. Those who have mastered the human living experience are those who are growth experts. Because of the nature of our natural drives and *Optimizers*, to be a growth expert will automatically make us growth addicts.

Being growth addicts will motivate us to perfect the art of accelerated growth. Once you enter the naturality paradigm and growth becomes a way of life, growth is exponential by quantum leaps rather than linear. More about this in the *growth horizon* section later in this chapter.

The greatest *flow* states occur around meaningful learning and creations associated with our *art*. This tells us another direction in which to move for growth. We must liberate ourselves to a life of doing our *art*. For most people, the resulting addiction to the territory where they have natural talents and skills will lead to a life aligned with that territory. And with the accelerated growth path that results, you'll soon find yourself operating and creating in that field beyond anything you could imagine.

The projects you become involved with will increase in magnitude and meaning until there is nothing else you want to work on. You have found your territory of greatest contribution and greatest reward, your most enticing growth path, and the route to peak evolution.

Once you truly experience your life theme which draws from you the most meaningful creativity, you will find that you never actually work again. Instead you will use the "effortless effort" of *flow* to accomplish monumental amounts of throughput. To the outside world, this can appear to be extreme dedication. To you, however, doing anything else is not an option. Your system has reached its dynamic home. Home for us is a *flow* state of naturality fully integrated into naturality flow. Your life moves into simplicity around the meaningful life theme(s) of your *art*.

Human beings have a built-in emotional adaptation to stimuli. This demands that we must perpetually pursue new stimuli to sustain positive emotional states. There is no arrival. Our emotional goals therefore, actually flag our direction of growth. Emotional drives are one of the ten *Optimizers* that identify the naturality flow.

Passion, in particular is an indicator of naturality. Passion tells you something is "you." Growth will be supported in the pursuit of your passions. We use our creations, including reality creations, to assist us to achieve our emotional goals. The same self-growth/creation-growth process is invoked. Thus our emotional drives satisfy Growth Direction II needs for increasing our naturality.

Just as passion is an indicator of your naturality, so, too, is meaning. Pursuing a great cause means there is a significant reality you want to create. Therefore, the self-growth/creation-growth formula for growth is energized by pursuing what is meaningful to you. Advances along your natural growth path will automatically be triggered.

Your creations, including your reality creations, are the only measure of your growth. Desired creations are the motivation for growing. Creatively expressing your naturality through your authentic *art* is a profound way to expand and reinforce your naturality. Pursuing this creativity is an imperative direction for growth.

Become Internally Referenced

Many of us have been brought up to look for our identity or how we are going to feel from external events. How much money we have. Our job title. What parents think we should be. Or our employers and friends. However, when we commit to naturality, we are moving to an internally referenced state. There is a very definite trend from childhood to maturity to move from being externally referenced to internally referenced.

This means, there is a natural evolutionary path from an identity, beliefs, and self-esteem based on the views of others to operating in accordance with our own internal voice. This then is another part of Growth Direction II.

Become More Fluid

As your growth experience and growth expertise increases, you will become much more fluid with growth as it becomes a way of life. You will be able to routinely change beliefs as they no longer serve you. This means you will be more fluid in changing your beliefs in order to change yourself and your reality. So many of us have been brought up to seek and expect stability when this is not the way of a world. It is filled with continuously re-optimizing and co-evolving interactive systems.

As a result, we are in constant distress when our expectations are never met. We live for the expected stable state not realizing that the stability we want is dynamic. There is safety in mastering dynamic stability and being fluidly able to respond to it. The shift from rigidity to fluidity is a growth direction we want to proactively pursue.

Move from Linear to Nonlinear

Most of us have been conditioned to operate with clear logical linear plans even though we consistently find that "stuff happens!" Consequently, we don't always get to actually work our plan. Once you have the pathfinding, creation and growth technologies down pat, however, a truly more logical approach to achieving our goals is to operate nonlinearly in partnership with nature. Nature prefers to operate by nonlinear quantum leaps to resolve optimization challenges.

Therefore, if we operate strictly in the present simply actioning nature's ten *Optimizers*, we will be capitalizing on nature's nonlinear expertise. The growth horizon technique is discussed shortly to expand on this concept.

With coincidences, flow events, quantum leaps and spontaneous knowledge, your effectiveness in going into the unknown will exceed even experts with the best plans. We want to capitalize on nature's ability to get there faster. Nature seems to have infinite creativity for achieving a goal with its increased access to information. This is a partner worth having.

Follow the Optimizing Trends for the Human Race

In Chapter 12, *Designing Future Worlds*, we learned of the directions in which the entire human system is evolving. Just as reality creation benefits from "going with this evolutionary flow," so too do the pathfinding technology and the growth technology. Here again are some current evolutionary trends for humanity you might want to take into consideration for choosing directions in which to accelerate your growth:

1. The flow of the human system is towards oneness, wholeness, unification, interconnectedness, integration and cohesiveness. The terms "clustering," "convergence," "alliance," "networks," "networking," "internet," "internetworking," and "community" are increasingly used in business.
2. There is a continuous flow to optimization through creativity, the creative expression of naturality, and quantum leaps.
3. Individuality is increasing.
4. Creativity is increasing.
5. The race is evolving towards expanded consciousness, nondual or unity consciousness, and higher frequency

consciousness. We are progressing from egocentric to worldcentric and beyond.

GROWTH ACCELERATION

Knowing the direction of growth is a wonderful asset for accelerating growth. There are some other growth expert tools that can accelerate your progress.

Flow

Flow is not only the direction of growth, it is a primary accelerator of growth. *Flow* is always taking us to naturality. Growth is built in because of the requirement for us to be stretched to enter *flow*. You're in an egoless state that is pure naturality. Therefore, one of the best techniques for accelerating growth is to significantly increase your time in *flow*. As we learned in the last chapter, all *Optimizers* lead to naturality and hence *flow*. However, following our resonance is especially effective in increasing *flow* time.

Quantum Leaps and Coincidences

Quantum leaps, which include coincidences and spontaneous knowledge, are an incredible way to accelerate growth. Nature prefers to achieve evolution, re-optimization and growth by quantum leaps. It's much more efficient to move from one stable state to the next without having to survive all sorts of gradations in the middle. Transitions are highly stressful, less efficient, and require much more work.

Many optimization solutions are not even possible by gradual evolution. It is difficult to imagine how to evolve a human eye, for example. It may be that the problem triggering your re-optimization cannot be resolved in a gradual way. It takes a redesign to an end state which may not necessarily even be linked to the start state. However, suffice it to say that what may look like an impossible task to grow from Point A to Point B can suddenly be achieved effortlessly by coincidences and quantum leaps.

Because the quantum leap technology offers a new artform and a new way of living, this mode of growth acceleration has its own chapter. Nature is much better at quantum leaps than we will ever be. Therefore, the solution, as with growth, is simply to learn how to partner with nature rather than to try to duplicate what nature does.

Your Natural Growth Horizon — Living Precisely in the Present

Growth speed increases tremendously when individuals come into alignment with who they are meant to be and when they begin to narrow their horizon of vision precisely into the present as a way of life. The goal is not just operating in the present but within the smallest possible horizon in the present.

The vision of our growth horizon can be thought of as a teeny, tiny window of time in the present. The horizon need only be as wide as is necessary to read the current signals from the ten *Optimizers*. All future thinking is relinquished as you shift into pure activity fusion in *flow* around the activity of actioning *Optimizer* messages.

From this narrow focus, we can grow at accelerating rates yet it *feels* like we are growing at the same leisurely pace. With increased fluidity, growth expertise, and the construction of an infrastructure of supporting beliefs and identities, growth will become easier. Therefore, over time, your effective rate of growth actually increases exponentially yet feels consistent.

It's as if, without the past and the future, there are no signposts to show movement, and therefore, the speeds of growth do not register. Again, the metaphor of living in the calm center of the dynamism of a tornado seems appropriate. Comfort also comes from the fact that, without past and future thinking, fears do not enter into the picture. Unless you are in imminent physical danger, there is usually very little to fear in the present. The overwhelm that often accompanies growth also does not exist with our focus confined to actioning messages in the immediate present.

This *growth horizon modus operandi* is the way to feel safe and at home in the dynamics of the naturality flow. Just imagine what this comfortable, naturality-directed, growth is going to accomplish over time if it is accelerating exponentially! Further, if our focus is strictly on the *Optimizer* signals, we will automatically end up in *flow*. All *Optimizers* lead to *flow*, which, in and of itself, is a glorious growth state.

Also, the growth horizon technique, itself, leads to pure activity fusion around the activity of actioning the Optimizers as a way of life. With growth built into *flow*, this *Optimizer activity fusion* defines the underlying dynamic of both peak performance and peak experience. Peak evolution continuously raises our peak performance potential.

The *Optimizer* activity fusion or the *Optimizer flow* state is the height of our growth capability (the growth technology), our creation power (the reality creation technology), and our access to spontaneous knowledge (the knowledge technology).

This is the place where consciousness evolves beyond the prevalent state for the rest of humanity. This is the point in which we move to our highest frequencies where we can hold more information and light. One could speculate that there could come a point where our frequency can ultimately cause us to cease to be visible.

Just like other information defined by quantum physics, we, as systems of information, could, theoretically, become nonlocal and distributed throughout the universe. We could access conscious awareness beyond our bodies. This could explain the phenomenon we call death.

There is no need for having a big plan about your growth or where you're trying to evolve to since we will always be evolving to intensified expressions of our *art* and our naturality. And nature knows how to do this best. It is more strategic to partner with nature through the *Optimizers* than to try to duplicate nature's expertise.

For this, we need simply tap into the optimizing dynamic acting on all systems. All the things we think we are pursuing are just our attempts to achieve this end anyway. Nature's communications tell you precisely what you need to do, message after message.

I developed this concept of the *growth horizon* initially on the basis of my work with Carl, a fifty-something marketing executive in a Fortune 500 company that was continuously downsizing. Carl lived in perpetual fear of being de-hired. He hadn't grown or changed in a long time and the whole prospect was quite formidable. His last performance review had labeled him "Not promotable."

To circumvent his continuous fear, we worked on taking Carl totally into the present by only having him action the messages from the ten *Optimizers* as they happened. He just had to focus on acting on each drive, each message event from his resonance, the blocks and flows as they happened, and so on. That's all he had to worry about. He didn't even have to think about the future. Gradually, all of Carl's fears began to fall away. He felt safe for the first time.

At first, we didn't realize Carl was growing to alignment with his naturality at such an accelerating pace because he wasn't experiencing any growing pains. Carl was just happy. As his naturality alignment began to *automatically* create adaptive realities for him, the CEO was fired and Carl was made acting CEO while an executive search firm recruited a replacement. Carl did such an incredible job during the six-month search that he was presented to the Board of Directors with the final shortlist of candidates. Carl was unanimously selected.

As Carl's alignment increased, he eventually reached the point of no return, where growth became an addiction. He was staying in the dynamic safety of his *growth horizon window*, but his effective growth rate was increasing exponentially. When Carl and I started, he was afraid of going into any new territory and couldn't wait until he arrived at some craved stable state again.

Once he became a growth expert and a growth addict and reached this point of no return, things reversed. He disliked the static states. They would trigger an emotional nosedive for him. Depression, fear, low self-esteem, frustration and anxiety all arose when he wasn't stretching himself into *flow* state to conquer a new territory.

Flow contains no negative emotional static and it would appear that it is biochemically addicting. Therefore, the new Carl felt most alive and happiest trekking into the unknown where *flow* was invoked. Stable states which could not incite *flow* were no longer appealing. In fact, he dreaded them.

Carl was now co-evolving with an advancing world rather than falling behind that progress. He had become an adaptive human being. To Carl, his stability was now dynamic. There was no context in which he could not feel safe. This trait alone drew the loyalty and respect of his followers.

The Reality Creation Technology

With the link between self-creation and creation, the reality creation technology can be used to accelerate growth. It is possible to simply create a reality of ideal growth. You can control the speed and direction of growth and the degree of support you want from reality using the reality design technology. The best reality design is always in the direction of the naturality flow, as is the case for nature-supported growth.

As you gradually become addicted to your natural growth path, you will want to receive your growth "fixes" on a regular basis. Therefore, you will want to begin to build an infrastructure of instructions creating a reality of accelerated growth. I recommend having standing growth blueprints for how you want your growth to be; what speed you want; whether you want a quantum leap per week or per day; and so on.

Reincarnation is a self-initiated form of quantum leap. However, it's an ideal technique for quickly internalizing a whole new set of beliefs in order to quickly change reality. Therefore, it would be advantageous to reincarnate yourself as a growth expert in order to quickly move to the level of expertise promoted through the growth technology.

Reality can be set up to support you. Why go through a painful transition if you can quantum leap from one stable state to the next. Rather than transitioning slowly into a growth expert, why not go direct? I've already described the end state in the growth horizon section. Why wait!

The reality design technology discussed in the Designing Future Worlds chapter includes a technique of "visualizing to the point of experiencing the emotions" the reality you want to create. You cannot experience the emotions of the new reality unless you have the relevant beliefs since you can't have one thought, one emotion, one symbol or one event in your reality without the underlying beliefs.

We need to feel the emotions in order to shift the beliefs in order to create the new reality. And this new reality can include re-creating us as well. Therefore, this same reality design technique can be used to accelerate our growth process. It helps us to lock in the belief changes that are necessary for growth to have occurred and to be sustained.

Growth by assimilation is another tool like reincarnation that is a self-initiated means for dramatic growth. It is a subset of reincarnation. It is another means to experience the emotions in the "visualize to the point of emotion" intervention because sometimes we can't visualize how it will feel to have a desired reality. It's too far beyond our world of experience. We need some help.

Can you find someone who has already achieved your next growth goal and absorb his/her emotional structure, thoughts, experience, knowledge and passion for that goal? Assimilation goes beyond having "empathy" or even "modeling" to actually assimilating or internalizing the emotional/belief complex of someone else to speed the creation of a new reality for yourself. It is an emotion-based exercise rather than an intellectual one. Clairsentience is a means to assimilate more effectively.

In the *Power of Identity* chapter, we learned about how to use your creations to strengthen your identity through identity-affirming creations. This is the foundation of the self-creation/creation growth dynamic. Because reality is 100% self-created, we can use it to strengthen our naturality.

Proactively pursue creations you are passionate about because passion is an indicator of naturality. That means they will be supported by nature. As those authentic creations come into being, they will reinforce your naturality so that even greater creations are possible in the future: self-creation, creation, self-creation . . . . Just doing what you are passionate about can therefore catapult you along your natural growth path.

The Knowledge Technology

You can also use the knowledge technology or, specifically, the pathfinding technology to accelerate your growth. Pathfind what you need next to either remove interferences or to strengthen your naturality. Reality can become a gigantic computer giving you the growth answers you need next. Knowledge derives from information. We are evolving in our individual lifetimes and "evolutionarily" as a race to holding higher frequencies. We can hold/access more information as a result. Growth is the process of adding to and changing the information of our system.

Find the Route of Least Resistance

Because, as a civilization, we have not had expertise in growth, many people have come to associate growth with struggle. How many times have you known how you must change in order for your life to work again, but fought to resist that inevitable change. This just prolongs the unpleasant transition state. How much smarter does it seem, in 20/20 hindsight, to have simply proactively embraced the obvious.

Now that you know about the naturality flow, you can partner with nature's expertise, processes and mechanisms to minimize disruptive transition states. You can know the direction of growth from the

Optimizers. If you are moving with this natural optimization dynamic, it should be without resistance. Blocks tell us we are going in the wrong direction. Blocks which invoke a negative emotional charge are actually struggle events which require us to resolve conflicting beliefs. There is no need to fight nature anymore.

Nature always chooses the route of least resistance for its progress. The route of least resistance tells us we are on the right path. Struggle means we are resisting growth, re-optimization, and evolution. We are resisting making the changes indicated by nature. We are fighting nature. We are not reading and complying with the messages.

Yes, admittedly, there will be some anxiety until you accept and have experienced growth and continuous re-optimization as a way of life for you. The sooner you get started, however, the sooner growth will be comfortable for you. You and nature want the same thing for your system. It's time to join forces. This is the route of least resistance.

"Through loyalty to the past, our mind refuses to realize that tomorrow's joy is possible if today's makes way for it; that each wave owes the beauty of its line to the withdrawal of the preceding one."
Andre Gide, Journals, 1928, TR Justin Obrien

16

TROUBLESHOOTING GROWTH

"Life is like riding a bicycle: you don't fall off unless you stop pedaling." Claude Pepper

A s our focus and priority becomes growth, we will begin to grow at accelerated rates. Consequently, we will begin to encounter new, more sophisticated growth problems. By identifying some of these special circumstances that can really throw "growth novices," I am hoping that you can move quickly to experiencing effortless, fast and safe growth.

Making growth a way of life requires growth to be safe. I want to give you an arsenal of troubleshooting tools every would-be growth expert should have. These will enable you to avoid problems, diagnose them when they do occur, and recover as quickly as possible. The intent is to keep growth trauma to a minimum.

Also, it is easier to maintain a growth momentum than to restart from a stopped position or after backsliding. I want to make certain you won't be sidelined by an easily rectified growth mishap. Forewarned is forearmed.

WHEN WONDERFUL PROGRESS SUDDENLY STOPS

As your growth expertise and your growth addiction compel you along your natural growth path, you can get very comfortable with the thrill of growing at this pace. Previously, you might have related to change like an ocean liner with the anchor dragging. Now, you have learned experientially that you were made for change. You've become a "growth Ferrari." However, all of a sudden, all this glorious growth and change and learning and advancement just stop.

This can be very unnerving, to say the least. All those emotional highs from growth and creativity and learning and pioneering disappear. You go from a state of knowing precisely what to do each moment to having no idea. You were operating on automatic pilot and never had to plan anything. Now everything has stopped.

The stream of flow events that were magnetizing you in a particular direction is gone. It is similar to following one bread crumb after the next through the forest and then all of a sudden there are no more breadcrumbs going forward or backwards. You have been deserted right in the middle of territory you have never been in before.

Relax. I am going to give you several explanations for what may be going on and what to do about each situation. It is important to remember that the growth and reality creation processes can never stop. You are always creating reality even when you are not consciously sending instructions to reality. Nor does the re-optimization process stop.

The chance of all systems interacting with your system not having to make any creative changes in order to re-optimize is almost nil. Therefore, your system's context will always be changing, requiring you to re-optimize. Accordingly, the explanations below are to help you deal with the *appearance* that one or both of these processes have stopped.

Rest

Nature may be stopping the interplay between you and reality and the other *Optimizers* because your growth addiction is about to overextend you. It's time to rest. It's time to stop and build up your reserves for your next growth spurt.

Sometimes, we get so high on the exhilaration flamed by the flow of exciting synchronicities facilitating our progress that we fail to notice that our body needs a rest. We may be on an adrenalin high. Nature will simply stop the speed of reality creation periodically to remind you to check in with your body to make certain that its needs are being met.

It may take the experience of several rest states before you are able to handle them without depression or fearing that something is wrong. We have all experienced the emotional drop that occurs after periods of great accomplishment or highs.

As you become a growth expert, you will take these breaks in your stride as with any other messages from the naturality flow. Rest is part of the growth cycle. You will learn to proactively work with nature and rest in preparation for future events.

As you experience the coincidences and events after the rest period and *know* that you could not have handled them as well without rest, you will come to trust these sudden breaks in the flow and take the time to prepare. This will become another of the indicators that the *Optimizers* do indeed operate with future knowledge.

Consolidate Past Growth – Assimilate Belief Changes as you Grow

One way to become a growth expert is to aerial view the process of growth – to understand its repetitive cycles. You are always going to have to periodically stop to rest, to consolidate your growth and learning periodically, and to restructure or lay the foundations for future growth. Growth is a period of new learning and new being followed by a period of consolidation to permanently integrate the new identity and beliefs into your system as new information.

Every time you grow, all your new learning and new beliefs need to be integrated into your system's current information infrastructure. There is no growth without new beliefs. Beliefs are the storage units for information. You need to absorb new realities, new identities, new beliefs, new modi operandi, expansions of your identity and your *art* and what is meaningful.

You'll want to consolidate your gains after new clearings of interferences. Periodically, all of these changes will need to be integrated into your existing structure so everything is cohesive and complementary. Gradually, you will come to know nature's signals to rest, grow, consolidate growth, and/or to restructure for pending growth.

Eventually, you will learn to do this on the fly despite rapid growth. But in the early stages of growth addiction, the emotional highs are so elating, you may forget all about doing this. Once your "buffer" is filled, however, like it or not, reality will grind to a halt until you reintegrate at your new level of evolution.

If you have really overextended yourself, this could require an illness or injury to get you flat on your back for the reintegration to occur. Or it could just mean a weekend as a couch potato in front of the television. As you commit to growth, you will gradually become highly sensitive to coming out of balance and therefore know when you need some downtime to do the necessary reintegration. Or, as I've suggested, to take 15 minutes to reintegrate on the fly.

The consolidation phase is an opportunity for expanding beyond your old habits and patterns. It is a time to reconnect with your natural self, and to strengthen the base from which you are creating your external environment. Here, your connections to others and external events is not as critical as a deeper connection with yourself.

Accordingly, as you begin living in alignment with your authentic core and your growth path, you will be blocked from people and events that would interfere with your consolidation period. Accept the temporary isolation and inactivity as benevolent and adaptive.

Rather than a continuation of the flow of synchronicities or coincidences catapulting you to your goals, you will find synchronicities supporting the assimilation process. Comply with the Optimizer signals that are enticing you to do the internal activity that is necessary for you to prepare to move to your next stage of growth.

If you really get going way too fast without assimilating, you will have stronger and stronger, perhaps more unpleasant reasons for suddenly going into the consolidation phase. But if you stay on top of the assimilation and proactively consolidate yourself, growth will be a painless process.

Restructure for Future Growth

In addition to consolidating past growth, downtime may be required to prepare your system for future growth built into your growth path or your current goals. This is especially prevalent for pending quantum leaps and periods of rapid growth. You will come to differentiate the feel of the downtime requirements for consolidating versus restructuring.

As a growth expert, it would be ideal to proactively cause the consolidation and restructuring phases on a regular basis in order to keep growing at rapid speeds. As you become more fluid and more able to make belief and identity changes at will, you can flow through these growth-cycle phases at high speeds without interrupting the growth process.

Remember, as well, that growth is expansion by concentric circles around your authentic core. Knowing the direction of growth will help you to understand what nature is trying to communicate. Increase your fluidity and spontaneously recreate yourself at the next level to eliminate uncomfortable transitional states. These are elements of the quantum leap technology you will learn about in the next chapter.

You may end up sleeping more during the consolidation or the restructuring phases of the growth cycle. It's easier to re-integrate at a new level in an altered state of consciousness such as occurs during sleep. In fact, if events in reality suggest you have to restructure very quickly, then you may even proactively decide to take a "growth nap."

If you have to continue to function out in a world created by the "old you" during a major restructuring, it makes it that much more difficult to morph into a new stage of growth. Just "reality design" the identity you need to have and go to sleep with the intention of waking up as that person. Again, this becomes easier as you become more fluid and as you gain the necessary beliefs experientially.

Simultaneous Reality Design and Creation – Instantaneous Creation

If there is no time between what you blueprint for reality and the creation of that reality, it will seem you have stopped. You will not have a measure of your progress. This is the most wonderful reason for the appearance that growth has stopped. It signifies we are actually in one of our most powerful states. This is the way we were designed to operate at optimization. Reality creation will be moving at the speed of your requests or needs.

This will naturally evolve out of a progressive increase in your reality creation capabilities and beliefs in compliance with the naturality flow. The time between each iteration of reality design and its creation will become smaller and smaller until it is simultaneous. We have all visited this state in flow. Now we can aspire to live in it permanently.

If you want to test to see if you are, in fact, in the powerful state of instantaneous creation, design bigger realities. This will increase the separation between the time you blueprint and the time you receive. You will see this separation between reality design and reality creation again, so you can experience progress again.

Another way to look at instantaneous creation is that you are operating in the "omnipotent NOW." You are operating 100% in the present. It is a little disorienting to slip into this state – a little like sliding into the eye of a tornado from the torrential outer winds. Begin experiencing past or future thinking again and you will click out of simultaneous reality design and creation. You will no longer experience the apparent inactivity of instantaneous creation.

Your time in this powerful state of instantaneous creation will increase as you sustain alignment with your natural growth path and the naturality flow, especially if you are doing your art in *flow*. In this state, your true identity beliefs are driving your reality creation without you being consciously aware of it or having to have your hands on the wheel, so to speak.

In the *Designing Future Worlds* chapter, I discussed the automatic reality creation that results from living in alignment with your naturality and your natural growth path. I mentioned that you could actually get to the point of not having to consciously design reality at all. This too is instantaneous creation.

It's a little unnerving to some when you suddenly move into automatic reality creation. If you are used to struggling to get what you want or meticulously visualizing your desired new reality because you believe it's hard to get, you may have trouble coping with all of the wonderful coincidences that start occurring to accelerate your progress. Some people aren't used to being looked after so well by a benevolent universe. It's alright to be overwhelmed now and again by tears of joy.

Fear and Future-Thinking

You can snap out of rapid growth and/or instantaneous creation the second you come out of the present. Fear is anxiety about the future and, as such, it may trigger you to slip out of the present and the activity fusion of *flow* state.

Let's say you're moving at this terrific pace where reality seems to be harmoniously "handing" you precisely what you need next for growth and instantaneous creation. You scan recent events and see the pattern of events indicates a very definite pathway that reality seems to have been guiding you along. You project that pathway out into the future and you suddenly move into overwhelm.

You feel you could not possibly cope with what seems like the inevitable direction of your growth. You fear you will not be able to cope with that impending reality, as wonderful as it may be. It is too big for you. Therefore, you immediately stop the growth with your fear.

Of course, if you use any of these past events as a viewpoint for your current state of evolution or progress, you will no doubt find that you would have had the same fear about achieving your current status. You would not have expected to feel this good or be handling the situation so well. In other words, taking your hands off the wheel, staying in the present, and letting nature drive your growth one moment at a time.

The only time it felt unsafe was when you wanted to take control back from nature. When you no longer wanted to follow what excited you moment after moment and what you resonated with. When you lost your connection with your naturality, NOW, this moment, in the present. This is where your power is and where you are safe.

So returning to the NOW is one way to restart your progress because all that exists is the immediate action indicated by your resonance and the blocks and flows. Another way is to clear your fears in the ways we discussed in Chapter 8, *Reclaim Your Reality*. A third way is to simply expand your identity – to reincarnate yourself – as a person who has had that projected reality for ten years. Then, rather than stretching yourself to handle a new reality, you are dealing with a reality with which you have been dealing expertly for the past ten years.

Reality is Waiting for Instructions

Growth and creation are linked. Growth can therefore stop if the requested reality has been delivered and there are no more requests. Has reality completed all outstanding instructions you have for it within your territories of activity? Is it time to issue another reality design? Think of reality as a computer. Within the confines of the naturality flow, you decide what that computer will be doing.

Are you no longer interested in a goal you have been pursuing? Check your resonance and enthusiasm. Is it time to pursue a new goal? Issue new Instructions to reality through the reality creation technology. This is a good time to reexamine your growth strategy, your emotional goals, and your desired reality designs. If you could reincarnate in a more evolved state, what would that look like?

Timing

Occasionally, the reason your progress grinds to a halt is because the necessity of orchestrating a number of streams of events requires it. Certain things have to happen before you can move to the next step. If you push through the halt of the flow states associated with growth, you will likely not only have to struggle uphill to do the work of the task you think has to be done next, but your efforts will likely be wasted.

For example, the requirement for the task could be completely eliminated in the future by a coincidence or a better direction becoming available or by creativity by another person altering what has to be done. It could be that an entirely new channel for your progress is being constructed as the resolution to an optimization challenge of another system.

You will want to keep your experience of negative events to a minimum to avoid damaging your system. Therefore, trust your blocks and trust the feeling of resonance and naturality at all times. Eventually, you will understand when nature and your resonance are communicating that an activity is delayed or eliminated. Growth stops won't be so disconcerting and you won't be tempted to push through them.

Multitasking - Wait for Events to Occur

Without question, one of the hardest things to do as a growth addict is to wait. Gradually you will shift over to a multitasking mode in harmony with nature so you never stop experiencing the joy of *flow*.

Here's a way to think about this. Assume there are 20 channels you feel are possible avenues for you to achieve your most recently requested emotional goals. You have no idea how to get to the goals and you have no idea what the 20 channels are. You use your resonance to select the first channel you are going to action. Let's say it's channel 18. You start taking the actions of channel 18 and flow event after flow event confirm you are going in the right direction.

Let's say this "hypothesis channel" seems to be leading to the preparation of a proposal to your boss for additional resources. All of a sudden, either the flow events stop or blocks begin to occur. For those who don't trust nature, you might push ahead to prepare the proposal. Experienced growth and pathfinding experts, however, would stop and poll the other channels. It could be that something has to occur before it's right for you to proceed with channel 18 again.

Let's say that through your polling, your resonance now tells you to proceed with actioning the hypothesis represented by channel 2. Again, flow event after flow event occurs and then, suddenly, it too stops. You poll the 20 hypothesis channels one more time. The flow events now suggest going back to channel 18. When you begin channel 18 again, you find the proposal you were going to have to make to your boss for resources to move ahead is not necessary. Some emergency has occurred that makes it everyone's priority to do what you wanted to do.

Had you pushed ahead on channel 18 previously, you would have wasted a lot of time and effort and possibly been "damaged" by the struggle. By the blocks signaling you to delay – and you listening to them – reality restructured effortlessly to support your progress.

Alternately, nature, with its broader knowledge of events occurring in multiple systems, had you stop to wait for events which were already in process. You must experience nature's intelligence – the knowingness of your resonance, the creativity of the blocks and flows – in order to have enough trust to relinquish the control of your own limited intelligence, knowledge and creativity.

Keep experimenting so that you have your own examples of nature orchestrating your progress and your growth in safety. I can tell you thousands of stories demonstrating this process but it is your own stories that will convince you. It is your own experiences which will change your beliefs so that the whole process operates even more quickly and effectively in the future.

Because of the ability to read the blocks and flows, you will find yourself working on multiple projects or themes simultaneously. This will occur even if you have always been a person who, in the past, has focused on one task at a time. When you partner with nature, blocks on one task mean wrong time or wrong direction. Look for what else is flowing or supported by nature.

If the original pathway was correct, in 20/20 hindsight you can often discover why nature delayed your progress. You will discover that something else had to happen before you proceeded. Nature's switching you over onto some other task helps to capitalize on and maintain your *flow* state and peak performance. In no time, you'll learn to multitask without blinking an eye to sustain maximum achievement.

Let Go of the Old to Make Room for the New

If you are a growth expert, you will always be bringing new elements, new ideas, new beliefs, new people and new realities into your life. As such, people, things, ideas, identities, beliefs and realities that no longer suit you will be leaving your life to make room for the new. You should allow this exodus to occur naturally. That means there should be a steady stream of things into your life and out of your life.

If you do choose to facilitate that process, there should be lots of flow events to help you, if it's the right time and the right action. If you attempt to hang onto parts of your old world that are no longer relevant to the growing you, you may inadvertently stop the flow of new things into your life. You may stop your growth. There will be no room for new things to come in.

This is particularly unnerving to people who fear abandonment or have tendencies towards being a packrat or who fear change or loss. Many of us want to hang onto everything out of beliefs in scarcity – just in case we need it or them in the future. We want to keep all of the old stuff and add new things as well.

The greatest dilemma occurs around letting new people into your life and letting others leave. One approach is to keep aerial-viewing your progress along your growth path. If you have just released the conflicting belief complex around powerlessness, for example, you are strengthening beliefs you are valued, capable, and respected as well.

Therefore, if there are people whom you associate with not valuing and respecting you, then one of two things will happen. They will either restructure to valuers or remove themselves from your reality. If you no longer have a belief of not being valued and valuable, you cannot create people who don't value you. Sorry, you'll just have to let these non-valuers leave.

If you fight it out of some sense of loyalty, or rules about what is required with respect to friends and family, for example, you will create struggle events in your reality.

It should not be necessary for you to take action to get rid of people. This is a relief to those of us who don't want a confrontation. All you have to do is get out of the way so it can happen. It is inadvisable to prevent someone from leaving who is being orchestrated out of your life by optimizing systems as a result of your growth.

GOAL-RELATED PROBLEMS

There are a few growth problem situations to be aware of with respect to goals: when you set a new goal; just before you achieve your goal; and right after you achieve it.

New-Goal Syndrome

The neutral dumping of problem events into your reality as a result of activating previously unused conflicting beliefs with a new goal was discussed in the last chapter with respect to removing interfering beliefs. The solution is to accept this occurrence as part of the growth and creation cycles and routinely resolve your conflicting beliefs whenever you set a new goal.

Problems When you are About to Achieve your Goal

When you are about to achieve a major new reality that you have been pursuing, things may suddenly go wrong. This is due to a conflict between the old identity that didn't have the new reality but craved it and the new identity that will have it. Simply quantum leap to a level of identity, and hence reality, beyond that which you are seeking – as if you had had the new reality for ten years, for example. The disruption or upheaval can also be because you've had a taste of the new reality and fear you won't get something that feels so great.

Also you may have some old conflicting beliefs relevant to creating your new reality that are dumping out. Just clean them up so you can hang on to the level of growth represented by the new reality in the offing. The old part of your belief blueprint was not designed to have the new reality and it hasn't quite faded out yet while the new part is fast creating the new reality. You are literally split between the old and new identities and the old and new beliefs all creating your reality simultaneously.

This is the point at which you are most vulnerable in your growth and reality creation processes. You just need to do some cleanup and keep energizing the emotional feeling of the new reality. Keep moving forward.

Problems Right After you Achieve your Goal

Being stretched beyond your existing capabilities is what creates and sustains your flow states. If you don't plan your next goal before you finish your current goal, you may risk going into downtime without flow. Flow is addicting and if you have spent a great deal of time in flow to pursue your last goal, you are going to be experiencing a major biochemical, electromagnetic and emotional withdrawal. Our goal is to be perpetually in flow. Plan ahead to avoid flow withdrawal.

REALITY "ZAPS" DE-ALIGNMENT

You will be zapped by major "struggle" events if you try to come out of alignment after living your true identity for a period of time. Reality can be brutal if you stray off your natural growth path after living in alignment. Alignment is home to us. It is natural and fully supported by the naturality flow.

Once your system has had a taste of being in alignment, even for a couple of weeks, it is very resistant to coming out of it. That resistance is reflected in reality as struggle events and major blocks. Since they seem to come out of the blue, I call them "zap" events. It's as if you get an electric zap from nature to get back to naturality. The solution, of course, is to quickly follow nature's *Optimizers* back to *flow* in the naturality flow.

IDENTITY-REALITY MISALIGNMENTS

In the self-created reality of the naturality paradigm, it is important for growth experts to keep their self-growth and reality-creation-growth in balance. This is tricky if you haven't yet experienced *growth-creation flows* or naturality-driven, automatic reality creation.

Coping with a Reality Larger than your Identity

Creating a reality too large or successful for your identity can invoke negative emotions like fear and overwhelm which can sabotage your progress. This is the imposter phenomenon. It is a psychological syndrome based on intense, secret feelings of fraudulence in the face of success and achievement.

Imposter phenomenon sufferers believe they don't deserve their success. They believe they are phonies who have somehow "gotten away with it." They feel they aren't the people they appear to be to the rest of the world. Imposter phenomenon victims are driven to achieve, yet live in fear that each new success will reveal them as fakes.

If you have beliefs that you don't deserve a successful reality, then those beliefs are going to eliminate the successful reality you have created. It would be a shame for you to lose ground in this way. I would rather you didn't sabotage your success. Instead, let's use a conditioned reflex again as we did with powerlessness. Use the event of creating a reality that is too large to trigger us to reincarnate with an identity far beyond the reality that exists.

You could redesign yourself as a person who has had the new reality for ten years, for example. That way this reality that was a stretch for us will be old hat. Instead of the successful reality disappearing, our reality will continue to advance and grow us right along with it.

When you've had a dose of success, pay attention to events in reality reflecting your fears and clear them. Your fears may be reflected in the voice of someone you consider a judge or a saboteur of your progress. If struggle events emerge, resolve the conflicting beliefs behind them as well.

This is business as usual anyway for a growth expert. We always want to clear toxicity as quickly as possible so we don't create events that will damage our system further. Our goal, again, is to have only beliefs which support our naturality. Intimidating success can be another opportunity to clear dysfunctional beliefs out of our belief blueprint.

Typically, what happens when you create a reality too large for your identity is that part of you has created events in reality that suggest you are ready to move to a new level. The other part is afraid of the change. Beliefs of the "new you" and the "old you" are beliefs in conflict. This is the recipe for creating the sandcastle syndrome, where one set of beliefs creates the success and the other set wipes out the new reality created. Both parts need to be brought into alignment.

Unfortunately, I have never seen anyone successfully "de-grow" the part that's the most advanced and be happy about it. Therefore, if you don't bring the other part up to the level of the more advanced part, you will have conflicting beliefs and conflicting identities creating struggle events in your life.

If parts of you accidentally create sudden levels of success, make it a habit to quickly reincarnate yourself as a person who has had that larger reality for over 10 years. Visualize all the things such a person would have experienced until you can not only "feel" all of the emotions but they are permanently ingrained and integrated into your emotional infrastructure.

From this more evolved state, you will successfully accommodate and sustain your new reality. You will again have an identity larger than your reality. As a growth expert, we don't want you to ever backslide but, rather, to pull yourself forward to hold any new reality you create. Increase your fluidity and spontaneously recreate yourself to eliminate the transitional state.

It would also be appropriate to revisit the judged-judging reflex intervention to eliminate judgment-related fears. In addition, creating a reality larger than your identity could also be considered business as usual for a growth expert. The underlying dynamic of human existence is self-growth then creation-growth. We grow ourselves to grow our creations. We then use our creations to help us grow even more.

If part of your belief blueprint and your identity beliefs has created the larger reality, you will want to quickly bring the other parts of yourself along so that the reality you created does not suddenly degrade back to your old level. You will want to use your creation to grow yourself. Your strengthened position will then empower you to create more significant realities again in the future. Your growth momentum will be sustained.

Coping with an Identity Larger than your Reality

The safest state for growth novices is to keep their identities ahead of their realities. In other words, the safest strategy is to start with the self-growth side of the equation first and let that drive the creation growth. We tend to strive for realities beyond where we are right now which means the growth is built into the process. This is consistent with the design of our systems.

However, where we go wrong is in hoping a new reality will give us emotional goals we don't have the beliefs for, or make us into the people we have not yet become. We hope a reality of fame, money, or success, or love, or being valued will make us into the person we want to be and give us the feelings we want to have – self-love, self-esteem, freedom, and the like. In a belief-created reality, we must *be* the person first in order to create the corresponding reality.

If I had to generalize as to the strategy which causes people some of the greatest unhappiness, it is in hoping that a new reality will create a new "you." Now that you know that a new reality can only be created by a new you, you know that striving for the reality before the identity is futile and a prescription for unhappiness.

Coexistence of Old and New Identities creates Conflicts

If we are growing gradually to alignment with naturality, then there will come a point where part of us is in alignment and part of us is not. Our natural identity is coexisting with our old identity. These are two conflicting belief complexes which will interfere with each other. When you have been doing your art and living in compliance with the Optimizers and the naturality flow, you will want to watch for struggle events to emerge from this clash.

If you aren't really making the progress you'd like in unraveling each of the conflicting beliefs in order to clean up your belief blueprint, here's a rapid approach. Simply reincarnate yourself entirely as the authentic you. The fastest solution is to simply quantum leap the rest of the way over to complete alignment with your naturality.

When half of you has changed, you can speed through the discomfort of the transition by simply yanking yourself all the way over in one watershed event like instantaneous reincarnation. You'll bypass all of the messy transitioning experience. When you know where nature is trying to take you, you can proactively accelerate your progress to get there by the fastest route.

I have already flagged the problem of co-existing old and new realities and old and new identities at other spots. Obviously, both of these are growth problems. The weakest point is when you are creating both the old and the new simultaneously and equally. "Growth novices" are quick to think they have failed to create their desired new reality because they don't realize that the continuance of the negative elements of the reality they are trying to replace is only temporary. The old creations from old instructions are still fading out as the new beliefs are gaining in dominance.

The answer always is to continue to "feel" emotionally the reality you are trying to bring into existence to continue to energize those instructions. Keep "wearing" the new reality of naturality. Keep blueprinting your desired new reality and try not to be distracted by the reality on its way out. It is important not to re-energize, in any way, the old reality.

Do not re-absorb its beliefs because they will reissue instructions to reality which will, in effect, sustain that reality in your life. Always assume that the new reality is coming and each item that is standing in the way is presented to you benevolently for clearing.

As a subset of this growth challenge, let me point out to growth novices a problem to watch out for as you're transitioning into alignment. As part of you is operating creatively around what you love to do, the other part is trying to maintain the old tasks that you used to do.

Work that you used to be able to do begins to cause you great discomfort and is wrought with problems. What's happened is that you've had a taste of the emotional highs of doing your art in flow, being authentic, growing and learning. Creativity is highly addictive. As a result, previous "have-to-do" tasks now seem intolerable by comparison.

Obviously, you want to turn yourself over to naturality as quickly as possible by operating with your resonance. Your resonance will help you to release the old tasks and shift into a life around your art. You know where nature is taking you. If you fight nature, you will simply prolong the uncomfortable transition state which may end up damaging your system.

Overwhelm: Stay in the Present

Overwhelm can creep into your growth process and quickly become a disabling state. While you may be enjoying the new growth experiences in your life as you become a growth expert, your progress along your growth path may be at speeds that are a little unnerving. In other words, you are overwhelmed by the sheer speed of your growth and the magnitude of the new realities you are experiencing.

Let me just remind you that, at all times, you are in complete control of your speed of growth. The moment you identify the new "slower growth" reality you want to experience you have started to bring it into existence. There is no need to return to your old state of powerlessness vis-à-vis the events occurring in your life. You are in control. Faster growth, slower growth, either is your choice.

Another instance of overwhelm relates to the fear that can occur when you suddenly realize that a reality you consider too large for your current identity is on its way into your life. As your consciousness expands, you begin to see the orderly patterns of your direction of optimization, your growth path.

With 20/20 hindsight, you can see precisely where the naturality flow has been channeling you from past events. However, when you project that direction out into the future, the future reality looks too big for you to handle. You choke. The solution is to stay in the present and allow nature's flow to continue to shape you through safe growth to be the person with the projected reality.

You can't create that future reality until you have the necessary beliefs and identity. Again, you are in control. You are not powerless and plunging towards danger. You are in precisely the same safe place in the present with your growth formula that you were several stages back on your growth path where your present position also would have looked scary to the person you were then.

Of course, then a third trigger for overwhelm would be if you had already created a reality too large for you, rather than just fearing it might come to pass. And again, to summarize my previous discussion, you will want the parts that are afraid of this reality to join those parts of you that created the larger reality. The faster the merger, the sooner you can get rid of the discomfort of experiencing the overwhelm of this transitioning situation.

Fluidity and reincarnation are by far the best ways to go. You want to have the identity of someone who's mastered that new reality ten years ago. You can also use the reality creation technology to create support mechanisms to assist you or to keep you safe.

Most executives I meet these days are already in overwhelm so it is difficult for them to contemplate adding growth, learning, and more creativity to their agenda. Scarcity of time and resources, fears about their capabilities, performance anxiety and the like all create the experience of overwhelm.

The fastest solution is to begin to live your life in the present with your resonance. That's all you have to concentrate on. You can only take one action at a time and your resonance will tell you which one is the best for you. This is the way of life you want to have in the naturality paradigm anyway so why not just quantum leap to this formula of existence. If your resonance is not yet developed enough on its own, you can read all of the *Optimizers* using the *growth-horizon-window* approach.

Overwhelm is just a habit you can release. There are some belief changes that will also help. Rather than believing in a scarcity of time and resources and rewards, you will want to convert to a belief in abundance – that this is an abundant world. And speaking of abundance, do you remember the definition? The ability to create what you want when you want it. This is a great belief to have and it totally eliminates the possibility of overwhelm.

Also, hopefully you have been experiencing the safety and benevolence of operating with nature in the naturality paradigm and have been growing those beliefs to the point of trusting the messages from nature to keep you safe. When you know how to read all of the signals, there's nothing to fear. You can trust that the growth process will grow you in time.

Coping with Clairsentience – Beyond Empathy to Absorption

Clairsentience is a stage of evolution. It is the ability to quickly absorb the emotions of another as your own. It results from the gradual expansion of consciousness en route to unity consciousness. With clairsentience, emotional intelligence goes up dramatically. Individuals become increasingly familiar with their own emotions and emotional goals. As their resonance leads them to be in the right place at the right time and to focus solely in the present, their empathy with others increases to the point that they have quite intense connections with them.

This would be great if it stopped there. However, as they come to "own their realities," to internalize identities which include everything in their reality, they begin to experience oneness inside and out. They will quite often end up "wearing" the emotions of others without realizing it.

There is a wonderful side to having clairsentience because of the increased sensitivity and connection to others. On the positive side, you can use clairsentience to better connect with people; to read them better; to acquire new information about them; or to assimilate the emotional structure of someone else for the purpose of creating a particular reality.

However, this chapter is about troubleshooting growth. It is very important to be aware that, in all likelihood, the development of clairsentience will creep up on you as you increasingly pursue naturality in the naturality flow. That means you can be humming along your natural growth path, again, without a care in the world, when all of a sudden you're experiencing major depression or major fear or major anger or major powerlessness.

Before you wonder what you did wrong as a growth expert, review the people you just had conversations with or even people you have just been thinking about. Whose emotions do you think you absorbed? As soon as you realize these toxic emotions are not yours, they usually clear right out of your system. I have seen very capable executives totally de-railed by clairsentience – even going into a tailspin for several days.

Hopefully, forewarning you about clairsentience will enable you to avoid the problems yet experience its benefits. You will want to protect yourself from it but also to use it. Get to the point of being able to differentiate your own emotions from someone's foreign toxicity in your system.

Also, watch for tapping into global sentiments on various subjects. You may stop reading the newspaper or watching the news for this reason. You can do this safely because you can have a standing reality design in which you will have information coincidences that will bring you the information you need when you need it. Having the beliefs to allow you to operate at Level III of the Knowledge Technology will accomplish the same thing (see Chapter 5, *Spontaneous Knowledge*).

You need to have the necessary beliefs in order to become a growth expert in partnership with nature. These beliefs will need to be gained experientially. As much as I would like it to be possible for me to simply give you the knowledge for you to immediately have the capability, there is too much unlearning for that to be the case for the majority of people.

Peak Evolution offers a completely integrated approach to an entirely new paradigm in which to live. Begin to operate in some part of the naturality paradigm and the other parts will also start to work for you. Make nature's expertise your own and you'll discover how truly exciting growth as a way of life – a life theme – can be.

17

QUANTUM LEAP LIVING

"You can't solve many of today's problems by straight linear thinking. It takes leaps of faith to sense the connections that are not necessarily obvious."
Matina Horner, PhD, Psychology; President, Radcliffe College

Our culture is generating changes in our world faster than we are able to adapt to those changes. Our quality of life depends on our ability to become more adept at growth, especially its acceleration. The naturality paradigm offers numerous techniques for partnering with nature to evolve more quickly.

None are more powerful and life-changing as the quantum leap. I am proposing we not only learn how to master quantum leaps but to make them our modus operandi for living.

Because everything is interlinked in the naturality paradigm, it's possible to parlay one quantum leap into a cascading series of quantum leaps by the domino effect. Rather than transitional growth, this is transformational growth at exponential rates. This is peak evolution.

Quantum leap living offers the means to not just survive but thrive and strive in today's tumultuous world. Quantum leap living is a state of mind as well as a modus operandi. It is a philosophy for living which goes beyond hitchhiking on the naturality flow to proactively skipping ahead to the most evolved states possible in the naturality paradigm. Growth and "quantum leaping" will be critical skills for the future fitness and adaptiveness of the human race.

Quantum leaps increase the speed of growth while reducing the pain of growth. One of our most serious failings with respect to growth is our tendency to resist change. As we fight change, we prolong our experience of unpleasant transition states before order is once more restored. Quantum leaps allow us to bypass this negative transition. Instead, we can quantum leap from one stable state to the next. We can progress by wholes.

From *Peak Evolution*, we know the direction of growth as prescribed by the naturality flow. We also know the key quantum leaps required to get us to our most evolved state. A quick review of the quantum leaps listed at the end of this chapter will confirm that. We know what to look for in the *Optimizers* to know when nature wants us to change. We know the techniques to make the changes. We know how to troubleshoot growth. With this chapter, we have the final piece for accelerated growth – mastery of the art and science of the quantum leap.

The quantum leap technology gives us the means to master the art of continuous and progressive re-invention. Quantum leaps will get you there faster. Nature is already masterful in advancing by quantum leaps. Now, there's a way to make nature's expertise your own. Learn how to become a quantum leap expert by partnering with nature. With the slightest whisper of our next stage of growth from the *Optimizers*, we can simply quantum leap to incorporate the change. We can simply embrace the inevitable end state, bypassing all transition stages associated with gradual evolution.

Whenever individuals are hooked into the naturality flow through compliance with the *Optimizers*, they all start to experience the same group of quantum leaps. Surprisingly, as I worked with executive after executive in partnership with the naturality flow, each experienced a collection of identical quantum leaps en route to peak performance and naturality. The order may be different, but we appear to all be moving along the same evolutionary path.

By learning what these quantum leaps are, you can proactively accelerate your own growth. Not only will you learn which quantum leaps to proactively pursue, but how to continuously quantum leap with finesse . . . . *as a way of life.*

WHAT IS A QUANTUM LEAP?

Dictionaries usually define a quantum leap as a sudden advancement that bypasses intermediate steps. Quantum physics refers to quantum jumps with respect to an electron moving from one stable orbit to the next around the nucleus of an atom.

The electron stays at its current orbit until it has *a full quantum of energy* or a *full energy packet* before leaping to the next higher-frequency orbit. It bypasses all transitional states to move directly to the next stable state.

In the naturality paradigm, quantum leaps are a means to progress by wholes from stable state to stable state as well. Using the electron metaphor, we can, for example, leap from one intensity of our naturality to the next intensity as we expand our authentic core by concentric circles.

Quantum leaps are also events of spontaneous creation, spontaneous knowledge and coincidence. Quantum leaps are the way nature quickly re-optimizes us when a linear transition won't resolve the optimization challenge. Their underlying dynamic is the process of emergence we learned about in Chapter 2, *Dynamic Stability*.

Progress by Wholes

Science seems to be uncovering an increasing number of demonstrations that progression in nature is not linear. Instead, nature appears to progress by *wholes* – systems with irreducible properties. Many disordered systems seem to spontaneously self-organize into a new level of order.

For us, this means our system can leap from one stable iteration to the next with no interim steps. There is no linear evolution between the pre-leap and post-leap states. The two states may not be visibly connected. Evolution appears to have occurred, and to be occurring, by a number of abrupt leaps to new levels of order.

Advancement appears to entail a series of iterations of completely integrated, whole systems in which significant change has occurred. We thought there were missing links in the fossil records of living history. Instead, those transitional beings may never have existed.

Quantum leaps appear to be nature's more efficient form of growth, evolution and re-optimization. Werner Heisenberg, the father of Quantum Theory concurs: "It is very difficult to believe that such complicated organs as, for instance, the human eye, would build up quite gradually as a result of purely accidental changes." Nobel Prize-winning chemist, Ilya Prigogine, believes that spontaneously self-organizing systems are the norm in the universe and scientists from many other disciplines are proving it.

Charles Darwin's revolutionary theory of evolution presented in *The Origin of Species* suggested that new species evolved gradually through small continuous adaptations (re-optimizations). Stephen Jay Gould, Harvard biologist and geologist, is one of a new breed of evolutionist who is convinced that "change occurs in large leaps following a slow accumulation of stresses that a system resists until it reaches the breaking point . . . . Change is more often a rapid transition between stable states than a continuous transformation at slow and steady states."[49]

Re-Optimization

Optimization is a dynamic state representing the best compromise between opposing forces among a system's internal components and between these internal components and the external environmental system. In the naturality paradigm, quantum leaps are nature's means to resolve optimization challenges. Often the re-optimization cannot be accomplished by simply adding a patch onto a system or advancing it linearly. Rather, the solution to the optimization problem requires a quantum leap to a new iteration of the system.

As nature is re-optimizing the universe and all its interacting component systems, there will be points when nature is prompting a quantum leap in you in order to resolve a larger optimization problem. There will also be times when your system must quantum leap to re-optimize the interaction of your internal components and information. If we knew what to look for, we could read nature's signals and make the leap with support from natural forces.

Knowing "why" we must leap – that is, for re-optimization – may eliminate our natural resistance to change. It may entice us to work with nature since the need for the change is not going to go away. Prolonging the change means that we have to move through unstable transition states to evolve to the change linearly – if indeed the solution can be linear. It could be that, when you attempt to slowly progress to the inevitable change, you reach a dead end and the growing pains you endured were for naught. You end up having to quantum leap after all.

We generally would rather stay in our current "safe" environment. When we don't know how to deal with change, we try to keep things static. The more you use the peak evolution science, the more you will harmonize with the natural optimization process. There will come a point where you will discover a new stability – a dynamic stability – through your re-integration into the ongoing natural optimization movement of the universe.

Instantaneous Creation

In the naturality paradigm, a quantum leap could also be viewed as an instantaneous creation. Aren't we really moving from one iteration of self-creation/reality creation to the next? The formula then would be to simply define who you want to be and be the person with those beliefs to create the new reality. If we believe our realities can change by quantum leaps, they will. If we believe they must evolve linearly, we will be confined to that experience. Transformation need not be a process but rather an instantaneous event – an event which can be triggered by intent rather than waiting for traumatic circumstances.

Coincidences, Spontaneous Knowledge and Intuitive Inspiration

A coincidence is also "a sudden advancement that bypasses intermediate steps." Therefore, they too are quantum leaps. Since they are the same thing, coincidences and quantum leaps emerge together. If you experience a cluster of coincidences, check to see if nature is encouraging you to make a quantum leap.

Both coincidences and quantum leaps occur along the naturality flow or natural growth path for your system. This is because both coincidences and quantum leaps are nature's attempts to resolve optimization challenges expediently. Since the naturality flow is the pathway of the universal optimizing dynamic, coincidences and quantum leaps increase as you align with it.

As their name suggests, the Optimizers signal the pathway for re-optimization. By following them, you are pliable for inclusion in the optimization dynamics acting on all systems. You become part of an orchestration of universal optimization. You can benefit from co-optimization solutions that are occurring across multiple co-evolving systems. Coincidences are simultaneous, multi-system, optimization events.

The sudden conscious awareness of a complete system of information that occurs with spontaneous knowledge and the experience of intuitive inspirations means these too are just different names for the same "progress by wholes" that occurs in quantum leaps and coincidences. Inside our heads or out in our realities, the same process is occurring in our system for the purpose of re-optimization.

"There comes a point where the mind takes a leap – call it intuition or what you will – and comes out on a higher plane of knowledge."   Albert Einstein

Computer Software Installation Metaphor

When you download new software (new information systems) into your computer, it has no effect until you reboot your computer system. When you re-start your computer, all of the connections are made with the new material and the system is transformed by the inclusion of the new information systems. There is a quantum leap to a new iteration of your computer system which now includes the new information.

As a user, we don't really know all of the intermediate steps. We simply see the sudden advancement to the software having spidered all relevant directories and other software in our computer. A quantum leap for us works in the same way.

> *"There is nothing in a caterpillar that tells you it's going to be a butterfly."*   Buckminster Fuller

THE ANATOMY OF A QUANTUM LEAP

As soon as we link ourselves to the naturality flow, we will be exposing ourselves to how nature likes to operate – nonlinearly by quantum leaps. Quantum leaps are re-optimization solutions which reflect nature's superior knowledge and intelligence.

The principle behind the quantum leap technology, and indeed all of the peak evolution science, is that it's easier to partner with nature's intelligence, expertise, and powerful forces than to try to duplicate them. As you turn yourself over to nature, you will discover nature's re-optimization solutions are incredibly more effective than what we might have developed.

If we knew the anatomy of a quantum leap, we could better tap into and proactively support the process. Or, with experience, we could begin to proactively initiate our own quantum leaps using what we learned from nature-initiated quantum leaps as the model.

Overview of the Quantum Leap Cycle

Most of us normally choose a goal, identify the steps to that goal and then move through the steps – 1,2,3,4,5,6,7,8,9,10 – until we achieve that goal. That is linear. Nature tends to bypass this and move from a stable stage 0 to a stable stage 10 variation or even an unknown stage X. Nature uses a quantum leap to bypass the unsettling transition steps in between. Once nature has figured out what the post-leap state needs to be to solve the optimization challenge, it takes our system directly there . . . . much like the computer software installation metaphor.

It would be illogical for nature to also create safe interim steps when they are superfluous. Why would we want to install each stage of the software when we can push one button to install it all? In addition, it may not be possible to gradually move towards some re-optimization solutions. The software, for example, may be so integrated that it could not even be divided out into gradual implementation steps.

Science is about finding new levels of order. Accordingly, perhaps we will find out there is order and linear steps linking the pre-leap and the post-leap states. For now, we will need to partner with nature's quantum leap expertise to help us get to an ideal, yet usually unknown, post-leap state. Most of us have been conditioned to take an ostrich approach to change and hence have negative experiences that make us resist change even more.

Accordingly, it will take a little trust of nature, its Optimizers, processes and mechanisms, to feel safe going through the unknown interim step of a quantum leap. Trust can only come with experience. After you've done a few, you'll be able to recognize the telltale signs of quantum leap stresses building up in your system and be ready to support the quantum leap process. You'll also know that if you fight the process you'll simply remain in the uncomfortable pre-leap state longer. Better to embrace the inevitable change.

To understand how the cycle of the quantum leap proceeds, assume your system is in a stable state and fully optimized. Next, assume systems sharing a context with yours have made some changes in order to re-optimize. As a result, the context for your system is now changed. New information resulting from the creativity of these interacting systems enters your system. It interferes with your system's stability and de-optimizes it. Your system shifts to the edge of chaos where stresses and strains move you to a breaking point. Your system must change. It must leap to re-optimization. This is the pre-leap state.

New and old information are recombined using the creativity of emergence to resolve the optimization challenge. A new iteration of your system results. This quantum leap moves us from one stable iteration to the next. We don't know precisely what happens in the middle to achieve the originality of our next iteration. This is very different than our usual linear approach in which each stage is an advance on the previous stage.

Emergence, on the other hand, seems to put all of the old and new information pieces into a hat, shake them up, and let them link up in a new and original way to solve the current adaptation problem. Nature seems to be trying to keep the disruptiveness of the transition states to a minimum while allowing for the greatest possible problem-solving creativity in between the two stable states. If an optimization challenge can't be resolved through linear evolution, this provides a creative new iteration of your system.

The pathfinding technology and other Optimizers provide the necessary new information for this emergence process. On average, it takes from three to seven information coincidences to facilitate a moderate quantum leap. The result may be predictable – much as would occur when rebooting your system to include the new information of a software package. More likely, however, the results of the creative recombining of the new and old information will be a surprise.

As a "growth novice," the leaps will appear to be more developmental in the beginning – more of a linear transition. As your expertise builds, the same amount of effort on your part will cause increasingly larger transformations. As your prowess, your experiential beliefs, and your fluidity increase, your post-leap forms will increasingly bear no connection to your pre-leap form.

Once you have made quantum leaps safe, you will find yourself doing them more often. Anything else would be too slow and boring – too primitive. The quantum leap technology could be seen as the *automatic growth process* and everything previous in *Peak Evolution* is the manual growth process. It is automatic because we capitalize on nature's ability to make all the new connections between the new and the old information in the quantum leap rather than us having to make each connection manually.

Our fluidity and the degree of our alignment, first in the task and second in our lives, determine the magnitude of our quantum leaps and our speed of growth. The first quantum leap is the hardest. It becomes easier with each quantum leap as we build up beliefs that we can make this process happen.

With experiential learning, you'll have new beliefs about your expertise, your ability to read nature, and the support nature can provide. You can be investing the same amount of energy in your tenth quantum leap as your first quantum leap but be accomplishing so much more in your tenth one. The degree of change in you and hence your reality will increase substantially.

An Example of Nature-Initiated and Self-Initiated Quantum Leaps

An example may help to communicate the anatomy of a quantum leap. In his stable pre-leap state, Dirk was a middle manager accountant in a corporation. Suddenly, new information entered his system. Through a cluster of coincidental events, he realized that he wanted to lead a humanitarian endeavor. Dirk really resonated with this next expansion of his naturality and began to obsess about doing it. He unsuccessfully tried to initiate a number of social responsibility programs within the corporation under the guise of generating revenues through cause marketing.

As a result of his needs not being met, his dislike of his old job increased dramatically until his system was at the edge of chaos. Stresses and strains were building up in his system much like the electron accumulates a quantum of energy before it jumps to the next orbit.

Dirk had a wife and baby at home, so he knew he could not irresponsibly leave his job. He felt like a prisoner. Being proficient at the reality creation technology, Dirk developed a reality design in which he would be discharged from his current job with a large settlement package.

Further, he blueprinted that a new job, which pays more, would spontaneously appear that provided an opportunity for him to make his greatest contribution to the world – in other words, to do his art. Dirk wanted the old reality to be cleared away and the new reality brought into existence as quickly as possible to keep his transition state to a minimum. He wanted a quantum leap.

Dirk held the *emotional feel* of his desired goal reality. He was an aspiring growth expert, so he used reincarnation to grow himself to be the person with his desired new reality. He used reality to clear all of his interfering beliefs and fears: you can't do what you love; you can't have a job at the level you want in a new career without paying your dues or getting the credentials; you aren't capable enough for the kind of job you want; you have no freedom to do what you want; you would have to take less money in a humanitarian role; it will take you a long time to find a new job and you will run out of money; you and your family will starve . . .

Dirk's naturality and humanitarian identity were strengthened both by his increasing commitment to his goal as well as by his clearing any interferences and internal conflicts about having what he wanted. Since beliefs create reality, Dirk's reality design materialized with another flourish of coincidences.

In a downsizing project, Dirk's job was eliminated and he received almost a year's salary as severance. Unexpectedly, about two weeks later, Dirk's previous employer recommended Dirk for running a major new social responsibility organization that they and a number of other companies were establishing. Dirk's attempts to start social responsibility projects had paid off after all. They had helped him to consolidate his new humanitarian identity so those identity beliefs could cause reality to shift. You must be the person first in order to create the reality in which you are that person.

The salary was more than Dirk earned previously. The job stretched him in every way resulting in his being continuously in *flow*. In *flow*, doing what he loved for a cause he believed in, Dirk performed beyond past levels of peak performance to achieve dramatic change for his community. In the space of a few weeks, Dirk had completed a major quantum leap. His internal quantum leap had been reflected outside in a quantum leap in his self-created reality.

His system was now in the stable post-leap state. Having experienced the complete cycle of a quantum leap successfully, Dirk felt he could do it even faster in the future. With 20/20 hindsight, he saw that he could have minimized the uncomfortable pre-leap buildup of stresses in his system if he had understood the inevitability of his having to make the changes in his life that nature was flagging for him. Because of his increase in quantum leap expertise, he would not be so fearful the next time. Each time he did it, he knew his increasing expertise would increase his safety.

To get to the level of safety he wants, Dirk continues to proactively construct quantum leaps for himself. You will learn more about the techniques for nature-initiated and self-initiated quantum leaps in this chapter. In brief, Dirk sets up goals he has no idea how to achieve yet which are consistent with the *Optimizers* and his natural growth path. He uses the growth technology and the reality creation technology to reconstruct himself to be the person with the goal reality.

Dirk uses the Optimizers to complete the quantum leap as efficiently as possible. He uses the pathfinding technology to find the three to seven pieces of new information to incorporate into his system to energize the quantum leap. He goes through cycle after cycle of quantum leaps from pre-leap to adding new information; to emergence recombining that information to energize the quantum leap; and then to the post-leap stable state again. Dirk has shifted into quantum leap living. He has accelerated the self-growth/creation-growth cycle.

NATURE-INITIATED QUANTUM LEAPS

By simply reintegrating into nature's expert processes, we can capitalize on nature's intelligence and experience to be in the right place at the right time with the right information for the quantum leap to a new iteration of our system. We can move from one stable state to another in pace with the naturality flow.

Each quantum leap is triggered by the ingestion of new information that invalidates or interferes with the balanced way in which current information is interconnected in our system. This new information needs to be internalized as new beliefs – the information storage units of our system – and all our current beliefs need to be reconnected to create a new cohesive whole. A quantum leap permits a spontaneous reconnection of all the dots to include the new information.

Once you master quantum leaps, they'll become a normal modus operandi for you. You'll recognize nature's signals when it's time to make a leap instead of trying to fight nature to keep your life the same. Re-optimizations that might have taken you months or even years to complete previously, may proactively be accomplished through quantum leaps in an hour or two. It's just a matter of how fast you can internalize the new information and make all of the reconnections to your belief systems.

Mastering the "Pre-Leap"

Our biggest problem with quantum leaps is the pre-leap stage. Because we resist it, we stay too long in this unpleasant transition state at the edge of chaos. Let's look at it more closely so you can recognize it and facilitate the process. Assume you have been in a stable state. Everything has been smooth sailing.

Gradually struggle events begin to emerge and you experience negative emotions and anxiety. You might be more tired than usual. Or you could be chomping at the bit for change yet see nothing on the horizon. There may be a very pronounced feeling that something big is pending that you both desire and fear. Conflict inside is reflected as conflict outside in your reality. Therefore, the problem events in your life reflect the co-existence of both the pre-leap and the post-leap state, and the desire for the leap and your resistance to it.

You'll want to learn to recognize the feeling of the pre-leap. It is the feeling of accumulating stresses and strains in the current iteration of our system until we reach a breaking point and can spontaneously make the leap to a more optimized form. The trick is to speed through the pre-leap stress so we don't have to endure the discomfort for long. Once you recognize the telltale feelings, you will want to scan your reality's landscape for patterns of Optimizer messages that might identify what the quantum leap might be.

All quantum leaps – whether nature-initiated or self-initiated – are always in the direction of the naturality flow. Always. Why else would quantum leaps occur? Their sole purpose is to resolve optimization challenges, especially for those challenges that cannot be resolved by a slow gradual evolutionary process. The naturality flow is the direction of the universal optimizing dynamic co-optimizing all systems. Therefore, you will want to comply with the *Optimizer* messages when choosing the direction of your quantum leaps. Quantum leaps are tricky enough without also trying to do them in conflict with nature.

Take an inventory of past events and *Optimizer* messages to determine your current themes from the patterns. Project these themes into the future and you will see your options for the possible directions of your pending quantum leap. Let your resonance rather than your intellect choose the likely quantum leap that is trying to happen.

Your resonance is attached into the same naturality flow. It knows better. Since quantum leaps are not linear, we may not always know everything about the likely post-leap state. However, we can at least use the reality design techniques to emotionally blueprint the feel of the post-leap state.

Look through the list at the end of this chapter to see if you can see what quantum leap is trying to happen. Since quantum leaps are so important to the optimization of your system, they tend to travel in packs. When you identify your current quantum leap you may also see what quantum leaps it will trigger. For example, you may quantum leap to believing that you can create your reality with your beliefs and thus view yourself as a creator.

However, while this is a major quantum leap, it will trigger an even larger one – that you and your reality are one, that everyone and everything in your reality is a reflection of you and can therefore be used to know yourself better. This leap in turn will trigger an even larger one to oneness and unity consciousness.

In addition, the quantum leap you are focused on may be accompanied by a series of coincidences which, of course, are also quantum leaps – sudden advancements that bypass intermediate steps. Clusters of coincidences are a telltale sign that a significant quantum leap is about to occur. Coincidences, like quantum leaps are evidence of nature trying to re-optimize your system and co-evolving systems interconnected with yours. Follow the coincidence trail as if they are breadcrumbs leading you through your quantum leap.

Use a combination of the pathfinding technology (blocks, flows and resonance) and reincarnation to feel/create your way to the post-leap state. Comply with all of the Optimizers which are guiding you along the naturality flow and hence in the direction of any quantum leap. They will increase your momentum for making the leap.

New information is often required to energize the quantum leap and the creative resolution of optimization challenges. Therefore, we can use the pathfinding technology to find the three to seven pieces of information that normally give us what we need for the emergence process in those unknown interim steps of a quantum leap.

If you don't do this proactively, then at least be compliant as nature orchestrates your "collisions" with the various relevant pieces of information needed for the quantum leap. If we are hitchhiking on the naturality flow, we will find ourselves being taken from information coincidence to information coincidence until the emergence creativity occurs that triggers the quantum leap. Lock these into information units in your system as they occur. In other words, change your beliefs.

If you are fairly confident in knowing which quantum leap on the list nature is inciting, it's possible to simply recreate yourself in the post-leap form. What could be easier? Redefine yourself and thus your reality. *Feel* who the "post-leap you" will be. The emotional complex of that *feeling* is your reality design. That's what you will want to keep reinforcing.

Wear this "post-leap identity" as if you've been this person with this reality for the last ten years. This will take the stress out of your leap by reducing your fears. Next, commit to this post-leap state and then simply "throw" yourself over to the new reality and identity. The faster you do it, the less time you'll have to spend in the stressful pre-leap state and the faster you'll come to love quantum leaps. Over time your beliefs that you can do this will increase and "quantum leaping" will become easier and easier.

Finally, you will want to check the "new you" as reflected in your new post-leap reality. Growth has not occurred unless we have new beliefs – new units of information incorporated into our system. New beliefs mean that reality will be changed. You can therefore use reality as a mirror to discover who you now are.

Lock in your changes using events and creations in your new reality to reinforce the new you. This is the usual self-growth/reality-growth theme. Review how well you accomplished your quantum leap to reinforce your quantum leap beliefs and to decide how to do them better in the future.

Major Categories of Quantum Leaps

After watching the *Optimizers* flag the need for quantum leaps in the lives of many people for over a decade, I began to see some patterns as to the categories of nature-initiated quantum leaps. These categories should help you to identify what nature is up to, so you can assist with the process.

Also, these would be good categories for self-initiated quantum leaps when you want to proactively accelerate your growth. Nature will participate. As we might expect, most quantum leaps have to do with the two growth directions – expansion of our naturality and removing interferences to expressing that naturality.

Quantum Leaps for Naturality Expansion

The naturality flow is very consistent about expanding our authentic core by concentric circles. Strategically, then you will want to keep intensifying your naturality as a way of life. If you don't, you will incur negative messages to pressure you to do exactly that.

Should you delay the expansion of your naturality, you will extend your transition period unnecessarily. The post-leap state will start to co-exist with the pre-leap state. Your old level and its corresponding reality will try to co-exist with the new strength of your naturality/reality. These conflicting beliefs create conflicting realities. This is the formula for struggle events.

There is no point fighting the inevitable. When part of your system is ready to leap and the other part isn't, you'll have to bring the resisting part along. The greatest traumas are created by letting the resisting part win – by curtailing the expansion of your naturality. You will be fighting everything the naturality flow can throw at you. Is this really how you want to live your life?

Quantum leaps to increasing intensities of one's naturality are easy to facilitate if you use the pathfinding technology to help you identify the fastest route through the unknown. Because we expand our naturality by concentric circles, there is rarely a linear progression with this category of quantum leap. The post-leap is rarely predictable from the pre-leap.

Unfortunately, we often resist the pressure to these quantum leaps the most, generating lots of growing pains. This again is a cultural problem. Because our cultures support only linear growth – requiring us to be an extension of the person we were before – we resist nature's attempt to have us quantum leap to re-optimization through re-invention.

Dirk's quantum leap from accountant to humanitarian leader was an example of a quantum leap to a greater intensity of expression of his naturality. It was not the expected next step on his growth path. However, once his system was consciously aware of the new information he knew about his naturality, there was no denying the change. To delay the inevitable quantum leap would cause problem events in his reality and introduce toxicity to his system.

Quantum Leaps to Clear Naturality Interferences

Sometimes clearing the interferences to naturality cannot be achieved through a linear transition. There are too many new beliefs to be added and too many beliefs to be reconnected. The powerless and judged-judging reflexes are examples. These are two large convoluted masses of interfering beliefs. A gradual evolution to resolving these optimization problems is not possible.

Clearing is accomplished with greater ease, speed and effectiveness using conditioned reflexes and quantum leaps. Internalize the post-leap state emotionally, "throw" yourself over to the inevitable post-leap state, and use the reality reflecting the new you to reinforce your leap and prevent backsliding.

Given the havoc that these two belief complexes create in your reality, is there any question that these leaps must be made? It may be easier to clear all of the fear beliefs, limiting beliefs and conflicting beliefs discussed in the *De-Creating Undesirable Realities* section of the reality creation technology by quantum leaps. Wouldn't we rather move from one stable state to the next rather than endure negative events in our reality any longer?

Quantum Leaps for Increasing Naturality Expression

This category of quantum leaps relates to creation and doing our *art*. We only know our naturality by the creative acts, the creation process, and the creations which express that naturality. Therefore, there will be pressure from nature for quantum leaps to increase our ability to create realities which will both express and strengthen our naturality. Naturality strengthens naturality.

Creativity is one of nature's techniques for re-optimizing our systems. The growth dynamic is one of self-creation/creation or self-growth/creation-growth. We grow ourselves to grow our creations. These creations will, in turn, reinforce our growth and stimulate more. Next time around, our creations and thus our contribution to the world will be that much greater. Quantum leaps in our creations or reality creations are another of nature's major categories of quantum leaps.

Break the Linear Connection to the Past

There are two elements that will enhance your quantum leap expertise dramatically: fluidity and a willingness to break your linear connection with the past. Each of these requirements is itself a quantum leap. Our need to progress linearly often means we will be fighting nature's pressure to quantum leap nonlinearly. Our need to be a linear projection from our past is the reason we do not fluidly re-optimize through quantum leaps when necessary.

The insistence of our cultures for us to be a linear extension of our past causes us to retain all sorts of damage from the past in the present rather than passing into a more evolved form. We can be more adaptive than that! If you truly want to experience the peak performance and peak evolution of your system, break with the past. Emerge as the optimal person you need to be for what is meaningful for your system right now.

Fluidity

What we're really talking about if we release our linear connection with the past is increased fluidity. If you are going to commit to quantum leaps as a way of life, then you are committing to a process of continuous adaptation to your environment. Our degree of fluidity will determine how successful we will be with our quantum leaps. I recommend setting the goal to be more fluid each time you quantum leap.

Once you've identified the quantum leap to be actioned, you will want to embrace, with increasing speed, the post-leap state. Fluidity is a sure sign of a growth expert. Rigidity and growth are, of course, mutually exclusive. The key to leaping is to fluidly redesign yourself and then become that person until reality begins to reflect that redesigning back to you in such a way as to support you in locking that new identity in.

SELF-INITIATED QUANTUM LEAPS

Once you master quantum leaps, they'll become the preferred modus operandi for you. You'll start to proactively trigger quantum leaps every time you crave growth or progress. If you target instead to move from one quantum leap to the next and the next as a way of life, you'll immediately have new power over your life and your future.

Growing without quantum leaps and coincidences in the old way with its stressful transition states, or not growing at all, will seem quite primitive once you've mastered the art of quantum leap living.

We have learned about how to help nature with nature-initiated quantum leaps. Now let's look at how we can initiate quantum leaps ourselves. The concept of reincarnation is an easy one for proactively facilitating quantum leaps. This technique requires you to simply become a new person this moment. You can bypass the transition. Whoever you were a moment ago is gone.

Just define it and be it! Reincarnation is one of the most powerful belief engineering techniques presented in Peak Evolution. It means you no longer view yourself as a linear extension of the person you used to be. You release your history and simply become, this moment, the person you want to be from here on in.

There is no need to include any of your past limitations. We sustain past damage in our system because we insist on transitioning linearly to the resolution of these problems rather than simply quantum leaping. Past traumas, toxicity, defects and limitations can simply be left out of the new iteration of your system.

Simply define yourself in one moment as you need to be for your current self-creation/creation goals and become that person in the next. Operate as if you already are that person and live your day and take decisions accordingly. Hold this new identity until reality restructures, reinforcing the new identity until it is locked in.

Why commit to the belief that one must evolve by some slow arduous process rather than being one way one moment and redefined in the next? Think of the process of creating ourselves in reality in comparison to a computer monitor. The image on the screen is refreshed so quickly that we don't even see the gap.

What if between one refreshing of the "you" you are this moment and the one you are in the next moment, you snipped the linear connection with the previous you. You did not own those problem events in the childhood of the previous "you" that were interfering with your optimization in the present.

What if you didn't have to go back and "deal with them" as so many psychiatrists and psychologists suggest? What if at the moment of refreshing the "you" in present reality, you simply dropped those toxic events, conflicting and limiting beliefs and defective identities? What if you clearly defined the person you wanted to be and simply allowed that blueprint to determine the "you" that flicked into reality the next time the image had to be refreshed?

Transcendence is the power to be born anew, to make a fresh start, to turn over a new leaf, to begin with a clean slate, to enter into a state of grace, to have a second chance. Transcendence is more than just the realization that the past is over. It is also a realignment of all dimensions of yourself with the very source of your life. Reincarnation is transcendence. It is a quantum leap to the "you" that you choose to be. As you begin operating at a new frequency, you will not be able to access the toxicity of the old frequency. Problem solved.

Creation reincarnation empowers dramatic reality change with minimal interim steps. It can trigger major coincidences and quantum leaps. *Growth reincarnation* accelerates your progress by quantum leaps along your natural growth path to increasing intensities of your naturality. If you know where you want to go with your growth or creation and you want to bypass the transition stress, then, in the naturality paradigm, you can use reincarnation to quantum leap from one stable state to the next.

The closer you blueprint your *growth* or *creation reincarnation* to the naturality flow and your natural growth path, the faster and more dramatic the self-initiated quantum leap will be. Nature will respond to support you.

Simply define who you want to be in your post-leap state. Commit to becoming the person with the reality defined. Walk around as that person. *Hold, hold, hold* until reality shifts and helps you to lock in this new self-definition. This is a time to try to duplicate nature. Just re-write yourself in one moment and become the new you in the next. Give up the requirement to evolve gradually. *Just begin.*

In a paradigm in which beliefs create reality, *creation reincarnation* is used to quickly change a multitude of beliefs in order to quickly change reality. An identity is shorthand for a system of interlinked beliefs. Wear a new identity to communicate new instructions to change your reality. The identity of having your desired goal reality, for example, is internalized so that all of the right belief changes, and hence reality changes, occur.

We can use this same technique for *growth reincarnation*. The process is the same except that the reality you want to create is based on your self-creation into a more evolved form. *Growth reincarnation* can be used to simply reincarnate yourself at the next level of growth you want to achieve.

Growth, like creation, just requires the storage of new beliefs in your belief blueprint – a change in the information database creating your system. As soon as the *Optimizers* indicate the next way that nature is trying to grow/optimize you, simply reincarnate yourself with the change. Quantum leap to bypass the transition state.

Speaking of reincarnation, here's a neat trick. Reincarnate yourself as an expert in growth, an expert at pioneering new territory, and a quantum leap expert. Quantum leap to being the expert you want with the peak evolution science. *Design it. Feel it. Be it.* Now that you know about "quantum leaping" as a segue to growth, why not bypass all of the interim anxieties and development time required to master the growth process. Just begin operating as if you have all of these growth mastery identities and let them restructure your day and your life.

PROGRESS BY COINCIDENCES

According to quantum physicist, David Peat, when we experience a synchronicity, what we are really experiencing "is the human mind operating, for a moment, in its true order and extending throughout society and nature, moving through orders of increasing subtlety, reaching past the source of mind and matter into creativity itself."[46]

A synchronicity is what scientists call a meaningful coincidence or significantly related patterns of chance. Carl Jung coined the term as "the coincidence in time of two or more causally unrelated events which have the same meaning." Quite simply, coincidences are quantum leaps. They offer progress by wholes – moving from one stable state to the next without the intermediate steps. They are the means to resolve optimization challenges. That is their purpose.

Coincidences and quantum leaps are the same thing. They are sudden advancements by our system and therefore our reality. They result from co-evolving systems clicking simultaneously back into optimization. From the viewpoint of expanded consciousness, nature surveyed the needs of multiple systems and saw a way to quantum leap them to a better form simultaneously as a creative way of resolving multiple optimization challenges. As a result, coincidences may be so dramatic that, in a split second, your world is entirely changed.

We all like to have these magical events in our lives. The formula for increasing the magnitude and frequency of coincidences in your life is simple. Creating coincidences requires reintegration into the naturality flow using the ten Optimizers. Comply with any or all ten of them, and the frequency and magnitude of the coincidences in your life will increase. This is because coincidences and the ten Optimizers are all reflections of the same optimizing dynamic of the universe.

When you reintegrate into that dynamic order, you will experience the coincidences that are part of that optimizing process. You will rejoin the orchestration of the co-optimization of all systems, gaining the benefits of optimization solutions occurring beyond your system. Proactively courting coincidences is an important part of the commitment to quantum leap living. You can help nature by courting coincidences with the "identity" of being able to create numerous and large coincidences effortlessly.

Clumping is a recurring theme in the universe as, for example, planets clump around the sun; atoms bond to form a molecule; molecules align in a cell; and similar beliefs cluster around a major belief thus reinforcing that primary belief. Therefore, the clumping of events in time and space as synchronicities is a natural extension.

Where there is a pattern of coincidences, a quantum leap is not far away since nature is using both to try to resolve an optimization challenge. If you encounter a pattern of coincidences in the pursuit of any goal, that goal is on your natural growth path. Coincidences tell us we are operating in alignment with our naturality and our optimization. Track the pattern of coincidences in the past in order to identify the path into the future which will be supported by more coincidences and flow events – in other words, by nature.

The speed of your progress when using the peak evolution science derives not only from operating as if you have total knowledge but also from bypassing linear process through coincidences. How many coincidences did you experience in the last month?

Try targeting twenty or thirty a day as you align your life with your naturality and pursue projects which express your art. Even top experts in any discipline using optimal linear process cannot compete with someone aligned with their naturality who has mastered the art of colliding with coincidences along the naturality flow.

As you use the peak evolution science, you will connect with the underlying dynamic order of the universe. As a result, there will be times when coincidences occur that are so dramatic, so meaningful, and so facilitating to your life that you might actually weep with the specialness you feel. As your beliefs increase that you can create coincidences, that will become your reality. Accordingly, you will build them into your reality designs, even for the most mundane processes of living. You will be amazed at the creativity with which coincidences can meet your goals.

CASCADING QUANTUM LEAPS

I invite you to find the pieces of the peak evolution science you relate to most for reintegrating with the naturality flow. Increase your use of them in order to augment your experiential learning and alignment with the flow. Once you achieve a critical mass of knowledge and beliefs about the naturality paradigm, you will automatically leap to operating entirely within the new paradigm.

This is because the naturality paradigm is fully integrated in the same way that nature is fully integrated. Hence, every part is interconnected and triggers every other part. No matter which segments you choose to learn, there will be a point where you will "quantum leap" to understanding the whole paradigm.

The three major technologies of the peak evolution science are each based on an uncommon belief. The knowledge technology is founded on the belief that we have the means to operate as if we have access to total knowledge. The reality creation technology is based on beliefs creating reality and hence that our realities are 100% self-created. The growth technology derives from the belief that our natural growth path is towards increasing expressions of our naturality.

These three beliefs each require a quantum leap because numerous other beliefs must be changed in order to internalize them. The reconnection of your beliefs around these three beliefs will generate a dramatically transformed worldview. Quantum leap to any one of these three beliefs, for example, and a cascade of the quantum leaps listed below will land you firmly in the naturality paradigm. Align your life to any one of the ten *Optimizers*, and you will initiate another cascade of quantum leaps reintegrating you into nature's optimizing flow in the naturality paradigm.

For some people, the fastest way to accelerate growth is to actually concentrate on a single leap to the totality of the naturality paradigm – to be fully integrated into the naturality flow. This reality design will automatically drive the orchestration of all the various sub-quantum leaps identified at the end of the chapter that occur as anyone evolves to peak performance and peak experience.

At the opposite end of the spectrum, others find grasping the naturality paradigm just too large for their current state of consciousness. They want to operate totally in the present in their *growth horizon window* responding to nature's *Optimizer* instructions as they occur.

Still others prefer to begin with nature's immediate instructions. They will support the quantum leap that is trying to happen in their life first and then look for the related quantum leaps to occur. One need only begin in whatever way you are comfortable and a cascade of quantum leaps will take you to peak performance, peak experience, and peak evolution. All roads lead to the *flow* continuum which will take you to increasing depths of *flow*, altered consciousness, expanded thinking and the oceanic experience of oneness with the universe.

> *"In a universe in which things are infinitely interconnected, all consciousnesses are also interconnected."*[46] Michael Talbot

> *"Deep down the consciousness of mankind is one."*[47]
> Einstein's protégé, quantum physicist, David Bohm

Humanitarianism will emerge spontaneously at this evolution of consciousness. As you move to full power with your *art*, you will make your greatest contributions to the world *accidentally on purpose*. They will be the byproduct of your activities in deep *flow* while pursuing your natural urges to increase the expression of your naturality. They are the natural consequence of individuals focused purely on the basic human dynamic of self-growth/creation-growth in a dimension where creation is the sole theme.

> *"As human beings we are made to surpass ourselves and are truly ourselves only when transcending ourselves."* Huston Smith

And what of a world composed of individuals thus evolved? If each of us is operating at our peak, doing what we do best, society will be enhanced and transforming at an accelerating pace. If we are all in the unity consciousness of pure activity fusion, creativity for the human system will be synchronized and harmonized.

What power of creation is possible if large percentages of the world population are not just in alignment with their naturality but operating in unity consciousness in the greatest depths of *flow*? And if we are all in alignment with our naturality and creating adaptive realities automatically, what will our unified reality look like? What reality design would we choose together as reality creation experts? As the sole creator of your reality, what is *your* reality design for the world?

If each of us is free to be the person we are naturally, we will have world freedom. Individual freedom defines world freedom. And, wouldn't worldwide freedom result in world peace? And, with the spontaneous emergence of humanitarianism that occurs as naturality alignment is achieved, won't an unimaginable theme of benevolence emerge? Are these not inevitable cascading quantum leaps?

In the pure activity fusion of *flow*, all experience of self as a separate entity disappears. All that exists is the pure creative act. One planetary consciousness inhaling and exhaling in the growth/creation dynamic – pulsating to new levels of self-growth and creation-growth. What would be the inevitable cascade of global quantum leaps . . . . ?

"Never doubt that a small group of thoughtful, committed citizens can change the world. Indeed, it is the only thing that ever has."   Anthropologist, Margaret Mead

"All religions, arts and sciences are branches of the same tree. All these aspirations are directed toward ennobling man's life, lifting it from the sphere of mere physical existence and leading the individual towards freedom."   Albert Einstein

NATURALITY PARADIGM QUANTUM LEAPS

This list identifies some of the most common leaps I've noticed as individuals evolve to peak performance, peak experience, and peak evolution. This should help you to recognize quantum leaps that are "trying to happen" as you progress along your natural growth path with the technologies. They should also suggest opportunities for proactively reincarnating yourself to accelerate growth and bypass uncomfortable transition periods. In keeping with these goals, the common categories of quantum leaps again are:

1. quantum leaps for naturality expansion
2. quantum leaps to clear naturality interferences
3. quantum leaps for increasing naturality expression

Any of these quantum leaps may trigger a cascading effect whereby multiple quantum leaps result. This is because they represent entrances to the naturality paradigm and, since the paradigm reflects nature, all of the quantum leaps are interconnected. Since we are all in different pre-leap states, there is no set order in which the quantum leaps must occur. Go with the naturality flow.

GROWTH LEAPS

1. The leap to the naturality paradigm and our integration into the naturality flow as part of the underlying dynamic order of the universe
2. The leap to continual optimization through creativity
3. The leap to systems thinking
4. The leap to a nonlinear modus operandi where growth is by wholes, quantum leaps, coincidences, emergence, and spontaneous knowledge. Release the need to be a linear extension of your past
5. The leap to being a growth expert and growth addict
6. The leap to being a reincarnation expert with the ability to fluidly reincarnate yourself at will – to change yourself to change your reality
7. The leap to the next expansion of your naturality
8. The leap to continuous growth and learning
9. The leap to evolving along your natural growth path – the expansion of naturality by concentric circles
10. The leap to aligning your life with your naturality and the naturality flow
11. The leap from externally referenced to internally referenced
12. The leap to pursuing emotional goals directly as our most basic purpose
13. The leap to eliminating the powerless belief complex
14. The leap to eliminating the judging reflex
15. The leap to living 100% in *flow* and advancing to the greatest depths of *flow*
16. The leap to *growth-creation flow* and *art-based flow*

17. The leap to the self-growth/creation-growth iterative process as a way of life, our ultimate purpose, and the underlying dynamic of human existence
18. The leap to oneness, nonduality and unity consciousness
19. The leap to unconditional acceptance, non-separation, and non-fragmentation
20. The leap to expanded consciousness and the ability to see the interdependence and patterns within large territories of focus
21. The leap to fluidity
22. The leap to growth by assimilation
23. The leap to quantum leap expert and quantum leap living
24. The leap to clearing each of a society's major conflicting beliefs:

- Valued *versus* not valued
- Respected *versus* not respected,
- Worthy *versus* not worthy
- Loved *versus* not loved,
- Valuable *versus* not valuable

Powerful *versus* powerless
Abundance *versus* scarcity
Capable *versus* not capable
Money is good *versus* money is bad
Power is good *versus* power is bad
Safe *versus* not safe
Free *versus* not free
Effortless progress *versus* struggle
Included/accepted *versus* excluded/isolated/judged

CREATION LEAPS (Not Covered Under Growth Leaps)

1. The leap to operating as if beliefs create reality
2. The leap to owning your self-created reality. The leap to extending your identity to include all of your reality
3. The leap to organizing your life around doing your *art* or your authentic creative expression to maximize your growth, contribution, and rewards
4. The leap to abundance – the power and freedom to have what you want when you want it
5. The leap to reality design expert
6. The leap to reality creation expert with the ability to create any reality at will
7. The leap to creativity and creation as the ultimate focus and purpose of your life. We are creative beings

KNOWLEDGE AND PATHFINDING LEAPS

1. The leap to a belief in the ability to access all knowledge by merely focusing consciousness
2. The leap to assuming spontaneous access to all information through blocks and flows
3. The leap to Level I: Being taken to desired information through blocks and flows
4. The leap to the knowledge technology Level II: (Information coincidences) The information will come to you
5. The leap to the knowledge technology Level III: spontaneous information through the assessment of the pattern of information coincidences
6. The leap to the knowledge technology Level IV: the ability to receive spontaneous information, especially complete systems of knowledge of a subject
7. The leap to being a clairsentience expert
8. The leap to being an expert at the unknown, the ambiguous, the new.
9. The leap to being an expert at pathfinding and pioneering
10. The leap to coincidence creation expert
11. The leap to operating in the present as directed by your resonance

NOTES

1. Seneca, Letters to Lucilius (1st C.) 41, TR. E. Phillips Barker

2. Barth, A., *The Creation In the Light of Modern Science* (Jerusalem: Jerusalem Post Press, 1966) p. 144

3. Van Valen, Leigh, "A New Evolutionary Law," *Evolutionary Theory 1*, 1973, pp. 1-30.

4. Ilya Prigogine and Yves Elskens, "Irreversibility, Stochasticity and Non-Locality in

5. Classical Dynamics," in *Quantum Implications*, ed. Basil J. Hiley and F. David Peat (New York: Routledge & Kegan Paul, 1987) p. 214

6. Michael Talbot, *The Holographic Universe* (New York: HarperCollins, 1991) p. 293

7. Seneca, *On a Happy Life*, Moral Essays (1st C.), TR, Aubrey Stewart

8. Wilber, Ken, *No Boundary* (Boston: Shambhala Publications, 1979) p. 47

9. R. Buckminster Fuller in Simpson's *Contemporary Quotations,* compiled by James B. Simpson (Boston: Houghton Mifflin, 1988) p. 227

10. Friedrich Nietzsche, *The Will to Power*, Trans. and Ed. Walter Kaufmann and R.J. Hollingdale. (New York: Vintage, 1967)

11. Freud Sigmund, "The Freud Reader," Gray Peter Ed, (New York: W.W. Norten & Co, 1989) p. 36

12. Candace B Pert, M.D., *Molecules of Emotion* (New York: Scribner, 1997)

13. Michael Talbot, *Beyond the Quantum* (New York: A Bantam Book, 1986), p. 174

14. Larry Dossey, M.D., *Recovering the Soul* 1989 Bantam Books, p. 182

15. Bill Moyer's five-part PBS television series called *Healing and the Mind* (1993)

16. Candace B Pert, M.D., *Molecules of Emotion* (New York: Scribner, 1997) p. 179

17. Dr. Ian Wilmut, Roslin Institute, Multiplicity, February 24, 1997, Transcript, PBS

18. Online NewsHour. http://www.pbs.org/newshour/bb/science/jan- june97/cloning2_2-24.html

19. Michael Talbot, *The Holographic Universe* (New York: HarperCollins, 1991) pp. 113-115

20. Michael Talbot, *The Holographic Universe* (New York: HarperCollins, 1991) pp. 115-116

21. Michael Talbot, *The Holographic Universe* (New York: HarperCollins, 1991) p. 169

22. Michael Talbot, *The Holographic Universe* (New York: HarperCollins, 1991) p. 14

23. Russell Targ, Harold Puthoff, *Mind-Reach: Scientists Look at Psychic Ability,* New York: Delacorte Press, 1977

24. Russell Targ and Harold Puthoff, *Mind-Reach: Scientists Look at Psychic Ability*, (New York, Delacorte Press, 1977), p. 51

25. Bayard Webster, "Are Clever Animals Actually Thinking?" *New York Times,* May 31, 1983, p. C1

26. Ayn Rand, *Atlas Shrugged* (New York: Signet, 1957) p. 979

27. Placebos: innocuous treatments which a patient is told will cure him

28. Michael Talbot, *The Holographic Universe* (New York: HarperCollins, 1991) p. 91

29. Saint-exupery, *Wind, Sand, and Stars* (1939), 2.2, Tr. Lewis Galantiere

30. Jauregui Jose, *The Emotional Computer* (Blackwell, 1995)

31. Daniel Goleman, *Emotional Intelligence*, 1995, p. 27 quoting from Prefrontal cortex: Antonio Damasio, *Descartes' Error: Emotion, Reason and the Human Brain* (New York: Grosset/Putnam, 1994)

32. Fritjof Capra, *The Tao of Physics,* Shambala Publications, Inc. Boulder, Colorado, 1975, p. 131
33. Candace B Pert, M.D., *Molecules of Emotion* (New York: Scribner, 1997) p. 257
34. Robert Fritz, *Creating*, Page 3
35. William James, *Letters of William James* vol. I (1878)
36. The research bulletin "Multiple Personality − Mirrors of a New Model of Mind?" Vol. 1, no. 3/4, is a double issue and is available from: Institute of Noetic Sciences, 475 Gate Five Road, Suite 300, Sausalito, CA 94965; 415-331-5650
37. Mihaly Csikszentmihalyi, *Flow, the Psychology of Optimal Experience* (New York: Harper and Row, 1990)*The Creative Spirit*, by Daniel Goleman, Paul Kaufman, Michael Ray, 1992, p. 46
38. Mihaly Csikszentmihalyi, *The Evolving Self* (New York: HarperCollins, 1993) p. 193
39. Robert A. Monroe, *Far Journeys*, (New York: Doubleday, 1985), p. 64
40. Kenneth Ring, *Life at Death*, (New York: Quill, 1980) pp. 238-239
41. Michael Talbot, *The Holographic Universe* (New York: HarperCollins, 1991) pp. 174-76
42. Mihaly Csikszentmihalyi, *The Evolving Self* (New York: HarperCollins, 1993) p. 189
43. Mihaly Csikszentmihalyi, *The Evolving Self* (New York: HarperCollins, 1993) p. 201
44. C.S. Lewis (Selected Literary Essays)
45. Henry Miller, *The Absolute Collective*, The Wisdom of the Heart 1941
46. Havelock Ellis, preface, *the Dance of Life* 1923
47. F. David Peat, *Synchronicity: The Bridge between Mind and Matter* (New York: Bantam Books, 1987), p. 235
48. Michael Talbot, *The Holographic Universe* (New York: HarperCollins, 1991) p. 60
49. Renee Weber, "The Enfolding-Unfolding Universe: A Conversation with David Bohm," in *The Holographic Paradigm*, ed. Ken Wilber (Boulder, Colo.: New Science Library, 1982) p. 72
50. K.C. Cole, *Sympathetic Vibrations*, (Bantum, New Age Books, 1985) p. 342

INDEX

ABOUT LAUREN HOLMES

All of Lauren's books speak to a new level of human potential possible through a partnership with the biological infrastructure of which we are a part and with which we have co-evolved to operate.

Lauren's education and career were designed to allow her to develop and test her achievement technology based on exploiting this internal-external partnership. She has a biological anthropology degree from the University of Toronto.

Lauren defines how to partner with this bio-infrastructure in her 2001 bestseller *Peak Evolution: Beyond Peak Performance and Peak Experience* and in *BioMaxed* (2019). She introduces a more advanced way to exploit the partnership through the lives of fictional characters in *The Encore: A Transformational Thriller* (2018) as they fight to save the planet.

She then attempts to illustrate the internal-external partnership in action in the lives of real people in *Savanting: Outperforming your Potential*. Here, Lauren retrofits the internal-external partnership onto some very well-known lives: successful entrepreneurial CEOs Bill Gates, Steve Jobs, Jeff Bezos, and Mark Zuckerberg, media mogul, Oprah, entertainer Jim Carrey, and others.

After first becoming a change leader in global banks, Lauren launched an executive search firm for change leaders for the boards and C-suites of large multinationals. This evolved into providing executive change leaders on contract before that field existed.

Recruiting executives evolved into coaching executives before that field existed. Coaching matured into co-creating new companies ventures, projects, jobs and frontiers customized to client talents, passions, and strengths to ensure their success. Lauren has been the CEO of Frontiering since 2002. She may be reached through laurenholmes.com or frontiering.com.

www.ingramcontent.com/pod-product-compliance
Lightning Source LLC
Chambersburg PA
CBHW060305030426
42336CB00011B/949